Capi

Capitalism since 1945

Philip Armstrong
Andrew Glyn
John Harrison

BLACKWELL
Oxford UK & Cambridge USA

First published in 1984 by Fontana Paperbacks under the title *Capitalism since World War II*
First published by Basil Blackwell in 1991
Reprinted 1994 (twice)

Blackwell Publishers, the publishing imprint of
Basil Blackwell Ltd
108 Cowley Road
Oxford OX4 1JF, UK

Basil Blackwell Inc.
238 Main Street
Cambridge, Massachusetts 02142
USA

British Library Cataloguing in Publication Data
A CIP catalogue record for this book is available from the British Library.

Library of Congress Cataloging in Publication Data
Armstrong, Philip.
    [Capitalism since World War II]
    Capitalism since 1945 / Philip Armstrong, Andrew Glyn, John Harrison.
        p.   cm.
    Previously published as: Capitalism since World War II. 1984.
    Includes bibliographical references and index.
    ISBN 0–631–17935–6 (pbk.)
        1. Economic History – 1945–   2. Capitalism – History – 20th century.
    I. Glyn, Andrew, 1943–   . II. Harrison, John.   III. Title.
    HC59.A817   1991
    330.9′09′045 – dc 20   90–45691   CIP

Typeset in 10 on 12pt Ehrhardt
by Hope Services Ltd., Abingdon
Printed and bound by Athenæum Press Ltd.,
Gateshead, Tyne & Wear.

This book is printed on acid-free paper

Contents

Figures

Tables

Preface

This book is about the economic history of the advanced capitalist countries since 1945. It is not a history of the capitalist system as a whole, since attention is largely confined to the United States, Western Europe and Japan. We have limited consideration of the less developed economies to events which impinged forcefully on the advanced countries. We believe that the advanced countries constitute a group with its own dynamics, and even four hundred pages is little enough space into which to compress forty years of the development of a substantial part of the world.

We have divided the period into three distinct phases: postwar reconstruction (1945–50), the great boom and its disintegration (1950–74) and the years of slower growth (1974 onwards). The very different character of the three periods has dictated a distinct approach to each.

Reconstruction involved the formation of the basic relationships between labour and capital within each country, and of the relations between the various countries, which were to underpin the subsequent boom. Part I discusses in detail developments in each of the six biggest advanced capitalist countries – the United States, the United Kingdom, Germany, Italy, France and Japan – during those five years. This crucial and exciting period of history is not widely known about, despite many excellent studies of particular countries, on which we have drawn heavily. We have also included many eye-witness accounts. Reports from the *Economist*, in particular, show how events were assessed at the time by a magazine devoted to providing serious information for those concerned to preserve capitalism. The discussion ventures beyond the economic indices to grapple with political programmes, international relations and many other issues. We hope to have shown that the generation of the boom was neither preordained nor trouble-free.

The great boom of the 1950s and 1960s displayed capitalism in full swing. Political differences became submerged into a social-democratic consensus, accepted more or less enthusiastically by parties of both left and right. Part II reflects the reduced political turmoil of this period and focuses on the economic dynamics of the boom. Here, the advanced countries are considered as a group, rather than as individual countries. For this purpose we have constructed data for the seven largest capitalist countries taken together (the six on whose development we focus in part I plus Canada), which contribute some 85 per cent of the output of the 24 countries which comprise the Organization for Economic Cooperation and Development (OECD). Figures for the advanced capitalist countries as a whole (ACCs) in the tables refer to those seven countries; those in the text sometimes refer to the OECD as a whole. Attention is paid, however, to changing relations between the different blocs (the United States, Europe and Japan), especially to the eclipse of US domination and to the rise of Japan. Figures for Europe in the tables refer to the four largest Western European economies taken together (West Germany, France, Italy and the United Kingdom); those in the text sometimes refer to all of Western Europe. Figures for the EEC (now EC) refer to the total for member states.

The beginning of the break-up of the boom in the late sixties is examined in a more blow-by-blow fashion. For it was in those years that the ideas generated by the boom – of the end of class conflict, the permanence of prosperity – were shattered. The forces underminirtg them and the turbulent events which these forces unleashed are discussed in some detail.

The period since 1974 has seen much slower growth, the return of mass unemployment, a partial and uneven recovery of profitability and capital accumulation and serious problems of financial fragility. Part III analyses these developments and discusses how they have affected and reflected the balance of power between capital and labour and relations between the advanced countries. Japanese work organization and industrial relations – widely regarded in other countries as a model – are discussed in some detail.

The outstanding political development was the break-up of the social-democratic consensus. Right-wing parties adopted aggressive policies to restructure the economy and redistribute income in favour of business. Workers' parties sought to preserve the gains of the boom and to ensure that the costs of slower growth and restructuring were broadly spread. To exemplify these developments we discuss the policies of Thatcher and Reagan on the one hand and those of the British Labour government (1974–9), the French Socialist government (after 1981) and Swedish social democracy on the other.

We have tried to explain economic terminology and, more importantly, real economic mechanisms as we go along, although some sections may still prove difficult for readers with no knowledge of economics. Many of the more important economic facts are presented in tables, but these can safely be skipped by readers who find them distracting. We have presented the more important trends in figures. We have seldom contrasted our interpretation with other writers', even those on whose work we have drawn heavily. This is not because such differences do not matter. Important debates rage about many events discussed: the role of Marshall Aid, the causes of falling profitability in the late sixties, the gains for the United States from the international position of the dollar, the role of government policies of deficit spending in sustaining the boom and so forth. But numerous subplots involving differences of interpretation would make it harder to keep hold of the main strands of an already complex story. The notes on sources indicate where some rival interpretations can be found. The Appendix presents the data on profitability and capital accumulation we have assembled, which form the statistical background for parts II and III. It also gives the various and diverse sources for statistics used in part I. Since the text frequently refers to flows of exports, loans and so on in billions of dollars, the Appendix also contains a table showing GDPs and imports in billions of dollars to provide some frame of reference.

For this edition part III has been entirely rewritten and some changes have been made to the rest. Andrew Glyn was primarily responsible for the drafts and Philip Armstrong for the assembly of the data on profitability and capital accumulation. Circumstances prevented John Harrison from contributing. Bob Sutcliffe drafted the section on the less developed countries in chapter 16; Wendy Carlin commented in detail on the drafts and supported the project in numerous ways; collaboration with Bob Rowthorn had a major influence on part III; Makoto Itoh provided advice and comments; joint work with Alan Hughes, Alain Lipietz and Ajit Singh, as part of Stephen Marglin's WIDER Project on Macroeconomic policies, clarified ideas about 'Fordism'; Stuart Reid undertook excellent research assistance; officials at OECD and the European Commission helpfully provided data; members of the staff of the library of the Oxford Institute of Economics and Statistics chased books; Mark Allin, Brigitte Lee and John Taylor gave us editorial support; many friends and colleagues provided help or encouragement in various ways now and when we were preparing the edition published in 1984. We are very grateful to all of these people.

PART I

Postwar Reconstruction, 1945–1950

1
Chaos and Despair

Japan and continental Europe were in chaos as hostilities ceased in 1945. Millions of people were on the move: occupying troops, defeated troops, evacuees, slave labourers, those expelled as borders were redrawn; refugees of every description. Food was hopelessly insufficient. The military administrations were ill-equipped to deal with huge civilian problems. Civilian administrations were inexperienced, disorganized and often without much authority.

In Japan, half the housing in the major cities had been destroyed. Evacuation had reduced the number of people living in Tokyo, Osaka and Kobe by one-half. Food supplies had broken down. The black market was the main source for food other than rice. On one Sunday in September 1945, a month after the end of the war, nearly a third of Tokyo's 3 million people left the city to try to buy food in the countryside. Since the purchasing power of wages was less than one-tenth of the prewar level, savings were run down and possessions sold in order to obtain food. Many failed in this struggle to survive, as a survey of the period explains:

> Indeed food was in extreme shortage, and many people were literally starving. In the days immediately after the war it was not uncommon at all to see hungry and malnourished people collapse and die on the streets. On 18 November 1945 the major Tokyo dailies reported that since the end of the war a total of 300 people had starved to death in Kyoto, 148 in Kobe, 100 in Fukuoka, 72 in Nagoya and 42 in Osaka. . .
>
> Most of them were homeless and jobless people who had become extremely weak and infirm. In the daytime they wandered around towns in search of leftover food, and at night they slept on the bare concrete floor of railway stations or underground tunnels with only a thin blanket to keep warm. Even if there were a job for them, the result was much the same. As a day labourer a man could not get paid more than 1 or 2 yen a day – but a small rice ball cost 10 yen and a bun 15 yen. (Quoted Moore, 1983, pp. 89–90)

In Europe there was a deficiency of 16 million houses, due to war damage and dilapidation. A reported 8 million refugees were in the Berlin area, where the struggling German administration could only try to minister to the dying, while pushing the rest on into the countryside. *Picture Post* published photographs of German women and children hunting for food on a vast US army garbage dump, and predicted, 'German misery this winter will be on a scale unknown in Europe since the Middle Ages' (8 September 1945). But the desperate situation that winter was not confined to Germany, as the *Economist*'s description makes clear:

> [The] tragedy is vast. It may vary in intensity; the peasantry are reasonably well provided and the rich can use the black market, but the poor urban populations of Europe, perhaps a quarter of its 400 millions, are all condemned to go hungry this winter. Some of them will starve. The plague spots are Warsaw, where, according to Mr Lehman, Director-General of UNRRA [the United Nations Relief and Rehabilitation Administration], ten thousand people will die of starvation; Hungary, particularly Budapest, where deaths from famine may reach a million; Austria, particularly Vienna and Lower Austria, where the rate of calories is below 1000 a day (the rate needed to maintain reasonable health is well over 2000), and where in some towns, Wiener-Neustadt for instance, there is already starvation; the Saar, where children are reported to be dying of hunger; Northern Italy, the Ruhr, Berlin, and most large towns in Germany, where it is proving difficult to keep the calorie rate up to 1200. Greece and Western Holland are improving, but are still below full subsistence level. Paris and the larger towns of France face a new food crisis. Nor does this bare recital of calories and diets cover those grisly companions of starvation – tuberculosis, dysentery, typhoid and typhus, rickets – nor the appalling figures for maternal and infant mortality.
>
> One person in ten in Poland has TB – the figure for Warsaw is one in five – it is rampant in Jugoslavia, and the Czechs say that out of 700,000 needy children 50 per cent have been discovered to be tuberculous. Infant mortality in Berlin has doubled. In Budapest it has risen from 16 to 40 per cent since September. There are no figures for the Ruhr, but English visitors have been told that very few newborn babies are expected to live this winter. (26 January 1946)

Nor, for those with time to think about such matters, were the precedents for postwar economic reconstruction and recovery encouraging. The years immediately after the First World War had seen a feverish postwar boom quickly collapse, in some countries after degenerating into hyperinflation. In Europe as a whole, manufacturing production fell by 9½ per cent between 1920 and 1921. In the United Kingdom, earliest and worst affected, unemployment rose from 2 per cent to 11 per cent; in the United States, where the fall in production was 20 per cent, unemployment reached 11½ per cent. Between 1920 and 1922 prices fell by 27 per cent in the United Kingdom; over the same period they rose by nearly 15 times in Germany. Since conditions immediately after the First World War were reckoned, in a classic history of the period, to be 'on the whole not so bad as in 1946' (Lewis, 1949, p. 16), the prospects at the end of the Second World War were distinctly ominous. Paul Samuelson, who later wrote the bestselling economics textbook published in the postwar years, raised in 1943 the probability of a 'nightmarish combination of the worst features of inflation and deflation', fearing that 'there would be ushered in the greatest period of unemployment and industrial dislocation which any economy has ever faced' (Samuelson, 1943, p. 51). He was speaking, it should be remembered, about the United States, which was relatively unscathed by hostilities.

The political precedents from the period around the end of the First World War were equally suggestive of turbulence. Not only was the Bolshevik revolution in Russia carried through and consolidated, but enormous social turmoil shook every major country. There had been a real possibility at the end of the war that the revolution against the imperial regime in Germany would follow the same path as that in Russia. In Italy revolutionary workers had occupied the factories in an explosive challenge to capitalist rule. In the United Kingdom the level of industrial and political unrest in the years after 1918 had been without parallel. Joseph Schumpeter, an eminent economist, summed up the mood of alarm of the early forties: 'The all but general opinion seems to be that capitalist methods will be unequal to the task of reconstruction.' He regarded it as 'not open to doubt that the decay of capitalist society is very far advanced' (Schumpeter, 1943, p. 120).

2

Behind the Chaos

This chapter documents the deep disorganization of the capitalist system at the end of the war and the resulting volatile situation that lay beneath both the celebrations of victory in some countries and the miseries brought by defeat in the others. The pattern of reconstruction proved to be the basis of the greatest boom in the history of capitalism. In 1945, however, no one knew how the process of reconstruction would proceed and under whose control it would be.

Even in Europe and Japan the fundamental problem for postwar recovery was not the physical destruction wrought by the war. As this chapter shows, destruction of the stock of industrial plant was comparatively minor. Nor were war casualties the major constraint on production. The war had certainly left very serious bottlenecks in the productive process, most importantly in fuel, transport and food, which would have catastrophic consequences if not removed. But they could be cleared away fairly rapidly if the available resources were mobilized with sufficient authority.

Much more serious for the long-term prospects of the capitalist system than the *physical* destruction was the challenge to its effective functioning as a *social* system. In the defeated countries the war had discredited the capitalist class: its association with the horrific consequences of fascism and war had undermined its authority in the political sphere and industrially. At the same time, organized labour was enormously strengthened in the victorious countries. Everywhere, with gathering momentum, people were demanding radical social and economic improvements.

Moreover, it was not only the internal structure of many of the capitalist states which was in turmoil. The old hierarchy of nation states was overturned, the continued domination of the colonial world was under challenge, and capitalism was confronting a hostile social system, that of the USSR, whose prestige had been enormously increased by the war.

The means to produce

The prerequisites for producing goods in any social system are workers and the means of production (factories, equipment, machinery – the capital stock) for them to operate. Only if the war had destroyed a significant part of the labour force or capital stock would the capacity to produce have been seriously diminished. During the war, governments had tried to maintain morale by exaggerating the extent of damage inflicted on the enemy; air forces connived in order to obtain a bigger share of resources. Newsreels of flattened cities seemed to confirm the picture of massive destruction of plant and machinery. Yet, more dispassionate studies have shown that in most capitalist countries the capacity to produce was as great or greater at the end of the war as at the beginning. This claim is so contrary to popular ideas about the economic effects of the war, and so important in our interpretation of what happened subsequently, that it must be backed up in some detail.

Workers

Despite the appalling numbers of people killed and wounded, none of the advanced capitalist countries (ACCs) ended the war with a significantly reduced labour force. Three factors account for this. First was the 'natural' increase in the population of working age which exceeded casualties by a substantial margin everywhere except Germany. Second, wartime mobilization raised the proportion of the population of working age at work. In the United States civilian employment rose by 5 million between 1940 and 1945. Despite an 11 million person expansion of the armed forces, male civilian employment fell by only 1 million as previously unemployed men took jobs. Female employment rose by 6½ million as women were encouraged to take jobs outside the home. In the United Kingdom increased female employment made up for 1 million of the 5 million men transferred to the forces. In Japan as many as 2 million extra women may have been employed. Many of these women, who under prewar conditions would not have looked for jobs, were available for postwar employment. In Germany fascist ideology dictated a far smaller increase in women workers. Finally, at the end of the war huge influxes of people started moving west. By 1948, 8 million expellees and refugees from areas incorporated into Poland, Czechoslovakia and the Soviet zone of Germany had flooded into Germany's western zones. Six million refugees from Japan's Asian empire had also returned home, contributing to a rise of 15 per cent in Japan's labour force as compared to before the war. In the United States, the labour force had increased by a similar percentage. In Germany the labour force of the British and American zones rose by 7 per cent. In the United Kingdom the rise was about 5 per cent. France and Italy's numbers of workers remained more or less stable.

War damage

Industrial war damage was almost certainly heaviest in Japan where around one-quarter of the factory buildings and one-third of plant and equipment were destroyed. The incidence of the damage was very uneven. About one-seventh of electricity-generating and steel capacity was destroyed, but as much as six-sevenths of oil-refining capacity. In Germany during 1944, when air attacks were heaviest, about 6½ per cent of machine tools were damaged or destroyed, but most of them (one estimate is 90 per cent) were repaired at the time. Around 10 per cent or less of steel capacity appears to have been lost. The most careful estimate puts Germany's total war damage at 17½ per cent of the prewar capital stock.

In Italy the steel industry lost about one-quarter of its capacity and engineering 12 per cent, but destruction in most other sectors was put at only 4–5 per cent. The Bank of Italy estimated damage to the total capital stock at 8 per cent. In France, industry lost around 10 per cent of its capital stock, 15 per cent in engineering. War damage in the United Kingdom was described by the UN as negligible. From August 1940 to December 1941, when air raids were at their peak, only 1.7 per cent of machine tools were damaged or destroyed.

Investment

The damage inflicted by hostilities is only one aspect of the way in which the war affected the stock of means of production. Another is that much new plant and machinery was installed. The expansion of munitions production required heavy investment, as well as a diversion of capacity from civilian to military uses.

In Japan throughout the period 1939–44 private industrial investment ran at around double the rate of the mid-thirties. In Germany between 1936 and 1943 the volume of investment in industry grew continuously to an unprecedented level. By 1945 this investment, allowing for normal scrapping of old equipment but not war damage, would have increased the capital stock by 38 per cent. At the beginning of 1945, 34 per cent of equipment was five years old or less as compared to only 9 per cent in 1935.

In the United States investment grew rapidly during the early years of the war. The peak in 1941, however, still represented a lower level than that achieved in 1929, and it then declined and stayed at a rather low level (less than half the 1929 peak) for the remainder of the war. Investment in plant and machinery in the United Kingdom rose by nearly one-half between 1938 and 1940, but then declined to well below half the previous rate for the last three years of the war. In Italy a high rate of investment was recorded until 1942, after which it sank to very low levels. In France investment declined earlier, averaging only half the 1929 peak (or two-thirds the immediate prewar level) for the whole period 1940–4.

The change in the stock of equipment during the war depended on the net effect of additions, through investment, and losses, through war damage and scrapping. Estimates are at best rough and ready, but nevertheless indicate how the stock of machine tools and total means of production changed during the war period (table 2.1).

Clearly engineering capacity increased substantially in many of the major countries despite war damage. Even in Britain, where the increase in the number of machine tools was quite small, the total engineering capital stock doubled. Numbers of machine tools are obviously a crude indicator. In Japan, in particular, shortage of materials led to deteriorating quality – one manufacturer put the life expectancy of machines produced in the last years of the war at only 6–12 months – and in France the average age of machine tools was 25 years, the more modern ones 'having taken the road to Germany' (Rioux, 1980, p. 35). But even by the end of the war only 15 per cent of Japanese machines were special-purpose and therefore hard to convert to peacetime production. In Germany many technical advances resulted from increased specialization, introduced to facilitate the mass-production techniques made necessary by the shortage of labour (especially skilled labour). Assembly-line production was extended in a variety of industries ranging from machine tools to furniture and clothing.

Table 2.1 Wartime changes in the stock of means of production (percentage change)

	Machine tools	Total stock of fixed capital
USA	100	10
UK	15	0
France	5	n.a.
Italy	40	0
Germany	50	20
Japan	25	0

Figures show percentage change between 1938 and 1945 and are only very approximate. n.a., not available.
Source: see Appendix.

Conversion to peacetime production proved less difficult than expected, despite the fact that engineering sectors were very heavily biased away from civilian production. In the United States, for example, by 1945 only 30 per cent of the industry's output was of the kind delicately titled '1939-type goods'. Other sectors inevitably suffered from the concentration on munitions. Perhaps the most dramatic example is the Japanese cotton industry, where the number of spindles fell from 12 million to 2 million. War damage accounted only for 7 per cent of this decline; the rest resulted from scrapping due to lack of access to cotton imports and to markets. But in those countries for which data are available, it appears that the total capital stock in 1945 was at about the prewar level (table 2. 1).

Bottlenecks

This productive capacity could not be fully exploited until certain strategic bottlenecks were overcome. Workers had to have food, factories required fuel, and the transport system had to permit the movement of materials and finished goods.

Inland transport was very seriously dislocated by bombing, especially in Germany. Less than 10 per cent of the German railways – which prewar had carried two-thirds of all goods transported – were still operational: 2395 rail bridges (including every one over the Rhine), 10,000 locomotives and more than 100,000 goods wagons had been destroyed. Less than 40 per cent of the remaining locomotives were immediately operational. But total stocks of locos and wagons were actually greater than before the war. Large numbers had been looted from elsewhere in Europe. In France too the railways were badly hit. The stock of locomotives was about three-quarters of the prewar level and less than half of the track was operational: 7500 bridges had been destroyed – for example, none remained over the Seine between Paris and the Channel. Italy had lost 10 per cent of its locomotives and around one-fifth of the wagon stock. In Japan railway losses were relatively light because the Allies had not seriously tried to paralyse the system through bombing. In the United States the railways had been very profitable during the war and were in good shape, having received priority for materials.

The deliberate creation of bottlenecks – destruction of bridges being the clearest example – could, when peace came, be reversed rapidly by diverting resources towards clearing them. By the first quarter of 1946 European railway traffic had regained its prewar level. Even in Germany 90 per cent of the main lines were operating within a year. The hard winter of 1946–7 brought a renewed crisis as the poorly maintained locomotives and rolling stock creaked under the strain of loads transferred from the frozen canals. A crash programme of repairs, instituted after that winter, succeeded in eliminating the transport problem, demonstrating that it was not a fundamental brake on recovery.

Shipping was essential to bring into Europe and Japan urgently needed supplies. Yet construction in Europe and Japan had made up for only a small part of wartime sinkings. European shipping tonnage had been reduced by nearly 40 per cent and the Japanese merchant fleet was cut by more than 80 per cent. However, US shipping capacity had trebled, practically offsetting European and Japanese losses. So the bottleneck in international transport lay not in the size of the shipping stock but in its ownership. Thus the difficulty for Europe and Japan was to find the dollars to pay for the shipping space.

The second major bottleneck was fuel. In the first quarter of 1946 European coal production was only 70 per cent of the prewar level. Here the major problem was not direct war damage but the deterioration of equipment run at full stretch during the war, combined with exhaustion of the miners, who in many countries were being required to work on inadequate rations. Imports from the United States were at a very low level, because of transport bottlenecks in American ports. Again, lack of fuel was no longer a constraint after the winter of 1946–7. Coal production improved in Europe as manpower was encouraged into the pits. The flow of imports was also increased. By 1947 coal consumption reached nearly 90 per cent of the prewar level, and less than three years after the war the UN could claim that the European coal shortage had largely been overcome. In Japan coal production in November 1945 fell to less than the amount required to run the railways. By the end of 1947 production was back to the prewar level though well below the wartime peak. Productivity (output per worker) was still only one-third of the peak level, reflecting in part the incapacity of the government to reorganize the industry.

Food shortage not only killed tens of thousands, it also threatened to undermine production more generally through reducing workers' capacity to work. In the 'crop year' June 1945 to June 1946, European food production was only 60 per cent of the average prewar level, reflecting the cumulative effect of insufficient use of fertilizers, scarcity of agricultural labour, loss of livestock, deterioration of equipment and the weather. But again, these problems were remedied quite quickly, and in northern and western Europe agricultural production exceeded the prewar level in 1947–8, with food imports from outside Europe running at a similar rate to prewar. In Japan the postwar years yielded 'bumper harvests'; it was the lack of imports – such as rice and sugar, which provided one-fifth of prewar calories – that caused the food shortages. The government's inability to organize collection and distribution of food meant that the towns suffered most. In Tokyo in May 1946 calorie consumption was only 1350, less than two-thirds of the prewar level.

Capital and labour

The basic physical requirements for production were therefore available. But the reconstruction of a viable capitalist system required more than adequate supplies of workers and factories and a desperate need for their products. Capitalism is not a system geared to production of goods simply because they are needed; it is geared to production for profit. For production to yield a profit, the employers must be in a position to ensure that the working class produces a surplus for them: workers must produce goods worth more than the capitalists are obliged to pay them in wages. To secure production of this surplus the employers must be able to hold wages down to a level which yields them a profit. They must also control activity on the factory floor so as to set the speed at which production takes place, and when and how new technology is introduced. As a class the capitalists must also exercise sufficient political control to ensure that such improvements in conditions – or reforms – as the working class secures through political action do not challenge the employers' right to own the means of production and deploy their profits to their best advantage. A factory only becomes part of *capital* if its owner is able to hire workers, control their work and invest the profits received without fear of confiscation.

The domination exercised by the capitalist class over the working class, both in the factories and in political life, is the fundamental *social relationship* underlying the capitalist system. This social relationship was far more deeply threatened by the ravages of the war than was the physical productive structure.

The United States and the United Kingdom

In the United States the wartime boom had consolidated the increased strength of the organized working class which a wave of unionization in the 1930s had effected. Four million workers joined unions, bringing total membership up to 14 million by the end of the war.

During the war the trade union leadership had cooperated in a no-strike policy with compulsory arbitration to limit wage increases. The mine workers constituted an important exception; they struck four times in 1943 to break through the wage freeze. Elsewhere in industry wildcat strikes took place. A study of the Detroit motor plants reported that most of the strikes were protests against discipline, against company policies or against the sacking of one or more workers. In 1944 more strikes took place than in any previous year; the auto workers' union leader bemoaned the fact that strikes were destroying the union.

The working class gained substantially from the wartime boom. Between 1941 and 1944 the increase in average earnings in manufacturing, adjusted for inflation ('real' earnings), was 19 per cent and family incomes were further boosted by average hours of work rising from 40½ to 45, as well as by more married women working. Consumption per head had been prevented from rising by a sharp increase in tax and by rationing; but higher real incomes were reflected in high savings. The end of the war saw these gains threatened. Through loss of overtime and downgrading of workers the weekly wages of non-war workers decreased 10 per cent between the spring of 1945 and the winter of 1946; war workers were estimated to have lost 31 per cent and their take-home pay was 11 per cent down on the 1941 level.

Days occupied in strikes rose from around 1 million a month during the latter months of the war to 7–8 million in the last three months of 1945 to 20 million in January 1946 and 23 million in February when 175,000 electrical workers and 800,000 steel workers joined the 225,000 General Motors (GM) workers and nearly a million others out on strike. In all, 116 million days were lost in 1946, prompting the Bureau of Labor Statistics to comment that it was the most concentrated strike wave in the country's history. Glass workers, machinists in California, New England textile workers and the GM workers all struck for more than a hundred days. The government seized half the country's oil-refining capacity, the packing houses, the railways (where the workers only returned after being threatened with the draft) and the coal mines.

The key struggle took place at General Motors where the union demanded that the company 'open the books' to justify its assertion that it could not pay the 30 per cent claim – 'the 40-hour week at 48 hours' pay'. In the event the strikers secured a little over half the claim and fought off GM's attempt to secure union guarantees of no opposition to speed-ups and of absolutely no strikes. But the Ford management soon set the pattern, gaining the unrestricted right to hire and fire, promote and demote, fix production schedules, and discipline strikers and others charged with violating company rules.

Profits were high at the end of the war. In 1945 the share of profits in the value of output was 22 per cent. Since this measure will be used dozens of times in the course of this book it is important to make clear what it signifies. Out of every $100 of net output produced – that is, output after setting aside a sum to cover the wear and tear of fixed capital equipment – $22 went to the employers and $78 to the working class. Another way of visualizing this distribution of production is in terms of labour expended: out of every 100 days worked, 22 were devoted to producing the surplus for the employers (luxury goods, new investment goods) while the rest were producing the wage goods for the working class.

Even this is an oversimplification, and never more so than during wartime when the government bought nearly half of total production. To finance this spending, taxes had risen enormously: about 60 per cent of corporate profits were taken in taxation in 1945 as compared to 8 per cent in 1929. Thus, *after* taxation, the share of profits was actually 9 per cent in 1945 compared to 15 per cent in 1929, the peak prewar year for profits.

But employers are not primarily concerned with the share of profits in the value of output. Its main importance to them is as a determinant of the *rate of profit*, the percentage return on each $100 invested in plant and equipment, in stocks of materials and so forth. This rate of profit depends not only on the profit share, the ratio of profits to sales, but also on the value of output compared to the value of capital invested. In 1945 about $100 output was being produced for each $100 of capital invested; in 1929 around $66 of output was being produced for each $100 of capital invested. So, despite the fact that after taxation employers were receiving a smaller profit share on sales, the rate of profit on capital invested was boosted by the high level of sales and it was about the same level in 1945 as in 1929.

The high level of taxation of profits reflected the need to finance the war effort, and the fact that the employers had to be seen to be contributing a 'fair' share. The prospective ending of hostilities meant that this burden would certainly be lightened. But, as already pointed out, there was almost general agreement in the United States that the reduction of military spending would rapidly lead to a slump.

Despite these fears, US business strongly opposed an explicit government commitment to full employment, arguing that it would destroy private enterprise. A proposed Full Employment Bill was watered down to become the 1946 Employment Act. The right to 'useful, remunerative, regular and full-time employment' became the 'responsibility of the federal government to . . . promote free enterprise . . . under which there will be afforded useful employment for those who are willing and seeking to work'. One senator admitted that the bill simply 'promised anyone needing a job the right to go out and look for work' (quoted Apple, pp. 11, 12).

The level of share prices is an indication of the gloomy view taken of future profits – the value of a share depends on the stream of dividends expected to be paid on it. The level of share prices in 1945 was only a little over one-half that of 1929, and well below even that for 1930 when the Great Depression was well underway. A strengthened working class determined to defend wartime gains faced by a capitalist class anxious about preserving profits in difficult postwar circumstances, contained the possibility of serious confrontation. Months before the war ended, the mine workers had accepted a substantial pay offer only after the government had temporarily taken over the mines.

In the United Kingdom the challenge posed by organized labour was felt more on the political than the industrial plane. Not that industrial strength had declined: membership of unions had risen by about one-third during the war to bring it up to 8 million, around 45 per cent of the work force. The authority of the trade unions was officially recognized by their being heavily embroiled in the execution of wartime planning, paying out unemployment benefit for the Ministry of Labour, for example, and cooperating in the allocation of labour to individual firms. On the shop floor the power of workers was considerably increased by the strong demand for labour. In the Coventry munitions factories, management frequently negotiated contracts with elected representatives of sections of workers to produce a certain amount of output. These sections would distribute the work and discipline workers collectively; removing these tasks from foremen and supervisors meant they became 'more concerned with coordination of production flows than with the maintenance of managerial authority' (Friedman, 1977, p. 213).

As long as production was high, and buoyant profits were guaranteed by the 'cost-plus' system of awarding munitions contracts (the share of profit in the value of output was at the same level as in 1938), enhanced shopfloor strength posed no particular threat to management. It was prepared to cede some measure of shopfloor control in return for a guaranteed high level of production. Average earnings in real terms were 24 per cent higher in 1944 than in 1938, but this was entirely due to extra overtime and bonuses. Weekly wage *rates* had no more than kept up with the increased cost of living. The trade union leadership had accepted the continuation of the wartime Order 1305 which made arbitration of wage disputes compulsory and virtually eliminated the right to strike. But if the much-feared postwar recession were to cut heavily into overtime and bonuses, there was no guarantee that the trade union leadership could hold back the shop floor. Such unease was clearly set out in a leader in the *Economist*:

> Whichever political party is proved, in a fortnight's time, to have won the general election, it is becoming clear that a period of labour unrest lies ahead. Strikes in transport undertakings and 'go slow' movements at the docks are signs of a troubled mood. There is no need to be alarmist; nothing like the open industrial war of the uneasy post-Armistice months after the last war is to be expected. But at a time when the fullest effort is still demanded from skeleton staffs after the immediate incentive has passed, when manpower shortages are, for the moment, intensified rather than relaxed, when the first reductions from high wartime rates of pay are beginning to appear – this is hardly the time to expect serene and unbroken industrial peace. If the Conservative Government continues in office and gives an appearance of lack of sympathy with what the workers regard as their just grievances, there might be an epidemic of 'grudge strikes'. And if a Labour Government takes office, then – if all British and foreign precedents are followed – there is likely to be even more industrial unrest, not indeed to coerce the workers' government, but to assist in breaking down resistance to its policy. (14 July 1945)

In the event the election produced a landslide majority for a Labour government committed to a radical programme. This included:

- the restoration of trade union rights, lost in the Trade Disputes Act of 1927 (contracting 'out' rather than 'in' for payments of the political levy to the Labour Party and the right of civil service unions to affiliate to the Trades Union Congress);
- 'a tremendous overhaul, a programme of modernization, and the re-equipment of land, factories, machinery, schools and social services';
- 'drastic policies of replanning, keeping a firm constructive hand on the whole productive machinery';
- that 'Labour will not tolerate freedom to exploit others, to pay poor wages, or to push up prices for private profit';
- 'a firm public hand on industry in order to get jobs for all';
- public ownership of fuel and power, in land, transport, iron and steel;
- public supervision of monopolies and controls;
- land planning and a major housing programme;
- implementation of the 1944 Education Act and the raising of the school leaving age to 16 as soon as possible;
- introduction of the national health service;
- extension of social insurance.

This series of reforms promised improved social conditions for the working class. But they would clearly be expensive. The effective taxation rate on company profits had risen during the war from around one-quarter to one-half. While business was calling for the immediate abolition of this extra tax as military spending was reduced, the chance of achieving it appeared seriously threatened by the need to finance social reforms.

Nationalization of some industries, and a wide-ranging series of controls over the rest, promised a much-diminished freedom to allocate capital where it was most profitable. The capitalist class had accepted many such restrictions during the war, as necessary to mobilize the resources for a project which it supported (fighting Hitler). In any case the wartime planning and controls, at the industry level, were carried out by representatives of the big firms. To acccept similar restrictions from a Labour government in order to mobilize resources for a massive improvement in social welfare, under conditions in which it might not be possible to exclude trade unions from a say in the details of the planning, was a much more threatening proposition.

In the United Kingdom and United States, then, growth in the strength of organized labour flowed fundamentally from the full-employment conditions generated during wartime. It was reflected in demands for reforms in the fields of social welfare, employment and wages, and channelled through trade union or social-democratic party structures which did not pose any immediate threat to the continuation of capitalist domination of the economy. What was in doubt was the extent to which the boom conditions necessary to satisfy these aspirations could be maintained. If the economies faltered and slump conditions returned, demands for the economic controls proposed by Labour in the United Kingdom to be toughened could grow into a real threat to capitalism. And, in such a context, what could guarantee that the US labour movement would be immune to socialist contagion?

Japan and Germany

In these countries the threat was of a very different kind. With the regimes discredited after their catastrophic defeat, big business discredited for its support for those regimes, the people suffering terrible privations, and the old reformist leaderships in a weak position to reassert control, the situation apparently contained many of the ingredients for revolutionary changes. But there were formidable obstacles to such changes. The organized labour movement had been smashed years before, both politically and industrially. Workers' organizations and parties had to reconstitute themselves from scratch and establish their authority among workers. State power was in the hands of powerful occupying forces, committed to restoring bourgeois rule in one form or another. Initially, at least, they were regarded as much as liberators from fascist oppression as a foreign occupation. Besides, the terrible physical conditions in the aftermath of defeat demanded that all efforts be devoted to survival, focusing attention on immediate tasks rather than on sweeping political change. Such a complicated situation passed no straightforward death sentence on capitalism. But even in Japan, where the historical basis for a challenge to capitalism seemed weakest, there was soon cause for alarm.

The Japanese labour movement had no lengthy tradition of broad organization. The trade unions, whose peak prewar membership was less than half a million, had been wiped out in the late 1930s. There are no reported cases of Japanese workers taking action against their employers or the regime before the surrender, or even in the interregnum before the occupying forces arrived, though in one or two cases Chinese or Korean forced labourers rose up in revolt. But as soon as the occupying powers made trade unions legal again, membership spread like wildfire. Within four months it reached double the prewar peak.

Within a few weeks of the ending of the war the first 'production control' struggle took place at the *Yomiuri* newspaper. Its militaristic president refused to accede to workers' demands for better conditions, democratization of the company's organization and acceptance of responsibility for militarism by senior officials. The workers, both editorial and printing staff, decided to produce the paper themselves: 'If we do that we don't have to worry about bankrupting the company. And if we gain the support of the readers by putting out an excellent newspaper, then we can reconstruct the *Yomiuri* as a democratic paper' (quoted Moore, 1983, p. 51). After publishing the paper for several weeks they won an agreement which included the resignation of the president, and formation of a management council on which they had equal representation. This latter position they used to continue the paper's exposure of government incompetence and business manipulations.

Workers were being laid off on a huge scale. In January 1946 sacked employees of the Itabashi Arsenal in Tokyo demanded the handing over of food and other goods stored there which were being effectively looted by businessmen to whom the government was selling them off at knockdown prices. Faced with a determined Communist Party leadership, and slogans such as 'People's control over the distribution of rationed food' and 'Kick out the military men: send them to the coal mines', the military commander was forced to hand over large quantities of food. From this springboard a regional Democratic Council on Food was formed with 300 organizations claiming 1½ million members. It was chaired by the *Yomiuri* union chairman. In the same month 50,000 people demonstrated to welcome back from exile the communist leader Nosaka; 20,000 surrounded the prime minister's residence demanding the resignation of the Tokyo police chief and of the whole cabinet, which was composed of old right-wing politicians acting under the occupation's orders.

Production control struggles were spreading rapidly at this time. They varied considerably in the extent to which the workers challenged management's rights. In the case of the Kanto electric power company, although workers elected by the union took over the jobs of senior management, 'actions which needed the decision of the president were all forwarded to the president and disposed of with the approval of the president' (Yamamoto, 1972, p. 69). On the Keisei railway in Tokyo, workers collected no fares for the first three days of their struggle. Management was at first intransigent in the face of union demands for a big pay increase, shorter hours, union recognition, equal union participation in a management council to run the firm and dismissal of corrupt supervisors. Management gave in, however, after a union decision to pay out very large wage bonuses from the fares now being collected. Workers at a Mitsui mine in Hokkaido decided to follow the *Yomiuri* and Keisei examples and engage in production control rather than a strike because 'the workers themselves must shoulder the burden of industrial reconstruction in Japan' (quoted Moore, 1983, p. 60). Despite reducing working hours from twelve to eight, output was doubled. At a Mitsubishi mine nearby, a 'People's Court' arraigned the management in a ten-hour 'People's Trial' where rank-and-file miners and their families denounced management for feeding their pets better than the workers. Improvements in pay and conditions, recognition of the union and formation of a management council were typical settlements. By March 1946 the number of production control struggles underway had built up to nearly 40.

These developments did not add up to an articulated challenge to the restoration of bourgeois rule in Japan. But they did suggest the possibility that the social relations underlying capitalism could come under severe strain.

As the Allied armies advanced through Germany they frequently found factories and mines in the hands of plant-based workers' committees. These had sometimes driven out SS units which had been ordered to destroy the plants. Work restarted within days and the provisional workers' committees procured food, clothing and housing and were the point of contact with the military authorities. Broader antifascist committees (antifas) sprang up in many towns. In Bremen the antifas circularized all the local plants calling for the formation of antifascist workers' councils where this had not already happened, their recognition by the management and the removal of all Nazis. On occasions antifas arrested notorious local Nazis, confiscated food hoards, and so forth.

The occupation authorities banned the antifas, depriving them of facilities, and refused requests for the open revival of the old political parties – a stance maintained until the autumn of 1945. The workers' factory councils were in most cases the only labour movement bodies allowed to operate. These works councils were frequently in effective control of the plants, the management having disappeared or been discredited. Their immediate tasks were practical: keeping the plants going and looking after the workers' welfare. In the disorganized conditions this required contact between the works councils within towns – one of the few reported attempts at cooperation beyond a local basis took place between works councils in four Ruhr towns in 1945, and was exclusively concerned with organizing barter transactions between the firms.

These practical, but extremely pressing, questions dominated their activity, but the councils also made widespread demands for nationalization, especially of war industries. In a conference held in November 1945 in the Ruhr, the foremen from the coal industry demanded the expropriation without compensation of the mine owners, and the transfer of the mines to the regional government. Krupp workers demanded in a memorandum to the military governor that Krupp's plants be expropriated and retooled for peaceful purposes. Similar demands were put forward by workers in other major plants.

Memories of the disastrous divisions in the trade union movement before the war led to strong demands for unity. Representatives of the old trade unions in Cologne, meeting before the US army arrived, called for the formation of one union, with industrial branches. This call was endorsed in September by a meeting of union representatives from all the Rhine towns. In the Hanover area a unified local union organization was actually formed soon after the war ended.

A parallel desire for unity existed on the political front. In Hamburg, in the summer of 1945, the military government's refusal to allow political parties to reconstitute themselves led to the setting up of a Socialist Free Union. It demanded full employment, state control of key industries, nationalization of the land, trade union control of labour exchanges, state control of foreign trade, extensive denazification and a new democratic constitution. Within five weeks it was reported to have attracted 50,000 workers. Social democratic leaders persuaded the military government that it was politically suspicious and it was dissolved. The *Economist* (19 January 1946) noted that the union 'had become too strongly political in character'.

In the early days after the defeat, the German Communist Party (KPD) was a major force, especially in the Ruhr where half the members of works councils in the mines also belonged to the KPD and where, by the end of 1945, its membership is said to have reached 50,000.

In fact the KPD's programme was less radical than contemporary Social Democratic Party (SPD) statements. It called for the expropriation of 'Nazi bosses' and war criminals, the breaking up of the nobility's and the Junkers' large estates and the nationalization of utilities such as electricity, gas and water. But reconstruction was to take place on the principle of 'completely unrestricted development of free trade and private entrepreneurial initiative on the basis of private ownership' (quoted Graf, 1976, p. 43). It was no more radical than the Christian Democrats' (CDU) programme which actually called for state ownership of natural resources and 'key monopoly industries', as well as for the elimination of large-scale capitalist enterprises. Such was the strength of the reaction against fascism that even the CDU contained a radical wing which was able to commit it to the abolition of capitalism because it had not been 'adequate for the vital national and social interests of the German people' (quoted Graf, 1976, p. 50).

Italy and France

On any scale of postwar dislocation Italy and France occupied an intermediate position between the Anglo-Saxon 'victors' and the main defeated powers. France had suffered its defeat five years earlier; and Italy ended the war fighting the Germans. But it was in these countries that the position of the capitalist class was most threatened. Both contained mass resistance movements. Their status as co-belligerents also made an extended period of Anglo-American occupation much more problematic.

In Italy the working class played a leading role in the resistance, first to Mussolini's government until its fall in August 1943, and then to the puppet regime in the north and its German masters. As early as March 1943 a strike wave began at Fiat in Turin and spread to Pirelli and other factories in Milan, gaining substantial wage increases. A general strike in Milan at the end of March saw workers' councils set up in the factories. In August, Badoglio's government, which replaced Mussolini's, was forced under threat of further strikes to legalize these councils. In November and December 1943 a further strike wave started in Turin, halting production for nine days. On 1 March 1944, a mass general strike was called in the German-occupied areas. Perhaps as many as a million workers came out. In Milan, many industrialists agreed to pay workers for the days they struck, despite German orders to the contrary. 'Premature holidays' were declared in some places to circumvent the strike.

As the Allied armies moved up Italy the resistance in the north, directed by the multiparty Committees of National Liberation, struggled against the German occupation. More than 150,000 resistance fighters tied down as many as 14 Axis divisions during 1944. Observers agreed that 'workers were in the forefront of the actual fighting' (*Economist*, 9 June 1945).

Striking workers played an important role in the liberation of Genoa, Milan and Turin. Factory liberation committees helped to preserve plant from destruction or removal by the Germans. The Committee for National Liberation issued a decree before the Milan insurrection calling for the organization of management councils for firms, composed equally of owners and workers. The councils each nominated a 'works commissar' and a technical manager. In Turin a general strike was in progress a week before the insurrection. On May Day of 1945 a Communist Party leader demanded that workers, clerks and technicians participate in the administration of production 'on a level of absolute equality with the owners' (quoted Dalzell, 1961, p. 557). Communists and socialists were in a majority in the resistance, and constituted an overwhelming majority among workers. The following quotation gives a flavour of how precarious and unstable the position appeared at the end of 1945:

> The Italian employer today has genuine grievances. He is forbidden to dismiss his workmen unless they were active Fascists, were taken on after June 30, 1943, or

have other resources at their disposal – this at a time when Italian industry is working at about 25 per cent of its average peacetime capacity. Labour's output is poor because the workers are hungry and tired; they expect to be provided with cheap food and clothes by their factory for the good reason that food and clothing can only be purchased at quite fantastic prices. Finally, the employer resents the 'councils of management' which have been appointed in every big factory by the local Committee of National Liberation. These councils are intended to ensure that the notions of anti-Fascist patriots of Resistance days shall not now be flouted by the captains of industry; but it is certain that they concern themselves with politics instead of confining themselves to technical considerations. . .

The wage crisis has been chronic in Italy ever since the liberation last spring. The employers are right when they say that further wage increases only accelerate the inflation of the currency, but the workers are right when they insist that the wages paid at present are less than half what the barest subsistence level would dictate. (*Economist*, 24 November 1945)

In France the communists were recognized even by non-sympathizers as the most dynamic part of the resistance. In Paris the liberation took the form of an insurrection, described by Albert Camus as follows: 'Four or five thousand men, with a few hundred firearms between them, came out in accordance with a well worked-out plan, in order to hold up the retreating remnants of the German 7th Army. After less than a week 50,000 Parisians were on the barricades, in the districts of the Revolution (i.e. the working-class areas), and were fighting with arms captured from the enemy' (quoted Werth, 1956, p. 218). The National Council of the Resistance published a Charter committing those active in the movement to secure a formidable programme of social reform. It demanded 'the removal from the management of France's economy of the great economic and financial feudal forces'; the intensification of production in accordance with a plan to be decided upon by the state, after consultation with all those concerned with this production; and the nationalization of 'all the great monopolized means of production which are a product of common labour; of the sources of power; of mineral wealth; of insurance companies; and of the big banks'; a share of responsibility for the workers in the economic direction of enterprises; a guaranteed wage to bring 'security, dignity and the possibility of a fully human existence'; a complete plan of social security; adequate old-age pensions; the fullest educational possibilities for all French children, in accordance with their ability and wholly independent of their parents' social or financial position (quoted Werth, 1956, pp. 222–3). In Marseilles the Commissaire de la République appointed from Paris began to implement these measures, applying a regional programme of nationalization. Many firms were being run by workers' committees which took over what they regarded as collaborationist property. The first election, in October 1945, saw the left win more than half the vote: the communists 26.1 per cent and the socialists 24.8 per cent.

It is hard at this distance to capture the real alarm that swept the capitalist class after Hitler's defeat. A quotation from the *Economist* expresses it well:

> The collapse of that New Order imparted a great revolutionary momentum to Europe. It stimulated all the vague and confused but nevertheless radical and socialist impulses of the masses. Significantly, every programme with which the various Resistance groups throughout Europe emerged from the Underground contained demands for nationalization of banks and large-scale industries; and these programmes bore the signatures of Christian Democrats as well as of Socialists and Communists. The maxim of French Socialism in the nineteenth century was Proudhon's 'La propriété c'est le vol'. The corresponding maxim, during the resistance era, was 'La propriété c'est la collaboration' (1 December 1945).

International relations

Since capitalist production takes place within a system of nation states, the smooth functioning of the system requires that the relations between countries assume a reasonably ordered and stable shape. Between capitalist countries this means a trade and payments system within which the international division of labour can develop. Because they depend upon worldwide imported materials, the advanced countries must also have a relationship with the rest of the world that allows access, under favourable terms, to these sources of supply. Finally, the existence since 1917 of a non-capitalist part of the world posed the problem of containing the latent antagonism between the capitalist and non-capitalist blocs. The war had profoundly dislocated all these dimensions of the international system.

Relations between the advanced countries

During the war the major capitalist powers had fought for markets with tanks rather than tariffs. World trade had shrunk and was concentrated in basic materials and munitions. In 1946, world exports were three-quarters of their prewar (1937) level, and less than 60 per cent if the United States is excluded. Trade within Europe was running at less than half the prewar rate. The pattern of production had been shifted towards armaments, leading to a gross overexpansion of engineering and a rundown of such consumer industries as textiles. This would make it difficult to establish a new international division of labour once the web of bilateral agreements under which trade took place by the end of the war had been dismantled.

The most important change, however, was in the relative economic strengths of the major capitalist powers. In the autumn of 1945 industrial production in Germany and Japan was less than one-fifth of the prewar level, whereas in the United States it was one-half greater. But appearances were deceptive to some extent, reflecting more the immediate postwar dislocations in the defeated countries than a longer-run reduction in their capacity to produce relative to that of the United States. Indeed, the total stock of means of production appears to have actually risen more in Germany than in the United States, although the stock of machine tools expanded more in the United States than in Germany, and much more than in Japan (table 2.1).

While the potential capacity to produce, after overcoming bottlenecks, was very high in Germany and Japan, it was unclear whether they would be permitted to use this capacity to produce for world markets. This decision rested in the hands of the Allies.

The United States' relative economic position among the Allies had enormously strengthened. Its capital stock, and especially the stock of machine tools, had expanded markedly as compared with the United Kingdom and France. The immediate position was of sharper contrast still. At the beginning of 1946 industrial production in Northern Europe (excluding Germany) varied from two-thirds of the prewar level to around the same as prewar, while in the United States it was 50 per cent higher. And even that level of European production was heavily dependent on imports from the United States. These had doubled as compared with prewar. Europe was running a payments deficit with the United States of $4 billion in 1946, eight times as much as in 1938. The increased imports were mainly of food and manufactures (especially vehicles); materials imports were only one-third greater than prewar.

European and Japanese dependence on US imports emphasizes the crucial role the United States would have to play in any new financial system. The United States had not piled up huge claims on its allies. The $35 billion aid it extended through Lend-Lease was in the form of grants rather than loans. But more than two-thirds of the world's gold reserves were held in Fort Knox, while the United States' prewar rival for financial dominance, the United Kingdom, was in a much-weakened position. It had disposed of many foreign assets and incurred large debts with its former colonies in the Sterling Area.

In the aftermath of the war, then, the United States was in a dominating economic position among the advanced capitalist countries. The immediate figures for production and trade reflected the chaos elsewhere and so exaggerated the extent of such dominance. But whether or not the other capitalist countries would recover rapidly and could use all their capacity depended to a very substantial extent on the policies pursued by the United States.

The colonies

The war had given a major impetus to the struggle for colonial freedom, especially in those countries invaded by the Japanese. Much the most important case was China which, although formally independent, had been dominated for decades by imperialism. The collapse of Japanese control over much of China made it likely that the fundamental antagonism between Chiang Kai-shek's nationalist forces and Mao's communists would erupt into civil war. External support was strongly in favour of Chiang. The Americans were backing him and the USSR also signed a treaty with him, agreeing to give aid only to his government and to hand over to him Chinese territory liberated from the Japanese by the Red Army. But China's future remained problematic.

Elsewhere in the Far East, the colonial powers (Britain, France and Holland) had to cope with the strengthening of the nationalist forces in Malaya, Indo-China and Indonesia which the Japanese had encouraged. Initially the Japanese had pretended to offer liberation from imperialism. When in retreat, they further fomented nationalist struggles in order to disrupt the reimposition of the old imperial order. The *Economist* warned: 'However spurious the present Japanese-sponsored uprisings may be, nationalism is a profound and deeply rooted force in the Far East and it must be satisfied' (6 October 1945).

At first, it seems, there was little anxiety that a change in colonial status would limit economic relations with the advanced countries. Unilever, heavily involved in India, where the move to independence was by then accepted as inevitable, 'appears to have had remarkably few fears about the effects of Indian independence and took appropriately few precautions' (Fieldhouse, 1978, p. 185). Its first internal report on the subject in 1944 waved aside calls for Indian ownership of basic industries and Indian access to foreign companies' technology as 'more irritating than harmful, and transitory than permanent' (quoted Fieldhouse, 1978, p. 185). It assumed that India would retain close commercial and trading links with Britain.

The United States believed that colonial powers should prepare their colonies for independence, which should be granted 'progressively' and at the first 'practicable' moment. This liberal approach was clearly aimed at securing for US business access to natural resources on the same terms as the old colonial countries. Such a policy of heading off the more radical nationalist movements by concessions, while pressing for the breakdown of the exclusivity of colonial economic relations, might well be the best strategy for the capitalist system as a whole. The old colonial powers, however, would suffer from the loss of economic control and would face the difficulty of placating white settlers and limiting the radicalism of the nationalist movements.

Relations with the USSR

'Somebody . . . made an awful mistake in bringing about a situation where Russia was permitted to come out of a war with the power she will have . . . England should never have permitted Hitler to rise . . . The German people under a democracy would have been a far superior ally than Russia . . . There is too much difference in the ideologies of the United States and Russia to work out a long-term programme of cooperation' (quoted Yergin, 1980, p. 118). This remark, made in a private conversation by US secretary of state Byrnes in the summer of 1945, sums up the problems posed for the capitalist world by the enormously enhanced power of the USSR.

Truman, who became US president in 1945, had bluntly stated in 1941: 'If we see that Germany is winning the war we ought to help Russia, and if Russia is winning we ought to help Germany, and in that way let them kill as many as possible' (quoted Horowitz, 1965, p. 61). Although the United States had not followed this policy, the USSR had nevertheless borne the brunt of Hitler's onslaught for years.

From the beginning of 1941 most of Germany's forces were engaged in fighting the USSR. When the long-delayed second front was opened, and at the peak of Anglo-American military involvement, the Russians still confronted almost 60 per cent of German divisions. Even in early 1945 the British and Americans were desperately appealing for the USSR to launch its winter offensive in order to relieve the pressure on their forces from Germany's drive into the Ardennes.

Although the devastation suffered was vast, with perhaps 20 million killed, the USSR was not fought to a standstill. By 1945 industrial production was running at its prewar level and the Red Army had been transformed into an enormous fighting machine. It controlled much of Eastern Europe and substantial parts of what had been Japan's mainland empire. Stalin summed up the implications in a conversation with Yugoslav communist leaders in the summer of 1945: 'This war is not as in the past. Whoever occupies a territory also imposes on it his own social system. Everyone imposes his own system as far as his army can reach' (quoted Djilas, 1977, p. 437).

Churchill had indeed agreed a division of 'spheres of influence' with Stalin in Moscow in October 1944 – Romania: 90 per cent for the USSR; Greece: 90 per cent for Britain (in cooperation with the United States); Bulgaria: 75 per cent for the Russians; Hungary and Yugoslavia: 50 per cent for the Russians. Significantly, Stalin also agreed to Churchill's request that the Soviet Union should 'soft-pedal the Communists in Italy and not stir them up' (quoted Yergin, 1980, p. 60).

But this sphere of influence agreement left many questions unanswered. If Stalin was right about armies imposing their social systems, as his capitalist allies feared, where did this leave Yugoslavia over which the USSR and Britain were supposed to share influence 50:50? Were part-socialist, part-capitalist countries possible? Moreover, the United States was not a party to the carve-up between Churchill and Stalin. Churchill told Stalin that it was 'better to express these things in diplomatic terms and not to use the phrase "dividing into spheres" because the Americans might be shocked' (quoted Yergin, 1980, p. 60). Many in the US administration remained unreconciled to Soviet domination of Eastern Europe, and the US government argued with the Russians throughout the second half of 1945 about the future of the governments of Poland, Romania and Bulgaria, ignoring the fact that 'they had their own new spheres in Italy and Japan where the Soviets had agreed to give them a free hand' (Yergin, 1980, p. 124). The future of Germany, divided into zones of occupation, was also highly uncertain. The USSR immediately pressed for the implementation of an earlier agreement specifying $20 billion of reparations from Germany. In dealing with the USSR, the Americans' confidence was greatly boosted by the 'successful' use of the atomic bombs. This had not only ended the war in Japan, but also removed the need to involve the USSR in a frontal assault on Japan, which would have strengthened Russia's position in the area.

In summary, the prospect of a redivision of the world into relatively stable spheres of influence was clouded by uncertainties. Where would the dividing lines be drawn? How would the social system develop in the Soviet sphere (with important implications for capitalist access to its markets)? How would the USSR use its influence with the greatly strengthened Communist parties in Western Europe?

The United States would clearly play a decisive role in settling these questions. It was bound to be the dominating capitalist power for some years and to shape the new trade and payments system. US occupation policy would control the fate of Japan and dominate that of Germany. Its decisions over aid to Western Europe would strongly influence the pattern of recovery there. Its attitude to the USSR would dominate one side of whatever new relationship would emerge between capitalism and the Eastern bloc. US attitudes towards the old colonial powers would shape any new forms of economic domination of the old colonies by the advanced countries. Conversely, the attitude taken by the Soviet Union would, through its influence on the Communist parties in Europe and Japan, deeply affect what happened there. The next chapter outlines the basic policies pursued by the two great powers.

3

Great Power Policies

Uncle Sam out for himself

The fundamental interests of US capital were to secure the largest possible markets for US exports and freedom to invest abroad wherever was most profitable, particularly where that was necessary to ensure access to raw materials. This was the cornerstone of postwar US policy. The reasons why are clear: fear of postwar depression, the consequent need for export markets to maintain demand and profits, and the memory of the impact of trade restrictions in the 1930s. So in 1943 a US State Department report pointed out that, 'A great expansion in the volume of international trade after the war will be essential to the attainment of full and effective employment in the United States as elsewhere' (quoted Kolko, 1969, p. 252). Secretary to the Treasury Morgenthau told a Senate Committee in 1945 that America required a world system 'in which international trade and international investment can be carried on by businessmen on business principles' (quoted Kolko and Kolko, 1972, p. 16). A year later, assistant secretary of state Clayton said: 'We need markets – big markets – around the world in which to buy and sell. We ask no special privileges in any of those markets' (quoted Kolko and Kolko, 1972, p. 13). 'Special privileges' were hardly needed, of course, given the productive and financial power of US capital.

Precisely what policy towards Western Europe and Japan flowed from these objectives was less obvious. At one extreme was the option of exploiting to the hilt the position of economic dominance achieved by the United States. This would be reflected in insistence on absolute freedom of penetration of US goods, with no attempt to help the reconstruction of production inside these countries. At the other extreme the United States could concentrate on the fastest possible recovery in these economies on the grounds that this would be the best guarantee of an expanding market for US trade and investment in the long term. Both options carried their own risks. If the economies of Western Europe and Japan failed to recover rapidly, the market for US goods would stagnate. More threatening still, popular demands for effective policies would strengthen the appeal of socialist measures leading perhaps to the abolition of capitalism itself in one or more of these countries. The USA might be left with little or nothing to dominate. On the other hand, giving maximum aid in order to hasten recovery would be expensive. It would involve accepting limitations on access to foreign markets for US products which competed too strongly with domestic industry. In the longer run it would risk building up industrial rivals to the point where they posed a serious competitive threat to US industry.

That the United States would use its economic might to gain concessions was clear enough from its dealings with the United Kingdom early on in the war. In February 1942 the United States insisted that the proposal to give Lend-Lease aid to its allies included agreement on the 'elimination of all forms of discriminatory treatment in international commerce'. In other words, eventual free entry of US goods should be guaranteed. Moreover, the US government decided that the amount of aid given should be enough to keep the United Kingdom's gold and dollar balances above the $600 million mark, to ensure some stability, but not enough to push the reserves above the $1 billion mark which would leave the United Kingdom with too much independence.

In terms of the two extreme options for US policy described above, the thrust adopted during the final years of the war and the early years thereafter was definitely towards taking full advantage of US dominance to achieve the most advantageous immediate position for US capital. This was felt most quickly in Europe and Japan where US aid was limited largely to emergency relief, without systematic planning for rebuilding production. Wherever possible, conditions thought favourable to US business were imposed on recipient countries, including pressure to give up colonial markets. In Germany and Japan the occupation authorities made little or no attempt to stimulate the process of economic recovery. While this had a perfectly understandable long-term political and military justification (fear of the resurrection of militaristic regimes), there was a strong undercurrent of more immediate economic self-interest (fear of renewed economic competition). Finally, the plans for the postwar world monetary and trading system drawn up by the United States enshrined both the central role of the US dollar and the principles of reducing balance of payments and trade restrictions. These principles could hardly be put into effect immediately, given the disorganized state of Europe and Japan, but the plans still represented an important registration of what the USA regarded as its vital interests and the extent to which it was prepared to use its economic muscle to further them.

Aid to Europe and Japan

The original US proposals for the postwar economy, released early in 1943, had contained a plan for a 'Bank for Reconstruction of the United and Associated Nations'. It was to have capital of $10 billion – half paid in immediately by members in gold and local currencies – and it could borrow extensively so that its total resources would have been much more than this capital. Its main purpose was 'to supply the huge volume of capital to the United and Associated Nations that will be needed for reconstruction, for relief and for economic recovery'.

Conservatives in the US administration succeeded in restricting the scope of the plans for the Bank by the time they were circulated. The British were keen to downplay it as well, since they expected to be making contributions rather than receiving loans. As agreed at the conference on international payments held at Bretton Woods in 1944, the Bank was limited in its lending to its nominal capital of $10 billion. Only one-tenth of its capital was paid in, and only the US contribution and one-tenth of the rest was in gold or dollars. So the Bank was left with only $¾ billion of resources, which could be used to purchase US commodities, plus what it could persuade the New York money market to lend. By the middle of 1947 all it had lent out was $92 million out of a $250 million loan to France; it was not until 1953 that it had lent out $1 billion.

The other body which seemed likely, at its inception, to play a major role in providing reconstruction aid was the United Nations Relief and Rehabilitation Administration. However, before the end of the war Congress forced rehabilitation to be defined as equivalent to relief, so that UNRRA's role as a provider of medium-term reconstruction aid was ruled out.

In the event the United States made some $10½ billion available during 1946 and 1947 in the form of grants and long-term government loans. This involved a series of pragmatic arrangements including Lend-Lease settlement, UNRRA and the Anglo-US and Franco-US loans. Only a fraction was in the form of grants. In 1946 these dollars financed nearly half of Europe's imports from the United States (figure 5.1, p. 69), and considerably more in 1947. More than two-thirds of total Japanese imports (mainly food) were covered by US aid. Harsh conditions were imposed, especially in the case of the Anglo-US loan of $3.75 billion negotiated at the end of 1945. This required that sterling be made fully convertible so that any overseas holders could cash their pounds in for dollars at the Bank of England in order to buy American goods. Moreover, the British were forced to agree that no discriminatory import quotas would be applied against the United States. The secretary to the treasury said: 'Its most important purpose from our point of view is to cause the removal of emergency controls exercised by the United Kingdom over its international transactions far more speedily' (quoted Kolko and Kolko, 1972, p. 66). According to a recent historian, generally rather sympathetic to US policy, 'the effect was to subordinate Britain to an American-dominated international economic order' (Yergin, 1980, p. 177).

Just after Lend-Lease was ended the *Economist* commented bitterly:

> To replace Lend-Lease by the offer of loans on commercial terms, and to forget about Bretton Woods, the commercial proposals, and the stimulation of American exports makes sense. Or to preach expansion and non-discrimination, and to offer

assistance of the dimensions and/or the terms that would make it possible to dismantle the economic defences also makes sense. But to thrust Britain back on its own resources and, as the rations are cut, to talk of non-discrimination and expansion does not make sense. (1 September 1945)

The US government worked hard to replace British capital's domination over the Empire. One example was in the Middle East where Britain's control of oil production had already been diminished during the war. In 1946, with government backing, the US oil companies broke off the prewar production and marketing arrangements with Britain. The US share of Middle East oil output, which had risen from 16 per cent to 31 per cent between 1939 and 1946, leaped up to 60 per cent by 1953.

International money and trade systems

Planning of the trade and monetary systems reached a far more advanced stage during the war than did planning for reconstruction of the war-damaged economies. The main debate was between the United States and United Kingdom. The United Kingdom wanted the new international financial institution – the International Monetary Fund (IMF) – to have very large resources ($26 billion), with contributing countries having automatic rights to substantial overdraft facilities. There would obviously be tremendous hunger for dollars, for dollars were now the only currency which could be turned into whatever goods were desired, that is US goods. Under the British plan drawn up by Keynes, the United States could have found itself contributing $23 billions of exports in exchange for credit balances at the IMF which paid hardly any interest. Such long-term aid to Europe was not the function the United States envisaged for the IMF. It was scarcely surprising, then, that the United States insisted on a much restricted plan. The final agreement at the Bretton Woods Conference of 1944 specified that the fund would only have $9 billion of resources, and that access would only be in order to 'shorten the duration and lessen the degree of disequilibrium' in the balances of payments of members. Exchange rates were to be pegged to the dollar, and to be changed only when there was a 'fundamental disequilibrium'.

On trade both the United States and United Kingdom agreed on the desirability of an international convention to draw up precise rules and a trade organization to police quantitative restrictions (fixing imports at certain levels). These were only to be employed for balance of payments reasons and should be non-discriminatory between sources of the imports. The United States wanted the abolition of the United Kingdom's system of proportionately low tariffs for their goods in the Empire and for Empire goods in the United Kingdom; the British were only prepared to consider the abolition of this Imperial Preference in the context of a big general reduction in tariffs (especially the USA's high tariffs). In the event, when the General Agreement on Tariffs and Trade

(GATT) was finally ratified in the spring of 1947 the United States made concessions (frequently 50 per cent cuts) on tariffs on items making up $1¾ billion of prewar imports, receiving concessions on $1¼ billion of exports. The United Kingdom eliminated some 5 per cent of preferenced trade. The GATT rules set up a forum and machinery for future modifications of the agreements.

The monetary and trade agreements had comparatively little effect in the short run. The desperate payments difficulties of Europe and Japan meant that any attempts substantially to liberalize trade and payments had inevitably to be postponed. In any case the dollar shortage meant that the hunger for US commodities hardly had to be stimulated by forcing down artificial barriers. US capital was able to sell abroad whatever it was prepared to finance. Even by the end of 1952 only one-tenth of European dollar imports were free of quantitative restriction, and the first move to liberalize intra-European trade had to wait until 1949 when 30 per cent of trade was freed from restrictions.

The United States' hopes of removing exchange controls rapidly were just as illusory. Slow progress was made towards freeing intra-European transactions beginning at the end of 1947 and culminating in 1950 with the European Payments Union which organized multilateral settlement of payments balances.

The United Kingdom was the only major country to maintain the value of its currency, in relation to the dollar, unchanged in the years before 1949. France and Italy devalued hugely, and Japan and Germany were without official rates for some time. But the rates at which foreign exchange transactions were made were at least pegged on a day-today basis and adjusted infrequently, in contrast to the experience after the First World War when rates fluctuated wildly. The rates fixed generally left European countries rather uncompetitive in relation to US industry. But over the period in which an excess of imports from the United States for reconstruction needs was inevitable, such an overvalued exchange rate was to the Europeans' advantage since it meant that US supplies cost less.

US occupation policy

US occupation policy was of central significance because it shaped the course of events in the most important capitalist economies of Europe and Asia. It also illustrates particularly sharply the United States' attitude towards the rebuilding of the other advanced capitalist countries. Japan, where the United States was in sole control, presents the purest case. US policies had to pay only the scantest regard to the attitude of the Soviet Union, Britain and France, which, rather than occupying zones, as in the case of Germany, were merely represented on a toothless Far Eastern Commission.

The Supreme Commander of the Armies of the Pacific, General MacArthur, received blunt instructions from the US government: 'You will not assume any responsibility for the economic rehabilitation of Japan or the strengthening of the Japanese economy. You will make it clear to the Japanese people that you assume no obligation to maintain any particular standard of living in Japan (Basic Initial Post-Surrender Directive, quoted Cohen, 1949, p. 417).

The initial policy on reparations was, in the words of a US government report, that the Allied powers should 'take no action to assist Japan in maintaining a standard of living higher than that of neighbouring Asiatic countries injured by Japanese aggression' (quoted Cohen, 1949, p. 420). Bearing in mind that such 'neighbouring Asiatic countries' included China, huge reparations seemed indicated. The recommendation was that these should be in the form of removals of equipment. Reparations in the form of current production would require the building up of Japanese industry to the extent necessary to generate massive export surpluses, which would re-establish Japanese industrial predominance in the area. The removals contemplated were vast: 20 million tons of pig-iron, steel-making and rolling capacity, more than three-quarters of the machine tool stock, the entire aluminium and magnesium industries, and three-quarters of ship-building facilities. The United States rapidly back-pedalled away from the devastating implications of the report and only a handful of machine tools was actually handed over. The original reparations plan would have destroyed for decades Japan's capacity to be a serious industrial competitor. Whatever its attractions, such a course would have cut off a market as well as competition, and would have made Japan's internal affairs very difficult to control.

Although reparations plans were never carried through, important reforms were initiated to break up the highly concentrated industrial structure and to improve workers' rights and conditions. Why should the United States engage in an aggressive policy of trust-busting and encouraging trade unions?

The Trade Union Law of December 1945 was modelled on US legislation and 'guarantees the right to organize and bargain collectively and recognizes the right to strike; laws and regulations infringing on the activities of labour unions are made invalid, and employers are forbidden to discharge workers for union activities' (Cohen, 1949, p. 437). The subsequent course of trade unionism led to allegations of communist influence in the relevant departments of the Occupation in Japan, yet the development of unionism in Japan was perfectly rational from the point of view of US business. Japanese industry would gain an 'unfair advantage' if it could avoid the costs and problems of trade unionism incurred by US firms.

The paper prepared to guide the occupation authorities on the 'Treatment of Japanese Workers' Organizations' was extremely explicit on this issue:

As soon as conditions are favorable, the Japanese trade unions, both by day-to-day negotiation with the employers and by pressure for national legislation, will undoubtedly press for an increase in the general wage level and the elimination of sub-standard wages. The achievement of such an objective could have important results internationally. Prewar Japan's foreign trade policies and practices had aroused widespread resentment. With relatively high technical efficiency in many lines of production and extremely low labor costs due to low wages paid to even the really skilled among her workers, she was able to undersell her commercial rivals in a wide range of goods in many parts of the world. This low wage level, it should be understood, was a product of the peculiar political, social and economic forces existing in the country, among which should be listed the violent opposition by government to genuine labor organizations. . . . Higher labor costs, therefore, would not only move in the direction of eliminating the unfair advantage long enjoyed by Japanese manufacturing and exporting interests, an advantage maintained to the detriment of the laboring classes in that country as well as to the legitimate business and labor interests of other lands, but the redistribution of income resulting from it would be a step in the desired direction of turning Japanese productive energies towards meeting the long neglected demands of the domestic consumers. (Quoted Moore, 1983, pp. 64–5).

The Occupation's breakup of the Zaibatsu – the giant holding companies that dominated industry – can also be explained by the fact that the competitive power of Japanese capital was concentrated in these enterprises. While the justification was always couched in terms of their role in Japanese militarism, this militarism was in reality the most concentrated expression of the outward economic thrust of Japanese capital. Breaking down the giant enterprises, especially in the context of massive reparations and unions able to negotiate better wages and conditions, would obliterate the competitive threat posed by Japanese capital. The Edwards report on Japanese combines, written for the Occupation at the beginning of 1946, makes very clear the relevance of these considerations:

Japan's industry has been under the control of a few great combines, supported and strengthened by the Japanese government. The concentration of control has encouraged the persistence of semi-feudal relations between employer and employee, held down wages, and blocked the development of labor unions. It has discouraged the launching of independent business ventures and thereby retarded the rise of a Japanese middle class. In the absence of such groups there has been no economic basis for independence in politics nor much development of the conflicting interests and democratic and humanitarian sentiments which elsewhere serve as counterweights to military designs. Moreover, the low wages and concentrated profits of the Zaibatsu system have limited the domestic market and intensified the importance of exports, and thus have given incentive to Japanese imperialism. The combines have been so dependent upon government favour that . . . they necessarily became instruments of their government in international politics. They necessarily served its purpose in order to be loyal not only to Japan but to their own profits. (Quoted Halliday, 1975, p. 178).

The directive sent to MacArthur on the basis of this report called for a ferocious policy: 'The dissolution of all excessive concentrations of economic power' covering any enterprise 'if its asset value is very large . . . or if it controls substantial financial institutions and/or substantial industrial or commercial ones . . . or if it produces or sells or distributes a large proportion of the total supply of the products of a major industry' (quoted Halliday, 1975, pp. 179–80). In the event, although the major Zaibatsu groups were broken up through the dissolution of the holding companies and by removing the major families' controlling interests, the banks were not included in the final dismantling plans and were able to play a big role in the groups' later reformation. The great trading companies of Mitsui and Mitsubishi were fragmented, however; the Mitsui Company employed some 700,000 people and was split up into 170 companies. Breaking up the trading companies provided 'the chief ground for the Japanese conviction that the policy was aimed primarily at weakening their country's competitive power in foreign markets' (Allen, 1958, p. 133).

The British and American governments had originally favoured operating the occupation of Germany through a German government. The administration set up by Admiral Doenitz was in fact maintained for about three weeks after the surrender, but adverse press criticism in the United States led to its removal at the end of May 1945. The exercise of state power then fell directly on the Occupation military government. Initially it was understaffed, of doubtful legitimacy in the eyes of most of the population, and faced problems even from the occupation forces themselves. US troops staged mass demonstrations in Germany, as in Italy, in the summer of 1945, demanding to be sent home immediately.

Supported at first by the French, US policy was designed to destroy German capitalism rather than to rehabilitate it. Before the surrender, Roosevelt had considered, and for a brief period apparently adopted, proposals from within his administration to de-industrialize Germany and turn it into a predominantly agricultural economy. One motive for supporting this scheme was to ensure that the USSR would find difficulty in seizing part of German output as reparations for war damage. The British moved quickly towards favouring the revival of German industry.

After considerable vacillation (different sections of the administration were pushing different lines) Truman eventually approved, on 10 May 1945, a Joint Chiefs of Staff directive (JCS 1067) which laid down basic policy: 'Except as may be necessary to carry out [your basic] objectives, you will take no steps (a) looking towards the economic rehabilitation of Germany or (b) designed to maintain or strengthen the German economy.'

Output was to be limited to a level sufficient to provide a minimum standard of material welfare. All plant over and above that required to produce such a level of output was to be dismantled and shipped abroad for reparations. Large industrial empires and cartels were to be broken up. These measures were originally justified in terms of preventing the possibility of future aggression. Thus deconcentration of the banks, for example, was argued on the grounds that a centralized banking structure had made it easier to finance war expenditure.

The level-of-industry plan of 1946 prohibited production in excess of half the 1938 level. Eighteen hundred plants were scheduled for dismantling in the Western zones. Contrary to the case of Japan, substantial reparations got underway. In 1946 plant comprising around 2 per cent of the capital stock was dismantled, one-quarter going to the USSR. The heads of the Krupp and IG Farben empires were arrested and the firms placed under the control of trustees. A 'liquidation commission' was set up to carry out deconcentration measures. Eventually the IG Farben concern was split into four separate companies (in 1953), the 12 major steel firms were divided into 28 units, with limitations on their coal interests, and the three biggest banks were split temporarily into 33 regionally based banks.

The chief respect in which policy in Germany differed from that pursued by the Occupation in Japan concerned the labour movement. German labour posed a more immediate threat to the restoration of normally functioning capitalist relations. It had a long history and a capacity to organize rapidly, as the antifas and works councils showed. If the immediate practical goals of restoring production and distribution of basic necessities could not be realized then demands for the socialization of production, already widespread, would become more insistent. The basic policies in both the British and the American zones were suppression of the radical and broad-based antifas, refusal to allow immediate reorganization of unions or parties at a national level and, after this period of quarantine, slow build-up of an 'acceptable' structure.

The authorities' nightmare was that a single union covering all workers might develop, its centralization enhancing its power. The British Trades Union Congress (TUC) was sent to Germany to convince the SPD trade union leaders that unions should be organized industry by industry with only a loose national federation, on the grounds that this would limit the KPD's influence. Initially local unions were not even allowed to levy contributions or hire offices, and were only allowed to link up with others in the same industry after the leadership agreed in August 1946 to the industry-based structure.

Uncle Joe in control

Just as the US government's policies were to be decisive for the countries liberated by its armies, so the policies of the Soviet government were decisive where the Red Army held sway. History determined which considerations dominated policy. For the United States, where the Great Depression had threatened the very survival of capitalism, economic access to Europe and Japan and their colonies was the paramount consideration. For the Soviet Union, where Hitler's invasion had almost crushed the Stalinist system, establishing a ring of allied 'buffer states' as a bulwark against future imperialist attack was the overriding necessity. These dominating concerns clearly had consequences for the type of social system which could be acceptable to each major power in its sphere of influence.

The socialist transformation of society in Western Europe or Japan was obviously inconsistent with the United States' economic ambitions. Similarly the restoration in Eastern Europe of the old regimes, which had collaborated with the Nazis and were implacably hostile to Russia, was quite unacceptable to Stalin. Both major powers had an interest in the failure of the designs of the other. The United States stood to lose access to the markets of Eastern Europe if those countries were fully integrated into the Stalinist system. The Soviet Union would have to deal with a more united powerful enemy if Western Europe and Japan were consolidated into a United States-dominated bloc. Each major power confronted internal opposition inside their zones of influence, which looked in turn towards the other. The United States faced a radicalized mass movement in Western Europe, generally led by Communist parties faithful to Moscow. In Eastern Europe Russia faced substantial sectors who were opposed to socialism, distrustful of the Soviet Union and oriented more to the United States. Of the two, the opposition faced by the Soviet Union was undoubtedly less of a threat, being on the defensive, fragmented, with its leadership discredited and generally disoriented by the outcome of the war. The left in Europe, with the partial exception of Germany, was on the offensive, cohesive, with a strong and tested leadership, and determined not to miss the opportunity for implementing important measures of social reform.

The Soviet Union, it seemed, was in a much better position than the United States to implement its own designs in its sphere, and to frustrate its opponent in the other. While the USA had the greater economic strength, which it could deploy to steer developments via aid and loans, the USSR had the military advantage of close proximity to its sphere of influence. Most importantly, socialist forces in both Eastern and Western Europe were much stronger than those favouring all-out capitalist restoration.

People's democracy

The crucial question was how Stalin proposed to take advantage of this apparently favourable position. The method devised was to oblige the Communist parties (CPs), in both Eastern and Western Europe, to follow the theory of 'people's democracy'. The CPs were to enter 'national democratic' coalitions which would include all antifascists, from Communists through Socialists and Liberals to Christian Democrats. These coalition governments would carry out measures of national reconstruction which would include nationalization of industries and distribution of land owned by Nazis or collaborators and their purging from the army, police and civil service. According to Stalin, the building of socialism in the USSR together with Soviet victories in the war provided a framework, safe from intervention by imperialism, for a different road to socialism from the Russian one:

Once the political power of the financial and landed oligarchy had been destroyed by the liberation, which cut it off from its economic basis by expropriation and nationalization, long-term cooperation became possible between the working class, small peasant proprietors and the middle bourgeoisie, industrial, commercial and agricultural, as part of a gradual transition to socialism. The nationalized sector would continue to grow and the capitalist sector to decline, and small peasants would gradually and voluntarily go over to cooperative forms of production, until the whole economy rested on a socialist basis. The class struggle would go on, but would take peaceful and evolutionary forms within the democratic parliamentary system. (Claudin, 1975, p. 461)

Stalin went so far as to tell Tito: 'Today Socialism is possible even under the British monarchy. Just recently a delegation of the British Labour Party was here and we talked about this in particular. Yes, there is much that is new' (quoted Djilas, 1962, p. 104).

The implications of this for Western Europe and Japan were profound. The 'popular front' tactic in Europe and elsewhere, in which CPs participated in coalition governments with capitalist parties, served Stalin's purposes admirably. It provided a way of dousing revolutionary enthusiasm in Europe by channelling it into parliamentary politics. At the same time it gave the labour movement maximum leverage against possible aggressive moves by the capitalist countries aimed at the Soviet Union. As we shall see in the next chapter, the influence Stalin wielded through his control over the Japanese and Western European Communist parties played a vital role in determining how reconstruction proceeded.

4

The First Two Years

In the first two postwar years the pattern of recovery varied from country to country. The United States and United Kingdom reconverted industry to peacetime uses rapidly. France and Italy raised production steadily towards prewar levels. Germany and Japan made little progress.

Reconstruction required high investment to eliminate transport and fuel bottlenecks and to renovate consumer goods industries neglected during the war. This was achieved everywhere except Germany, where investment was still very low in 1947 (table 4.1).

Table 4.1 Production and investment, 1937–47

	Industrial production (1938 = 100)		Non-residential investment[a] (1937 = 100)		Share of total fixed investment in GDP[b] (percentages)	
	1946	1947	1946	1947	1937	1947
USA	156[c]	175[c]	161	193	15.7	17.2
UK	106	115	85	102	16.1	13.1
France	84	99	119	132	16.1	21.2
Italy	61	92	81	113	21.4	29.3
Germany	29	34	35	46	19.6	n.a.
Japan	31[d]	37[d]	80	93	18.1	28.7

[a] Total fixed investment less housing investment, except for Germany (manufacturing and mining investment) and Japan (total fixed investment).
[b] At constant market prices. For Italy, includes stockbuilding.
[c] 1937 = 100.
[d] 1934–6 = 100.
Source: see Appendix

Investment and wages

Under capitalism, high profits are normally a precondition for high investment since they provide the motive and much of the finance to invest. But in the immediate postwar years firms could finance investment by running down financial assets accumulated during the war. And fears about their future value could make building up machinery and stocks preferable to hanging on to financial assets. With production limited by shortages and uncertainties, high investment financed in this way would pull up prices and eat into real wages. So high profits would still tend to accompany high investment, but as effect rather than cause.

With production low, the working class could achieve tolerable real wages only by accepting widespread dismissals and speed-up on remaining jobs. Successful resistance to dismissals would result in low productivity. Satisfactory profits for employers would then imply very low real wages.

Two other groups complicate the picture. One is middle-class savers or rentiers (people for whom a significant part of their income is returns on financial assets). Governments had financed much wartime spending by selling bonds to this group, which thereby accumulated enormous savings. If these savings were spent then prices would rise further, screwing down real wages and boosting profits. This could be avoided only by wiping out these savings. Monetary reform often sought to do exactly this, by replacing hoarded cash with smaller amounts of new currency. This was obviously unpopular with the middle classes (although attempts to spend their savings would have had similar effects since the resulting inflation would have severely devalued remaining savings).

The other main complication was the peasantry. Chronic food shortages raised the price of food relative to manufactured goods (especially on the black market). This meant higher real incomes for peasants. If they spent these on consumption (buying more manufactures or eating more) then this would squeeze workers' consumption further. But if they saved their extra incomes, say, then this would allow high investment without high profits. In effect, capitalists could finance investment by running down financial assets, which would finish up under peasants' mattresses.

The final squeeze on wages came from high government spending. There were pressures to repair dilapidated social capital, such as housing, and to improve social welfare programmes. If these were to be paid for from taxes then much of the burden would have to fall on workers so as not to jeopardize investment. Where taxation was limited by political considerations, governments would have to borrow more. Surplus profits and middle-class incomes would have to be that much higher to provide the funds. Government investment in nationalized industries also had to be financed, implying high profits in those industries or borrowing from other sectors. Resources would only be available if real wages were low enough.

These pressures would be eased only if available resources exceeded production by a substantial margin, that is, if imports ran well ahead of exports. Such a balance of payments deficit would imply borrowing from abroad. In effect, capitalists could then continue to invest heavily with low profits and high workers' consumption. But this possibility was severely limited. Dollar reserves were low and credit difficult to obtain. The interconnection of these various pressures and constraints is illustrated in figure 4.1.

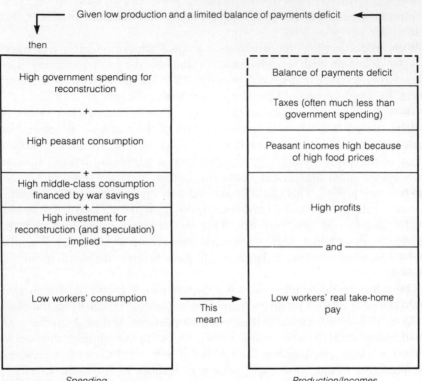

Figure 4.1   Pressures on wages.

One result was inflation. The excess of purchasing power over production pulled up prices. This helped to keep real wages down as money wage rises lagged behind prices (limiting workers' consumption). It reduced the value of cash hoards and financial assets (limiting middle-class consumption). It also made it hard for governments to sell more debt, since no one wants financial assets whose real value is falling. Governments were forced to pay for expenditure (finance deficits) by printing money. Inflation also meant that capitalists could often make more by hoarding commodities (investing in stocks) than by accumulating productive assets (investing in plant and equipment). So inflation twisted and distorted the whole pattern of reconstruction. Where it was repressed by price controls and rationing it both discouraged production and diverted much of it into black markets.

Whether or not workers would passively accept the severe hardships facing them in the aftermath of the war depended crucially on how far they felt – or could be persuaded to feel – that the reconstruction which their deprivations were underpinning was being carried out in their interests. The situation varied considerably in each country. In Germany and Japan, where no real reconstruction was taking place, demands arose within the labour movement for workers to intervene directly, gaining a real measure of power in government or the factories, or both. In France and Italy working-class parties were in coalition governments. Discontent accordingly centred on opposition to attempts to make workers redouble their efforts while black markets flourished, middle-class consumption was given more or less free rein, and speculative stockpiling proceeded unchecked. In the United Kingdom, where Labour had won a landslide victory in 1945, workers concentrated on trying to prevent backsliding by their party.

Japan

During the first months of the occupation, the Japanese government allowed big companies to plunder its funds and stocks of materials while industrial production stagnated at one-tenth the prewar level. The government then responded early in 1946 by launching a plan for more effective controls over the economy. Credit, agricultural deliveries and hoarded goods in particular were singled out. Six months later a new finance minister proposed massive subsidies to key sectors of industry to stimulate recovery. But successive governments, all solidly linked to big business, proved incapable of forceful reorganization. The Occupation became frustrated with the situation, which it euphemistically ascribed to 'government incompetence', and reversed its original policy of 'non-responsibility in the economic sphere' (Cohen, 1949, p. 419). From then onwards, any effective action flowed from its instructions.

By 1947 industrial production had only risen from one-tenth of prewar levels to a third. Petrol output was 6 per cent of its prewar peak, machine tool output 9 per cent, steel 12 per cent, cotton fabric 14 per cent and cement 20 per cent. One constraint was electricity. Demand outstripped supply despite the fact that electricity production (mainly hydroelectric) was running at almost double the prewar level. Demand was so high because coal production remained well below prewar levels even by 1947. Productivity in the mines was hardly one-third of the prewar level, partly because of union resistance to work speeds. Coal was also being used much less effectively on the railways, presumably due to lack of maintenance of the rolling stock. Imports of coking coal for steel production were no longer obtainable from prewar Asian sources.

Foreign exchange to buy imported raw materials was a crucial bottleneck. Cotton textiles, a major prewar export earner, is a good example. The Occupation considered the rehabilitation of this industry as a priority: 'Possibly the existence in the United States of large government held stocks of raw cotton influenced this determination' (Cohen, 1949, p. 484). Even though only one-sixth of prewar capacity remained, some spindles were still idle in 1947. The industry was in an impossible situation. It needed to export some 60 per cent of output to earn the dollars to buy the US cotton. Traditional markets, in the Sterling Area for example, were starved of dollars. Japanese textile exports to the United States were banned. The Americans were slow to release Japan from the double bind of having to buy cotton for dollars while being effectively prevented from earning them with textile exports.

Agriculture was much less dislocated than industry. Production was at about the prewar level, but the number of mouths to feed had risen by around one-tenth. Daily calorie consumption in Tokyo was 1350 in 1946. By mid-1947 it had risen only to 1700. Rapid inflation made peasants reluctant to sell rice to the government. Urban inhabitants made treks to the countryside to barter household goods for rice. In desperation the government followed suit in 1947; it began delivering fertilizers, textiles, cigarettes (eight for 72 litres of rice) and other goods, exchanging them for rice. Even the official figures show real farm incomes 20 per cent up on prewar.

The food problem was eased by around $300 million of food imports, paid for by US aid. But the relief was strictly limited. The balance of payments was in deficit to the tune of about 4 per cent of total output, or gross domestic product (GDP), in 1946 and 1947.

Inflation ran at a phenomenal 42 per cent a month in the 6 months after surrender. Production collapsed, while the huge stock of financial assets was further bloated by various handouts to big business ('compensation' payments for war damage and so forth). A currency reform instituted early in 1946 involved compulsory deposits of banknotes and limitation of withdrawals. Prices did decline at first, but reversed only half the increase of the immediately preceding weeks, when expectations of the reform had fuelled a spending spree. By the turn of the year the inflation was in full swing again. The government's borrowing requirement was some 9 per cent of GDP. Prices were three times as high in 1947 as in 1946. The basic inflationary mechanism is clearly explained by an American observer:

> Spiralling prices, due to an inadequate supply of raw materials and consumer goods, excess purchasing power, etc. tend to make the cost of living outrun the wage level at any time. The resultant pressure for higher wages, made possible by the new strength of the unions, the real economic basis for their demands and the weakness and disorganization of management, caused a higher wage level than the one upon which the government based its calculations in the prior fixing of official prices. . . . The increase in industrial costs in the face of fixed official prices forced a firm either to divert its output in whole or in part to the black market in order to realize a profit or, if it sold in legitimate markets at official prices, to incur a deficit which could only be made good by a government subsidy or a deficit-covering bank loan . . . in effect, government-related funds have been funnelled via the

Reconstruction Finance Bank to finance industrial deficits. (Cohen, 1949, pp. 448–9).

Recorded profits were less than one-tenth of company output in 1947 (table 4.2), less than one-quarter of the prewar level. With high overheads, and productivity so low, companies only managed to make any profits at all because real wages were hardly a third of the prewar level.

Table 4.2 Profits, wages and productivity: Japan, 1936–47

	Profit share[a]	Real wage[b]	Industrial production	Industrial employment	Industrial productivity
1936	38	100[c]	100[c]	100[c]	100[c]
1946	10	25[d]	31	86	36
1947	8	30	37	95	39

[a] Net profits as percentage of net corporate product.
[b] In terms of cost of living.
[c] 1934–6 = 100.
[d] Very rough estimate.

Source: see Appendix.

Recorded investment was high in relation to recorded profits. More houses were being built than in the 1930s. Government investment on infrastructure was twice the prewar level and comprised nearly half of total investment in 1946 and 1947. But private investment was also high. Investment in rebuilding stocks (of materials, food, goods, etc.) was estimated at an enormous 11 per cent of total production (reckoned at prewar prices). Private fixed investment (in plant and factories) was lower – a little over half the 1938 level (but was above that of the twenties and early thirties). The cotton textile industry invested heavily, increasing capacity by one-third in 1946 and 1947. Quite what the rest of the investment consisted of is unclear. Production of most investment goods appears to have been very low and imports non-existent.

A good deal of recorded investment may in fact have been in repairs or concealed stockbuilding. Clearly capitalists stood to gain from borrowing from banks to finance stock accumulation. And bigger and surer profits could often be made by hanging on to stocks rather than using them to raise output or invest in extra plant in a situation of heavy excess capacity. So fixed investment may not have been as high relative to profits as the figures indicate. To the extent that total investment really was high, it was financed by firms running down financial assets.

The inflation was catastrophic for rentiers. The proportion of the national income (itself a third lower than prewar) received as interest fell from 9 per cent in 1936 and 12 per cent in 1944 to 1 per cent in 1947. The share taken in rent fell from 4 per cent to 1 per cent. A capital levy was carried out, ostensibly to hit those with such 'real' assets as shares. But it was a farce, being based on prewar asset values when by 1947 the price level had risen a hundred times.

Inflation also kept real wages low. In 1947 they were only about 30 per cent of the prewar level even if calculated on the basis of official prices. The existence of an extensive and expensive black market means that the postwar figure exaggerates real purchasing power. The disparity in living standards was less than that in incomes since, in contrast to prewar, workers were making no savings (and spending such wartime savings as were still worth anything).

Roaring inflation and starvation wages made pay a major issue. By the end of 1946 membership of unions had rocketed to nearly 5 million, well over a third of the work force. 'At most factories or shipyards . . . the blue-collar workers organized unions first, with white-collar staff following suit several months later. At NKK's Kawasaki mill, initial talk of forming a single all-employee union was rejected by blue-collar workers, who felt they would be unable to co-operate with their supervisors' (Gordon, 1985, pp. 342–3). The key wage agreement was negotiated in the electric power industry in autumn 1946. This 'Densan wage system', which embodied most union demands, linked wages to the cost of living. It was calculated after tax and included a basic wage, a strong age-related element (giving a single man of 40 twice the pay of a 20-year-old) and a substantial allowance based on family circumstances (giving a married man of thirty with three children double the basic wage of a man with no dependants). The principle was that wages should reflect living costs, with age and family circumstances regarded as relevant. But an additional element (equivalent to the basic rate for a 30-year-old) was to be determined by 'ability', judged on criteria of skill, experience and educational background. This element was apparently accepted as just by both workers and management, and its determination in individual cases was not a matter of contention. The workshop supervisors who fixed it were in many cases elected by workshop meetings of union members. Other workers in less favourably placed industries struggled for comparable deals. Miners in Kyushu, lacking an effective regional organization, were defeated. But in Hokkaido a strong regional organization led an effective strike and forced the mine owners to concede.

Workers also resisted redundancies fiercely. Despite the low level of production, industrial employment was barely below its prewar level in 1947 (though a third less than its wartime peak). It also rose nearly as fast as production during 1947, even though productivity was less than 40 per cent of the prewar level (table 4.2). Workers struck for more than 6 million days in 1946 and 'the Labour unions won all their strikes against discharges' (Okochi et al., 1974, p. 319). Government plans to dismiss 43,000 seamen and 75,000 railway workers were beaten off by rank-and-file pressure, which forced the unions to call a ten-day seamen's strike and to fix a date for strike action by railwaymen. After a 55-day strike 40,000 Toshiba workers won an agreement that 'the company will absolutely not fire anyone for reasons such as "rationalization" '. Many managements were obliged to agree to 'consult and gain the consent of the union in virtually all matters relating to personnel policy and wages' (Gordon, 1985, p. 345), on occasion this specifically included the issue of work rules. A quarter of a million workers engaged in 'production control' (chapter 2). A few actions developed beyond struggles over union recognition and pay and conditions into battles for workers' control and planning. Workers in the Toyo Gosei chemical plant, faced with closure, excluded company executives, borrowed funds to expand capacity, bartered the ammonium sulphate they produced with a farmers' association, took on more workers and introduced a new wage system embodying a 50 per cent increase.

Massive numbers of workers took to the streets in the spring of 1946. In April, just before the first general election, 70,000 demonstrated in Tokyo, calling for the overthrow of the government. They disarmed police who fired warning shots. Order was restored only after American armoured cars appeared. On May Day half a million demonstrated in Tokyo, and some 1½ million throughout the country, demanding a 'democratic government' and 'control of food by the people', and opposing suppression of workers' control. Two weeks later a quarter of a million, organized by trade unions and the Kanto District Council on Food, held a 'People's Rally to Secure Rice' (the average daily intake in Tokyo had reached a low of 1064 calories). The rally called for citizens' committees to control food distribution, for a 'democratic government with the Socialist and Communist parties as its nucleus and with trade unions, peasant organizations and democratically oriented cultural associations as its basis' (quoted Yamamoto, 1980/1, p. 26). The leaders sat in at the prime minister's residence, but left after MacArthur issued a statement denouncing these mass demonstrations as 'a menace not only to orderly government but to the basic purposes and security of the occupation itself' and said the occupation forces would take 'the necessary steps to control and remedy such a deplorable situation' (quoted Yamamoto, 1980/1, p. 30).

The Occupation intervened not only to threaten demonstrators; it also encouraged management at the *Yomiuri* newspaper to sack workers' leaders controlling the paper. The workers fought off company thugs who tried to prevent those sacked from entering the building. On 21 June 1946, 500 armed police forced their way in and made 50 arrests. Workers' leaders were charged with serious crimes. Both management and the Occupation threatened to close the paper. Faced with such powerful opposition the union retreated, abandoning control over the paper's operations. But it continued to demand recognition, initiating court action. Management then transferred union leaders outside Tokyo and organized a pro-management 'reconstruction council'. The union struck and reoccupied the paper. Management thugs threw them out while the police stood aside. Plans for a national press strike fizzled out. In October the union admitted defeat and dissolved itself. Workers taken back on the paper had to join the company union. This was an important defeat.

But struggles continued elsewhere. A mass rally of half a million in December 1946, called to coincide with a no-confidence vote in parliament, demanded the overthrow of the Yoshida cabinet. Following the motion's defeat, the 2½-million-strong government workers' union federation called for a general strike on 1 February 1947, defying a law passed the previous autumn denying their right to strike. Public sector workers were under particular pressure; their wages were lagging far behind inflation. They demanded wage rises, no dismissals, the conclusion of collective contracts and less authoritarian management. The Communist Party, announcing its support for the demands of the unions, called for the strike to aim at establishing a 'democratic people's government' – that is, a Socialist-led coalition cabinet. It also stated 'its confidence that SCAP [the occupation authorities] would not suppress a political strike of this nature and criticized the trend in the labour movement towards direct action and a frontal attack upon the rights of the capitalist owners of the means of production' (Moore, 1983, p. 234).

MacArthur initially pressed the government to concede to some of the strikers' economic demands, including a 50 per cent wage rise and a resumption of negotiations. But he then denounced 'the use of so deadly a social weapon in the present impoverished and emaciated state of Japan' (quoted Cole et al., 1966, p. 15), prohibited the strike and told the union that defiance would 'provoke action of the most drastic nature against individual and organized labour interests' (quoted Moore, 1983, p. 239).

Even after this setback, the Socialist Party won 26 per cent of the vote in the April 1947 election on a programme including nationalization of the mines. The situation was highly unstable: 'The collapse of a Japanese cabinet as a result of a communist promoted general strike would indeed have greatly strengthened the communists and gained credit for their direct-action methods at the expense of constitutional processes. It is understandable that the American authorities should fear the development of a revolutionary situation which might have a sharp anti-American tendency' (*Economist*, 8 February 1947).

The Communist Party provided the leadership for the most militant workers. Although it secured only 4 per cent of the vote in the April 1946 and April 1947 elections, and had a membership of only 7500 in April 1946 (70,000 by the end of 1947), the CP led the mass demonstrations and campaign for a general strike. The union confederation Sanbetsu, founded in August 1946 with 1½ million members, was the most militant labour movement organization and under CP control.

Although there were divisions in the party and fluctuations in its pronouncements, the leadership was committed to a parliamentary road to socialism. Its demand for the downfall of an unpopular reactionary cabinet was not the first step towards insurrection. It even distanced itself from 'production control'. In December 1945 it called for 'workers' control over essential enterprise' as a prerequisite for restoring production. But by February 1946 it had amended this to a call for 'the heightening of the general efficiency of industry by employing a system of management councils' (quoted Moore, 1983, pp. 118, 124).

In sum, the situation in 1946 and 1947 did not provide a stable and healthy basis for capitalist reconstruction. High inflation, rampant speculation, high government and balance of payments deficits, were symptoms of instability (shared with Italy and France). Low production and profits represented further problems. Japanese workers, with only a minimal history of organization, were showing an extraordinary capacity for struggle. They had established strong shopfloor organizations. In a number of industries individual enterprise unions had welded themselves together into effective industry confederations. Moreover, the ruling class was unused to dealing with labour unrest.

Electorally, a 30 per cent vote for workers' parties posed something of a threat. But it proved easy to defuse. The peasants delivered a massive vote to conservative parties in the wake of a land reform, which increased the proportion of families owning more than half their land from 50 to 90 per cent. The Socialist Party was enticed into a coalition with one of the conservative parties and its programme was shredded. Its plan for coal nationalization was reduced to a bill which 'signified that the obsolescent machinery in Japanese collieries would be modernized at the taxpayer's expense and soon returned, with the mines themselves, to private hands' (Cole et al., 1966, p. 18). The crushing of workers' shopfloor strength, previewed at *Yomiuri*, was to prove a much tougher task.

Germany

The German economy's gradual emergence from the chaos of the summer of 1945 showed no more sense of direction than did the Japanese, but the problem was not the Japanese one of procrastination and vacillation by a weak national government. It was rather paralysis on the part of the occupying powers. They could not decide what they wanted a future Germany to look like. (From now on, when we refer to Germany we mean the postwar Federal Republic.) As long as the issue of eventual unification with the Soviet-occupied Eastern zone remained undecided, the Western occupation authorities did little more than maintain existing economic controls. They intervened decisively only on a few matters of particular interest to themselves, such as coal.

It is especially difficult to chart the exact course of recovery in Germany. Officially the wartime administrative system was used to control all prices, wages and the allocation of materials and consumer goods. But low production, inadequate rations and high stocks of liquid assets, amassed during the war, combined to produce tremendous excess demand for commodities. A black market flourished. According to one report, 'regular trade is the exception and exists only as a camouflage' (quoted Abelshauser, 1975, p. 5). In the autumn of 1946 it was suggested that only half of real production and stocks was being reported. Official estimates were that in 1947 at least one-tenth of production went to the black market. Obviously there is scope for a large margin of error. The best available estimates are that industrial production was growing rapidly by the middle of 1946. It fell back to little more than the level of the previous year during the winter of 1946–7 but then rebounded rapidly. By the end of 1947 it was around half the 1936 level.

As in Japan, fuel, materials and transport were the main bottlenecks. These constraints were often interconnected. At one stage there was a shortage of timber for shoring up mines. The foresters refused to work in the rain because they did not have good enough clothes and shoes. But the textile industries were dependent on coal to expand production, and so on.

Transport had been badly hit by bombing (chapter 2). By the middle of 1946 the railways and canals were functioning effectively and there was apparently no transport shortage. But the exceptionally hard winter of 1946–7, combined with overuse of rolling stock, brought a major crisis. In January 1947 only two-thirds of transportation requirements could be met. An emergency repair programme was launched and the system coped well next winter.

Coal was generally regarded as *the* key sector. Poor rations reduced output. The *Economist* noted: 'The situation in the Ruhr is becoming desperate. In the past week after the cut in rations a decrease in coal output by about 10 per cent was reported. By the end of March the decline in output was already nearly 20 per cent' (6 April 1946). By August 1946 miners' rations had risen to 4000 calories – about three times the average – and this, together with a 20 per cent wage increase, helped to boost the number of miners by nearly 40 per cent between 1945 and 1947.

But productivity per underground worker still stood at only about 60 per cent of prewar levels in 1947. In 1946, 24 per cent of coal from the US and UK zones was exported. Although this was only slightly higher than the prewar share, the coal was bought at less than half the market price, leading to an estimated loss of foreign exchange earnings of some $200 million by the end of 1947. Even more foreign exchange could have been earned by diverting coal, which made up three-quarters of exports in 1946, to domestic industry to permit production of other goods for export.

The iron and steel industry became a victim of attempts to demilitarize Germany. The initial industrial plan limited productive capacity to 5.8 million tons a year, less than one-third of prewar output. But the industry received such a low priority that even this level was nowhere near reached. Until early in 1948 the industry was forbidden to import Swedish iron ore, which had previously provided two-thirds of its supply. So it was forced to rely on inadequate amounts of poor-quality domestic ore. The British even shipped home half a million tons of scrap, bought at well below market prices.

Food production in the US and UK zones was only about 70 per cent of prewar levels in 1946–7; $660 million worth of food was imported in 1947, almost as much as in 1936. But it now consisted almost entirely of cereals whereas fat and meat imports had been important before the war. It was financed mainly by aid from the United States and Britain, totalling $470 million in 1946 and $600 million in 1947. Very little else was imported.

The United Nations calculated that in 1947 industrial employment in the Western zones stood at 89 per cent of the prewar level. Combining this with the production index suggests that average productivity was around one-half the prewar level. A figure of one-quarter was quoted for iron and steel in 1946, hit especially hard by low production. Hourly factory wages had typically fallen by one-quarter to one-third in money terms since the war had ended, and the 48-hour week had been reintroduced. The official cost of living index increased by 20 per cent between March 1945 and April 1946. But these figures underestimate the decline in living standards. Rationing limited purchases and the black market inflated prices. Periodically the situation became desperate. It was reported in March 1946 that rations in the British zone had been reduced to 1014 calories.

An estimated two-fifths of a worker's income was spent on black market food, clothing and tobacco at five to ten times official prices. Uncontrolled commodities prices were reported in the summer of 1946 to be from three (shoe-polish) to sixteen (bootlaces) times the prewar level. In the spring of 1946 skilled workers were reported to be financing 40 per cent of expenditure out of savings.

The pressures on firms to operate on the black market were well described by the *Economist*:

> Several conditions make it inevitable that a large proportion of output should tend to go directly from the factory to some form of black market. The first is the low level of production in comparison with capacity; this means that enterprises work at a loss which can only be made good by selling – or more often bartering – some of their output on the black market. The second is the artificially low controlled prices. . . . The controlled rates of wages are also artificially low, which makes it necessary for the employer to supplement them in kind. The absence of any currency reform, coupled with the knowledge that a proportion of the existing note circulation will sooner or later be cancelled, makes for a plentiful supply of money on the black market. And finally, lack of food drives works managers to barter part of their production in exchange for canteen supplies. (26 April 1947).

It is impossible to calculate profits. At official wages and prices the low level of productivity probably implied losses. But with many sales at black market prices, the real purchasing power of wages was extremely low and savings were run down to boost family expenditure. While much production must have been consumed by the masses of the population, part of this consumption involved the transfer of financial assets from workers to black marketeers – profits of a sort. There was also, according to the available figures, some gross fixed investment in manufacturing and mining; although this did not cover depreciation (so that the capital stock fell even before taking account of reparations) it suggests some gross profits. There was probably also substantial stockbuilding on the expectation that prices would rise when controls were removed. As in Japan, this represented concealed profits.

The extreme hardship did not provoke major working-class unrest until the spring of 1947. The trade unions, permitted to develop during 1946, were led mainly by officials from the pre-1933 period, usually social democrats. These people were seldom foisted on the unions by the authorities. Their experience and anti-Nazi stance gave them some authority among the workers. But they nevertheless saw their task as checking workers' aspirations and assured the military authorities that they were doing their best to keep their members at work.

Elections for regional parliaments were held in 1946. The SPD received one-third of the votes in the US zone and, together with the KPD, around half in the more industrialized UK zone (the KPD averaged around 10 per cent). In Hesse a referendum was included on the socialization of industry. US commander Clay insisted that it had to be voted on separately. When 71 per cent of the voters approved the proposal, he vetoed it. The trade union leadership tried to restrain such demands at the Bavarian Union Congress in 1947. One leader, Tarnow, produced an ingenious objection: 'The hour of the private capitalist system is passed, and therefore strikes which demand the handing over of concerns into common ownership are superfluous' (quoted Schmidt and Fichter, 1971, p. 29).

While nominally committed to socialization, SPD representatives combined with the right in the North Rhine-Westphalian regional parliament to vote down a motion put forward by 95 delegations, representing 100,000 workers, for the 'expropriation without compensation of the war-criminal coal barons of the Rhine and Ruhr'. The *Economist* described the situation in the Ruhr in the spring of 1947:

If only the theoretical daily calorie level of 1550 for basic consumers could be maintained and honoured, then the miseries of cellar life and overcrowding and shortage of goods would matter much less. Only half this level is being met at the moment, and for the four weeks ahead the bread ration will be cut by two-fifths, from 92 ounces to 55. As nearly half the bread grain to be received in the next two months consists of maize – which makes a heavy and indigestible loaf – and as most families living in the towns can eat hardly anything but bread, there is great hardship ahead. To honour the official bread ration, 5000 tons of grain daily must be imported, and the deliveries planned for May fall far short of this figure.

As for the rest of the diet, the fat ration nominally stands at seven ounces every four weeks; in fact, only two or three ounces were received on the last ration. Because of shortage of meat, fish and sugar have been substituted for two-thirds of the current meat ration. Families who were not lucky enough to lay in stocks of potatoes last autumn are now completely without them; even in the miners' canteens, which receive special issues, potatoes are often short. In these conditions it is not surprising that the mood of the people since the recent demonstrations has been explosive. A further strike of the miners to protest against the shortages is expected soon. If it comes, the effect on German exports and industry will be very serious. (26 April 1947).

Strikes swept through the Ruhr early in 1947. The demands initially concerned housing and food but soon spread to include nationalizations. Mass strikes over this issue took place in Düsseldorf and Essen. In February the factory councils organized ballots on nationalization without compensation. Voting in the mines was typically 90 per cent in favour. Strikes continued to spread: 85,000 workers came out in Wuppertal and 80,000 in Düsseldorf on 25 March. At the high point 350,000 workers were out and mass demonstrations held. Miners operated an effective 'go slow' when at work.

In a broadcast made during the strikes the US governor, Newman, said:

> In the US Congress there is a distinct inclination to oppose further shipment of food to Germany. This can be traced back to rumours of strikes, threats of strikes and a certain resistance in behaviour to the authorities. Strikes which endanger the policies of the occupying powers, or interfere with their plans, will not be tolerated . . . any person who behaves in such a manner will be punished, and do not forget, that under the laws of the military the guilty can be punished with the death sentence. Avoid agitators, and reject those who, out of selfish grounds, criticize the occupation. Be industrious! I have the power to cut the rations of anyone involved in work unrest . . . this would be drastic and extend for an indefinite period of time (quoted Schmidt and Fichter, 1971, pp. 28, 29).

Troops clashed with demonstrators in Brunswick on 1 April and armoured patrols began to prowl the streets regularly.

A report on the founding conference of the German Union Federation stressed the decisive role for the trade union movement: 'Hitherto, the union officials have exerted a restraining influence over the workers, and have both preached and practised a policy of cooperation with the British authorities. The present mood of the populace is such, however, that checks and restraints can be of very little avail. Only an improvement in food supplies and the clearing up of the administrative confusion can bring any change' (*Economist*, 24 May 1947). The Federation's constitution included the aim of 'ensuring for the workers an equal voice in the control of economic and social policy . . . and their participation on a basis of parity in all existing and future economic corporations' (*Economist*, 24 May 1947).

Trade unions in the British zone drew up model works council constitutions covering matters affecting wages, welfare and working conditions and providing for regular reports from the management on production progress and programmes. They stipulated that the council should have access to the firm's books, and should be consulted on all questions of staffing and promotion. 'It is not surprising that some employers should have only agreed reluctantly to what some must have regarded as the signing away of their managerial rights. In some cases, their refusal to agree with the trade union terms has led to strikes' (*Economist*, 24 May 1947). The conference also called for broader reconstruction measures, including the immediate socialization of basic industries (beginning with coal and steel), a halt to the dismantling of factories which could be put to peaceful purposes, land reform, a complete purge of the food administration and stricter measures to ensure deliveries from the farms.

Italy

In December 1945 the Christian Democrats toppled the coalition government led by the radical resistance leader Parri by withdrawing their support. A series of coalitions led by the Christian Democrat De Gasperi followed. De Gasperi's appointment prevented the radical aspirations of the liberation from being realized. It meant 'for the capitalist classes the end of the policy of factory works councils, the end of the fear of nationalization and of the equally dreaded changes in the currency, the end of state intervention in economic and social life to achieve greater social justice and the end of taxes on excess profits accrued from speculation and the war' (Catalano, 1972, p. 85). But the Communist Party stayed in the coalition in the name of 'national unity'. This line had been mapped out by CP leader Togliatti on his return from Moscow in March 1944.

Production reached 90 per cent of its prewar level in 1947. This rapid recovery flowed from high demand rather than effective government action, which, instead of using the much-expanded public sector as a motor for recovery, relied on private enterprise.

Basic public utilities – the railways, coal mining, telephones and part of the electricity supply – were already nationalized. The state had also acquired extremely important holdings in banking in the thirties. This gave it effective control over credit. Only 13 per cent of deposits were in private banks in 1945. The banks also owned strategic holdings in iron and steel, shipbuilding and engineering. IRI, the state company into which these holdings were concentrated, employed 233,000 workers in 1948 and undertook 5 per cent of investment. Although badly war-damaged, these firms had substantial excess capacity. Large state subsidies (about $30 million a year) were required to prevent wholesale redundancies. The government refused to use IRI as a 'pilot' of reconstruction as this would have been seen as an assault on private enterprise. Only the German Siemens interests and a few other engineering firms were taken over. On the other hand, privatization was impossible both politically and economically – as there were no private capitalists willing and able to buy the state holdings.

Nevertheless investment recovered strongly. By 1946 industrial fixed investment had nearly regained the prewar level. By 1947 it was 10 per cent higher. This suggests that profits must have recovered too; the fragmentary evidence available also supports this view. The law banning dismissals had, in the immediate postwar months, kept industrial employment above prewar levels. With production still very low in 1946, productivity cannot have been much over half the 1938 level. The major trade union confederation abandoned the ban on dismissals early in 1946, agreeing to reductions in employment of up to 20 per cent over four months. In return it received vague assurances of increased employment in healthy sectors. Industrial employment fell, and unemployment rose by ¾ million between March 1946 and March 1947. This, together with the recovery of production, allowed productivity to rise rapidly in 1947 (table 4.3).

Table 4.3 Productivity and wages: Italy, 1938–47 (index numbers)

	Industrial production	Industrial employment	Industrial productivity	Product wage[a]	Real wage[b]
1938	100	100	100	100	100
1946	61	115	53	58	60[c]
1947	92	105	88	86	88

[a] In terms of prices of manufactures.
[b] In terms of cost of living.
[c] Very rough estimate.
Source: see Appendix

Given productivity developments, real wages evolved favourably for the employers. They were around 60 per cent of the 1938 level in 1946 and still at about 90 per cent in 1947. But employers are not concerned with workers' incomes measured in terms of what they can buy. What matters to them is labour costs, measured in terms of the value of what their employees produce. However, these real labour costs (product wages) followed a very similar path to both real wages and to productivity (table 4.3). So real product wages seem to have constituted a share of output in 1946–7 similar to that in 1938, at the height of fascist repression. Profitability also depends on the cost of other inputs. The prices of fuel and transport (mainly state-owned) had grown only one-third as fast as manufactured goods, and white-collar salaries had fallen by one-third or more relative to wages. Both developments worked to boost profitability. But the low level of capacity utilization, especially in 1946, substantially increased overheads, such as depreciation. Overall, the share of profits in industrial output in 1947 can hardly have been much below that in 1938.

Rapid inflation prevented the working class from increasing living standards faster. Price increases were running at nearly 100 per cent a year early in 1947, according to the official cost of living index, and rather more if the black market is taken into account. Rents were tightly controlled and bread rations subsidized. But food prices rose especially fast, transferring about 10 per cent of the national income into the hands of peasants and capitalist farmers. The sliding scale of wages negotiated early in 1946 provided only partial protection and was accompanied by a 7-month wage truce.

High demand and big government deficits fuelled inflation. The budget deficit was 9 per cent of GDP in 1947–8 (down from 29 per cent in 1944–5). Social expenditure had doubled as a percentage of GDP since before the war and huge subsidies were forthcoming to keep the prices of public sector services down while maintaining employment. These deficits added to hoards of financial assets which had already risen, in relation to GDP, by about one-half during the war. These were either spent directly or lent by banks to capitalists to spend. The middle-class lobby was powerful and effective. Plans for a capital levy and currency reform were shelved. Tax concessions for property income swelled the deficit further. So excess liquidity burnt itself out through inflation. By 1947 the ratio of liquid assets to GDP had fallen to less than half its wartime peak. Inflation encouraged speculation; stockbuilding was high in 1946 and reached 6 per cent of output in 1947. Share prices rose six-fold. The foreign exchanges were substantially freed, allowing exporters to make enormous profits by using their foreign currency to buy imports which could be resold at huge margins.

The pressure exerted by successful middle-class resistance to monetary reform and the consequent deficits and inflation was relieved somewhat by a substantial balance of payments deficit, which rose to 8½ per cent of GDP in 1947. US aid and credits were an important source of finance, covering a third of the deficit in 1947 (emigrants' remittances also contributed). This permitted imports of essential fuel and food without corresponding exports. The resources released were available for investment. But inflation biased the pattern of accumulation towards stockbuilding. In 1947 the deficit was almost equal to stockpiling, so that much foreign borrowing was in effect squandered on speculation.

Despite the relief afforded by the payments deficit, the pressure on workers' living standards was enormous. In 1947 total output was 1000 billion lire (1954 prices) down on 1938, a fall of 11 per cent. Current public spending was 400 billion lire down (reflecting less military spending). But investment was 300 billion up. So 900 billion lire less domestic production was available for consumption, a fall of 15 per cent. The shift in the balance of payments provided an extra 400 billion lire, which reduced the decline in consumption to 9 per cent. But the population had grown. So consumption per head was 13 per cent less in 1947 than in 1938 (up from around 25 per cent less in 1946). Different groups were hit unevenly. Many peasants and small businesses faced much smaller cuts (if any) than working-class families. Salaried employees and those on fixed incomes fared worst.

Rising unemployment, cuts in consumption, accelerating inflation, rampant speculation and the lack of effective planning seems a recipe for working-class opposition. Reality had conspicuously failed to live up to the expectations held at the end of the war. But opposition was dampened and defused by the main workers' parties, particularly the Italian Communist Party (PCI).

From the moment that Togliatti collaborated with Marshal Badoglio's government after the fall of Mussolini in July 1943, the PCI followed a broad Popular Front policy. It maintained this line until it was expelled from De Gasperi's government in May 1947. Its conditions for participating in government were 'extremely moderate compared to the contemporary English labour party experience: a defence of the standard of living and employment and a few measures against war-time profiteering; it did not demand a radical redistribution of income, widespread nationalization or a welfare-state' (Salvati, 1972, p. 195). It even accepted postponement of the currency reform in order not to provoke a crisis before elections to the Constituent Assembly in spring 1946. The results disappointed the PCI. It secured only 19 per cent of the votes. Even combined with the Socialist Party's 21 per cent, the left vote was only marginally greater than the Christian Democrats' (DCs). After this setback, the PCI's attitude to the DCs became, if anything, even more conciliatory. The Communist-dominated union federation negotiated a wage truce.

Collaboration extended into the factories. Works councils were used to 'stimulate the rhythm of work, discipline and production'. In the Brida heavy engineering factory in Milan, a PCI stronghold, 'Stakhanov squads' of exemplary workers were formed to secure greater work effort: 'The militants collaborated because they were convinced they were working – not for the owner but for socialism' (Salvati, 1972, pp. 199–200).

In January 1947 Togliatti proudly affirmed in the Constituent Assembly that Italy had fewer strikes than other European countries: 'In the last years no political strike has taken place in Italy. . . . This is a country where the unions have signed a wage truce, a pact which is unique in the history of the working-class movement, because it determines a maximum wage, not a minimum one. This is really the striking and absurd feature of the economic situation in which we live: it is the working-class and the unions who are giving the best example and are taking all the necessary steps to preserve the discipline of production, order and social peace' (quoted Salvati, 1972, p. 197).

But the PCI found it difficult to sustain restraint. Although no national strikes took place, plenty of local walkouts occurred. In July 1946 a major strike wave among tanker drivers, printers, dock workers and hotel workers grew into a general strike lasting several days. Observers judged it to be a spontaneous reaction to the increasingly desperate economic situation.

The Communists' departure from the government was less dramatic in Italy than in France (see below). The three-party coalition had come under increasing strain. At the beginning of 1947 the Socialists split over increasingly close links with the Communists. The right wing of the party withdrew from the government. This incident highlighted differences between the Christian Democrats and the Communists, whose leader Togliatti maintained that the only options were his party's programme or perpetual crisis. De Gasperi proposed to broaden his cabinet into a government of national unity. The left refused to support the move, fearing increased opposition from the right to such measures as a capital levy. De Gasperi resigned. After more manoeuvrings he formed a government composed entirely of Christian Democrats. The *Economist* warned: 'Beyond the political quarrel, there is the economic crisis, insoluble without strong government' (17 May 1947). It also noted: 'Without the support of the Communists Signor De Gasperi, or for that matter any Italian prime minister, would find the trade unions unmanageable' (17 May 1947). Since, according to one report, 'there was not a factory in the North and few in the centre in the period 1945–48 that was not armed' (quoted Allam and Sassoon, 1977, p. 177), it was clear that even a strong government faced formidable problems.

France

De Gaulle led the early postwar coalition governments in France. But he resigned early in 1946 over left-wing opposition to high military spending. No individual dominated the subsequent series of coalitions, which included conservatives as well as the Socialists and the Communists. The last was marginally the largest party. Its share of the vote peaked at 28.8 per cent in the November 1946 National Assembly election. The Socialist Party's vote fell from 24.6 per cent in October 1945 to 18.1 per cent in November 1946. The CP tried to persuade the Socialists to join them in a Popular Front government, excluding the right. But they were rebuffed. As in Italy, the right-wing parties limited radical reforms and blocked action to check inflation by means of a capital levy, monetary reform and effective attacks on the black market. One journalist claimed early in 1947 that a fifth of the working population was engaged primarily in rackets: 'According to the authorities *everybody* today having anything to do with food or ration cards, or their control, at whatever stage of production or distribution, is certain to gain "illicit profits"' (quoted Werth, 1956, p. 321).

Despite the Socialist Party's unwillingness to exclude the conservatives from government, they, rather than the communists, 'most eagerly championed nationalization and most emphatically emphasized its socialist nature' (Kuisel, 1981, p. 50). The main union federation, the CGT, 'followed the communists closely when it portrayed nationalization as a continuation of patriotic resistance rather than the beginning of the destruction of capitalism. Trade union officials rejected the term "socialization" and said only provocateurs spoke of socialism and revolution in times of economic distress' (Kuisel, 1981, p. 51). Thorez, the CP leader, said that nationalizations were democratic and nothing to do with socialism or communism. In 1945, however, the Communists did help secure the nationalization of those mines remaining in private hands, and of gas, electricity and the banking system. They then fought to dominate the tripartite boards – representing the government, workers and consumers – which had been established to run the industries.

The French government made a serious attempt after 1945 to plan the modernization of industry. The Monnet Plan, published early in 1947, contained ambitious schemes for investment in transport, energy, and iron and steel. In 1947 investment in these industries ran at between 1½ times (iron and steel) and 5 times (coal) the UK level. Most of this investment was in newly nationalized industries, and since their prices were held down substantial state loans were required to finance it. By 1947 industrial investment exceeded its prewar level, and public investment constituted around one-fifth of the total.

The state also provided grants to reconstruct war-damaged property. But to qualify for such a grant a recipient had to install an identical item in the same place, so there was no opportunity for modernization or relocation. Otherwise the state provided little finance for industry. The nationalization of the big four deposit banks and 32 major insurance companies provided a potential lever to influence investment through credit provision. In the early years this control could hardly have been very effective because firms were making high profits and possessed many financial assets accumulated during the war. The government nevertheless accused the banks of 'excessive caution in their credit policy, caution often amounting to downright sabotage and of deliberate attempts to bring pressure on the state' (quoted Werth, 1956, p. 278). Nationalization did not change very much, one observer noting how the banks 'continued to work hand in hand with big business' (quoted Werth, 1956, p. 278).

Total production in 1947 was 1100 billion francs down on 1938 (in 1954 prices) – a fall of 9 per cent. Investment, including stockbuilding, was 800 billion higher than in 1938, and public current spending on goods and services 500 billion higher. So domestic production available for consumption was 25 per cent lower. The fall in actual consumption was held to 15 per cent by imports financed by borrowing from the United States and by running down reserves. Consumption per head was equally squeezed. Workers fared worst, while peasants and businessmen did best.

After the liberation, workers received wage rises which, according to the official price index, restored real wages to nearly 90 per cent of the prewar level. But the socialists abandoned a plan for monetary reform. Mendès-France, minister for the national economy, wanted to use the opportunity of a new banknote issue in March 1945 temporarily to block all bank accounts and limit individuals' expenditures to a level compatible with production. There was little parliamentary support for these proposals. As one commentator pointed out: 'In France the assault against the mountain of 600 millions of hoarded notes affects 18 million peasants – and that of course is a major political problem' (quoted Werth, 1956, p. 248). For electoral reasons, even the Communist Party opposed monetary reform. These cash holdings, built up during the war, boosted purchasing power enormously. Prices doubled between 1945 and

1946. According to official indices, real wages fell to only 60 per cent of pre-war.

In fact, these figures considerably overestimate real purchasing power because of the black market. Between 1945 and 1947 real wages hardly exceeded half of the prewar level. Working hours had also risen to around 44 hours, as compared with 40 before the war. J.-P. Rioux graphically describes the situation in Paris:

> The very bareness of the official figure makes it clear that the parallel market is essential: scarcely 900 calories a day in August 1944 for adults in Paris, 1210 in September and 1515 in May 1945 (in the same official publication it is discretely revealed that even low grade civil servants in the National Statistical Office in sixteen large towns including Paris had between 1840 and 2540 calories a day in May–June 1944 and between 2050 and 2870 in September–October, thanks to 'supplementary resources'). At the cost of waiting in endless queues when unexpected supplies of food arrived, of sometimes humiliating diplomacy towards the shopkeepers to whom the destiny of a family was linked by their ration cards, the rations are gathered and consumed without wasting a single gramme. Finally, to reach the 2000 calories necessary for survival, anything goes – exchange, food parcels from the family, gardens, allotments sometimes in the most unexpected places, discreet visits to the back of the shop, expeditions to farms of 'friends', exchange with neighbours or workmates. These harsh days in this way had their lighter moments which fed the family conversation for a long time afterwards. (Rioux, 1980, p. 40)

The process, already seen in Italy, whereby large amounts of money ended up in peasant hands is well illustrated by the French experience:

> How to make the peasants declare, and then sell their products at the official price, when the black market visits their home and makes a much more tempting offer. The producers have no interest in supplying food when they have no possibility of receiving the manufactured goods they need in return. The peasant table is, more often than not, well garnished and only the surplus is sold on the black market. . . . Savings are ample witness to the growth of deposits in the Crédit Agricole which grew from an index of 100 in 1938 to 743 in December 1944 and 1717 in December 1946. This reflects black market profits but also a transformation of part of their capital into money as it was impossible to replace fertilizers and depreciating machinery. (Rioux, 1980, p. 43).

Industrial productivity had fallen much less than real wages; it appears to have been 95 per cent of the prewar level in 1947 and nearly 90 per cent in 1946 (table 4.4). The prices of materials and other inputs probably rose less than those of manufactures and, again as in Italy, salaries rose less rapidly than wages. Both developments worked to raise manufacturing profits. So by the end of 1946 the pressure of spending on investment and on consumption must have pushed industrial profits up to a very high level. No figures are available, but an official survey noted that the 'fortunes made in textiles and food for example are not a myth' (Closon, 1950, p. 24). Nor did workers benefit from a radical restructuring of the tax system. 'Wage earners in particular, though their real income has risen considerably from the very low levels of the early postwar years, have certainly lost to farmers, industrialists and merchants' (UNECE, 1953, p. 80).

Table 4.4 Productivity and wages: France, 1938–47 (index numbers)

	Industrial production	Industrial employment	Industrial productivity	Real wage[a]	Real wage[b]
1938	100	100	100	100	100
1946	84	96	87	58	40
1947	99	104	95	63	50

[a] In terms of official cost of living.
[b] In terms of actual cost of living.

Source: see Appendix

As in Italy, the Communist Party exerted a key influence on working-class reaction: 'Communist leadership can to a large extent determine the speed and the extent of the vicious spiral of wages and prices. Communist leadership can also make or mar the campaign for production, without which neither the immediate stabilization of prices nor the ultimate modernization of the French economy is possible' (*Economist*, 8 June 1946).

In the coal mines, for example, the CP used its influence to encourage more production for scarcely increased wages. Faced by staunch resistance by the miners to working for the old owners, the state first controlled, and then nationalized, the mines. Absenteeism remained high. In June 1945, Thorez said to northern miners: 'I say frankly that it is impossible to approve a strike by miners in the present period, especially when it starts outside the union . . . 20,000 to 30,000 tons have been lost in this way; it is a serious crime against the country, against the union and against the interest of the miners themselves' (quoted Lefranc, 1969, p. 30). At the beginning of 1946 he again informed miners that, 'To produce, is the highest form of class duty, of republican and patriotic duty' (quoted Lefranc, 1969, p. 30).

De Gaulle said of Thorez: 'While still pushing forward the interests of communism, he acted in the public interest on many occasions. He never stopped giving the advice to work as much as possible whatever the cost. Was this simply a political tactic? That is not my affair; it is enough that France was served' (quoted Unir, p. 264). When the public sector workers threatened to strike at the end of 1945 Thorez blamed 'agitators'. Such action, he said, would 'be a crime against the fatherland'.

Workers were given no control in private enterprises in return for their restraint. The workers' committees which were set up 'were allowed to make suggestions about production processes, [but] nobody was obliged to take any notice' (Werth, 1956, pp. 278–9). The unions raised no objection to the key proviso in the Monnet Plan that hours of work should be increased from 44 to 48.

In 1946 workers, dissatisfied with the slowness with which conditions improved, struck spontaneously, with particular impact in printing and the Post Office. The Communist Party denounced the disputes as the result of 'provocation'. Strikes were, it said, a 'tool of the trusts'.

The main strike wave occurred from April to July 1947. It began at Renault, nationalized because of its owner's collaboration. The communist-dominated union there had 'promoted the battle for production and de-emphasized wage demands more vigorously than anywhere else in the country' (Ross, 1982, p. 45). Wildcat strikes broke out on 25 April. Three days later 12,000 people had downed tools. The CGT denounced the strike leaders as 'Hitlero-Trotskyite provocateurs in the pay of de Gaulle'. But the workers forced it to call a one-hour strike, over which it lost control. All the 30,000-strong work force came out. Concessions the union had obtained from management were voted down. The union was forced to back the strike, which was rapidly spreading through the Paris metal-working industry, although it failed to take up all the demands of the strike committee. The Communist Party was obliged to follow suit to retain working-class support. Its ministers, who opposed the government's wage control policies, were dismissed by the prime minister.

The Communist Party felt obliged to leave the government once its working-class support was threatened. It still sought to use working-class discontent to pressurize the Socialist Party into joining it in a Popular Front government. But it was a socialist prime minister, Ramadier, who with strong US support had dismissed the communists. This signalled a decisive attempt to roll back working-class strength in the voting booths and, most importantly, on the shop floor.

The United Kingdom

The United Kingdom faced no economic disruptions remotely comparable to those in continental Europe and Japan. Industrial production in 1946 was about equal to the 1938 level, with employment fractionally up and productivity down. There were three immediate economic problems: external payments, demobilization and the switch to peacetime production, and wartime accumulation of financial assets.

The current account deficit of the balance of payments was running at approximately 2 per cent of GDP. The basic problem was the massive turnaround on invisibles (income from services and from investment overseas). From the turn of the century to the Second World War the United Kingdom had run a deficit on visible trade (goods) of 5–6 per cent of GDP, more or less covered by a surplus on invisibles. By 1946, however, the invisibles account had run into deficit to the tune of 1 per cent of GDP. The turnaround was largely the result of a fall in interest, profits and dividends from abroad, from about 4 per cent of GDP in the 1920s and 1930s to 1 per cent in the late 1940s. Some £1000 million of external capital assets had been sold to help pay for the war, and £3000 million extra external debts incurred. The latter were mainly loans from the Sterling Area countries (mainly colonies whose currencies were tied to the pound). Another factor was the increase in the government deficit abroad (almost entirely military) which ran at over 3½ per cent of GDP in 1946 (falling to around 1½ per cent for the rest of the 1940s and 1 per cent for the 1950s). The overall deficit could also be expected to rise substantially once imports regained prewar levels, unless manufactured exports grew considerably. The problem of the external account became pressing when, on the surrender of Japan, US Lend-Lease aid ended.

Demobilization and the restructuring of production posed a problem on a vast scale. In 1944 and 1945 the armed forces employed about 20 per cent of the work force. Public authorities' current expenditure on goods and services had risen from 13.4 per cent of GDP in 1938 to an average of 43.0 per cent between 1939 and 1945. It remained 23.3 per cent in 1946.

More government expenditure had been financed by taxation than during the 1914–18 war (39 per cent in 1940 rising to 55 per cent in 1944). But with consumption limited by rationing, personal savings had risen massively, reaching a peak of 25 per cent of personal disposable income (up from less than 5 per cent before the war). The national debt had risen as fast, from £6½ billion in the 1930s to £21.4 billion at the end of 1945 (£25.6 billion by the end of 1947). By the end of the war it was approaching three years' GDP (twice the 1930s level). These financial assets posed a major (potential) inflationary threat.

The abrupt ending of US Lend-Lease coupled with the external payments situation made further US loans an urgent priority. The new government promptly despatched Keynes to Washington to negotiate one. The other economic priorities of the Labour government were rapid demobilization (and consequent reduction in government expenditure) and the restoration of peacetime production to provide resources for controlled expansion of private consumption, social reforms and, most urgently, increased exports (especially to the Dollar Area).

This last objective was made all the more urgent by the loan terms dictated by the United States. The $3.75 billion made available at the end of 1945 was conditional on the United Kingdom making sterling fully convertible within one year of ratification by Congress. Despite these pressures to open up the Empire the government exploited the colonies to the full. It required them to sell it their main export commodities at prices frequently well below world market levels. The government also accorded the colonies low priority for UK exports, preventing then from spending all their foreign exchange earnings. So the sterling balances grew in the late forties. Such high dollar earners as the Gold

Coast (Ghana) and Malaysia were particularly ruthlessly exploited, being forced to add their dollars to the Sterling Area's common pool, much of which was used to buy UK imports. India, which had more political leverage, was treated more gently. An Indian historian has commented in response to Harold Wilson's statement that the dollar pool was a 'rough and ready way of allocating dollars amongst several major countries according to their needs', that 'it certainly was rough and ready – rough on the dollar surplus countries because the others were only too ready to spend the surplus' (Gupta, 1983, p. 111).

Demobilization proceeded fairly smoothly. 1946 was the only year in which unemployment exceeded 2 per cent (most of the unemployed were service personnel yet to be officially demobilized but released to seek work). Between 1945 and 1948 employment in the armed forces fell by 4,242,000. Civilian employment plus total unemployment rose by 3,375,000, so that nearly 900,000 people disappeared from the labour force. These were mostly women and old people brought into the labour force during the war. Absorption was facilitated by a marked drop in average weekly hours worked, down from 52.9 in 1943 to 46.5 in 1948 for male manual workers.

Housing posed the biggest problem. Destruction and deterioration of the housing stock during the war had led to a considerable shortage. Many demobbed soldiers and sailors took to squatting and often resisted eviction violently.

The problem of financial assets was dealt with by a combination of low interest rates to minimize debt servicing (interest payments were about 9 per cent of GDP in the 1920s, fell to 6 per cent in the 1930s and, despite rapid growth in the debt, remained at that level in 1947) and the maintenance of wartime controls. Materials controls directed investment and production into priority areas (especially exports) while rationing held down consumer demand, thereby staving off rapid inflation.

The government could only achieve all its objectives if production grew rapidly. In the long run this required high investment. But in the short term the government emphasized 'production drives' – propaganda exercises aimed at persuading people to work harder. It managed to mobilize an extremely wide range of political support for these drives, from capitalists to the CP.

Less immediately pressing, but ultimately more menacing, was the stagnation of pay. In 1946 and 1947 real earnings were slightly lower than in 1943 and 1944 (though a fifth higher than prewar). But take-home pay had risen much less. The average male manual worker now paid around 9 per cent of his wage in taxes and social security contributions, up from 2 per cent prewar. The government also rigged the retail price index by subsidizing items whose weight in the index was disproportionate to their true importance. Average consumption per head grew by more than 10 per cent in 1946, but by only a further 2 per cent in 1947, to reach a level only 2 per cent above that of 1938. The higher purchasing power of real wages and accumulated financial assets was bottled up by rationing.

Workers were not rewarded for restraining personal consumption by being provided with vastly expanded social services. The National Health Service, which was to involve a big injection of resources, was only in the planning stages. A smaller proportion of GDP was being spent on education than prewar (table 4.5). Transfers absorbed a slightly higher share. Increased pensions and the family allowance cost more than was saved as a result of lower unemployment (in real terms the dole was no higher than prewar). Council housing was the only major area of public spending to leap ahead (doubling as compared to prewar), and even this should be judged against the wartime dilapidation of the housing stock. As late as 1947, military spending exceeded the 1938 level by as much as did spending on the welfare state.

Table 4.5 The British welfare state, 1938–51 (spending as percentages of GDP)

	Total transfers to persons	Health	Local current education	Local housing capital	Total[a]	Current military
1938	5.1	1.2	2.0	1.0	12.2	6.3
1946	6.8	n.a.	1.7	1.0	13.7	15.7
1947	6.4	n.a.	1.8	2.0	15.4	9.3
1948	6.0	2.0	1.9	2.3	16.8	6.3
1949	6.0	3.3	1.9	2.2	18.0	6.2
1950	5.9	3.5	1.9	2.1	17.6	6.3
1951	5.4	3.3	2.0	2.0	16.7	7.5

[a] Current civil expenditure plus local authority housing.
Sources: Feinstein, 1972, tables 2, 10; UK Government, *National Income and Expenditure 1946–51*, tables 27, 30 and 31.

Nor were workers benefiting from effective industrial planning in exchange for wage restraint. Planning amounted to a maze of pragmatic controls inherited from the war. The official criterion for controlling prices was that they should guarantee a 'reasonable return' to high cost producers. So efficient firms earned very high profits while the inefficient remained in business. Most of the top personnel administering the controls were employers, often seconded from major firms in the industry on an unpaid basis. Unilever employees filled 90 posts in the Ministry of Food, 12 of them senior; the director of the Iron and Steel Federation headed the steel rearmament panel; the match controller worked for Bryant and May – his office was on the firm's premises; and so on.

The Labour government also encouraged the formation and amalgamation of trade associations, often delegating the administration of controls to them (e.g. newsprint, imported meat, war surplus stocks, confectionery). Sometimes the task was entrusted to a single large firm (e.g. the Mond Nickel Company).

Allocations were normally determined by production shares. Trade associations expelled firms selling below government maximum prices. Harold Wilson, at the time president of the Board of Trade, summed it up: '[This system] perpetuates the pattern of a particular industry or trade, featherbeds the inefficient and unenterprising, freezes out the newcomers and penalizes the efficient, growing firm. It has, in fact, many of the vices of the old, prewar type of control, dividing out whole markets between producers on the basis of arbitrary quotas, and doing this with all the statutory sanction of the state behind it' (quoted Rogow, 1955, p. 67).

But Labour did believe that direct control of resources in the nationalized industries was crucial to economic development. Since the major nationalized industries began to operate as such in 1947, this is a convenient place to discuss the role that nationalization played in Labour's strategy.

The Labour Party had long argued for nationalization, on both ideological and pragmatic grounds. In 1934 it had drawn up a radical programme to nationalize banking, land and those 'basic industries' (fuel and power, transport, iron and steel) which had 'failed the nation'. Between 1945 and 1951 the Labour government implemented the whole of this programme, with the important exceptions of banking and land. Nationalization seemed to the government to offer a solution to many economic problems – indeed, to be a substitute for comprehensive economic planning. First, it could end strategic shortages hampering private sector industrial growth; hence the concentration on 'basic' industries. Second, control of basic industries could ensure that supplies went to high-priority activities.

This conception of nationalization satisfied to a large extent the needs of the capitalist class. Most of the industries taken over – coal and railways, for example – had been unprofitable for a long time. Their prospects under fragmented private ownership were poor, as a string of official reports since the First World War had made clear. The 1944 Reid report on the coal industry had said that the mines needed vast investment and comprehensive reorganization, and that a public authority empowered to force through mergers and rationalization should be created.

Capitalists in the industries concerned received fairly generous compensation on nationalization. Others hoped to benefit from the rationalized services and lower prices which, interwar experience suggested, would not have happened under private ownership. They felt that industrial relations – exceptionally bitter, especially in mining – might improve. So resistance to the early nationalizations was muted.

Initial plans for workers' participation, via trade union representatives on boards, were watered down to a system of 'worker directors' not responsible to the workers. But nationalization probably did reduce industrial unrest (although more days were devoted to strikes in the mines in the year following nationalization than in that preceding it). Prices were held down; the nationalized industries' share of total profits fell from 31.5 per cent in 1930–8 to 14.2 per cent in 1948–9. Productivity improved. In 1951 the British coal industry was the only one in Europe with a higher output per man shift than prewar. This reflected reorganization, and perhaps speed-up, as well as modernization. Investment in the nationalized industries was lower than prewar, suggesting that benefits to private industry from cheaper inputs would be limited.

Nor, indeed, did private industry invest much more than prewar. The ratio of fixed investment to GDP was a little higher in current prices terms, but this was more than offset by the fact that investment goods prices had risen nearly 30 per cent more than the average during the war. So in real terms the share of investment actually fell by 3 per cent of GDP to a level well below that of continental rivals (table 4.1). While the volume of manufacturing investment was some 50 per cent higher than prewar, the ratio of manufacturing investment to manufacturing output was hardly higher at all (at around 9 per cent). Engineering – crucial for the production of investment goods for domestic modernization and for export – was investing less of its output than prewar (7 per cent in 1947, down from 7½ per cent in 1937).

Profits slipped back a little in 1947, but the profit share was hardly below the prewar level, and high capacity utilization will have boosted the profit rate. In comparison, returns from investing in financial assets were very low. Around 40 per cent of company income went in tax compared to 15 per cent prewar. The proportion of income paid out as dividends and interest fell further, as a result of dividend control (from 60 per cent in 1937 to 28 per cent in 1948). So company savings were high and firms spent less than their current savings on fixed investment, despite large stocks of liquid assets accumulated during the war. Although new shares issues were controlled, it is hard to believe that lack of finance was the reason for relatively sluggish investment.

But finance was not the only aspect of government control. Building was under tight rein until the mid-1950s, and investment in plant and machinery was limited by export targets for the engineering industries and import controls. The UK *Economic Survey* for 1947 explained: 'Import is permitted if the machine is of essential significance and cannot be supplied in comparable conditions from UK production' (p. 17). 'The provision of new equipment and maintenance . . . cannot all be done at once. There is not enough manpower, steel and building and engineering capacity, especially as a large part of the latter must be used for export. The government must therefore retain close control' (p. 25).

If controls did limit accumulation, this resulted from working-class pressure on government to improve living standards. Physical constraints on construction and engineering could have been avoided by cutting housebuilding further and reducing home consumption of engineering products. Alternatively, cuts in consumer goods imports would have permitted higher imports (or lower exports) of machine tools. Also, if the controls really were holding back a huge pent-up demand for investment then their relaxation in the early fifties should have seen an investment boom. It did not.

It is impossible to establish how far low (by international standards) UK investment was the result of working-class pressure (reflected in shopfloor resistance to the effects of modernization or in high taxation to pay for social services, or physical controls on investment to free resources to allow consumer imports). But the complacent attitude of UK management was probably the more important factor. This was encouraged by the continuing wartime practice of amicably sharing out markets, both at home and in the colonies (which absorbed 50 per cent of exports).

The 1947 position was both unsatisfactory and unsustainable. The balance of payments deficit of 4 per cent of GDP had to be cut. Unless the government could increase production rapidly, it would have to divert resources from public services, from investment (which was in any case too low to generate rapid productivity growth) or from consumption (already growing too slowly to satisfy Labour's supporters).

Industrial struggle had been more muted than expected in the immediate postwar years. In 1945 less than 3 million days were occupied in strikes, half of which were accounted for by a dock strike, and there were a number of short strikes in the mines. In 1946 the number of days involved actually declined to just over 2 million, the motor industry accounting for half. Compared with the average number of days spent in strikes in 1919–20 (30 million) the situation appeared calm. But pressure was building up for continued reforms at just the time the government was facing equally compelling pressures to cut back. The *Economist* stated very clearly the disquiet that employers were feeling:

> When Parliament reassembled after the summer recess, the Government had just overcome the squatters' crisis. It meets again next week, after a short Christmas break, against the background of a strikers' crisis. To call in troops to safeguard London's food supply was undoubtedly the only course open to the Cabinet, although its immediate effect was not to stop the strike, but to spread it to the provinces and to the provision market workers and dockers.
> . . . 1947 has started badly, with the token strike of ship-builders in support of their claim for a five-day week, the 'work to rule' movement of LNER [railway] shopmen, and now the transport strike. It would be prudent to bear in mind the possibility that the usual postwar industrial troubles have merely been postponed and not avoided. The present depressed standard of living in this country cannot be raised – or at least not raised quickly – unless there is a sharp increase in output per worker. Without this, the standard of living will soon fall since the country is still, in effect, living on Lend-Lease. . . . Though they are not averse to any increases in wages, what the workers really want, as shown by what they will strike for, is more leisure – the only thing that is quite certainly disastrous to the country. . . . It is painfully apparent that the workers will not follow their chairborne leaders; they prefer to follow the shopsteward in the street. It is true that there was the same irresponsibility and turbulence – indeed, far worse – after the war of 1914–18 and that it then disappeared. But it did not disappear before full employment also disappeared. Every time there is one of these unofficial strikes, the conclusion seems to be reinforced that it is only when there is some unemployment that organized labour will behave responsibly enough to make full employment possible. (18 January 1947).

The extent of successful capitalist reconstruction achieved in Europe and Japan by early 1947 cannot be read off from indices for production or investment. Even where output and accumulation had grown rapidly, balance of payments deficits, government deficits and rapid inflation were the economic manifestation of powerful, and as yet unresolved, conflicts as the various classes struggled to maintain or improve their position. Workers' demands had so far been checked by the trade union and party leaderships, but patience was wearing thin. The working class might deploy its formidably increased industrial power at any time. Such an offensive would almost inevitably transcend simple wage demands since the economy still was manifestly incapable of granting big rises. The obvious alternative to continued self-restraint was to press for workers' governments to take effective control over the economy. Even in Britain, where the situation was much less severe, Labour was finding it difficult to satisfy its supporters' aspirations.

In Germany and Japan, where effective recovery had hardly begun, workers suffered more severe hardships. If the occupying powers continued with their dismal failure to launch a determined assault on the obstacles to recovery then workers might attempt the task themselves, by methods, and along lines, quite inimical to capitalism. The deep crisis which had gripped the system in the immediate aftermath of the war had yet to be resolved. In the spring of 1947 the capitalist class still faced enormous difficulties. But help was at hand.

5

Marshall Aid: the United States Changes Tack

People who recall the immediate postwar years usually think first of the Marshall Plan and the beginning of the cold war. President Truman formally launched the cold war in a speech to Congress on 12 March 1947. He called for economic and military aid to Greece and Turkey and outlined what came to be known as the Truman Doctrine: 'It must be the policy of the United States to support free peoples who are resisting attempted subjugation by armed minorities or by outside pressure' (quoted Yergin, 1980, p. 283).

On 5 June Secretary of State Marshall proposed a European Recovery Programme. The United States should help to draft it and provide support 'so far as it may be practicable for us to do so'. A week or so later he suggested that $5 or $6 billion a year might be required from the United States for several years. While the Marshall Plan was confined to Europe, a similar shift of policy towards Japan soon followed, with the US government calling, in November 1947, for the Japanese government to formulate a plan for economic recovery to ensure that 'the Japanese economy will be balanced at the earliest possible time' (quoted Halliday, 1975, p. 187).

These shifts in US thinking were to influence reconstruction decisively. They were also interlinked. One White House aide called the Marshall Plan 'a Truman Doctrine in action' (quoted Yergin, 1980, p. 321).

Europe's crisis?

Historians disagree about precisely why the United States decided to commit itself to participate more actively in European reconstruction. What is not in dispute is that reconstruction required continued American aid at existing levels. The crucial point is that before Marshall the United States had no plans to provide such aid. During 1946 food aid was channelled through UNRRA. But the United States decided in the autumn to terminate UNRRA, apparently justifying the move on the grounds of the extent of industrial recovery in Western Europe.

Although food and materials were now readily available on world markets, Western Europe lacked the dollars to buy them. It was running a huge deficit with the United States. In 1946 exports covered no more than one-quarter of imports, and the balance had not improved by 1947 (figure 5.1). Europe's deficit with the rest of the world rose from $5.8 billion in 1946 to $7.5 billion in 1947. Much was financed by US loans. Stringent conditions were often attached (for example to the British loan). Gold and dollar reserves were running down rapidly. In the two years before Marshall Aid was agreed, they had fallen by one-third. New sources of finance were essential to maintain vital imports.

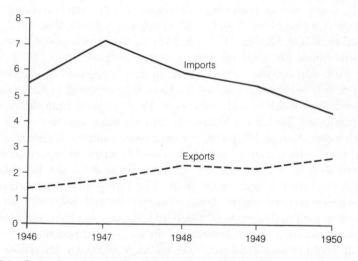

Figure 5.1 Europe's trade with the United States, 1946–50 ($ billion).
Source: US Government, *Balance of Payments*.

Neither Europe nor Japan was collapsing (contrary to many later accounts). The terrible winter of 1946–7 had set back recovery. But this was a far cry from economic collapse. Even in the first quarter of 1947 – badly hit by the weather – European industrial production was 16 per cent up on the same quarter of the previous year. It also recovered rapidly: by the last quarter of 1947 it was some 12 per cent above the last quarter of 1946. But this level of production, let alone further increases, could be maintained only if dollar aid for the purchase of vital imports continued. The European crisis was *potential* rather than actual.

It is obviously difficult – if not impossible – to decide how Europe and Japan would have fared without continued US aid. The apparently simpler issue of what Washington believed would happen, and why it regarded the prospect as unacceptable, also turned out to be a minefield of different interpretations. J. M. Jones, a senior US diplomatic officer, privately summed up the prospects in Europe at the time thus:

If these areas are allowed to spiral downwards into economic anarchy, then at best they will drop out of the United States' orbit and try an independent nationalistic policy; at worst they will swing into the Russian orbit. We will then face the world alone. What will be the cost, in dollars and cents of our armaments and our economic isolation? I do not see how we could possibly avoid a depression far greater than that of 1929–32 and crushing taxes to pay for the direct commitments we should be forced to make around the world. (Quoted Horowitz, 1965, pp. 126–7).

It has been argued forcefully that independent nationalistic capitalist development in Europe was a real possibility – that 'the real issue at stake was less the condition of Western European capitalism than its form, and whether it would be cooperative or competitive', and that 'Washington correctly perceived that recovery without United States participation was a basic threat to American interests' (Kolko and Kolko, 1972, pp. 337–8). But the claim that America was being shut out of European markets cannot be sustained.

The European economies were far from developing into an insulated unit, trading mainly between themselves. In 1947 they exported to each other only just over half as much in real terms as in 1938. Imports from the rest of the world (excluding the United States) ran at only three-quarters of the prewar level. However, Europe bought 90 per cent more from the United States than prewar. Its exports accounted for 27 per cent of European imports in 1947, as compared with 10 per cent in 1938. Every available dollar was being spent on US food, raw materials and capital goods. The European capitalist class was in far too precarious a position, both economically and politically, to cut an independent path of development. Such an approach would be a desperate last resort, to be adopted only if American help was not forthcoming.

Britain might be seen as an exception. Its economic and political position was far less unstable than that of the main continental countries or of Japan. Indeed the British Treasury had examined the implications first of failure to secure a US loan and then of failure to secure substantial Marshall Aid. Early in 1946 a section of the Treasury floated a plan for a 'multilateral system based on sterling, excluding the USA'. The basic idea was a widened Sterling Area – including the French, Belgian and Dutch empires – within which dollars would be strictly pooled and imports controlled. But the paper admitted that the support of the European countries would be 'rather worthless economically' and that 'our policy would have to be based upon the fact that in a world of bankrupts the half-solvent is king' (quoted Clarke, 1982, p. 141). Keynes had poured scorn on the idea, asking rhetorically, 'What motive have [the other European countries] to rupture trade relations with the USA in order to lend us money they have not got?' (quoted Clarke, 1982, p. 135).

By mid-1947, when discussing the implications of 'inadequate Marshall Aid', the same Treasury officials had become far more pessimistic about going it alone. Talk of a general European dollar pool had given way to a more modest proposal for a series of bilateral arrangements 'primarily with the stronger countries (e.g. Australia, New Zealand, Eire, Denmark) rather than with countries which would be likely to be a drain on our resources and which would raise difficult questions of allocation of scarce supplies' (Clarke, 1982, p. 178). While recognizing that the United Kingdom would be unable to fulfil its obligations to free trade and payments, the new paper had abandoned talk of 'walking out' of the IMF and the International Trade Organization, and of setting up parallel organizations centred around the Sterling Area.

It acknowledged that the import programme would have to be trimmed, although 'radical cuts in this programme will be extremely difficult to make, and if made, confront us with the prospect of a decay of industrial activity – a downward spiral towards the plight of Germany today' (quoted Clarke, 1982, p. 177). It also foresaw the need for 'drastic action, equivalent to national mobilization; to expand export production (e.g. coal and textiles), stimulate import-saving production (e.g. agriculture) and stop long-term capital projects . . . the building and investment programmes generally should be drastically cut down, to save timber, steel and man-power. We should not have resources for satisfying our elementary consumption needs plus exports plus investment' (quoted Clarke, 1982, pp. 175, 180).

So even the best placed potential recipient of Marshall Aid was in too feeble a position to envisage a future without such aid as anything other than desperate. In the Treasury's words, it would be a 'backs to the wall' situation. Marshall Aid was no bribe to lure Europe away from an emerging viable capitalist road of mutual cooperation, and independence from the United States.

Nor was it a bribe to keep Europe from toppling immediately into the Russian orbit. The European Communist parties were hardly poised to launch a Moscow-inspired insurrection. Only in Greece did the CP make a serious bid for state power, and in so doing broke with the Kremlin line. Stalin had ceded Greece to the Western sphere of influence in his discussions with Churchill. Early in 1946 the influential US foreign policy adviser, George Kennan, had admitted that the Soviet leaders envisaged 'revolutionary upheavals within the various capitalist countries' only after another inter-imperialist war. In the meantime, 'Democratic-progressive elements abroad are to be utilized to bring pressure to bear on capitalist governments along lines agreeable to Soviet interests' (Kennan, 1967, p. 548). He had added that the CPs would be used to 'increase social and industrial unrest', urging those with economic or national grievances 'to seek redress not in mediation and compromise, but in defiant violent struggle for destruction of other elements of society' (p. 555). But the Communist parties' behaviour during 1946 had proved him wrong on this score (chapter 4).

Despite later rhetoric, the US administration clearly did not 'see communist activities as the *root* of the present difficulties in Western Europe' (emphasis added). Kennan's background paper to Marshall argued that 'American effort in aid to Europe should be directed not to the combating of communism as such but to the restoration of the economic health and vigor of European society' (quoted Kolko and Kolko, 1972, p. 376). But it also observed that 'the Communists are exploiting the European crisis' and that US aid 'should aim, in other words, not to combat communism but the economic maladjustment which makes European society vulnerable to exploitation by any and all totalitarian movements and which Russian communism is now exploiting' (Kennan, 1967, p. 336).

So the United States did perceive a communist threat in Europe even though this existed despite, rather than because of, the policies pursued by the CPs. The fundamental point was that if working-class conditions did not improve – let alone if they deteriorated further – then mass struggles would inevitably erupt. The Communist parties, which had so far done their best to defuse such a response, might then be forced by rank-and-file pressure to lead the struggles. To do otherwise would jeopardize their influence within the working class. Where the CPs were less powerful, Socialist parties would experience the same pressures. The 'Communist Threat' was real. But the danger was that deteriorating economic conditions would breed demands for socialization, planning and workers' control, despite the policies of the CPs.

The capitalist class in Europe and Japan was in no state to deal with such pressures on its own. Speculation on what form of socialism, if any, might have emerged in Western Europe, had the United States washed its hands of the class struggle there, would probably be fruitless. President Truman was oversimplifying when he told a group of Congressmen in September 1947 that 'we'll have to provide a program of interim aid relief until the Marshall program gets going, or the governments of France and Italy will fall, Austria too, and for all practical purposes Europe will be Communist' (quoted Yergin, 1980, p. 328). But it was not an absurd scenario.

A US official put the essential point more clearly at a businessmen's meeting in February 1947: 'If the American program for world trade were to fail, its failure would hasten the spread of nationalization among the other countries of the world. . . . We cannot insulate ourselves against the movements that sweep around the globe. If every other major nation were to go socialist, it would be extremely difficult, if not impossible, to preserve real private enterprise in the United States' (quoted Kolko and Kolko, 1972, p. 338).

So the fundamental task for the United States was to restructure provision of the resources necessary for European recovery – to replace existing pragmatic arrangements with ones designed to ensure the restoration of effective capitalist control. Kennan, a leading foreign affairs adviser, discussing the situation in France and Japan in early 1947, summarized the problem succinctly. It was, he said, a matter of imposing 'stringent measures of financial and social discipline' (Kennan, 1967, p. 330). J. M. Jones later wrote: 'There was no confidence to spare. *World Report* published on January 21 [1947] a survey of the state of European recovery. It concluded that industrial recovery was beginning to stall. Lack of confidence and shortage of productive labour were partly responsible, but even more so was the feeling of helplessness and frustration which reduced and undermined government authority' (Jones, 1955, p. 83).

Economic problems in the United States

The United States adopted the Marshall plan mainly because it was concerned about the future of Europe (and Japan), with all that that implied for American interests. But economic problems at home also played a role.

As we have seen (chapter 2), in early 1946 profits in the United States were high. But unprecedented numbers of workers were striking for improved living standards. The US Department of Commerce's *Survey of Current Business* echoed widespread fears of economic instability: 'The existing volume of cash deposits and liquid securities is often described as providing the seeds for a reflationary boom and collapse such as was associated with previously postwar periods. A disruptive inflation is of course a real possibility' (February 1946, p. 31).

In the event the shift to peacetime production proceeded more smoothly than had been feared. Output fell by $82 billion (1972 prices) between 1945 and 1946, with practically all of this fall accounted for by government payments to the forces. Private sector production fell by only $12 billion or 3 per cent, despite a $102 billion cut in government purchases from the private sector (largely munitions). The shortfall was made up by a rise in consumption and housebuilding ($30 billion and $13 billion respectively), a sharp rise in business fixed investment and restocking ($15 billion and $16 billion respectively), and an $18 billion increase in net exports (largely to Europe and Japan). Private spending was buoyed up by the release of pent-up demand when controls were abolished.

Liquid assets had grown considerably during the war. Personal savings had exceeded 20 per cent of personal income. Although upper income groups held most of these savings, there was nevertheless a widespread hunger for consumer goods. The real post-tax profit share fell from around 9 per cent in 1945 to 7 per cent in 1946. But this probably went unobserved, being masked by rapid inflation. Profits seemed higher because increases in the value of stocks, resulting solely from rising prices, were wrongly considered as profit, and because depreciation provision was insufficient, being based on the price paid for the machinery rather than on the current cost of replacing it. Calculated in this incorrect way, profits appeared to be both high and rising rapidly. Firms also had plenty of liquid assets and little debt. Demand for new capital goods was strong.

High spending allowed a fairly smooth reabsorption of ex-service personnel. Between 1945 and 1946 employment in the forces fell by 8 million, while the number of civilian jobs rose by nearly 4 million. Unemployment rose from a low point of 0.8 million at the end of the war to 2.7 million in March 1946 (down to

2.1 million by the end of the year). So around 2 million people apparently disappeared from the labour force. Numbers in higher education rose and some older war-workers retired. Most importantly, 2¼ million women workers left their jobs.

The film *Rosie the Riveter* provides a fascinating insight into the ways in which many women, who only a few years before had been pulled into the wartime factories, were suddenly despatched back home to rear children. The rise in private sector employment was almost exactly offset by a decline in hours worked – down from 45.4 in January 1945 to 40.4 in 1946 – as overtime wound down, especially in war-based industries. So total civilian hours changed little from those worked at the end of the war.

Marshall Aid affected the US economy most directly in the export field. The rise in net exports in 1946 had accounted for nearly one-fifth of the total rise in non-government spending. This rise prevented the fall in military expenditures from generating a major recession. Net exports (exports minus imports) of goods and services constituted 3.7 per cent of GDP in 1946. In the second quarter of 1947, when discussions over the Marshall Plan were most intense, net exports were running at an annual rate of $12.4 billion, or 5.4 per cent of GDP. And their importance was even greater than this figure suggests. Nearly 70 per cent of GDP was realized by consumption expenditures, most of which depended on workers keeping their jobs. Had exports fallen, workers producing them would have been put out of work. In 1946, 16 per cent of agricultural machinery, 20 per cent of freight cars and motor trucks, 10 per cent of steel products and 40 per cent of wheat production were exported. If workers producing goods for export had lost their jobs then their spending would have fallen. Demand for consumer goods in the United States would have been hit, leading to job losses there. The likely extent of these 'multiplier' effects is difficult to calculate. But the importance of exports to overall employment was certainly far greater than their percentage of GDP. So spending in the United States was vulnerable to European countries' ability to buy US exports. Senior US officials were well aware of the changes. *The Economic Report of the President* (1948) said: 'The rate at which foreign countries were utilizing United States credits and their own gold and dollar assets was depleting these resources rapidly and the ability of some countries to import from the United States was being exhausted. Many of these countries were forced to put more rigid restrictions on their purchases from the United States' (p. 26).

In a speech in the spring of 1947, delivered some weeks before Marshall's, Dean Acheson had stressed graphically the importance of US exports:

It is difficult to imagine $16 billion worth of commodities. This represents one month's work for each man and woman in the United States . . . when the process of reconversion at home is completed, we are going to find ourselves more dependent upon exports, than before the war, to maintain the levels of business activity to which our economy has become accustomed . . . continued political instability and 'Acts of God' are retarding recovery to a greater degree than had been anticipated. The extreme need of foreign countries for American products is likely, therefore, to continue undiminished in 1948, while the capacity of foreign countries to pay in commodities will only be slightly increased. Under existing authorizations considerable sums will be available to offset next year's deficit. But these funds will taper off rapidly during the latter part of 1948 . . . we must push ahead with the reconstruction of these two great workshops of Europe and Asia – Germany and Japan – upon which the ultimate recovery of the two continents largely depends. (Quoted Jones, 1955, pp. 277–8).

Jones says that 'the President's Council of Economic Advisers expected a slight business recession within twelve months; if the expected export decline, due to foreign inability to pay, coincided with weakness in the domestic economy, the effect on production, prices and employment in the United States, might be most serious' (p. 207).

US labour

In the month that Marshall announced his Plan, Congress passed the Taft-Hartley Bill, radically curtailing trade union rights. Four months later, Marshall addressed one of the two major union confederations, the Congress of Industrial Organizations (CIO), which represented nearly half the organized working class. He warned against the 'enemies of democracy' who would 'undermine the confidence of the labour element in the stability of our institutions and the soundness of our tradition' (quoted Preis, 1964, p. 340).

While the Truman Doctrine and Marshall Plan were intended primarily to help re-establish 'social discipline' in Europe and Japan, they also had a domestic component. The 1945–6 strike wave (chapter 2) had shown up weaknesses in domestic social discipline. The new initiatives were to help create the climate for an assault on organized labour at home to parallel those the United States was underwriting abroad.

The great strikes of early 1946 were contained only by wage increases of 15 per cent or more. The government sought to offset the effects on employers by easing price controls. Thus the steel settlement, in February 1946, of an extra 18½ cents a hour followed government authorization of a $5 dollar per ton increase in steel prices. This settlement, the first made by the giant US Steel in the face of a strike, set the pattern for the mass-production industries.

Truman responded to the May 1946 rail strike by pressing Congress to pass a law granting 'emergency powers to break strikes in any industry held by the government'. Strikers and union officials could be 'inducted into the Army . . . at such time, in such manner . . . and on such terms as may be prescribed by the President' (Preis, 1964, p. 290). The strike was called off just before the bill would have become law. At the end of May the mine workers struck, even though the government had taken nominal control of the mines. They won a substantial wage increase and, more importantly, a five-cent levy on each ton of coal to finance a health and welfare fund to be administered jointly by the union and the government. In the autumn the mine workers' leader, John Lewis, called for a renegotiation of the contract. The government responded with an injunction instructing Lewis to withdraw his announcement terminating the contract: 400,000 miners struck in protest. The judge fined the union $3½ million and Lewis $10,000. The strike was called off pending an appeal to the Supreme Court. On 12 December (well over a year after the end of wartime hostilities), Truman said that 'the recent soft coal strike makes it impossible to declare war formally at an end now' (quoted Preis, 1964, p. 299).

In March 1947 the Supreme Court reduced the fine to $700,000 provided the union withdrew its cancellation of the contract, which it did. In April the miners came out for six days' mourning after 111 of their members had been killed in a pit disaster. Most refused to re-enter mines which violated the safety code. Lewis instructed them to go back as soon as each mine was certified as conforming to the federal mining safety code, and they did so. When the contract finally ended in June, the employers conceded a 44 cents per hour wage increase, a doubling of the welfare royalty and acceptance of the federal mining safety code. Most other major unions accepted considerably smaller increases (between 7½ and 15 cents per hour) without strikes.

Business organized a massive campaign for the abolition of price controls, arguing that they were responsible for meat and bread shortages in the spring of 1946 – shortages which it may have partially contrived. Consumer prices rose 28 per cent and the wholesale price index by 25 per cent (faster than after the First World War). A worker with three dependants had seen real earnings rise by some 4½ per cent between September 1945 and April 1946. With the ending of price controls they began to fall. By 1947 they were around 15 per cent below January 1945. Profits also climbed sharply in 1947, to around 9 per cent of the value of production.

Business also pressed Congress to move beyond such crisis measures as seizing industries, obtaining injunctions and so forth, and to launch a more fundamental attack on the union movement. It did so with the Taft-Hartley Act of June 1947. This:

- outlawed the closed shop and permitted states to pass laws banning union shops;
- made illegal secondary strikes or boycotts to force management to recognize a non-certified union;
- required a 60-day cooling-off period before a contract was ended;
- allowed employers to sue unions for breach of contract or for illegal strikes or boycotts;
- prohibited strikes by federal employees;
- allowed the President to seek an injunction to postpone for 80 days any

strike deemed to affect 'national health and safety', pending conciliation, and to require a ballot before the strike could proceed;
* required union officers to swear they were neither members of the Communist Party nor supporters of any organization advocating 'unconstitutional' means of overthrowing the government;
* forbade union contributions to candidates in federal elections.

Truman opposed the bill but used its provisions 12 times during its first year on the statute books. The miners and Ford workers secured contracts which expressly protected them from damage suits under the act. But most union leaders, other than Lewis, signed the Taft-Hartley affidavit.

The common thread linking foreign policy initiatives and the offensive against labour was a stress on the 'Communist Threat'. Surprising as it may now seem, the Communist Party had built up a powerful position in the US labour movement. In 1946 it controlled unions making up roughly one-third of the CIO's membership. Its main bastions were in the half-million-strong United Electrical Workers (UEW), the food and tobacco, non-rail transport and agricultural machinery unions, and in local union coalitions in major industrial cities. It was also influential in the Union of Autoworkers (UAW).

The attack on the CP was not in response to any recent industrial militancy on its part. During the war it had helped moderate industrial conflict. *Business Week* commented astutely: 'Since Russia's involvement in the war, the leadership in these unions has moved from the extreme left wing to the extreme right wing. Today they have perhaps the best no-strike record of any section of organized labour; they are the most vigorous proponents of labour management cooperation; they are the only serious advocates of incentive wages. . . . In general, employers with whom they deal now have the most peaceful labour relations in industry' (quoted Brecher, 1972, p. 221).

Nor did the end of hostilities produce a shift to militant class struggle. In the General Motors strike in early 1946 the electrical workers, in the CP-controlled UEW, settled before the UAW did. As the UAW president explained, this 'put us in an awful spot since GM now will come to us insisting that we settle on the same terms' (quoted Preis, 1964, p. 279). When Walter Reuther won the presidency of the UAW in the convention which followed the strike, he was opposed by the CP, despite support from the most militant sections.

The attack on the CP in the unions began in earnest at the November 1946 CIO convention, which passed a policy statement containing the words: 'We resent and reject efforts of the Communist Party or other political parties and their adherents to interfere in the affairs of the CIO' (quoted Preis, 1964, p. 332). This opened the way for unions to ban communists from holding office. The witch-hunt helped to defuse the strike wave, ease the implementation of Taft-Hartley and consolidate the position of union leaders prepared to reach an accommodation with business. Union organizations in the electrical and farm machinery industries were split. Within a year of its launch, Reuther had used a 'Get the Commies' campaign to win undisputed control of the crucial UAW and to suppress all opposition.

The adoption of the Truman Doctrine and Marshall Plan obviously helped the attack on the United States CP, which could now be presented as an enemy fifth column. But the emphasis on the Communist Party as such was mainly a device to link industrial militancy with political subversion. This allowed a far wider ranging assault directed at all left-wingers and union militants. Again, the foreign policy parallels are clear.

How the Marshall Plan worked

As soon as the Marshall Plan – or European Recovery Programme (ERP) – was announced, the IMF eased its tough lending conditions. Together with the World Bank, it lent more than $1 billion to Europe in the next twelve months. In December 1947 Truman persuaded Congress to agree $600 million in emergency aid for France, Italy and Austria to tide them over until Marshall Aid came on tap. Congress finally sanctioned $13 billion Marshall Aid, to be spread over four years. This was less than half the amount the Europeans had asked for. But they, and especially the United Kingdom, nevertheless responded quickly and enthusiastically, establishing a Committee of European Economic Cooperation (later converted into the OEEC) to devise a recovery programme. Much to the relief of the United States, the USSR declined to participate on the grounds that the sovereignty of individual countries in making their own reconstruction plans would be violated and that German reparations would be set aside.

The European governments sat down to draw up these plans in a relatively relaxed economic climate. Prospects had improved considerably since the first half of 1947. Industrial production had regained its prewar level (and was well above if Germany is excluded). Agricultural production was improving after the bad winter of 1946–7, though more slowly than industry. Despite worsening terms of trade (import prices rising faster than export prices) worth $1500 million, the trade deficit with the United States had been cut by almost a third (and the overall deficit by only slightly less).

Table 5.1 Receipts of US non-military grants and government long-term capital, 1946–50 ($ million per year)

	UK	France	Germany	Italy	Japan
1946–47	1722	948	371	474	419
1948–50	857	668	847	378	373

Source: US Government, 1962, *Balance of Payments*, table 46.

Only Germany received a major increase in US assistance after 1947 (table 5.1). The United States insisted on recipients drawing up four-year reconstruction plans to help it systematize and monitor aid flows (and see a clear end to them). William Clayton, US under-secretary for economic affairs, wrote to his government from Paris at the end of August: 'In determining requirements of coal and steel, account should be taken of relative efficiencies of available plants and other related matters . . . attention must be given to an initial selective utilization of productive capacity, without regard to national boundaries' (quoted Balfour, 1981, p. 84). Such international planning to secure maximum production and to distribute the output was both unacceptable to the European governments concerned, and, as Clayton and the United States ambassadors in Paris and London admitted a couple of weeks later, was not in the United States' interests anyway: 'Such a procedure and organization would result in a planned economy to a dangerous degree. It is almost certain to lead to international cartels which would stimulate nationalism and frustrate the ultimate restoration of natural economic forces' (quoted Balfour, 1981 p. 84). The 'nationalism' they referred to was not the nationalism that was preventing European-wide planning, but the assertion of European interests against the United States and the 'natural economic forces' of free trade and capitalist competition. Accordingly, the United States accepted that the overall plan should be based on separate four-year plans submitted to the OEEC by each country.

In fact many of the national plans were mutually incompatible. For example, the continental countries aimed at a surplus of £50 million on trade with the United Kingdom, while Britain envisaged no equivalent deficit.

European output was expected to reach 120 per cent of the 1938 level by the end of the plan period (a 35 per cent increase over 1947). Exports were to rise from $6 to $10.6 billion (leaving a dollar deficit of $1.4 billion). But the OEEC was sceptical about this figure – derived from individual national plan targets. It argued that unless imports were held down to 75 per cent of national plan targets a deficit of $3 billion would result. US aid was expected to total a sum equivalent to around 5 per cent of European production.

Marshall Aid brought a clear shift in the form of US aid. From 1947 loans repayable with interest dropped sharply. Non-military grants rose correspondingly (figure 5.2). In line with this commitment to greater support for European governments, the Americans also relaxed pressure on them to open up their economies to US capital.

Free trade hawks had wanted to use Marshall Aid as a lever to break open the Sterling Area. One had written: 'We have in our hands bargaining weapons we may never possess again. . . . If we cannot now obtain the liquidation of the Ottawa System [Sterling Area controls against dollar imports] we shall never do so' (quoted Kolko and Kolko, 1972, p. 366). But the US government rejected this approach, recognizing a prior need to support the British and other European economies. Even so, the Americans tried to persuade the Europeans

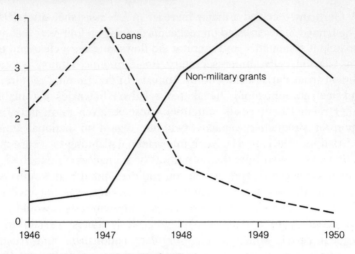

Figure 5.2   US aid to Europe, 1946–50 ($ billion).
Source: US Government, *Balance of Payments*.

to accept IMF consultation as a precondition of devaluation, and a binding assent to the principles of the proposed International Trade Organization. They succeeded in getting unprecedented agreements with each country 'to stabilize its currency, establish or maintain a valid rate of exchange, balance its governmental budget . . . create or maintain internal financial stability' (Kolko and Kolko, 1972, p. 380). Congress also inserted a 'counterpart' provision, requiring aid recipients to set aside a sum of domestic currency equivalent to the aid, to be spent in ways agreed with the United States. Moreover, although easing the pressure to liberalize trade, the Americans insisted on a number of provisions advantageous to US business: 50 per cent of goods financed by aid were to be shipped in American boats and covered by American insurers; aid-financed food imports must come from the United States, even if they could be bought more cheaply elsewhere; US oil interests were also to receive preferential treatment. According to an official involved, these arrangements 'maintained outlets for American oil in Europe . . . which otherwise would have been lost' (quoted Kolko and Kolko, 1972, p. 447). While Marshall Aid aimed primarily at making Europe safe for US business in the long run, there was no reason to forgo short-term advantages.

6

The New Turn in Europe and Japan

The years after 1947 saw no marked acceleration in the pace of expansion, other than in Germany. Total European production grew at a rather steady 7 per cent or so a year, and industrial production at around 10 per cent (figure 6.1). In most countries of Western Europe prewar output levels were exceeded in 1948 (1951 in Germany). Japan did not find the impetus to escape the stagnation which set in during 1949 until the Korean war (chapter 7). In 1951 output was still well below the prewar level.

European investment grew no faster than production as a whole (figure 6.2). In Japan it stagnated. Accumulation rates showed no great upward spurt. In Germany, where the capital stock fell in 1947, the subsequent strong rise in investment drove the accumulation rate only to some 4 per cent in 1950 –

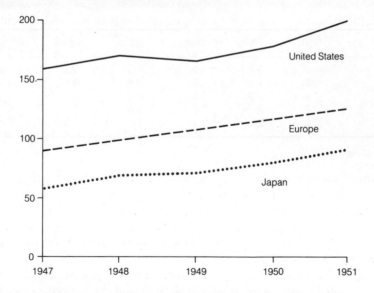

Figure 6.1 Gross domestic product, 1947–51 (index numbers, 1938 = 100).
Source: see Appendix.

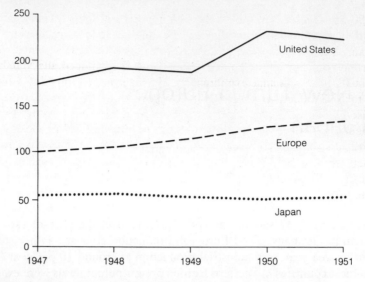

Figure 6.2   Gross fixed investment, 1947–51 (index numbers, 1938 = 100).
Source: See Appendix.

similar to elsewhere but hardly remarkable when compared to subsequent experience. Accumulation was generally maintained at around the rather moderate rate established by 1947 (Table 6.1).

Table 6.1 Accumulation: growth of the business capital stock, 1947–51 (annual percentage growth rates)

	USA	UK	France	Italy	Japan	Germany
1947	3.9	1.7	3.9	1.5	4.2	−1.9
1948	3.9	1.8	3.9	0.6	4.6	−0.5
1949	2.9	2.0	3.8	0.2	4.4	3.9
1950	3.6	2.7	3.6	0.6	4.7	4.1
1951	3.6	2.1	3.2	1.5	5.3	5.2

Source: see Appendix

Neither European nor Japanese expansion was markedly faster than that in the United States. In 1951 the United States was still producing at double the 1938 rate, whereas European output had only grown by one-fifth. In 1950 the rate of US accumulation was comparable to that of France, Japan and Germany, and well above that of the United Kingdom and Italy. No one was yet 'catching up' the United States.

Nor was continued European expansion based on massive import growth from the United States or elsewhere (table 6.2). Indeed, imports fell in 1948 and only regained 1947 levels in 1951. Meanwhile exports steamed ahead and by 1950 had regained prewar levels, with imports still some 10 per cent below. So although Marshall Aid allowed the flow of necessary imports to be maintained, it did no more. The increase in exports was reflected in a reduction in Europe's deficit with the United States (figure 5.1). Indeed, the Marshall Aid was not all used to finance extra imports. Having dropped from $10.5 billion in 1945 to $7.3 billion in June 1948, the reserves of ERP recipients actually increased by $2 billion by 1950. So growth after 1947 was neither especially spectacular nor based on a massive increase in Marshall Aid financed imports. Nevertheless, substantial productivity gains were achieved. European industrial productivity rose by 42 per cent in the four years after 1947. In Japan it practically trebled (figure 6.3). These rises ran well ahead of those to be expected from accumulation.

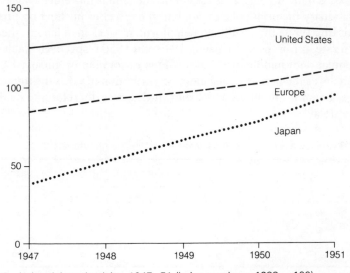

Figure 6.3 Industrial productivity, 1947–51 (index numbers, 1938 = 100).
Source: see Appendix.

Table 6.2 Volume of trade, 1947–51 (index numbers, 1938 = 100)

	USA		Europe (with outside Europe)		Japan	
	Imports	Exports	Imports	Exports	Imports	Exports
1947	130	227	98	60	11	5
1948	150	182	88	78	15	8
1949	147	182	89	90	24	16
1950	174	163	88	105	26	35
1951	180	195	97	119	35	47

Source: see Appendix

Much labour must have been underutilized in 1947. Throughout most of Europe and Japan industry was producing less than prewar with more workers. Where materials shortages limited output, workers were often kept on. Even where there was acute overall labour shortage, as in France and Britain, it was difficult for employers to reduce employment levels. The common thread in this bewildering tapestry is the employment of workers surplus to management requirements. In other words, many more workers were employed than would have been required to produce the same output at maximum productivity levels. Productivity was held down by effective worker opposition to dismissals and to the implied speeding-up and intensification of production.

The most important feature of the three or four years after 1947 was a general attempt, particularly in continental Europe and Japan, to reimpose managerial control by dismissing workers, especially trade union militants, and by attacking trade unions. This assault on the labour movement was backed up by deflationary financial policies and had the effect of pushing up productivity dramatically. While the resulting unemployment weakened labour, the reduced inflation rate in Europe and Japan in 1949 and 1950 respectively (table 6.3) was very popular with middle-class savers. This restoration of 'financial and social discipline' was the period's outstanding contribution towards the foundations of the great boom of the fifties and sixties. It deserves, therefore, to be discussed in some detail.

Table 6.3 Consumer prices, 1947–51 (annual percentage growth rates)

	Europe	Japan
1947	25[a]	151
1948	11	68
1949	4	17
1950	2	−2
1951	11	15

[a] 1947 figure is average for UK, France and Italy during 1947.

Source: see Appendix

France

French governments introduced deflationary policies piecemeal, rather than as a coordinated package. The government's current account, which had been in deficit to the tune of 6 per cent of national income in 1947, was in surplus in 1949 (equivalent to 1 per cent of GDP). Tax receipts rose as a share of GDP by one-quarter between 1947 and 1950. Subsidies to coal and other industries were cut in the autumn of 1947 and current civil spending was lower in real terms in 1950 than in 1947.

Credit expansion was brought under firmer control in the autumn of 1948.

Banks were required to hold a proportion of assets in government bonds, and limitations were placed on lending by the Bank of France to the commercial banks. The rate of increase of wholesale prices declined from 70 per cent during 1947 to 33 per cent during 1948; wholesale prices fell in the first half of 1949. Industrial production fell during 1949, and although unemployment only reached an estimated 50,000 (as compared with 10,000 in 1947), applicants per vacancy rose nearly threefold between 1948 and 1949.

Profits shot up, as production grew with little or no employment increase, boosting productivity (table 6.4). Real wages stagnated after 1948 at well below the prewar level.

Table 6.4 Productivity and wages: France, 1947–50 (index numbers, 1938 = 100)

	Industrial production	Industrial employment	Industrial productivity	Real wage[a]
1947	99	104	95	63
1948	113	108	105	78
1949	122	109	112	77
1950	128	110	116	78

[a] In terms of the official cost of living index. From 1948 product wages appear to be a few per cent lower.

Source: see Appendix

The communist union leadership had disciplined workers well enough to guarantee profitable production up until 1947. But rank-and-file resistance had increasingly undermined its effectiveness. From 1947 the employers increasingly took on the job themselves. Shortly after the expulsion of the CP from the government, the *Economist* described the situation as follows:

> The dream of the Resistance has faded and French society is back in the impasse which destroyed the Popular Front in 1936. The bourgeoisie are not reconciled to the passing of a large measure of political and even economic power to the organized working class, and their response today, as in 1936, is a sort of concealed strike. Then it took the form of a flight from the franc to foreign currency. Today exchange control restricts this possibility. The answer is therefore hoarding, tax-evasion, failure to invest and luxurious spending. The Government lacking sufficient revenue from taxation, and unable to induce saving, cannot balance the budget and has resorted to inflation. But the workers, pinched by rising prices and conscious of their greater political influence, resort to the weapon of the open strike for higher wages, and thus the inflationary spiral spins the faster. (26 July 1947)

This stalemate was broken over the next 18 months.

In the autumn of 1947 the CGT launched a campaign for a general wage rise, although the socialist minority denounced calls for a general strike as 'excessive'. Higher fuel and transport prices triggered a general strike.

On November 12, police, acting on orders from the new Gaullist mayor of Marseilles, broke up a CGT-organized protest against a rise in trolley fares. The arrest of several demonstrators prompted the CGT to call another protest in front of the Marseilles Palais de Justice. The police were called in again, and this time one protester was killed. By November 14 Marseilles was shut down by a general strike. Simultaneously the situation exploded in the North of France when Léon Delfosse, the PCF [Communist Party] miners' leader, was fired from the Coal Board, leading to a miners' strike. The occasion was seized by the CGT to begin its strike offensive. The Marseilles railroad strike became the core of a national railroad shut-down, spreading from railroad centre to railroad centre. Next, PCF-dominated federations and departmental unions went out in force. On November 14 the Paris metals sector shut down (beginning at Renault), then the building trades, then gas and electricity, the Post Office and the docks. In very short order 2 million workers were out. (Ross, 1982, pp. 52–3).

The CP employed exceptionally vigorous tactics to spread the strike. CGT members in the mines refused to hand out safety equipment and used the Coal Board's motor pool to transport flying pickets. The government responded ferociously: it introduced legislation carrying severe penalties for 'interfering with the right to work', and called up 80,000 army reservists. Police broke up picket lines and occupied Paris's power stations. Soldiers were used to break the railway strike. Police and army intervention then became general. Hundreds of workers were arrested and imprisoned. The number on strike fell to a third of the peak of 3 million, and on 9 December the strike was called off. None of the demands had been won.

In the aftermath of the strike the socialist minority in the CGT split to form the Force Ouvrière (FO), taking around one-third of the membership. (It was especially strong among civil servants.) A few years later, George Meaney of the American Federation of Labor boasted that 'it was thanks to the money of American workers – the workers of Detroit and elsewhere – that we were able to create a split, important to us all, in the French CGT, by creating the Force Ouvrière Fédération' (quoted Werth, 1956, p. 385).

In the autumn of 1948 the government issued a series of decrees to reduce employment in the nationalized industries by 10 per cent, and to implement a tougher system of work discipline. The CGT organized a referendum among the miners, who voted overwhelmingly to strike. But other workers were not persuaded to come out in support.

The CGT next called a 24-hour strike of mine safety crews in response to alleged police brutalities. The government then conscripted the crews, obliging them to stay on the job. The CGT responded by calling them out on indefinite strike, threatening pit safety. The government then despatched troops to mining areas, to remove strikers from the pit-heads. CGT officials were fired from the Coal Board and family allowances to striking miners reduced. The strikers began to drift back to work at the end of October. By mid-November, when the strike was six weeks old, over a thousand workers had been arrested, and nearly 500 policemen injured. The CGT called off the strike on 30 November, having won none of their demands. At least three thousand militants were sacked and the CGT's influence was seriously weakened. The miners were not to strike for another 15 years.

A contributory factor to the defeat of the strike was the division in the trade union movement which followed the strikes of the previous year. Attempts were made to replace local workers' representatives who belonged to the CGT, by FO supporters. In the middle of the strike a certain François Mitterrand was reported as offering, on behalf of the cabinet, negotiations 'notably with trade union organizations that have displayed in this period of crisis, a republican and patriotic attitude' (*Economist*, 30 October 1948). Socialist ministers were responsible both for the decrees which sparked off the strike and for the measures which broke it.

Labour movement divisions presented the employers with a golden opportunity to use divide-and-rule tactics. They had no effective organizations at all until the middle of 1946; by 1949 their organization covered 90 per cent of capital employed. They could settle disputes with non-CGT unions quickly and then use police to intimidate the now-isolated strikers. The FO's virulently anticommunist leadership opposed any unity of action with the CGT. The employers took every advantage of the weakness that these divisions brought. Their federation came out against the conclusion of any major collective bargaining agreements which were allowed under a law passed early in 1950. None was signed. George Ross, on whose account the foregoing is based, concludes: 'After 1944 the French labour movement had been more powerful than at any point in the history of French capitalism. During the cold war the whole atmosphere of French industrial relations changed, to the labour movement's detriment' (Ross, 1982, p. 67).

Italy

The Italian government began to deflate the economy soon after ejecting the PCI from the ruling coalition in May 1947. It tightened monetary policy sharply in the autumn, requiring banks to deposit substantial amounts with the central bank rather than lending to the private sector. Over the next year bank lending rose less than one-third as fast as in the previous one. Share prices halved. Many goods prices fell too, especially on the black market, as speculators unloaded stocks. Between 1947 and 1949 the share of tax receipts in national income rose from 15 to 22 per cent, while subsidies were cut from 5 to 1 per cent. The volume of current civil public expenditure fell by one-quarter between 1948 and 1949, but military spending was maintained. Investment in public works fell by one-quarter between 1947 and 1949.

Industrial production slowed down during 1948. Deflationary pressure also held prices down and caused a big jump in the real cost of employing labour

Table 6.5 Productivity and wages: Italy, 1947–51 (index numbers, 1938 = 100)

	Industrial production	Industrial employment	Industrial productivity	Product wage[a]	Real wage[b]
1947	92	105	88	86	88
1948	96	105	91	109	108
1949	105	104	101	117	109
1950	122	102	120	125	113
1951	138	104	133	124	114

[a] In terms of prices of manufactures.
[b] In terms of cost of living.
Source: see Appendix

(the product wage (table 6.5)). Fuel and transport costs rose, too, as nationalized industry deficits were reduced, intensifying the squeeze on private sector profits. Bankruptcies doubled from one-third of the prewar level in 1947 to two-thirds in 1949.

Over 2 million had been unemployed before the deflation, which seems to have boosted the number only marginally. But employers took advantage of the squeeze to launch an assault on the power of the unions, at shopfloor level, to resist redundancies and rationalization. The government refused to subsidize firms to keep on workers; although the ban on dismissals had been lifted, workers had previously successfully resisted redundancies. The *Economist* (13 December 1947) had written of the 'symbolic figure' of the 'workman whom his employer fears to lay off but refuses to pay', quoting press reports that thousands of engineering workers were in this position. An *Economist* report a year later (6 November 1948) symbolized the shift in conditions in its title:

Cold War in Italian Industry
Italian employers are now making serious efforts to reduce their staffs to reasonable proportions for the work in hand. This action has long been hanging over the already strained relations which exist in many parts of industry between employer and employee. But it is essential if excessive Italian production costs are to be reduced. The feeling is growing among employers that they are now in a stronger position to try their hand than a few weeks ago.

Workers, however, are putting up a stiff running fight. Last week the Fiat motor company's Mirafiore factory in Turin, the largest in Italy, employing 50,000 people, and of prime importance in the country's export drive, was reduced to operating on what has become known as a 'non-collaboration' basis, because seven workers were dismissed. 'Non-collaboration' means that a worker refuses to go one iota out of his prescribed routine. If so much as a screwdriver is needed, he will stop work until it is brought to him; he deliberately does nothing at all about getting it himself. When this system was first introduced for a week last December, production in Italian industry was estimated to have fallen by 60 per cent. The Fiat management has now retorted with a statement that the proportional loss of takings will be debited to wage-checks.

Many other big works are also suffering from resistance in this and other forms. Daily one-hour strikes are staged or planned over a period. Last week the Snia Viscosa management of the company's Pignotte works in Florence was completely frustrated by a stay-in strike of redundant workers who had been dismissed. It remains to be seen what the upshot of all this will be, but one thing seems clear. The present cold war in Italian industry will concentrate growing attention on the battle between the Communist and non-Communist trade unions.

This important union split took place in the summer of 1948. Expelled from government, the PCI had used its controlling influence to make the main union confederation (CGIL) adopt a more aggressive posture. At the beginning of December 1947 the 'big strike of the week' took place in Milan against the government's attempt to remove the mayor. A 'citizens' committee' took over the town hall for 24 hours. The government began moving troops northwards. Further general strikes were planned in Genoa, Turin and Venice. Fears grew that an 'occupation of the Northern Plain' by striking workers would cut 'Italy off from Western Europe' (*Economist*, 6 December 1947). But a general strike in Rome against unemployment and in support of public works was met by 'an effective deployment of the police forces'. It was called off on the second day (20 December 1947) as it was fizzling out. The left's weakness was shown in the April 1948 election when the Christian Democrats won 48 per cent of the votes, more than half as much again as the PCI and Left Socialists combined.

The biggest industrial upsurge occurred after an assassination attempt on Togliatti in July. The *Economist* (24 July 1948) described the reaction:

> In Genoa almost immediately, about 50,000 workmen, pouring in from the industrial suburbs to the centre of the town, disarmed the police en route, seized four armoured cars and established road blocks with machine guns. . . . In Milan, the local Chamber of Labour ordered all workers to stand at their factory posts, suspending all work. Later two factories, the Motta Confectionery Works and the Bezzi Engineering Works, both of which have been cleared by police of sit-down strikers, were entered by force . . . there was extensive sabotage to railway lines in Northern Italy.

There were allegations that the dreaded insurrectionary 'Plan K' (or 'Z': no one was sure which) had been launched. The CGIL proclaimed a general strike, but called it off after three days. Nevertheless, the decision by the Communist and Socialist majority to call the strike provided the excuse for the Christian Democrat section of the CGIL to split off. It formed the CISL. As with the Force Ouvrière in France, money from US unions helped in its formation. By 1950 the CGIL had lost around 1 million members. The employers systematically favoured the CISL, both in the few national agreements signed in following years and in local agreements, which were 'often granted by firms rather than having been exacted by the workers and made with national "non-communist" unions or the black-leg unions encouraged by many firms' (Salvati, 1972, p. 208).

The benefits of deflation and the employers' offensive showed up when production grew rapidly after 1949 (table 6.5). Production shot up without an increase in industrial employment; productivity was forced up to a level one-third higher than prewar. Since the industrial accumulation rate was low (table 6.1), work intensification must have accounted for much of the productivity gain. The temporarily unfavourable effects of deflation on profits were soon reversed. By 1951 the balance between what workers produced for their employers (productivity) and the cost of employing them (product wage) was more favourable to employers than under Mussolini in 1938.

In going for deflation, the government apparently opted to waste Marshall Aid. During the years 1948–50, ERP donations ran at $250–300 million a year but, rather than being spent on imports to reconstruct and expand capacity, all of this and more was simply hoarded as gold. The reserves rose from $70 million in September 1947 to $885 million in December 1949. Nor did the government strive vigorously to secure as much Marshall Aid as possible; the $1.3 billion received by the end of 1951 was little over half the sum acquired by France.

These deflationary policies provoked strong criticism. The mission administering Marshall Aid was particularly vehement. The Bank of Italy responded unconvincingly with long lists of state aids to industry (allegedly equivalent to 10–15 per cent of industrial investment over the years 1945–51, and one-third financed by 'counterpart' funds). Later commentators have presented the deflation as a triumph for the middle classes and peasants, whose salaries and savings were hit particularly hard by the inflation. These groups did swing behind the government in the 1948 election. But deflation also played another, more decisive role. It created an economic climate in which a degree of capitalist control adequate for future accumulation could be reimposed. This was the fundamental achievement in the years after 1947. Italy is the clearest example of how the need for social and financial discipline took precedence over physical reconstruction in these years. Marshall Aid was primarily symbolic of wholehearted US support for this project.

Japan

By successfully banning the proposed February 1947 general strike (chapter 4), the US Occupation had shown itself capable of intervening effectively against any major labour movement offensive. In July 1948 MacArthur greeted a threatened strike by government employees with a directive to the government declaring that public sector workers had no right to strike or engage in disruptive tactics. Again the response was ineffective. A planned postal workers' protest was called off because of lack of support.

However, the situation was one of stalemate rather than of consolidated capitalist control. The public sector workers had proposed the strike because their pay had lagged behind both inflation and private sector incomes. As the *Economist* explained at the time: 'Japanese private capitalism . . . has proved very adaptable to the new order of things; in order to avoid trouble many industrialists have not only granted substantial wage increases, but have maintained full-time union officials on their pay-rolls and provided them with office space and printing equipment. As a result, rates of pay and union privileges in private industry have risen well above those in state employment' (28 August 1948).

Such 'adaptability' was a sign of weakness rather than strength. Productivity remained low, reflecting the employers' inability to prune the labour force. In 1948 only one major company succeeded in imposing sackings, and then only after it was surrounded by 'four American army tanks, one cavalry squadron, three airplanes and 1800 armed police' (Okochi et al., 1974, p. 336). Company profits hardly rose at all. In 1948 they were hardly higher as a share of production than in 1947 (table 6.6). Retained profits (after depreciation) were non-existent. In May 1948 the employers' association issued a paper on 'Securing management authority' criticizing the excessive powers of the management discussion councils, in which half of all unions were participating, over personnel and even financial matters.

Table 6.6 Profits, wages and productivity: Japan, 1947–51

	Profit share[a]	Real wage[b,c]	Industrial production[c]	Industrial employment[c]	Industrial productivity[c]
1947	8	30	37	95	39
1948	9	49	55	96	57
1949	15	66	71	97	73
1950	22	85	84	98	86
1951	26	92	114	101	113

[a] Net profits as percentage of corporate product.
[b] In terms of cost of living.
[c] Index numbers: 1934–6 = 100.

Source: see Appendix

The government was carrying out more than half of investment, and providing much of the finance for the rest. The Reconstruction Finance Bank was an important channel for funds. During 1947 and 1948 it made loans equivalent to more than 40 per cent of private investment. The United States provided grants of around $400 million to finance essential imports. The government then, in effect, lent back the yen counterpart of these dollars to finance private capital accumulation (the payments deficit was equivalent to some 55 per cent of private fixed investments during 1947–8). Private fixed investment is recorded as 80 per cent of its prewar level, presumably because the inflation (80 per cent or so in 1948) made it cheap to borrow; but in 1948 more than half total investment was in the form of stocks – an estimated 9 per cent of GDP. Such stockbuilding both reflected and exacerbated the inflation. Food shortages were a further problem. The peasant, unable to secure in exchange for rice either enough consumer goods or money which would maintain purchasing power, tended to 'consume more of his produce within his family, or to direct as much as he can to the black market, where prices fluctuate between 10 and 100 times the official rates' (*Economist*, 17 January 1948).

So the position was deadlocked. The labour movement was not powerful enough to bulldoze away the block to decisive action imposed by the Occupation. Private capital was too weak to reassert control in the factories, and the government unable to act decisively to stabilize the financial system and promote accumulation.

During 1947 and 1948 the United States came round to the view that it should intervene to break the stalemate and revitalize the Japanese economy to strengthen the world capitalist system. In early 1948 George Kennan recommended ending deconcentration purges, promoting economic recovery and expanding police numbers in cities where 'the problem of Communist activity would be most acute' (Kennan, 1967, p. 390). At the end of 1948 the Occupation, advised by a prominent banker, proposed a nine-point stabilization programme including a balanced budget, wage and price controls, longer hours of work and mass lay-offs. Another banker, Joseph Dodge, was sent to Japan in early 1949 to oversee the programme. Government expenditures – especially payrolls, subsidies and unemployment pay – were to be cut to balance the budget. State handouts were to be restricted to 'those projects contributing to the economic stability of Japan' (quoted Tsuru, 1958, p. 9). Wage increases were to be granted only as a reward for productivity gains.

Some 700,000 workers were sacked 'as a direct result of the retrenchment measures' (Levine, 1958, p. 73). Dodge was quite clear about what he was doing. He noted that 'the standard of living has probably been permitted to go too high' and that higher unemployment 'will in turn lead to increased efficiency of labour and a greater production' (quoted Kolko and Kolko, 1972, pp. 522, 524). The private sector's response to this government lead was clearly set out by the *Economist*'s correspondent:

With hoarse democratic shouts of 'Down with Communism!' Japanese employers are rushing in to hold down working conditions and wage scales and to knock out the tottering Japanese trade union movement. They have been swift to scent advantages in the current labour retrenchment programme, imposed by the belated 'austerity' orders of Mr Joseph M. Dodge, the Detroit banker whom Washington dispatched to Tokyo to enforce the economic reforms . . . Unemployment in Japan is expected to reach the four million mark as the public services and big industries shed their tens of thousands of surplus employees, and the government fumbles apologetically the task of unemployment relief and reabsorption. . . .

The Communists threatened 'a summer revolution', 'an August labour offensive' (which has now been shifted to September, or it may be October) and a programme of strikes from one end of Japan to the other. But only words were violent as the dismissal notices were issued. And then even the words lost their violence when an elderly, inoffensive railway executive, charged with the technical responsibility of sacking surplus railwaymen, was found, cut to pieces, on a Tokyo railway track. . . . The public revulsion against the Communists in general, and dismissed railwaymen in particular, was bitter and spontaneous. That was seven weeks ago. There has been no arrest. The railwaymen, like other dismissed workers, wilted under horrified public opinion. . . .

Now employers, in common with the government, are exploiting the situation with Oriental expedience and mock-humble opportunism. This week the Japanese League of Employers' Associations in a long report full of pious phrases and unashamed hypocrisy, has drawn up recommendations for nation-wide adoption by all employers who are hampered by the existence of unions, whether Communist-infiltrated or not. They said among other things:

> It was for a time regarded as a legal issue whether or not an employer could dismiss his employees on the ground that they lacked the sincerity to cooperate with him. However, the latest mass discharge of railway employees has furnished a decisive precedent. We are authorized to dismiss all those who either have committed acts interfering with the normal management of enterprises or who have assisted others in the commission of such acts. . . .

> When a second union is organized for the purpose of improving the condition of the enterprise by means of adequate labour-management collaboration in harmony with the actual state of affairs, the employer should give priority to this second union, regardless of the number of its members.

Other useful suggestions are made for reducing retirement allowances 'in view of the present social and economic condition of the nation', for revising labour contracts, for restricting union membership and for 'otherwise democratizing labour unions'. The moral effect of including union officials among the first batch of discharged employees is gently referred to in passing. Finally, the League pays warm tribute to the remarkable legislation, proposed by the government, which will empower the police to arrest and punish equally all the leaders of any union of which an obscure member has committed a crime of violence. (24 September 1949).

There were also 'some successful efforts by employers to produce internal splits often by excluding middle-aged workers from displacement lists and providing them with augmented wage increases' (*Economist*, 24 September 1949).

In 1950 the Occupation instigated a 'red purge': 12,000 communists were sacked, 11,000 from private sector jobs, including 2500 union officials. Sanbetsu, the CP-dominated union confederation, was destroyed. A new federation, initially based on anti-communist 'democratization leagues', was set up. Days devoted to strikes fell by one-half, three-quarters of which were in mining, where employers managed to cut jobs by 10 per cent.

Production stagnated during 1949 as credit expansion halted. Recorded sackings rose from less than 20,000 a month in early 1949 to 85,000 per month in March 1950. Nevertheless, business fixed investment held steady, though stockbuilding fell sharply. Profits rose in 1949. But the real benefit was felt in 1950 and 1951 when production leaped ahead with virtually no increase in employment. By 1951 industrial productivity was well above prewar levels, while real wages were well below. The profit share was extremely high (table 6.6).

Germany

Germany seems the obvious case of a floundering economy rescued by Marshall Aid. In 1947 industrial production was only one-third or so of prewar; by 1951 it had overtaken the 1938 figure. But the recovery was only symbolically based on US dollars. The Allies' decision to work to restore German capitalism fully in the zones they controlled was the real key. Other consequences flowed from this. One was partition. Any system for integrating the Russian zone into the new Germany would have had somehow to incorporate the substantial state ownership and planning established in Eastern Europe. However, the labour movement in the Western zones had to be disabused of notions of the socialization of industry. This implied strengthening the market economy in the West. The maze of controls, black market deals and barter must be swept away and money restored to its role of prime arbiter of economic life. Most obviously, wages must be paid in cash, and spent on goods in the shops. But they should also be held down to a 'realistic' level in relation to workers' output. In other words, profits must be restored to a level sufficient to revive German capitalists' shattered confidence and restore adequate accumulation. Marshall's dollars, as in Italy, symbolized wholehearted American support for this project. But their direct economic contribution was secondary.

The June 1948 monetary reform was decisive. The year's gap between Marshall's speech and the implementation of effective measures to restore the German economy resulted from the need to secure French acceptance of a strong capitalist Germany, manoeuvres to blame the Russians for partition, and so forth.

The situation remained chaotic in early 1948. The *Economist* reported: 'For the third year in succession, a food crisis has reduced the Ruhr to rebellion and despair. The authorities' persistent failure in recent weeks to honour the fat ration has led to strike action in various towns, factories and mines. Had it not been for the remarkable restraint and responsibility shown by the leaders of the German trade unions, there might well have been a general stoppage of work' (24 January 1948). In fact, communist calls for strike action at the Ruhr trade union conference at the end of the month were defeated. SPD trade union leader Boeckler said that 'it would not bring a single grain or a single loaf of bread more' (quoted Schmidt, 1970, p. 141). The same *Economist* report explained why monetary reform was crucial:

> The story is told in Frankfurt of a German businessman in Hamburg who found the work of his factory held up for want of cement. So he set off in his car, and drove, on black market petrol, from Hamburg to Frankfurt. There he bought in the black market some packets of chocolate, such as are sold to GIs in their stores for $1.05 a box, and to Germans illegally for 250 marks. With these he drove to Munich, where he bartered the chocolate for silk stockings, smuggled in from the Soviet zone. He then went on to the Bavarian Alps, where he bartered the stockings to a peasant for butter. With the butter on board he drove all the way back to Hamburg. There he bartered his butter for cement.
>
> The tale might be continued further. The Hamburg manufacturer would produce in his factory just enough to enable him to secure by barter sufficient food and goods to keep his workmen and his family, and to offset the losses which he had incurred through selling a part of his output legally at the prewar fixed price. Then, bearing in mind that currency reform is planned for the spring, and that a large proportion of his cash and bank account will be cancelled, he would store his remaining goods and raw materials as far away from the eyes of authority as possible.

The Christian Democrats, who controlled the Bizonal Executive Council, had earlier claimed to support nationalization. But when it came to the crunch they refused to act, preferring to allow the chaos to discredit planning and pave the way for unhampered free enterprise. They found excuses to prevent Council meetings, claiming on one occasion that the building had been booked for amateur dramatics. A law requiring householders to declare stocks of goods was simply ignored: of 350,000 questionnaires issued in Frankfurt only 14 were returned. Some SPD leaders favoured 'postponing' (i. e. abandoning) demands for socialization and entering a coalition with the CDU. But the leadership opted to stay in opposition, fearing that a coalition might allow the communists to accuse the SPD of betraying workers' interests.

Although Boeckler had said in September 1947 that, whatever the implications of the Marshall Plan, 'the unions would continue the struggle for socialization with more energy' (quoted Schmidt, 1970, p. 116), the party did little to encourage such action. The trade union leadership forced through support for the Marshall Plan at a special conference held in June 1948, despite the fact that the leadership 'saw correctly that Marshall credits were conditional on abandonment or postponement of trade union plans for the socialization of key industries' (Graf, 1976, p. 59). The military authorities had indeed made their stance abundantly clear. They had continued to block all local attempts to pass laws to socialize industry or to extend radically the power of works councils. In the spring of 1948 the British authorities refused, under American pressure, to accept a law, passed in the region covering the Ruhr and North Rhine-Westphalia, to socialize industry (significantly, the Christian Democrats then withdrew their previous support for the measure). The US commander Clay also blocked a law passed by the Hesse government, supported by the CDU, giving works councils decision-making rights over such issues as production methods.

Economic stalemate prevailed. The market was not allowed to function freely to promote revival on its own terms. The monetary reform broke the deadlock. All individuals and institutions were obliged to register holdings in cash or bank deposits. These were then converted into Deutschmarks (DM) at what transpired to be a rate of $6\frac{1}{2}$ DM for 100 Reichmarks. All individuals were given 60 DM in two instalments, and businesses 60 DM per employee (roughly the weekly wage). The national debt was simply cancelled. Private debts were converted at a rate of 1 for 10. This harsh discrimination against holders of government debt was supposed to be offset by a scheme for 'equalization of war burdens' involving taxation of those holding assets whose real worth was not touched by the reform (such as shares). Almost all manufactures were freed from price and physical controls (clothing and shoes remained rationed but their prices were decontrolled). Price controls were retained for food, utilities, transport and rents (though often perfunctorily administered). Wages were decontrolled shortly after the monetary reform.

Money in circulation compared to production at existing prices fell to about one-third of its prewar level. Firms, initially short of cash, began unloading stocks. Barter disappeared. Black market prices tumbled. 'Housewives strolled down the streets gazing in astonishment at shop windows – at shoes, leather handbags, tools, perambulators, bicycles, cherries in baskets' (*Economist*, 3 July 1948). As the same report explained, absenteeism fell dramatically, from 18–20 per cent to 2 or 3, according to Nuremburg manufacturers, and 'makers of heavy engineering products, which could not be used for payment of wages in kind and were difficult things to barter with, had been starved of labour in the days of cigarette currency; within the first week of the new money a manufacturer of heavy transformers and electric motors was getting a steady trickle of applicants for jobs'.

But the collapse of the black market did not signify a collapse of prices. Consumers, starved of commodities and fearing further cuts in the value of financial assets in the wake of the reform, spent cash holdings pell mell. Firms borrowed from banks, which had been allocated surplus reserves. Prices rose 15 per cent in the first six months after the reform. The British military government hardly boosted confidence in the currency by remarking in November that 'the future of the D-Mark was a matter for considerable alarm'. The same report continued: 'Dr Erhard's hope that the removal of price controls would permit a normal competitive price structure to be found has been brought to nothing by the activities of the business people in whom he put his confidence. Rather than face price competition they have banded together to enforce "price discipline" – in other words, to ensure that profits are not reduced by outsiders who cut production costs' (*Economist*, 27 November 1948).

Profits were high. The balance between the cost of employing labour (product wage) and productivity seems to have been similar in the second half of 1948 to 1938 – both variables stood at around 60 per cent of the prewar level. This balance was to persist through the following couple of years of expansion, and then to become even more favourable to profits in 1951 (table 6.7).

Table 6.7 Productivity and wages: Germany, 1948–51 (index numbers, 1938 = 100)

	Industrial production	Industrial employment	Industrial productivity	Product wage[a]	Real wage[b]
1948 (second half)	61	103	59	64	75
1949	75	108	69	74	85
1950	94	114	82	84	101
1951	113	124	91	80	105

[a] In terms of prices of manufactures.
[b] In terms of cost of living.
Source: see Appendix

In 1948 lower costs of materials and other inputs relative to output prices also helped to maintain profits. Capitalists who had accumulated stocks also made vast windfall profits. The UN Economic Commission for Europe (UNECE) reported that during 'the first year after the monetary reform, profits were already higher in relation to wages and salaries than they had been before the war' (1953, p. 74). The central bank's report for 1948–9 also acknowledged that 'price increases in many branches of production soon went beyond mere adjustment to the higher costs, so that in many cases large profits resulted' (Bank Deutscher Länder, 1948–9, p. 5).

Given high profits, it is not surprising that investment more than doubled in 1948, with the increase concentrated in the second half of the year. Much of the investment was in 'palatial hotels, restaurants, movies and shops' (Balogh, 1950, p. 84). The UNECE noted that low wages 'permitted for a small class, a degree of luxury consumption unheard of in most other European countries and contrasting sharply with the low living standards of the wage earners' (1953, p. 75).

Living costs rose less than the prices of industrial output (rents, for example, increased by much less). So the purchasing power of the pretax wages in 1948 stood at three-quarters of prewar. But taxes had risen sharply, reducing net disposable pay by significantly more. By the end of the year the black market had reappeared in food and other controlled items, rendering the official cost of living index increasingly misleading. In August workers held demonstrations against profiteering, and purchasing strikes took place in the Ruhr. In Stuttgart feelings ran particularly high, and a total curfew was imposed for several days. On 12 November some 9 million workers took part in a 24-hour general strike against price rises and shortages.

The situation increasingly threatened economic recovery. The SPD and the labour movement favoured circumscribing the market with state ownership, workers' control, physical planning of production and price controls. Such a solution would at the very least have postponed restoration of untrammelled German capitalism. To achieve such a restoration, capitalist methods of 'social and financial discipline' were required. The authorities, aware of this, responded to the inflation by a monetary squeeze. Bank lending was restricted by increasing by one-half the reserves banks were obliged to hold and by an embargo on further credits. Production slowed down. Prices stabilized and then slid back; the cost of living fell by 7 per cent during 1949. Bankruptcies rose and unemployment soared.

Numbers out of work had already officially risen from half a million in June 1948 to three-quarters in December (employment had continued to rise but many more workers had sought official jobs now that they would be paid in cash of real value); during 1949, waged employment fell by one-quarter of a million, and official unemployment doubled, reaching 11 per cent of wage and salary earners. Unemployment levels were three times as high in the agricultural regions as in the industrial areas. But it rose faster in the latter, reaching 6 per cent. The rate for refugees was around three times as high as that for the indigenous population.

Employment did not fall because of a fall in output. Output merely stagnated for a period in the middle of 1949. Employers took advantage of the credit squeeze and slackening demand to reorganize: 'The process of rationalization of industry – involving re-equipment, adoption of labour-saving processes and machinery and substitution of more for less efficient labour – is going on apace, not only releasing labour but inhibiting reabsorption of those released' (Heller, 1950, p. 534). By the end of 1949 industry was producing one-quarter more output than a year earlier, with no more workers. Spare capacity abounded. The UNECE estimated in 1949 that industry could employ a million more workers, since it was operating at only 75 per cent capacity. An import liberalization policy, introduced in the summer of 1949, put employers under further pressure to rationalize. Half of Germany's imports from Europe were freed from controls, even during 1949 and 1950.

The jump in unemployment further weakened the unions, whose funds had been nearly wiped out by the monetary reform. Since only one-quarter of workers had secured the 15 per cent increase in wages authorized by the military government in April 1948, the abolition of wage controls in October – when unemployment was already rising – posed no threat. The position of militants in the unions was weakened by organizational measures against communists: for example, the metal workers' union, IG Metall, changed its basis of organization from work place to geographical area or industry; at the end of 1948 all KPD members were voted off the Ruhr miners' executive.

Low wages permitted high profits, which encouraged investment, production was increasing rapidly after the end of 1949, and the increases in productivity permitted increases in real wages without profitability being threatened. The weakened state of the trade unions and the growth of real pay ensured that money wage claims did not challenge these high profits. Business investment more than doubled in 1949 and brought the rate of accumulation up to about 4 per cent a year. Although Germany devalued less in 1949 against the dollar than did the UK and most other European economies (chapter 7), the very low level of real wages permitted a rapid expansion of exports in the boom conditions of the Korean War. The volume of exports increased by about six times between 1948 and 1951 to regain the prewar level, and this helped to maintain the expansion and ensure that the rising profits were invested. Exceptionally favourable tax concessions for investment and the wiping out of the burden of interest payments by the monetary reform also encouraged the ploughing back of expanding profits into increased investment; in the two and a half years after currency reform 70 per cent of investment was financed from firms' retained profits. By 1952 the rate of accumulation had been levered up to 6 per cent (table 6.1) – three times the rate in Germany's European rivals and twice that in the United States.

Marshall Aid played only a limited role. Foreign aid peaked in 1948, at just over $1 billion (little actually contributed under the Marshall Plan). This level was maintained in 1949 when Marshall Aid was in full swing. Aid in these two years was around 5 per cent of GDP, representing two-thirds of total imports in 1948, but by 1949 the proportion was less than one-half. By 1951 it was less than one-tenth. The dollars did finance imported raw materials, vital to the expansion of production in 1948 and 1949. But the real extent of aid was less than the gross figures suggest. Significant foreign exchange losses resulted from the underpricing of German coal exports (put at $100 million in 1950 and 1951). There were requirements to use more expensive Dutch and Belgian ports, and limitations on how Marshall Aid could be spent (chapter 5). By 1951 exports were quite adequate to meet the import bill.

The 'counterpart funds' played some role in financing investment. Given the authorities' extreme distaste for deficit financing, the availability of these Deutschmarks – the 'counterpart' of dollar imports – to the government may have made 'respectable' the financing of some investment in basic industries – fuel, transport and iron and steel. But even in 1950, when the use of these funds was at a maximum, they constituted only 9 per cent of total investment. Over the five and a half years after monetary reform they represented only 3 per cent of total investment. In any case the availability of these counterpart funds for investment was enormously outweighed by the occupation costs paid (in Deutschmarks) by the German authorities; these amounted to about 5 per cent of GDP over the years 1949–52, 12 times the value of the counterpart funds available for investment. Of course, Germany was thereby provided with 'defence' which cost a smaller percentage of GDP than was the case for the occupying powers, but this cannot disguise the fact that the costs were obligatory charges levied to pay for armies of occupation and far outweighed the counterpart funds available for investment.

So the dollars provided by Marshall Aid were only of temporary importance in 1948–9. Far more significant was the wholehearted commitment they signified on the part of the United States to the restoration of untrammelled (West) German capitalism. The first elections for the parliament, in August 1949, registered the success of this restoration. The SPD and KPD combined secured only one-third of the votes, compared to 44 per cent in state elections during 1946–8.

The socialization of industry, especially the basic industries of the Ruhr, was effectively ruled out after 1947. Despite IG Metall's threat in 1950 that it would bring business to a standstill if the old owners were restored, they did indeed regain control. The old shareholders were allocated shares in the new companies, though multiple holdings were restricted. So the ownership of Ruhr steel and coal merely became slightly more dispersed. But the workers clung stubbornly to the issue of codetermination in industry. The *Economist* reported: 'In Germany the trade unions, which have made a valiant effort to prune their ranks of communists, find themselves pushed into the background, and advised by the American military government to concentrate their efforts on questions of hours and wages; . . . the trade union leaders fear that industrial workers if they receive no satisfaction from the Western powers on codetermination, may drift in the direction of communism' (14 May 1949).

In 1950 IG Metall secured 96 per cent of the vote in the steel mills for strike action if their demands were not met; 93 per cent of miners voted to support the struggle. After intervention by Chancellor Adenauer, the employers conceded parity on supervisory boards. This was a tactical retreat. As the head of the Iron and Steel Control Board put it, works councils were 'claiming rights of interference in the conduct of the works without assuming corresponding responsibilities. Giving the workers and the trade unions a share in these responsibilities should go a long way towards forestalling labour trouble in industry' (quoted Spiro, 1958, p. 33). The authority of the boards was confined to local works and personnel matters. The key demands of 1946–7 had been parity with employers on issues of the type, methods and layout of production, investment, sales, price setting and mergers. None was conceded (chapter 9). These demands were inconsistent with the full restoration of capitalism. When they were laid to rest with the acceptance of the watered-down system of codetermination, the postwar challenge to the system had been definitely contained.

The United Kingdom

In the United Kingdom the shift in policy after the announcement of the Marshall Plan was milder than in continental Europe and Japan because the political and economic situation was less threatening. The government sought to divert resources away from consumption (private and social service) towards exports and investment (chapter 4), although workers' consumption was growing very slowly. By 1948 it was barely higher than before the war (table 6.8).

Table 6.8 Profits and wages: Britain, 1938–51

	Profit shares as percentage of net domestic product			Index numbers of living standards	
	Before tax[a]	After tax[b]	Undistributed profits[c]	Real wage	Real personal consumption per head of population
1938	12.5	9.8	7.7	100	100
1945	12.3	n.a.	n.a.	121	90
1946	13.0	6.2	6.5	120	100
1947	11.8	3.9	5.5	122	102
1948	14.0	6.1	7.7	124	102
1949	13.7	6.4	7.7	126	103
1950	13.2	5.0	7.9	128	105
1951	14.5	4.5	7.3	128	105

[a] Corporate profits net of capital consumption and stock appreciation.
[b] As (a) but net of taxes (UK) on company income.
[c] Undistributed profits net of stock appreciation, gross of capital consumption.
Source: see Appendix

The first moves came in the autumn of 1947 when the attempt to make sterling convertible into other currencies, which the United States had made a condition of the dollar loan, collapsed after a few weeks. The government introduced a deflationary budget to hold back consumption at home. It also cast around for ways of earning dollars.

Having previously limited the colonies' ability to borrow in London to finance capital projects, the government succumbed to a wave of enthusiasm for aiding colonial developments specifically geared to helping the British balance of payments. The schemes were more or less disastrous. The most spectacular was the Groundnut Scheme in Tanganyika (Tanzania). This cost some £40 million and yielded less groundnuts than had been bought for planting.

Vague calls for wage restraint were replaced in February 1948 by an altogether firmer statement on *Personal Incomes, Costs and Prices*. This proposed that manufacturers should not be allowed to justify price increases by wage rises. In practice this sanction was a less effective means of enforcing wage restraint than the strong support of the right-wing trade union leaderships.

At the time of the 1949 devaluation the call for restraint was replaced by a wage freeze, again supported by the union leaders. The TUC asked for various concessions in exchange for maintaining the wage freeze, including the continuation of food subsidies, rent control and expenditure on social services. Most were partially eroded over the final three years of the Labour government. But the wage freeze had a major impact. Real wage rates fell continuously from 1946 to 1951, though earnings rose slowly through overtime and local agreements. Consumption per head crept up. The policy was finally undermined by rank-and-file pressure. In September 1950 the Trades Union Congress annual conference rejected wage restraint against the advice of its General Council.

The continuation of Order 1305 (chapter 2) provided the backdrop to the wages policy. Its anti-strike provisions were first used in 1949 when gas maintenance workers were prosecuted and sentenced to one year's imprisonment. The other strikers returned to work and the sentences were reduced to £50 fines on appeal. In the following year an attempt to use the Order against London dockers failed because of spontaneous working-class resistance, and it was finally repealed.

As well as the clampdown on wages, 1948 also saw the beginnings of the erosion of Labour's social programmes. The house-building target was reduced, as were the plans for future expenditure on education and health. The principle of free medical services on which the health service had been founded was also abandoned: the budget introduced a one-shilling (5p) prescription charge. After the devaluation in the autumn of 1949, government spending was cut by a further 8½ per cent. Health expenditure increased as a proportion of GDP up to 1949 (table 4.5), but then stabilized.

In a White Paper published in December 1948 the government attempted to make explicit the planning of priorities in the shares of national expenditure. This was done over a four-year period, in line with the requirements of the OEEC as part of the run-in to Marshall Aid. It calculated the extent to which the rate of growth of consumption would have to be limited if the investment (public and private) and current state spending objectives were to be reached. A 12 per cent growth of GDP was projected. Consumption was to increase by 5 per cent. The investment share was to be 20 per cent.

The document had little or no practical effect. But it did reflect the fact that consumption was the main area of expenditure amenable to control, so that other expenditure objectives could be met. Hence the importance of wage control.

The Labour government made no attempt to institute economic planning, even of the indicative kind. It explicitly rejected real economic planning as being inherently anti-democratic: 'It is not possible to establish firm and definite plans. . . . No other method of progressing is possible in a democratic community. For . . . policies can be fulfilled only if they gain the voluntary cooperation of people as groups and individuals. The means of control which can be effectively used within a democracy are limited' (1948 White Paper, quoted Pritt, 1963, p. 283).

In September 1949 the pound was devalued from $4.03 to $2.80 after sterling export earnings (particularly raw materials exports from the Empire) were hit by the US recession (Chapter 7). This, together with the accompanying wage freeze and spending cuts, paved the way for a substantial improvement in the payments position. Profits rose sharply in 1948 and remained high during the rest of the Labour government's term of office.

Alongside the Labour government's retreat towards pro-business policies, a witch-hunt was launched against communists in the trade unions. The CP moved into a position of opposing the Labour government in the autumn of 1947, following the more aggressive line adopted by the Cominform, the newly formed international organization of Communist parties. At the end of 1947, the Labour Party national executive committee issued a circular which in effect invited trade unions to dismiss officials who were CP members: 'We can expect a campaign of sabotage by Communists and their fellow travellers . . . we can expect inspired attempts to promote discontent in the factories . . . we can expect intensified attempts to undermine and destroy the Labour Movement' (quoted Pritt, 1963, p. 160). In the spring of 1948 the government announced a purge of communists in the civil service. The *Economist* reported (23 October 1948): 'The question of communist influence and leadership in the British trade union movement has now become an issue of first-class importance. What has happened in France could happen here if communist influence was sufficiently strong.' It pointed out that the miners had a communist secretary, who had just described the Marshall Plan as 'the American pattern for the reconstruction of Europe at the expense of the working class', and communist leaders in Wales and Scotland. In the engineers' union two out of the national committee of seven, and three out of four national organizers, were communists. The electricians had just elected communists as president and secretary. Eight out of thirty-eight members of the transport workers' executive were communists, as was the president of the builders' union. The *Economist* urged the TUC to intervene 'to end the equivocal position of communist union officials'. In July 1949 the transport workers took the lead by debarring communists from holding office, in line with the letter and the spirit of the TUC's anti-communist circular. This signalled an important weakening of the left. It was noted that 'while the conference was passing a resolution banning Communists from holding office in the union, and while their general secretary was making a highly responsible speech about the necessity for wage stabilization, many of the union's members in the London docks were stubbornly resisting all exhortations to return to work' (*Economist*, 16 July 1949).

The same issue reported that 'among trade union officials there would be

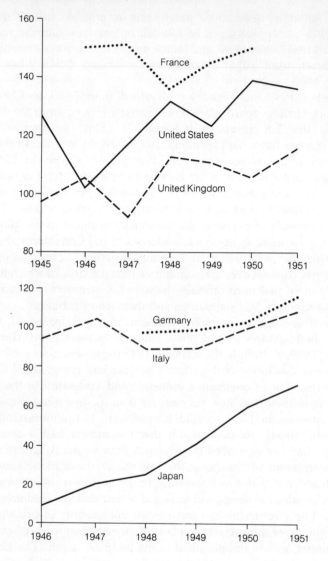

Figure 6.4   Profitability. Indices of the profit share, with the prewar share (usually 1938) = 100.
Source: see Appendix.

support for a legal prohibition of unofficial strikes' in essential industries, but that, given the mood of the dockers, legal threats would not work. 'No section of workers has had its conditions of work more radically improved at the community's expense than the dockers. Yet what is the result? A most marked decline in both efficiency and responsibility.' Despite the anti-communist witch-hunt, employers in Britain never launched a frontal assault on the labour movement comparable to those in France, Italy, Japan or even the USA. This may actually have weakened the employers in the long run. Complacent, with their markets carved up at home and in the Empire, they failed to launch the kind of 'rationalization' drive against the labour movement that was a precondition for the investment booms of the fifties in continental Europe and Japan.

Summary

Much had happened in the few years following the launch of the Marshall Plan. The United States had recognized that the reconstruction of an effective world capitalist system required its wholehearted support for the restoration of 'social and financial discipline' elsewhere, and had been prepared to delay prising open foreign markets to US business to this end. The USSR had been safely contained within its Eastern European bunker. While the USSR's sphere of influence had been more firmly consolidated than the United States had initially hoped, it was also more limited than the USA had subsequently feared. And hostility to the USSR was to prove a useful weapon against the labour movement. While the colonial revolution had achieved a great victory in China, imperialism had elsewhere begun successfully to combine moves towards political freedom with continued economic domination.

The continental European and Japanese labour movements had suffered crushing defeats. They had been forced to retreat enormously from the apparently commanding positions they had held in 1945 – both on the shop floor and politically. The balance between wages and productivity was extremely favourable to the employers. Profits were comparable to prewar levels, even in the countries then under fascism (figure 6.4). In the United Kingdom developments had been less dramatic, but, nevertheless, decisive. In 1945 many people had believed that the Tories would never govern again. In fact, the first ever majority Labour government was to be followed by 13 years of unbroken Tory rule and an erosion of socialist ideas. The US labour movement's postwar offensive was contained in a climate of virulent anti-communism.

So the basic conditions for renewed capitalist expansion had been established, and the basis laid for the great boom of the 1950s and 1960s. But it was to take a few more years to get really going.

7

Towards the Boom

The great postwar boom did not emerge easily from the stabilization in the late 1940s. Indeed, prospects initially appeared gloomy. Industrial production in OEEC Europe (excluding Germany) slowed down, its growth rate declining from 12 per cent between 1947 and 1948 to 5 per cent between the first halves of 1949 and 1950. Possibilities for rapid growth were far from physically exhausted. Unemployment rose in several countries and subsequent events were to show the existence of spare capacity which could be taken up rapidly to permit much faster growth. The slowdown rather resulted from deflation (chapter 6) and the onset of recession in the United States.

The US recession

Pent-up consumer demand in the United States had largely disappeared by the end of 1947. Low-income families had exhausted wartime savings. The 1948 *Economic Report of the President* noted that 'more than a quarter of all spending units and almost half of those with income under $2000 a year held no liquid assets in 1947' (p. 20). In 1948 the average proportion of income saved rose from 3.1 per cent to 5.9 per cent (a level roughly maintained for the next two decades). So consumption decelerated sharply. In 1947 investment was high in 'utilities, transportation and those lines of manufacturing, such as textiles, which had not undergone a normal rate of expansion or modernization of factories during the war period' (p. 22). But investment in many mass-production industries peaked in 1947. Total business investment stagnated from early 1948. Profits peaked then too. By mid-1948 exports were 20 per cent down on the previous year, despite emergency aid to Europe – a grim reminder of what would have happened without the Marshall Plan. Expansion was maintained, only because the government raised its spending by nearly one-half, boosting civil projects in particular (the budget surplus fell from $15 billion in 1947 to $3 billion in 1948).

This stimulus was not maintained in 1949 and production began to fall.

Business investment led the way down, declining by about 4 per cent of GDP, of which nearly two-thirds consisted of destocking. Unemployment doubled to 7.6 per cent.

The recession seemed to confirm the universal prognostications of doom (chapter 1). In fact, a major slump was not in the offing. But the United States was probably only saved from a bout of stagnation by the outbreak of the Korean war in the middle of 1950. Meanwhile the improvement in Europe was registered and consolidated by a substantial round of successful devaluations.

The 1949 devaluations

Europe and Japan could reduce their massive deficits with the United States only by improving their competitiveness. Otherwise increases in production would inevitably be choked off by payments constraints and the United States would see no end to the need for dollar aid. Improved European competitiveness would have a further advantage for leading US exporters: the elimination of the deficit would make it possible to resume pressure to eliminate European barriers to their exports, since the argument that they were necessary to reduce the deficit would no longer hold.

Devaluations can succeed only if workers in the devaluing countries pay the necessary price. Devaluation increases import costs, and hence the cost of living. If workers gain compensatory pay rises then the competitive benefit of the devaluation is soon eroded. The increase in export profits (as UK goods sold for dollars in the United States, for example, bring in more pounds) makes it even harder to persuade workers to accept a cut in living standards. 1949, with the labour movement in retreat throughout Europe and Japan, was an auspicious year for successful devaluation.

Aware of these considerations, the US Treasury began applying pressure for devaluations, especially of sterling, in that year. The US recession led to a sharp deterioration in the Sterling Area's balance of payments. Between January and mid-September of 1949 the United Kingdom lost half a billion dollars – more than one-quarter of its reserves. The government then carried out a 30 per cent devaluation. Amidst French cries of 'trade war', most European countries followed suit with more modest devaluations (a little over 20 per cent for France and for Germany, a little under 10 per cent for Italy; Japan had only established an official rate in April 1949 and it was not readjusted). Rough estimates suggest that (with the exception of France) the devaluations improved European competitiveness considerably compared to prewar (table 7. 1).

Wholesale prices in dollars had risen by less than 50 per cent in the United Kingdom, Germany and Italy while doubling in the United States. The establishment of competitive exchange rates was further evidence that real wage rates could be held down, and profitability jacked up, to the level necessary for

Table 7.1 Prices and exchange rates, end of 1949 (index numbers, prewar = 100)

	(1) Wholesale prices	(2) Dollar value of currency as percentage of prewar value	Dollar wholesale prices (1) × (2) / 100
USA	200	100	200
UK	246	57	140
France	1,944	11	213
Germany	195	59	127
Italy	4,747	3	142
Japan	21,886	1	219

Source: Bank for International Settlements, *Annual Report 1949–50*, pp. 95, 104, 154.

sustained accumulation. The immediate impact of the devaluations, however, was swamped by that of the Korean war.

The Korean upswing

The US economy revived on the expectation of hostilities in Korea. Stockbuilding took off at the beginning of 1950, reaching a massive rate by the end of the year. Business fixed investment recovered: by the middle of 1950 it had reached a level, above the 1948 peak, which was to be maintained for the next five years. Government spending on goods and services – this time military – began to shoot up at the end of 1950. By the end of 1951 it absorbed a phenomenal 7½ per cent more of GDP than in the middle of 1950. Taxes were increased rapidly so that the deficit only reached $5½ billion a year during 1952–4, 1½ per cent of GDP. Consumption hardly grew and post-tax profits did not exceed their 1948 peak since profits tax rose sharply. But the enormous increase in military spending boosted production considerably, simply by absorbing so many resources.

The Korean War generated a dramatic commodities boom. Wool, rubber, tin, cotton and other basic commodities more or less trebled in price. The terms of trade for raw materials against manufactures improved by 30 per cent between the first halves of 1950 and 1951. Raw material imports took off before hostilities began in June 1950. Between the first halves of 1949 and 1950 manufacturing production in the United States, Japan and the OEEC rose by 8 per cent and imports of raw materials by 20 per cent. 'Normal' restocking as output rose was boosted by speculation, encouraged by a doubling of US stockpile contracts in the first half of 1950. When the boom in production got underway materials supplies were limited and prices soared. Between the first halves of 1950 and 1951 manufacturing production rose by 17 per cent and raw material imports by 4 per cent. In the first quarter of 1951 stockpile contracts ran at ten times the 1949 level. In 1951 the rise in military spending accounted for half of the 7½ per cent expansion of production in the capitalist countries.

The raw materials boom subsided towards the middle of 1951. Commercial stocks reached saturation levels and consumer spending fell behind consumer goods production. Demand for raw materials for both consumer goods and military production fell off, while supply continued to grow. Prices fell sharply.

In 1952 the rate of stockbuilding halved, as did the growth rate of total production, which fell to 3½ per cent. Military spending accounted directly for three-quarters of the total expansion (the United States' share on its own accounting for 60 per cent). Unemployment continued to fall in North America (to 3.2 per cent in 1952, compared to 6.1 per cent in 1950); in Western Europe it rose a little as industrial production stagnated (to 6.2 per cent compared to 5.7 per cent in 1950). Inflation, which had been running at around 10 per cent in 1951, subsided very rapidly as the deterioration in the terms of trade (about 7 per cent in 1951) was reversed in 1952. In North America inflation was down to 1½ per cent in 1952. The decline took a little longer in Europe but by 1953 inflation on both sides of the Atlantic was a mere ½ per cent. The inflationary surge ebbed rapidly because trade unions put in only moderate wage claims. Real wages were maintained or slightly increased in 1951, but high inflation rate did not lead to further rapid pay rises. With the fallback in materials prices after 1951, this moderate bargaining yielded real wage increases of 3 to 5 per cent in 1952 and 1953.

The jump in inflation did boost profits in 1950 and 1951 (figure 6.4). But company reports exaggerated the increase by including inflated stock values. In France, for example, the share of profits in national income appeared to rise by nearly one-half between 1949 and 1951, whereas after adjusting for inflation the rise was less than one-tenth. In the United States and United Kingdom stiff tax increases on profits, levied to help finance military spending, actually pushed down the after-tax profit share (table 6.8).

Investment and the boom

In retrospect it might seem that the Korean war boom and subsequent rearmament should have provided the ideal impetus for a sustained boom. The deflations and assaults on the labour movement after 1947 had restored the conditions for profitable production. The expansionary effect of the war could have provided the prospect of expanding markets necessary to justify a major increase in investment, which in turn would have pushed production to greater heights.

In fact, the Korean boom generated only a small increase in investment which soon petered out. Investment in plant and machinery rose by just 5 per cent in 1951. Only in Germany, where reconstruction had been so delayed, was the rate of accumulation substantially higher in 1951 than two or three years earlier (table 6.1). Business investment actually fell a little in 1952 and its growth rate between 1950 and 1954 was less than 3 per cent a year, not much more than a third of the rate which was to be achieved over the following decade. For the advanced countries as a whole the rate of accumulation during 1954 was no higher than in 1951. The beginnings of an investment boom in Europe were apparent, but accumulation had yet to take off in Japan, and in the United States it was slipping back from the 1951 peak.

The main explanation for the sluggishness of investment, despite the high profits and booming markets in the early 1950s, must lie in a lack of confidence on the part of employers. While the most dangerous legacies of the previous decade had been dismantled or contained by 1950, further years of tranquillity and relative prosperity were needed to erase its memory. Stock markets are an indication of expectations about future profits. In 1951 the level of 'real' share prices (that is, adjusted for inflation) was everywhere below prewar, and far below in Europe and Japan. Even by 1954 stock markets outside the United States remained more gloomy than prewar (table 7.2).

Table 7.2 Real share prices, 1929–59[a] (index numbers)

	1929	1937	1951	1954	1959
USA	122	100	90	114	206
UK	88	100	72	80	108
France	300	100	63	112	178
Italy	150	100	38	53	114
Japan	n.a.	100	16	25	95

[a] Share indices adjusted by consumer price index. Data for Germany are not available.

Source: UN, *Statistical Yearbook*, 1960 and earlier issues.

The columns of the *Economist* reflected unease about the extent to which real stability had yet been achieved: 'In the third year of the Marshall Plan, which has succeeded beyond expectation in rebuilding European economies, in conditions of prosperity and restored standards of living – in short, in what ought to be a good year – a quarter of both the French and Italian electorates voted communist. . . . There is almost nowhere a positive faith in the possibilities of progress, such as the Russians and Americans in their different ways, both have' (7 July 1951).

Optimistic assessments of the situation in Japan were also discounted: 'The true picture is of the Japanese nation, facing a grim struggle for existence on the basis of somewhat artificial and distorted economic conditions, and of a Japanese people dazed and strained after all their chequered experiences in the last ten years' (10 November 1951). A couple of years later the problems of potential conflicts in Japan remained. 'Fundamentally Japan's difficulties are simple and backbreaking: costs are too high, hungry mouths are too many, markets are too few . . . costs, however, can be cut only if equipment is modernized, with consequent incitement – never very necessary in Japan – to staff retrenchment, which in turn must provoke industrial unrest, already strong and mounting' (6 June 1953).

Early in 1951 a report headlined 'Strike Pressure in France' reported that 'France was hit by a new wave of strikes the most serious since the big coal strike of October and November 1948. . . . It is a revealing fact that when the Communists tried to mobilize the workers behind political slogans – for instance, against General Eisenhower – they met with failure; but with a rapid rise in the cost of living they found it easy enough to start a strike about wages' (24 March 1951).

Some two and a half years later another strike wave involved '2 million strikers paralysing the public services of France and the movement spreading to private industry . . . unable to topple a centre-right government in the Assembly, they are trying to register the vote of no confidence outside the Chamber. It is a near revolutionary situation' (15 August 1953).

Italy was 'by no means in a state of boom. And the relative stability has been obtained at a level far too low to give every Italian an adequate standard of living' (19 June 1952). In the autumn of 1953 a major strike took place in support of a 10 to 15 per cent pay rise. 'The twenty-four-hour token strike of September 24th is regarded by many observers in Rome as the most imposing trade union demonstration since the war. Over 5 million workers of all three union organizations (Communist, Catholic and Social Democrat) came out. In the North the strike was almost 100 per cent effective in the bigger factories' (3 October 1953).

Germany seemed the outstanding success story in terms of political stability. In 1953 the *Economist* confidently wrote of the Christian Democrats' electoral success: 'For Germany's neighbours the outstanding fact of last Sunday's elections is that Dr Adenauer is established as the most powerful statesman on the continent. The disparity between his position and that of the politicians who temporarily govern France and Italy is startling. So, too, is the German vote that eliminated the Communists and the Communist success in the Italian elections; or between the stable labour conditions in Germany and the strikes in France' (12 September 1953). Within a year, however, it was reporting that widespread strikes involving public sector workers in Hamburg and metal workers in Bavaria were shattering such complacency: 'Peace in the labour world has lasted so long that everyone had come to feel that "Germans don't strike" ' (14 August 1954). A fortnight later its correspondent wrote: 'On the whole West Germany's economy can now bear increased wages, but its political structure would be shaken by class struggle. It is likely that extremism on the part of the unions is less to be feared than a stubborn attitude amongst a section of the employers.'

All these movements were successfully contained, but the essential point is that 'informed' opinion was still jittery. This bred poor business confidence and hesitancy over long-term investment plans. The UN Economic Commission for Europe, writing early in 1953, stressed clearly the link between economic confidence and political stability:

> At the beginning of 1953 there was stagnation in production and shrinking trade in Western Europe, in sharp contrast to the one-and-a-half-year-old resolve of the OEEC countries to secure an increase in production of 25 per cent in five years. It would be rash to attempt a forecast about cyclical movements in the near future: the developments over the seven post-war years . . . serve to stress the influence which political changes in Europe and elsewhere exert on Western Europe's economy' (UNECE, 1953, p. 52).

A year later the UN, with rather a rosy memory, reported a substantial decline in private investment, and commented: 'There was in general no return to the climate of confident expectations which had characterized the years up to 1950' (UNECE, 1954, p. 1).

Contrary to the UNECE's expectations, however, a general upswing started in Europe in 1954: 'The general impression was that, after the Korean boom, Western Europe – with the notable exception of West Germany – had entered a period, not of outright downturn, but rather of protracted stagnation. On top of this came, in the latter half of 1953 and the beginning of 1954, two new factors which added to apprehensiveness. One was the onset of American recession and the other was a pronounced weakening in European markets for coal and steel' (UNECE, 1955, p. 3). But the US recession proved less severe and protracted than had been anticipated (the *Economist* had feared a 'medium-sized slump'). It also had less impact than had been expected, since US military expenditures in Europe (running at about $2 billion per year) still more than covered Europe's increased trade deficit with the United States. So, paradoxically, the US recession may have boosted confidence in Europe by showing that stagnation in the United States did not necessarily imply stagnation in Europe.

Moreover, in longer-term perspective, Europe was proceeding in the United States' footsteps.

> One of the most notable features of the present upswing in Western Europe is the great increase in purchases of consumer durable goods. The expansion of the West European motor-car industry was largely destined for European markets, and concurrently there has been a growing sale of furniture, electrical appliances and other durable household goods which, when added to the increase in purchases of motor-cars constitutes a veritable wave of consumer buying. Much of this expanding demand has been financed by means of consumer credit (UNECE, 1955, p. 21).

Most fundamentally, the struggles of the early 1950s had shown that the challenge posed by the labour movement, already severely weakened by the onslaught of the late 1940s, could be contained by affordable improvements in living standards. Amidst widespread reports of the 'Investment Boom of 1955', the rate of accumulation climbed steadily in Europe to reach a rate of over 4½ per cent by 1956 – half as much again as five years before. Japan was to prove to be close behind (chapter 8). The great boom was on its way.

PART II

The Great Boom, 1950–1974

8

The Golden Years

The wealth of those societies in which the capitalist mode of production prevails presents itself as an 'immense accumulation of commodities'.

Those opening words from Marx's *Capital* could have been written about the long postwar boom, the most striking feature of which was a quite breathtaking growth in production.

By 1973 output in the advanced capitalist countries (ACCs) was 180 per cent higher than in 1950 – almost three times as great. More was produced in that quarter century than in the previous three quarters, and many times more than in any comparable period in human history (table 8.1).

Table 8.1 Long-term growth, 1820–1973 (average annual percentage growth rates[a])

	Output	Output per head of population	Stock of fixed capital	Exports
1820–1870	2.2	1.0	n.a.	4.0
1870–1913	2.5	1.4	2.9	3.9
1913–1950	1.9	1.2	1.7	1.0
1950–1973	4.9	3.8	5.5	8.6

[a] Arithmetic averages of individual country figures.

Source: Maddison, 1982, p. 91

With growth on that scale, output doubles every sixteen years. If these rates were maintained then, with population growing at the rate of 1 per cent a year, each generation could expect to be roughly twice as well off as its parents and four times as well off as its grandparents.

Moreover, figures of this sort understate the pace of development. Being purely quantitative measures, they fail to illuminate qualitative advances. People not only had more than their forebears; they also had revolutionary new products. By 1969 millions of people were able to watch on colour TV as the first human set foot on the moon.

The fifties and sixties were capitalism's golden age. As a British prime minister remarked at the time, people had never had it so good.

Workers and means of production

The increase in output was out of all proportion to the growth of employment. The number of people classified as in civilian employment rose by only 29 per cent between 1952 and 1973. So most of the extra production represented an increase in output per worker. Annual productivity doubled, a growth rate of 3.3 per cent a year. (See figure 8.1.)

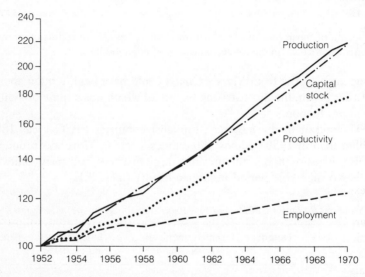

Figure 8.1   ACC production, capital stock, productivity and employment, 1952–70 (index numbers, 1952 = 100, log scale).
Source: see Appendix.

Longer working hours do not account for the increase, because on the whole the 'normal' working week was reduced and holidays grew longer. The number of married women employed on a part-time basis also grew rapidly. The Organization for Economic Cooperation and Development (OECD, expanded from the OEEC) has suggested that hours of work decreased by about 0.3 per cent a year during the 1950s, and by 0.8 per cent a year during the 1960s. Overall, therefore, hourly productivity probably rose significantly faster than yearly productivity, though measuring hours of work is difficult, especially in the self-employed sector.

The main cause of spiralling productivity was a phenomenal increase in the quantity and quality of means of production. The stock of these means of production was 2½ times as great in 1973 as it was in 1952. Since employment growth was relatively modest, the mass of means of production per worker more than doubled over the period. It was as though each worker was confronted by two machines where one had stood before.

The machines changed as well. Technological advances meant that the new generations of machinery embodied important innovations. By the end of the boom the machines confronting the average worker not only were more numerous than before but also bore little resemblance to those in use two decades previously.

These developments were accompanied by changes in work practices, shaped partly by the nature of the new machinery and partly by struggle on the factory floor. Since such changes are inherently unquantifiable, it is impossible to say whether or not people were generally working harder by the end of the boom. But there is no doubt that most were working differently, and that changes in the labour process were part and parcel of the explosion in productive potential.

Profits

A dissection of the relationship between employment, means of production and output does not, of course, explain the boom in any other than a purely statistical sense. Since the production of more goods and services is never an end in itself under capitalism but always a means to making profit, any attempt at an explanation of the boom must centre around the returns capitalists received on their outlays.

In Part I we examined in detail the ways in which the conditions for profitable production were reconstituted in the aftermath of the war. How did the rate of profit fare during the boom itself?

To answer this question we have constructed figures for the advanced capitalist countries' rate of profit (a weighted average of the best estimates available for the seven biggest capitalist countries). As described in the Appendix, we have done this both for the corporate business sector as a whole and for the crucial, and sensitive, manufacturing sector.

Profitability displays no trend between the mid-fifties and the mid-sixties, although it dipped in the recession of the late fifties (figure 8.2). From the mid-sixties onwards it moves into decline. This latter fall is discussed at length in later chapters. Here the focus is on how profitability was maintained until then.

Profit shares and rates

We shall examine the development of the rate of profit in terms of two statistical components. One is the share of profits in the value of output. The other is the ratio of output to capital.

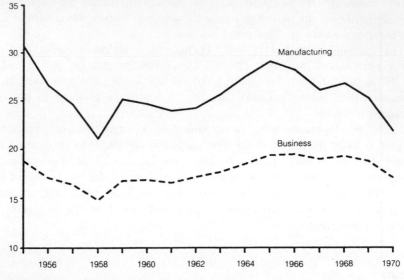

Figure 8.2   ACC profit rates, 1955–70 (percentage).
Source: see Appendix.

Changes in the profit share register relative changes in the costs of employing labour (wages inclusive of all taxes on labour incomes and employment) and the value of output produced. If real product wages rise more slowly than productivity then the profit share rises. If the growth of labour costs exceeds that of productivity, the profit share is squeezed. There was virtually no change in the profit share between the mid-fifties and mid-sixties. In other words, the real cost of employing labour rose at the same rate as productivity – over 3 per cent a year (figure 8.3).

Since the rate of profit is the percentage return on capital employed, a constant profit share maintains a constant profit rate only if the ratio of output to capital remains constant. This ratio in turn depends on the relative rate of growth of capital employed and of output produced.

We have already seen that both the quantity of means of production in use and the output produced by their operation grew enormously. In manufacturing and business, the two grew very closely in parallel until the mid-sixties, so that the ratio of output to capital remained fairly constant (figure 8.4).

Production and realization

Thus far, the account remains a statistical description of certain features of the boom. To get beyond this, and to try to understand the processes involved, we return to the basic requirements for profitable production. We have already

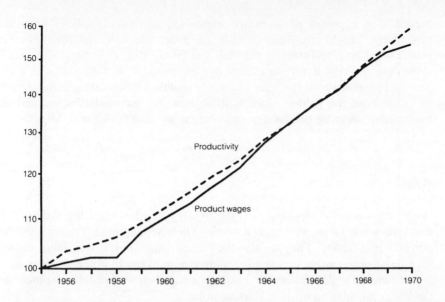

Figure 8.3 ACC business productivity and product wages, 1955–70 (index numbers, 1955 = 100, log scale).
Source: see Appendix.

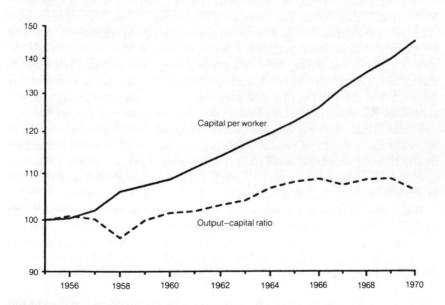

Figure 8.4 ACC business capital per worker and output–capital ratio, 1955–70 (index numbers, 1955 = 100, log scale).
Source: see Appendix.

argued that a period of sustained expansion can occur only if potential profitability can be maintained, that is, if an adequate balance between productivity and real wages can be sustained. But capitalists also need expanding markets if they are to sell their produce and thus *realize* their potential profitability in the form of money profits. The crucial question about the success of the golden years is thus: how did accumulation succeed in maintaining adequate production and realization conditions for so long?

Wages

Wages are a major component of costs for any individual capitalist and are the dominating one for the system as a whole. Their development is thus crucial to potential profitability. They are also the largest single source of income, and so spending from wage packets is a key source of markets. In other words, wages are also crucial to demand. So an examination of their role and development in the boom provides an obvious starting point.

We have already seen that real wage costs rose roughly in line with productivity at over 3 per cent a year – an extremely rapid rate by historical standards. It might seem at first sight that this pace was unambiguously beneficial to demand (being crucial to market growth) and equally un-ambiguously detrimental to profitability (being the only thing preventing a phenomenal profits bonanza). But rising wages played a more complex role. If accumulation is rapid then large numbers of workers must regularly be available to operate newly installed machinery. Some of these workers were provided by growth in the labour force, the rundown of unemployment and a reduction in the numbers of people on family farms (chapter 11). But these sources were quite inadequate. The boom would have run out of steam very quickly indeed if capitalists had been forced to find extra employees to operate all the new machines. Much more important was the transfer of workers from old machines to new ones. If means of production remain in use for 20 years (a reasonable figure) then the scrapping of old ones releases some 5 per cent of the work force to work with new equipment every year. This figure exceeds the annual growth in the labour force during the boom by a factor of more than four.

Wage rises are the main immediate cause of scrapping. The criterion for capitalists to scrap old equipment is not whether the machine is physically serviceable – most machinery is withdrawn from use well before it has worn out – but whether it can any longer be operated profitably. And the key factor which renders unprofitable the operation of older vintages of machinery is a rise in wage costs.

Thus, paradoxical as it may seem, the rapid growth of means of production during the boom depended upon much scrapping of means of production. If this scrapping had not occurred then capitalists would have been unable to find workers to operate new machines and would have been forced to cut back accumulation sharply.

The rise in wages was therefore not basically damaging to profitability. Given labour constraints, it was essential to the pace of accumulation and hence to the rate of growth of productivity. The growth in average productivity resulted from a combination of two processes: the rapid installation of new, high-productivity machinery and the fast scrapping of old, low-productivity machines. If wages had not risen, most of this scrapping would not have happened and productivity would have grown much less quickly than it did.

Rising wages were important for markets primarily because workers' additional spending accounted for the bulk of the growth in consumption expenditure. Rising spending on consumer goods in turn allowed the industries producing them to grow more or less in line with those producing means of production. Indeed, an important element of the boom was the mass production of durable goods and the improvement of the technologies required to produce them. This growth of consumption was essential to stability. If real wages had remained constant between 1955 and 1970, with productivity growth unaffected, then the share of profits would have doubled to around one-half of the value of output. With consumption growing at only about 1 per cent a year (the rate of growth of the labour force), the system would have become one in which machines were being installed at hectic rates in order to produce other machines.

The example is absurd because, apart from anything else, workers would not have been available to operate the new machines. The process could never have gone that far. But that is precisely the point: the boom would have been pulled up sharply if consumption had not grown fast enough, and rising wages were essential to that growth. The phenomenal Japanese expansion of the late 1950s, in which production outstripped consumption and accumulation accelerated enormously, was altogether exceptional and only temporarily sustainable.

In the advanced capitalist countries as a whole the share of consumption declined far less than it did in Japan in those exceptional years – between 1952 and 1973 it only slid down from 62.9 per cent of GDP to 59.5 per cent. The part financed out of wages (and the incomes of the self-employed corresponding to the average wage) fell by rather more than this (figure 8.5). Consumption financed from government transfers (pensions etc.) rose from 5 per cent of GDP in 1952 to 10 per cent in 1973, and it was partly to pay for this that the average proportion of incomes taken by direct taxation rose from 16 per cent in 1952 to 22 per cent in 1973.

Despite this increased taxation, despite a rise in the proportion of incomes saved from 6 per cent to 11 per cent and despite a probable slight rise in the share of total incomes in the form of rent, dividends and interest and high self-employment earnings, consumption out of wages still constituted some 45 per cent of GDP in 1970. If wages per head had not increased, the share of GDP accounted for by consumption out of wage earnings would have fallen from 52

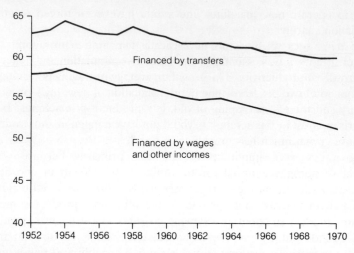

Figure 8.5   ACC consumption, 1952–70 (percentage of GDP).
Source: see Appendix.

per cent in 1952 to 31 per cent in 1970; this would have required an inconceivable rise in other types of spending (by capitalists and government) if the increase in production was to be sold.

Regardless of their importance in sustaining accumulation by providing a growing market for consumer goods, wages must be regarded as a basically passive element in the process of realization. The development of wages is largely a product of the process of accumulation itself.

A capitalist boom requires potential profits to be realized. Workers' spending as a whole provides the demand which realizes the profits of capitalists producing consumer goods. But the pay of their employees is an expense which reduces profits, not a source of demand which realizes them. Only the spending of workers employed elsewhere realizes profits in the consumer goods industries. These workers will only be employed if there is demand for the products they make – for export, from the government or from the employers themselves. So the realization of all the potential profits ultimately depends on sufficient spending by the employers (on investment or consumption), by the government or by those purchasing exports.

Why wages rose

It is one thing to describe the key role played by rising labour costs and another to explain why they rose. But the functions provide clues to the mechanisms. On the production side, labour constraints in the context of rapid accumulation will tend to pull up wages as capitalists compete for workers. Those with new, more productive equipment are prepared to pay higher wages to attract labour than are those with older machinery because the former can operate profitably at higher wage levels than the latter. And they may need to pay more if enough workers are to be available – unless sufficient old machines are forced out of operation there will be a shortage of workers to operate the new.

On the demand side, firms with new capacity will tend to cut prices in an attempt to win markets from their rivals with older equipment. Productivity gains on the new equipment allow such cuts without a fall in profits. The effect is for labour costs to rise relative to the price of the product. Real wage rises were thus a product of the competitive process whereby more efficient firms drove out weaker rivals to obtain both labour and markets, which less efficient producers would otherwise have hung on to.

A question which arises from this analysis is whether competition for labour or for markets was the more fundamental in pulling up wages. Real wages vary according to the net outcome of competition in the labour market, which determines changes in money wages, and competition in the product markets, which determines price changes. At any point in time a shortage of either labour or markets is likely to be the dominant factor constraining accumulation at the existing real wage level. It then makes sense to ascribe the subsequent rise in real wages primarily to whichever of the two markets sees the more intense competition.

In a number of countries a distinct shift took place during the course of the boom. Labour markets tightened noticeably as reserves of unemployed labour and underemployment on family farms were progressively exhausted (this development is discussed in later chapters). As a broad generalization, it is thus reasonable to say that the role of tight labour markets in driving up real wages eclipsed that of competition in product markets as the boom progressed. But that is a generalization. There was considerable variation between countries and between industries.

Emphasizing the role of competition between firms in raising real wages may appear to fly in the face of the everyday reality of pay negotiations. But in the golden years institutionalized pay bargaining constituted one of the transmission mechanisms through which the requirements of accumulation, and the competitive struggles bred by them, generated the necessary real wage increases.

Negotiations over pay are about changes in money wages. What happens to real wages depends on changes in both money wages and prices. Unions do not negotiate with employers about the prices of the products they produce. So they can only raise real wages if product markets are tight enough to prevent the employers from passing all money wage increases on in higher prices. And the tightness of product markets is out of union control.

The need for a certain amount of scrapping if accumulation is to proceed smoothly determines a necessary rise in product wages. If collective bargaining yields less than the required rise then firms will not be able to find enough workers to operate all newly installed machines and will have to pay above the settlement. This will result in a further rise in wages. If negotiations yield more than the required rise then too much scrapping may result, generating unemployment. This did not happen significantly during the boom; the trend was for unemployment to fall. Alternatively, firms will pass on the 'excess' component of the settlement in higher prices, and real wages will rise by less than expected. This was a factor in the development of inflation from around the mid-1960s.

Exports

If wages cannot realize the potential profits, this leaves sales of exports, and spending by the government or the employers themselves, as sources of demand. The advanced capitalist bloc could have realized profits by running a positive trade balance with the rest of the world (i.e. the less developed countries and the Eastern bloc). By selling more outside the advanced bloc than was bought in, capitalists could have increased their assets (in the form of third world factories, gold or financial assets) without accumulating means of production at home.

Exports to less developed countries rose from $20 billion in 1958 (the earliest year for which data are available) to $42 billion in 1970, and those to centrally planned economies from $2 billion $8 billion. The 1970 total represents only 2½ per cent of OECD GDP, a slightly smaller proportion than in 1958. And most of the money coming in was offset by spending on imports into the bloc. The export surplus of the industrial countries in 1970, for example, was only $9 billion. This represented less than ½ per cent of OECD output, or 3 per cent of investment. So it was of trivial significance as a means of realizing surplus.

Government spending

Civil spending on goods and services (health, education and so on) increased by 50 per cent more than total output, and grants to persons (e.g. pensions) grew. twice as fast. Both rose by some 4 per cent of GDP. More than half of this increase was offset by a declining share of military expenditure. The share of government investment was fairly steady (figure 8.6). The effect was a more rapid rise in government spending than in output.

The impact of an increased share of government expenditure depends on the way it is financed. If the money is borrowed, then capitalists can accumulate without investing in means of production. They stock up on financial assets such as government bonds, and the government realizes profits by spending its borrowings on buying commodities. Demand rises and, providing higher real wages do not cut into profits, the economy expands, justifying higher investment. This Keynesian process of governments pumping up demand for

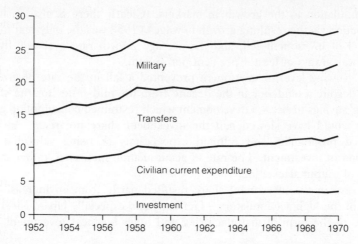

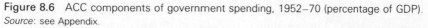

Figure 8.6 ACC components of government spending, 1952–70 (percentage of GDP). *Source*: see Appendix.

commodities has disadvantages: government interest payments grow and attempts to finance them by taxation tend eventually to threaten profits. But these problems are not immediately apparent, and so need not inhibit accumulation for some time.

In any case, this was not, by and large, the way state spending was financed in the boom. Total government deficits fluctuated between 1 per cent of output in the recession years of 1958 and 1967 and minus 1 per cent in the boom years of 1955, 1960 and 1969. Despite rising interest rates, debt interest rose only from 2¼ per cent of personal income in 1952 to 2½ per cent in 1973. So, contrary to those who ascribe great importance to Keynesian policies, the boom was in no sense based on government deficits.

The overwhelming bulk of state spending, then, was financed by taxation. So increases in state spending were largely offset by corresponding reductions by taxpayers. With workers' real gross incomes determined primarily by accumulation, higher taxes bit into take-home pay. But the balanced-budget method of financing extra expenditure by higher taxation is still expansionary to the limited extent that tax bills are met by reduced saving rather than by cutbacks in spending. So increased state spending did increase demand. Without it, even higher investment would have been needed to achieve the same growth of demand.

Investment

Since the level of investment measures the level of demand for means of production, the growth in the investment level measures the direct contribution of accumulation to the growth in markets. (Clearly there is also an indirect contribution via the resulting growth in wages.) 1958 was the only year in which the level of investment fell, and the average growth rate over any five-year period was always at least 4 per cent per annum.

The growing level of investment prevented a fall in the rate of growth of output despite a tendency in the decade from the mid-fifties for the share of workers' savings to rise – a development which restrained consumption growth. Output would have slowed had the investment share not risen. As it was, improved profitability and fulfilled expectations of rising sales led to an expansion of investment. The rate of accumulation increased, rather than the growth of output slackening.

The rise in the investment share resulted partly from an increase in the weight of the high accumulators – Germany and especially Japan. Most of the rise was in the form of manufacturing and other business investment (figure 8.7).

In 1961, 78 per cent of corporate business investment was financed by retained earnings. The remainder, equivalent to 2.8 per cent of GDP, was paid for by borrowing from the personal sector (i.e. workers' savings and rentier incomes). By 1973 this self-financing ratio had fallen to 64 per cent, and 5.6 per cent of GDP was borrowed by firms to cover the shortfall. This offset the tendency towards stagnation generated by increased workers' savings.

So accumulation played the decisive role in maintaining favourable demand conditions. The boom in accumulation was essentially self-sustaining. It simultaneously increased the surplus produced by the working class and ensured that this surplus found a market, generating steadily rising profits for the employers.

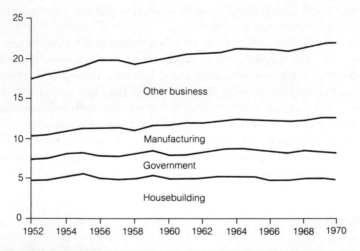

Figure 8.7 ACC components of investment, 1952–70 (percentage of GDP).
Source: see Appendix.

The Japanese economic miracle

The boom was most powerful in Japan, and the period 1955–61 was decisive. Over those years accumulation built up the phenomenal momentum which it was to sustain through the sixties. This period – the most glittering episode of the golden years – illustrates the fundamental dynamics of the boom particularly well because it shows them in operation in top gear and with enormous effect.

We left Japan under the screws of the deflationary Dodge stabilization plan (chapter 6). The Korean boom pulled the economy out of stagnation. Exports trebled between 1949 and 1952, and the share of profits doubled. The expansion allowed employers to reap the benefits of the deflation-induced rationalization.

But the expansion was pulled up sharply by a balance of payments crisis. Imports rose by one-third while exports stagnated. The problem was Japanese capital's competitive weakness. The government's *Economic Survey of Japan* for 1952 noted that the products of heavy industry were typically 30–40 per cent more expensive than in other countries, because of high materials costs and low productivity. It also reported that 'equipment is often old-fashioned, decrepit and inefficient and will not easily permit standardization and mass production' (p. 114). Modernization of the industrial structure had hardly begun. Only 7 per cent of machine tools were less than five years old, and under one-third less than ten.

The government responded to the payments crisis with a credit squeeze. This prompted further rationalization. By 1955 export prices were down to world levels, a development which must have accelerated the scrapping of old plant. And while investment stopped growing, it remained at quite a high level. The accumulation rate remained about 4 per cent, implying substantial further modernization. By the mid-1950s productivity in steel was around half the US level. But wages were still only around one-fifth of US rates. So Japanese wage costs per unit of output were less than half of those in the United States, and below European levels. Productivity in cotton-spinning was almost equal to the US level, and much higher than that in Europe. Without this productivity increase exports could not have expanded fast enough to balance the additional imports required to sustain the 1955–61 expansion.

Over those six years non-agricultural business investment tripled, boosting the rate of accumulation from around 4 per cent a year to 10 per cent. Business investment grew to absorb about one-quarter of GDP. Production of investment goods trebled, while consumption (public and private) rose by less than 50 per cent. The rate of accumulation in those branches most closely tied to investment (machinery, metals, construction) reached 25–35 per cent per year, implying a doubling of the capital stock every three years or less. No industrialized country had ever achieved such a burst of accumulation before.

Myth has it that the accumulation was financed by frugal Japanese workers. Their savings were indeed high by Western standards (largely because of poor government welfare provision and high and escalating housing costs), and they rose over the period from 9 to 16 per cent of their income. But as a share of GDP, workers' savings rose by only 3 per cent while investment leaped up by 13 per cent. The rise in the share of fixed investment, from 19 per cent of GDP in 1955 to 33 per cent in 1961, was paralleled by one in the share of (pre-tax) gross profit incomes, up from 31 to 39 per cent. This latter rise generated much of the necessary finance.

The share of profits was able to rise quickly because real wages did not need to grow in line with productivity. Rapid accumulation maintained expanding markets – much extra output consisted of means of production bought by capitalists – so that demand shortage did not pull down prices and hence push up real wages. Since labour reserves were adequate, there was no need, either, for an acceleration of wages and faster scrapping in order to release workers for employment on new machines.

Employment rose by about one-tenth. Employment in industry and services, which gained 2½ million workers from agriculture, grew by only around one-quarter, which seems modest in relation to the increase in the capital stock. But the extra workers imparted a decisive flexibility to accumulation. Employment in construction rose by two-thirds over the six years, increasing its share of non-agricultural employment by more than half a million. Employment in electrical machinery trebled, again increasing its share by half a million. Such employment leaps in particular industries could not have occurred in a tight labour market with slow labour-force growth.

The labour market tightened considerably over six years. The unemployment rate and the ratio of job-seekers to vacancies both fell precipitately. By 1961 they had reached levels which were to persist, with minor ups and downs, for the remainder of the decade. Labour turnover rose, as did voluntary quits. Annual money wage increases rose to about twice those of the mid-fifties, and product wages (real wages in terms of the product) accelerated as well. The upswing of accumulation partially absorbed the huge pool of labour in backward sectors (including ex-agricultural workers drawn into service industries in the early fifties). As the labour market tightened, faster product wage growth limited the expansion of the backward sector, and thereby ensured an elastic labour supply for the dynamic modern sectors. This effect was accentuated by a squeezing of differentials, especially in large manufacturing firms. Product wages probably accelerated only about half as much in the largest firms as in the smallest, thus facilitating the expansion of the former as the latter were knocked out.

These developments prevented newly accumulated means of production from being starved of labour. They ensured that few of the extra workers entering the market were trapped in small-scale operations and provided an elasticity of labour supply essential to very rapid accumulation in advanced sectors. In 1955 one-third of manufacturing workers were employed in enterprises with less than 20 workers. By 1961 the proportion had fallen to one-quarter. The number of manufacturing plants with more than 30 workers had risen by two-thirds. Small-scale industry constituted a huge 'tail' of ancient means of production which could be scrapped without jeopardizing profits in modern enterprises. So the rise in product wages was both the clearest expression of tightening labour markets and the mechanism which prevented it from inhibiting accumulation.

New techniques of production were introduced at an accelerating rate. Initially, the rapid run-down of agriculture allowed employment to rise in line with the capital stock. But as accumulation accelerated, capital intensity increased. The rate of introduction of new techniques from overseas trebled in 1960. By the next year more than half of manufacturing production used foreign technology. The proportion was higher in the fastest growing sectors, such as electrical machinery, transport equipment and iron and steel. By the end of the six years Japan possessed a younger stock of machine tools than the United Kingdom or the United States: 40 per cent was less than five years old. Productivity had more than doubled in the chemicals, transport equipment and electrical machinery industries.

Fast productivity growth in the sectors producing means of production ensured a rapid reduction in the real cost of capital goods. This offset the effect of rising mechanization on capital costs, and, combined with a rise in capacity utilization, pushed the output–capital ratio up. So the profit rate rose faster than the share. The pretax rate of profit for business rose from about 17 per cent in 1955 to 24 per cent in 1961.

In sum, accelerating accumulation pushed up employment quite rapidly, but not as fast as the stock of capital rose, since mechanization proceeded apace (figure 8.8).

Ample labour supplies permitted the operation of new machines without the need for product wages to rise as fast as productivity. The situation was also eased by rapid mechanization (figure 8.9). Capitalists realized the rising share of profits by increasing investment at a faster rate than production (figure 8.10).

Since productivity rose faster than mechanization, the output–capital ratio rose, boosting the profit rate still further. By the end of the period, however, the tighter labour market forced product wages to rise as fast as productivity to ensure sufficient scrapping to provide labour to operate newly installed equipment. The share and rate of profit and the accumulation rate more or less stabilized at the very high levels established over the previous six years.

The speed and economic mechanics of this burst of accumulation were dazzling. But it is important not to become so mesmerized by them as to lose sight of the underlying social processes. The extra output was produced on the shop floor. Here the employers consolidated an industrial relations system which ensured maximum control. Relatively strong private sector unions were picked off one by one. The resulting disputes were bitter. But by the close of

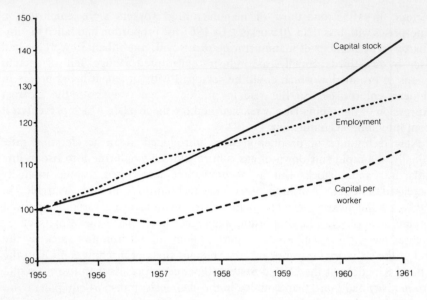

Figure 8.8   Japanese business capital stock, capital per worker and employment, 1955–61 (index numbers, 1955 = 100, log scale).
Source: see Appendix.

the decade militant trade unionism had been literally eradicated in the private sector.

At Nissan, management felt especially threatened by a shopfloor system whereby each group of 10 workers elected delegates to a shop committee. 'While the committees normally held meetings in working hours with management's permission, when disputes arose, chairmen frequently convened unauthorized meetings and excluded staff representatives if they disagreed with the positions of the union leadership' (Cusumano, 1985, p. 148). These committees assumed the authority to grant or refuse overtime requests. In the summer of 1953 the union carried out strikes and go-slows in support of a wage claim, but were locked out. The management had the financial support of the Industrial Bank of Japan, the Employers Federation ensured that Nissan's sub-contractors would receive alternative orders, and its rivals guaranteed that they would not steal its markets while the firm was out of production. After the management fired the union leadership, initially 86 per cent of workers voted to go on with the strike, but eventually they were cajoled into a 'second union' started by white collar staff who wanted to cooperate with the company (and many of whom were to receive rapid promotions from the grateful management – see also chapter 16).

A year later a major steel plant announced the dismissal of 901 of its 3700 workers:

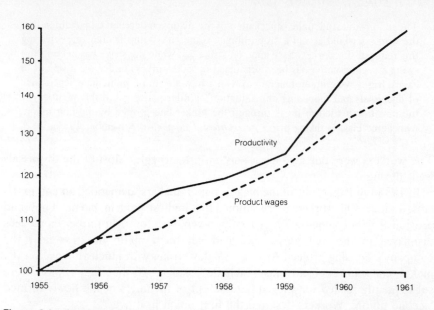

Figure 8.9 Japanese business productivity and product wages, 1955–61 (index numbers, 1955 = 100, log scale).
Source: see Appendix.

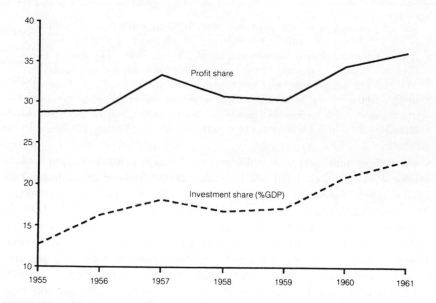

Figure 8.10 Japanese business investment and profits, 1955–61 (percentage).
Source: see Appendix.

> The unions demanded the cancellation of the dismissal decision on condition that the workers would accept a proportionate wage cut. With the company rejecting this request, the workers have gone on strike . . . while the strike has been in full swing a second union has been organized by 800 workers under the auspices of Zenro [right-wing union federation] with a new slogan of 'immediate acceptance of dismissals and reopening of production'. Under police guard the members of the new union tried to break through the picket line formed by the first union, with fierce clashes taking place. . . . (*Oriental Economist*, November 1954).

The workers were defeated after a six-month struggle. Most of the dismissals went through.

In 1958 Oji Paper, one of the biggest paper-makers, demanded an end to the closed shop. Oji workers were among the highest paid in Japan. They had previously won compensation of 1 million yen each for eight former employees dismissed in the 'red purge' and had set them up in business near the company's housing project. After a 145-day strike, with much violence on the picket line, a settlement was reached. Leaders of the 'first' union were subsequently sacked for alleged harassment of members of the newly formed 'second union'. Workers deserted the first union in droves.

These struggles culminated in a dispute at the Miike Coal Mines, owned by Mitsui Mining, the biggest mining firm in Japan. The company tried to sack 1300 workers, including 300 union leaders, for 'sabotage'. The *Oriental Economist* – whose sympathies mirror those of its occidental namesake – explained the situation:

> The mechanization of the mine has already been carried to an admirable point. . . . Nevertheless the per worker per month production of the mine is a lowly 14 tons in comparison with the usual 20 tons. Why? The answer is too obvious to miss. The majority of the workers there work only two or three hours a day. . . . The union's control of its workers is literally fabulous. . . . No one can break into the miners' housing area without 'security clearance' at the gate by the union guards . . . the orders from management are completely disregarded and the directions from union leaders are kept to the letter. . . . (January 1960).

The union took selective strike action. Management responded with a lockout. Picketing was violent. At its peak, 100,000 policemen confronted an equal number of union supporters, mobilized by the militant federation Sohyo. One striker was killed and 1000 were injured. But, with unions in all other coal companies, and in Mitsui's other mines, accepting management plans, the Miike workers were isolated. Finally they had to accept the dismissals. The struggle was seen as a trial of strength, and the employers' victory as decisive. No major strike has occurred in large-scale private industry since.

Aggressive tactics by management and state support are not the only explanation for the employers' victory. The trade union movement was immature. Its roots among workers were shallow and the tactics of its leadership weak. The ease with which management could organize 'second unions' cannot be explained simply by intimidation, important though that was.

The wages system furnished employers with an important weapon. Once the unions were in retreat, management increasingly used those elements of the pay packet based on age and ability to undermine them further. Workers feared that opposition to the employer would lose them the ability bonus, which was increasingly determined by cooperativeness rather than skill. If they were sacked they stood to lose old-age and long-service premiums. These features of the wages system were strengthened ('lifetime employment', 'seniority wages') as the anti-union offensive gathered strength through the fifties. By 1955, 39 per cent of pay was determined by 'ability' (up from 26 per cent in 1947). The wages system also helped to create a climate favourable for introducing 'second unions' through weakening worker solidarity. An American observer noted in 1958:

> In some cases companies introduced job classification and revised their wage structures based on job evaluations. . . . However in many cases it is doubtful whether these are anything other than the traditional wage system in a new disguise – for 'merit', 'loyalty' and 'cooperation', which are often tied to length of service have been used as major criteria for wage increases granted in this fashion . . . managements have not proceeded hastily towards full-blown wage rationalization because of their own concern with preserving worker identification with the enterprise. . . . Management has not been insistent on displacing the permanent/temporary worker system with job seniority procedures (i.e. first in/first out) because of its own sense of paternalistic responsibility and because of the flexibility of operations afforded by the employment of temporary workers. (Levine, 1958, pp. 117–19).

In 1958 workers aged 20 to 25 earned less than half as much as those between 40 and 50 years old, as compared with around 60 per cent in the interwar period and in 1948. Older workers, anxious to protect their ability bonuses, often supported the 'second union'. The successful introduction of these pro-management 'second unions' was as fundamental to Japan's subsequent economic success as the phenomenal accumulation rate.

9

A New, Managed Capitalism?

The astonishing economic achievements of the golden years led many to conclude that capitalism had undergone a qualitative transformation – that the bad old days of slumps and class antagonisms had been transcended for ever. The most important expression of this view was the development in many countries of a broad political consensus, embracing the major parties of both left and right, and subscribed to by trade unions and employers' associations.

Its central feature was acceptance of the so-called mixed economy – that is, a capitalist framework within which state enterprise was tolerated and the government held responsible for managing the economy. Broadly speaking, workers obtained certain rights and material benefits. The most important rights were those to free trade unions and certain forms of representation. The most important benefits were adequate job provision, regular pay rises and state welfare services. In return, they did not question capitalist ownership or control. Employers were prepared to tolerate these rights and provisions in return for a profitable economic environment.

Acceptance by the left of the basic parameters of the mixed economy was exemplified by Antony Crosland's book *The Future of Socialism*, published in 1956. He argued:

> Traditionally, or at least since Marx, socialist thought has been dominated by the economic problems posed by capitalism, poverty, mass unemployment, squalor, instability and even the possibility of the collapse of the whole system. . . . Capitalism has been reformed almost out of all recognition. Despite occasional minor recessions and balance of payments crises, full employment and at least a tolerable degree of stability are likely to be maintained. Automation can be expected steadily to solve any remaining problems of under production. Looking ahead our present rate of growth will give us a national output three times as high in fifty years (p. 517).

He also predicted that 'any government which tampered with the basic framework of the full-employment welfare state would meet with a sharp reversal at the polls' (p. 61). Three years earlier, Churchill had signalled a similar acceptance on the part of the Tories when he said, 'Party differences are now in practice mainly those of emphasis' (quoted Gilmour, 1977, p. 20).

The necessary analytic underpinning for the consensus was the belief that the state could manipulate the economy to achieve these goals, most importantly that it could always change spending to ensure full employment. In later chapters we show that this was unrealistic as a long-term perspective – that the processes which maintained the boom inevitably also undermined it. Here we look at some examples of attempts to reshape features of the economy within the parameters of the consensus.

The welfare state

The ultimate principle of the welfare state is well summarized by a French resistance declaration demanding 'a complete plan of social security, designed to secure the means of existence for all French men and women wherever they are incapable of providing such means for themselves by working' (quoted Saint-Jours, 1982, p. 122). The United Kingdom Beveridge report echoed the theme in more prosaic language: 'Social insurance should aim at guaranteeing the minimum income needed for subsistence' (quoted Rimlinger, 1971, p. 149).

The principle is no invention of the 1940s, and the practice no innovation of the 1950s. Large-scale social insurance – covering sickness, accidents and old-age pensions – was introduced in Germany in the 1880s following the Kaiser's announcement, inspired by Bismarck, that 'the cure of social ills must be sought not exclusively in the repression of Social Democratic excess, but simultaneously in the positive advancement of the welfare of the working masses' (quoted Rimlinger, 1971, p. 114).

The first state-run programme of unemployment insurance was introduced in the United Kingdom by the Liberal government in 1911, with flat rates of benefit and contributions by employers, employees and the state. A small non-contributory pension came in 1908 and health insurance in 1911. After the First World War the coverage of unemployment insurance was extended and a contributory pension scheme was introduced. In 1930 a scheme for social insurance was implemented in France, covering pensions, sickness and a system of family allowances.

Although not new, the welfare state did expand enormously in the postwar period. The share of gross domestic product absorbed by government civil spending (a rather broader category than welfare spending, though debt interest and subsidies have been omitted) rose from 15 per cent in 1952 to 24 per cent in 1973.

This huge expansion was by no means carried out solely by governments of the left. In the seven major countries the only periods of majority left governments between 1950 and 1973 were those of Wilson in the United

Kingdom (1964–70) and Brandt in Germany (1970–3), yet spending on welfare rose under Macmillan, Adenauer, de Gaulle, under both Nixon and Kennedy, as well as under a succession of Italian and to some extent even Japanese prime ministers of the right. The expansion of welfare spending was noticeably faster in the sixties than the fifties – especially in Europe. But, although this undoubtedly reflected increased working-class pressure as full employment was achieved, or approached (chapters 11 and 12), such pressure drew a response from right-wing governments as well as from those of the left elected as a direct result of it.

The welfare systems introduced in the immediate postwar years built on previous achievements. Existing prewar schemes were generally restored or consolidated. Even the United Kingdom Beveridge scheme had only a minor effect on unemployment insurance. In the United States unemployment insurance, accident compensation and public assistance underwent no major changes.

The continuity with prewar schemes created important international diversities. Thus the British scheme was based on flat-rate contributions and benefits, while the European and American ones varied with earnings. But gaps in previous schemes were often plugged by incorporating innovations from abroad. Family allowances, introduced in Britain in the Beveridge scheme, had been in operation in France since 1932. (They were not reintroduced into Germany until 1954 because of their associations with Nazi population policy.)

Coverage was often broadened. Schemes which had been confined to industrial workers before the war were typically extended to include the self-employed, farm workers and domestic servants. In many cases, reduced contributions qualifications meant that more people became eligible for benefit. (In the United States in the late 1940s, only one-fifth of the over-65s were insured or receiving pensions.)

Unemployment insurance in Europe generally became both more generous and easier to obtain. Comparing the situation in 1975 with the year of introduction (generally prewar), on average the ratio of benefits to earnings had risen slightly, the duration of benefits had doubled to nearly a year, the delay before eligibility to benefit had halved (to two days), and the period of disqualification (on account of dismissal for misconduct, for example) had halved to about three weeks.

The one really radical innovation was the replacement in Britain of sickness insurance by the National Health Service (NHS), free as of right without means test or contribution (although prescription charges were introduced in 1950). But this was unique in terms of universal supply based on need. Elsewhere, earnings-related insurance, plus 'social aid' at a distinctly lower level for those not covered, continued prewar traditions.

An important development in the fifties was the linking of benefits to rising living standards. This was most explicitly promulgated in the German pension reform of 1957, which Adenauer forced through to great electoral benefit, in the teeth of strong opposition from the central bank and the employers. But benefits were regularly revised upwards to similar effect elsewhere.

The same German reform reinforced the 'insurance' principle behind pensions, by tying them more closely to past contributions. This eliminated the minimum pension level which had survived since Bismarck, and substantially widened differentials. The British Labour Party also proposed replacing flat-rate contributions and benefits by a scheme aimed at raising pensions to a level equivalent to half of earnings. A scheme of this sort was finally implemented in the seventies. There was also a trend towards adding an earnings-related supplement to previously flat-rate unemployment benefits (for example, the United Kingdom) or moving to entirely earnings-related payments (Germany).

Pensions give some indication of the level of benefits by the early seventies. For a married couple they were reckoned to be between 50 and 60 per cent of post-tax earnings in France, Germany and the United States, about one-third in Britain and Italy, and probably barely one-fifth in Japan. For unemployment pay and sickness benefit the ratio averaged one-half higher.

Did the postwar development of the welfare state remould capitalism to give it a more human face, or were the changes largely cosmetic? The answer is complex.

The new measures did bring about a large flow of resources to the disadvantaged. By the early 1970s a typical continental European country was devoting a little over 20 per cent of GDP to social expenditure, the United States and United Kingdom 17–18 per cent, and Japan 10 per cent. The extension of coverage, plugging of gaps, index-linking and softening of contribution eligibility criteria, brought enormous gains to many people.

Wider coverage accounts for well over half of the increase in the proportion of output devoted to welfare provision during the 1960s. Cash benefits also rose faster than inflation, growing in line with average incomes (table 9.1).

But there were also important limitations. The welfare state never came close to eliminating poverty. On the basis of standardized poverty figures (a percentage of national earnings based on the average of national official poverty standards), in the early 1970s 3 per cent of the German population lived in poverty, 7½ per cent of the British, 13 per cent of the US, and 16 per cent of the French.

A crucial question about the growth of the welfare state is whether it undermined employers' control over labour by reducing the compulsion to work. Two cases should be distinguished. The one dear to the heart of the popular press is the possibility of individuals opting out of the labour market altogether to 'sponge' off the state. By depriving employers of potential labour, this could force up wages. The rise in real levels of social assistance which occurred in the boom could have made such opting out more feasible, even if the social assistance rates did not rise relative to earnings (which they generally did not – child benefit in particular fell substantially relative to average incomes). Relaxation in eligibility criteria would also reduce the pressure on

Table 9.1 Growth of ACC welfare spending in the 1960s

	As percentage of GDP	Resulting from		
		Demographic changes[a]	Coverage[b]	Real costs and benefits per recipient
Education	1.1	0.0	0.6	0.5
Income maintenance	2.0	0.8	1.2	0.0[c]
Health	1.9	0.1	1.1	0.8
Total	5.0	0.9	2.9	1.3

[a] The effect on spending of the changing age-structure of the population (old people, children).
[b] The effect on spending of welfare schemes covering an increasing proportion of the population.
[c] No change relative to average income levels.
Source: OECD, 1976, *Public Expenditure Trends*, table 7.

able-bodied recipients to look for work. However, the rise in pensions relative to incomes which occurred in most countries also increased the cost of not working – for the farsighted, at least – since pensions were generally linked to contributions from pay. In fact, 'social aid' (transfers to people not eligible for pensions, unemployment benefit and so forth) constituted only 5 per cent of all money spent on transfers in the early 1970s. In the two countries where it was more important, the United States and United Kingdom, the proportion of transfers going to social aid hardly increased during the 1960s. The low level of social assistance and the stigma attached to receiving it make it implausible that significant 'scrounging' took place.

However, the development of welfare benefits may well have reduced dependence on any particular employer. Unemployment benefits on average rose in line with pre-tax incomes during the sixties. But since the tax burden on earnings rose, there was probably some small rise in the net amount received while out of work, relative to pay received while working. The benefits sometimes received by strikers' families also rose in absolute terms. Health expenses were covered for those not in work. So the financial hardships imposed by temporary unemployment or strikes fell. This helped give workers the confidence to stand up to their employers – to quit or strike or be sacked seemed less daunting.

These developments should not be seen in isolation. They reinforced others. The most important factor reducing fear of the sack was the reduction in unemployment, which increased the chances of getting another job quickly. Higher living standards enabled many workers to save a little, providing additional insurance against the financial costs of the sack, of quitting or of striking. The important rise in some countries in the proportion of families with two adults working acted in the same direction.

The tax burden imposed on workers to pay for welfare services opened up a gap between the cost of labour to the employer (the wage gross of employers' and employees' social security contributions and of income tax) and what the worker received (the wage net of all these deductions). As the tax burden edged up, so did the gap widen between the sum that a pay settlement gave workers and what it cost employers. Unions bargaining with individual employers, or at industry level, sought to maximize the return to their members for working, welfare benefits being unaffected by the negotiations. So the rising tax 'wedge' heightened conflict over wages.

So, while growth of the welfare state hardly loosened the compulsion on workers to work, it did undermine dependence on any particular employer and provided an additional source of conflict, in the course of which such greater independence could be exercised.

German codetermination

The right of workers to organized representation was another important feature of the consensus. This usually took the form of institutionalized collective bargaining between trade unions and employers. But in Germany it also involved the apparently more advanced form of 'codetermination', which aroused considerable interest.

This interest stems in part from Germany's outstanding economic record in the boom. Did codetermination contribute to its 'economic miracle'? But there is also another reason for the interest. From the mid-1970s, left parties came increasingly to adopt a more radical approach to the consensus (chapter 18). One feature of this shift was an emphasis on industrial democracy, which drew heavily on principles of codetermination.

Codetermination – the right of workers to help direct the firms they work in – was a major preoccupation of German trade unions in the years after the war (chapter 6). At first they regarded it as a prerequisite for the socialization of large-scale heavy industry. Then, as the German economy was firmly steered towards a reconstructed capitalism, codetermination was presented as a substitute for socialization – an alternative way of assuring that big businesss would never again play the political role it had in the thirties. Codetermination received enormous support. In 1950 and 1951 well over 90 per cent of metal workers and miners voted in favour of strike action to secure a special codetermination law for their industries.

The system involved workers electing half of the members of supervisory boards, with the shareholders electing the rest and appointing a 'neutral' chair. The workers could also veto (in effect, nominate) the labour director, responsible broadly for personnel questions. Outside the steel and coal industries, workers could elect one-third of the supervisory board. In all industries works councils, elected by the employees, had the right to 'codetermine' some issues (working hours, holidays, implementation of pay scales), to veto others (hirings, job classification, transfers), to be consulted over yet others (mass redundancies, individual dismissals) and to receive economic information (profits, production, investment).

But workers' influence has been more constrained than these provisions might suggest. The labour director in steel and coal firms is a member of the management board which controls the day-to-day operations of the firm (the other members being the production and business managers). His or her mandate generally covers most of the issues over which the works council has codetermination rights but excludes questions of incentives and job evaluation. These labour directors may well have initiated enlightened personnel policies, but that is a long way from real worker representation in the overall direction of the firm:

> The labour director is charged in law with carrying out his function in the best interests of the firm as a whole. Since he is chosen by workers he is theoretically subject to extensive loyalty conflict. Most labour directors have resolved this conflict by operating as responsible managers rather than as worker agents *per se*. They have been most successful when they have been able to win the trust and acceptance of the other management board members. When they have not been able to do so they have been isolated and their influence has been drastically reduced' (Adams and Rummel, 1977, p. 12).

The worker members of the supervisory board are elected partly by the works council and partly by the trade unions. Outside steel and coal, minority representation means that the committees are usually balanced to favour the employer, and information is restricted. The general consensus is that worker influence on these boards has been limited. Furthermore, minimal communication between the board members and the workers seems to take place, with board members legally bound to secrecy over 'sensitive' company matters. So it would be hard, if not impossible, for worker representatives to mobilize the work force against the employers. Nor can the works councils do so. Failure to agree over 'social matters' in which they have codetermination rights, such as holiday schedules or welfare provision, results in arbitration. Disagreements over the important personnel issues of hiring, firing, classification or redeployment are resolved in the Labour Court. Works councils have to be consulted over mass lay-offs but have no right to call strikes.

Certain weaknesses are clear. Workers' representatives are often removed from the shop floor, which cannot mandate them. Their access to information is limited and their right to use it even more so, as are their areas of influence and the sanctions they can use.

Nor does codetermination appear to have done much to improve work conditions. 'Exhausting physical effort, excessive heat, hazardous safety and health conditions have been far less points of attention (and redress) than in the American steel industry, and at least straight-time workers endure a high measure of personal . . . coercion (speed-up in one word) by supervision' (Herding, 1972, pp. 329–30). This despite the fact that, as the same author notes, in codetermination plants 'work crews in the key operations enjoy a high degree of autonomy in setting their own pace, breaks, etc.' (p. 330). One survey reported that workers regard works councils as a part of management. But workers participate heavily in elections. Turnouts of 80 per cent are typical. Pressure for increased influence resulted in a 1972 Act which extended codetermination rights in a number of personnel matters, such as employment contracts and training. A 1976 Act extended a weakened form of parity codetermination to all firms with more than 2000 employees. It is weaker than in steel and coal because one of the worker nominees must be a senior executive and the chair, a shareholder nominee, has two votes.

The employers clearly had strong reservations. They went to court and tried, unsuccessfully, to have the 1976 Act declared unconstitutional. However limited, codetermination does serve to remind employers both of the days when their prerogatives were generally and seriously challenged and of the fact that such a situation could recur.

French economic planning

> The characteristic attitude in large-scale economic management, both inside government and in the private sector, which has made itself increasingly felt during the post-war period, is the pursuit of intellectual coherence. Its most obvious manifestation is in long-range national planning. . . . Economic planning is the most characteristic expression of the new capitalism (Shonfield, 1965, pp. 67, 121).

This view from the author of *Modern Capitalism* – at the time probably the most influential interpretation of postwar trends in the advanced countries – was fully in line with the consensus. If governments were to manage the new capitalism then economic planning was clearly of the essence.

Shonfield singled out France as the innovator in the field. So what was French planning? Most governments manipulated tax rates and government expenditure to influence the overall level of spending in the economy. But this Keynesian demand management could not dispel much of the economic uncertainty faced by business. Keynes himself had argued for 'the collection and dissemination on a great scale of data relating to the business situation including full publicity, by law if necessary, of all business facts which it is useful to know. These measures would involve society in exercising directive intelligence through some appropriate organ of action over many of the intricacies of private business, yet it would leave private initiative and enterprise unhindered' (quoted Estrin and Holmes, 1983, p. 8). Precisely this kind of 'generalized market research' lay at the heart of French planning. Its consistency and coherence were supposed to encourage a common view about the future to which firms would respond with bold investment plans – nudged, if necessary, by government tax and credit policies.

The process evolved from the Monnet Plan for the reconstruction of six basic sectors, formulated at the end of 1945 to persuade the US government that the French were sufficiently serious about modernization to justify a loan (chapter 4). Modernization Commissions, the basic planning units, brought together civil servants and managers (the trade unionists involved have never played a major role) to thrash out targets for output and investment.

This process continued to form the basis for planning. But hit-and-miss targets were increasingly replaced by sophisticated forecasts for individual industries' markets based on aims for the overall growth of the economy and its division into private consumption, government spending and so forth.

The Monnet Plan itself undoubtedly facilitated the reconstruction of the basic sectors. The Americans were persuaded to allow the 'counterpart funds' to Marshall Aid to be used for these purposes, and their backing helped Monnet to protect the investment targets from the deflationary policies of the time. The fact that three of the six sectors were nationalized – coal, electricity and railways – helped. Their own programmes were incorporated in the plan, which must have reduced scepticism and helped in obtaining priority finance. The impact on the private sector – the real test – is harder to assess. Proposals for 'state contracts with trade associations, groups of concerns or, in exceptional cases, individual enterprises' (Kuisel, 1981, p. 234) or even the nationalization of recalcitrant firms were never implemented. Nor could they have been after business regained its initiative in 1947. Controls over foreign exchange, credits and scarce materials could hardly force anybody to expand. Yet, one member of Monnet's team remembered that plan as having 'ably manoeuvred a reluctant steel industry to modernize' (Kuisel, 1981, p. 245).

Jacques Delors, later to be minister of finance in Mitterrand's socialist government, records that when Monnet first gathered the steel masters together and demanded the reconstitution of prewar production capacity within four years, 'Two or more cases of heart seizure reportedly ensued' (Delors, 1978, p. 15). Nevertheless, the target was reached only a year late. When in 1951 he demanded another 40 per cent expansion, 'that did not work at all, since these steel masters had been so nourished on Malthusianism that their dominant fear was over-production. In this case, the planning response was not simply financial incentives, but direct intervention to change the steel cartel itself. . . . If you reproduce this anecdote some ten or twenty times in different industries, you begin to explain the role of the Plan during this first period' (Delors, 1978).

Judging the effect of subsequent plans on the private sector becomes even harder as the number of commissions, and the equations in the planning models, grow.

The evidence shows that firms took notice of the plan, at least by the 1960s. In 1967, 79 per cent of firms knew the plan's forecasts for the economy as a whole and 50 per cent (85 per cent of those with more than 5000 employees) knew of the production and investment forecasts for their industry group; 24 per cent (51 per cent of the biggest) said that the plan forecasts affected their investment decisions.

There seems to be a consensus that the plan did encourage accumulation, at least up to the late sixties. 'According to the witnesses we have consulted, it seems likely that the growth expectations set forth in the Second National Plan (1954–57) were in contradiction to the conventional wisdom at the beginning of the 1950s, which expected that only low rates of growth were possible. . . . The picture of a growing economy provided by the Plan, in which production was sure of finding sales, probably played a significant part in the resumption of growth after 1952' (Carré et al., 1976, p. 471).

A sophisticated statistical evaluation suggested that in the late fifties and early sixties the plan provided better pictures of the evolution of the economy than would have been derived simply by extrapolating past trends. But it seems likely that the importance of the plan in creating a 'growth climate' diminished as the experience of rapid growth meant that business came to expect it anyway. This in itself, however, would be success of a sort.

Even if the Plan's effect on the *level* of accumulation was bound to diminish, it could still have significantly influenced its *pattern*. At least until the early 1970s, however, the government made no systematic attempt to shape the pattern of industry. The Fifth National Plan's objective of greater concentration to achieve two or three dominant firms – 'national champions' – in each sector, for example, was *entirely* non-selective. The government did not choose the firms; it simply changed legal and tax rules to help mergers.

Mechanisms for selective intervention were available. The planners could determine the availability of finance: 'Every single externally financed project was therefore meant to be scrutinized for conformity with the targets and if the projects passed this test the Commission would see to it that sufficient tax and credit incentives would be made available' (Estrin and Holmes, 1983, p. 179). But, since there was no overall industrial strategy, it is hardly surprising that the finance tended to be granted almost automatically.

What of the pattern of investment within each industry? According to one observer: 'There is in general no noticeable discrepancy between the target of the branch and the sum of the targets of the individual companies' (quoted Cohen, 1969, p. 68). This means that 'The French system of detailed target planning involves . . . the toleration of agreements between firms to fix the share each will take of the planned expansion' (Cohen, 1969, pp. 71–2).

During the 1950s and 1960s, Plan forecasts for business investment were always well below the outcome. Between 1965 and 1970, for example, business investment grew by 8.5 per cent a year, while only 5.8 per cent a year had been expected. The discrepancy was systematically much larger than that for production growth. This suggests that firms may have formally agreed to share out capacity growth, but then invested to increase their share. Such investment over and above plan targets must have speeded up modernization.

All in all, planning may have temporarily acted as a catalyst in launching French capital on its dynamic growth path. It certainly did not create the potential for that path, which was provided by the backward state of French industry, the strong position of the employers and favourable external circumstances (chapters 2, 4 and 6). It probably played only a small role in maintaining accumulation once that got going. And planning certainly proved incapable of maintaining accumulation once conditions became unfavourable. In the seventies, growth faltered in France as elsewhere. The credibility of the plan was undermined by its increasing unrealism, the clear political motivation behind its projections and the resort by governments to orthodox deflationary policies. By 1979 only 9 per cent of employers regarded the Plan as very important. Even recession-hit industries wanted less planning rather than more. In France, as elsewhere, capital preferred to ditch the consensus in favour of more traditional capitalist virtues.

But the trade unions strongly criticized the erosion of planning and 'regretted the lack of any attempt to articulate real priorities other than the need to submit to world market forces' (Estrin and Holmes, 1983, p. 116). This survey reported a 'nostalgia' among socialists for the Fourth National Plan of the early sixties. When elected in 1981, the Mitterrand government harked back to the legacy of planning in the first postwar decades (chapter 18).

Japanese industrial policy

The lack of an industrial policy is generally regarded as a weakness of French planning. Japan is often cited as the prime example of a successful industrial policy playing a key role in the dynamism of accumulation. Was Japan's industrial structure successfully orchestrated by the bureaucrats of its Ministry of International Trade and Industry (MITI)?

General measures to stimulate accumulation in Japan differed little in kind or degree from those employed elsewhere. The government provided investment finance directly through such institutions as the Japan Development Bank. But even at their early fifties peak, these funds constituted only 7 per cent of industrial finance (12 per cent of that raised outside the firm). By the second half of the fifties the proportion had declined to 4 per cent. The government also provided a multitude of tax concessions which at their 1955 peak probably reduced average corporation-tax liability by one-fifth, falling to around 12 per cent in the early sixties. Many were fairly standard provisions for bad debts, and so forth. The more innovative included accelerated depreciation on 'special machinery', 'special repairs' (to heavy plant), research and development, exemption from tax on income from sales of 'important new products', exemption from customs duty on 'important equipment' and exemption of certain exports from income tax. But they reduced tax payments by only 6 per cent during the years 1959 to 1963.

Such aggregate figures could be misleading, however. Both government lending and tax concessions were highly selective, being steered towards particular industries. Government favour also helped firms secure loans from private banks. Tariffs and prohibition of foreign firms from setting up in Japan were further important weapons.

The Japanese government decided on a number of occasions to foster particular industries, using a large armoury of policies. A few case studies illustrate the process.

It was clear after the war that Japan could no longer rely on textile exports for most of its foreign exchange earnings (chapter 2). So it adopted a policy of fostering basic 'heavy industries' (steel, chemicals, shipbuilding). After 1947 a policy of 'planned shipbuilding' operated. Every year the government announced the total tonnage to be built of each type of ship and selected which shipbuilders and (domestic) owners should be involved. A high percentage of the funds required (80 per cent or more in the early fifties) was supplied cheaply by the Japan Development Bank. The interest rate subsidy sometimes involved deferral of repayment for 15 years. Cheap loans to finance exports were 'perhaps the most significant assistance to shipbuilding' (Magaziner and Hout, 1980, p. 69). The companies also profited from a bizarre system whereby shipbuilders who exported were given import quotas for raw sugar, which could be sold at a hefty profit. The result was Japan's first 'miracle' industry. By the early seventies Japanese yards were launching over half the world's ships.

Steel, also designated as a key recovery sector immediately after the war, was a key input into major export industries such as ships (and in turn the development of huge ore-carrying ships allowed the Japanese steel industry to overcome a major disadvantage in transport costs for materials). In the 1950s the industry expanded under two five-year 'rationalization plans' developed by the industry together with MITI. Steel benefited from major government loans, accounting for half its borrowing during the first five-year plan. Ten per cent of its finances still came from government sources in the early sixties. It also received a host of tax concessions.

The government has been continuously involved in the process of capacity expansion:

Representatives of the privately owned steel producing firms gather under the umbrella of the Japan Iron and Steel Federation to present and discuss tentative investment plans for the coming year. (Often these representatives, usually managing directors, are MITI alumni.) The producers' plans are evaluated in relation to the demand outlook for the industry and the existing pattern of market shares. After these meetings and informal discussions among these managers and the officials of the Iron and Steel Section of MITI's Heavy Industries Bureau, the presidents of the steel companies try to reach a consensus on the rate and timing of the major investments of individual producers. MITI participates *ex officio* in these meetings. . . .

After consensus has been reached, MITI issues a report recommending a course of action to the industry. . . .

It has been said that no application from a major firm for a capacity increment has ever been flatly rejected, although some have been delayed. This, of course, is the mechanism of the consensus process: the expanding firm is persuaded either to delay its application or to accept a delayed approval. When this persuasion fails, consensus is frustrated. (Magaziner and Hout, 1980, p. 48).

Strikingly, MITI frequently tried to *slow down* the rate of accumulation to avoid overcapacity, a problem exacerbated by the increasing size of new plants which reduced the number to be built each year. In 1965, Sumitomo, which has tried to remain independent of MITI's 'administrative guidance', broke with an industry decision to delay all new investment in rolling facilities. MITI disciplined it by limiting its allocation of imported coking coal. In 1967 'eight steel makers sought approval to begin building new furnaces, but according to MITI's projections only two were needed. Five received approval, one with a year's delay' (Kaplan, 1975, p. 148). This prompted MITI to seek mergers. But the resultant creation of Japan Steel 'only served to consolidate two conservative producers. The impact on the other producers, at least Sumitomo and Kawasaki, who did not oppose the merger, may have been counter-productive in stimulating continued aggressive expansion' (Kaplan, 1975, p. 151).

The value of government support to the industry cannot be measured in terms of cash expenditures. By the judicious application of support in the areas where it could be most effective, government has done a great deal for the industry. Selective measures – help through the insurance of debt for building greenfield plants, assistance in procuring raw materials and forming anti-recession cartels – have provided support without extinguishing competition or stifling initiative in individual companies. Even capacity expansion co-operation has been carried out in such a way as to allow substantial continued internal competition and even greater market share changes than occurred in the United States. The actual flow of funds from government to the industry represented by loans, grants and tax allowances has been minimal, at least since the late 1950s. Per ton of steel, such assistance has been substantially less than that supplied by many European governments (often to subsidize the losses of uncompetitive plants)' (Magaziner and Hout, 1980, p. 54).

Steel was certainly another Japanese success story. By 1977 Japan had 25 blast-furnaces in operation with a capacity of over 2 million tons. The EEC had seven and the United States none.

In the early 1950s the Japanese motor industry consisted of a handful of clapped-out truck producers, rescued from bankruptcy by the Korean war. The Japanese central bank originally favoured car imports. But MITI argued that a domestic industry should be nurtured because of its critical importance, and won. The government's key role in the early days was to protect the industry. Foreign investment was more or less prohibited (it had to contribute to the development of the domestic industry). Quotas at first restricted imports to $½ million a year. In the mid-1960s quotas were replaced by prohibitively high tariffs. Import of foreign technology was encouraged, with the stipulation that 90 per cent of licensed parts be produced domestically within five years. Nissan was the only major producer to enter into a licensing agreement (with Austin). Toyota developed its own system of organizing work (see chapter 15). The industry benefited from access to Japan Development Bank loans, and various tax concessions. But MITI 'played little or no role in the investment policies or technological development activities of the producers' (Kaplan, 1975, p. 116).

MITI helped to promote streamlining in the parts industries over the years 1956 to 1966, aimed at modernization and rationalization of the number of suppliers. But it failed comprehensively to push through various plans for mergers between the assemblers. Instead of merging with each other, or one of the bigger concerns, in the early seventies three of the smaller firms signed affiliation agreements with the American Big Three as MITI opposition was overcome by political pressure for foreign capital liberalization.

Today Japan is the biggest car exporter in the world.

Finally, there is the computer industry, which 'MITI has unequivocally dominated' (Kaplan, 1975, p. 78). IBM was granted the right to manufacture in Japan in 1960 in return for licensing basic patents to Japanese manufacturers, and most major Japanese companies entered technical assistance agreements with big American manufacturers. By the mid-1960s MITI recognized the importance of the industry by increasing loans and subsidies and embarking on a series of attempts to rationalize the industry and/or organize cooperative ventures. The culmination was the Very Large-Scale Integration project involving MITI's electronics research institute, the state and telecommunications laboratory and five major computer manufacturers. MITI's attempts at consolidation failed to overcome the firms' competitive attitude (indicating limitations to MITI's 'dominance'). As well as assisting technology development, MITI organized a leasing corporation to lease only Japanese computers on competitive terms to those available abroad. The industry was protected until the early 1970s by the rule that foreign machines (including IBM machines produced in Japan) could only be purchased if a suitable Japanese model was not available. While Japanese computers were hardly a factor in the boom years, they were to become a major force in the 1980s.

It is difficult to draw a neat conclusion. MITI clearly pushed strongly to develop certain key industries. It provided finance, ensured protection and, on occasion, encouraged technological development. In a few cases, such as steel, it effectively coordinatated expansion plans.

On the other hand MITI seems to have been rather unsuccessful in securing rationalization through mergers. MITI sometimes held back accumulation in the steel industry. In the other cases it played a facilitating rather than a decisive role. Moreover, the case studies reported, where MITI was highly influential, were not entirely typical: 'Some of the rapidly expanding "new" industries, the products of which have been increasingly exported all over the world – such as motor cycles, bearings (especially miniature bearings), transistor radios, TV sets, tape recorders, pianos and zippers – received relatively little government assistance even in their infancy periods. By and large these industries were able to stand up by themselves, with little government protection or planning' (Komiya, 1975, pp. 219–20).

Clearly, industrial policy cannot fully explain the extraordinary dynamism of Japanese accumulation. Other factors were at work (Chapter 8).

Conclusions

The boom saw the generalization and expansion of state welfare provisions, unprecedented attempts by governments to plan for economic growth and shape industrial structures, and some experiments in worker involvement in the direction of enterprises. The most important point to recognize, however, is that these developments did not substantially undermine the essential relationships underpinning capitalist economies. Despite the increased strength of labour, as reflected in welfare provisions and moves towards 'industrial democracy', workers were still obliged to sell their labour power to employers whose freedom of action they might be able to limit, but certainly not control. Despite the growing importance of state intervention through macroeconomic planning and industrial policies, the essential decisions about investment were still taken by the controllers of private capital, on the basis of private profitability.

Perhaps the most important aspect of attempts to manage the 'mixed economy' during the golden years was that people believed they could work. This helped maintain confidence, which in turn helped maintain accumulation. Accumulation generated jobs, regular increases in living standards, resources for welfare and profits. These in turn reproduced the consensus.

When the boom conditions began to disintegrate, the economic logic of capitalist production reasserted itself in a very brutal fashion (chapter 14). But the development of state intervention in the course of the boom had an important effect on reactions to growing economic difficulties. Many on the right blamed the breakdown of the boom precisely on government interference (chapter 17). The left, by contrast, saw the greater worker and state involvement in the economy as a pointer to how the crisis could be resolved in the interests of working people (chapter 18). In this way the patterns set in the boom left their imprint firmly on the years of mass unemployment which followed.

10

The Eclipse of US Domination

Our discussion of the dynamics of the boom in chapter 8 focused on the advanced capitalist countries as a group. Of course the boom was very uneven between countries; the wave of accumulation in Japan was more powerful than elsewhere. By far the most important aspect of this uneven development was the undermining of the economic dominance of the United States. This chapter discusses some aspects and implications of this process.

At the beginning of the boom the economic might of the United States was overwhelming (table 10.1 and figure 10.1). In 1952 nearly 60 per cent of the production of the ACCs was located there, produced by around 33 per cent of the total number of workers operating over half of the business capital stock. Careful studies of the total level of output per head of the population in 1950 suggested that, taking the United States as 100, the United Kingdom scored

Table 10.1 Weight of the US economy, 1950–70 (percentages)

	1950	1970
US share of ACC output	58[a]	47
US share of ACC capital stock	60[a]	52
US output per head of population in relation to		
United Kingdom	180	170
France	220	130
Germany	270	130
Italy	400	220
US manufacturing productivity in relation to		
United Kingdom	230	200
Germany	310	170
Japan	860	240
US share of manufacturing output (big 10)	62[b]	44[c]
US share of manufacturing exports (world)	33	16

[a] 1952. [b] 1953. [c] 1971.

Sources: see Appendix; and Kravis, 1976, table 1; Prais, 1981, table A1; Branson, 1980, tables 3.8, 3.13

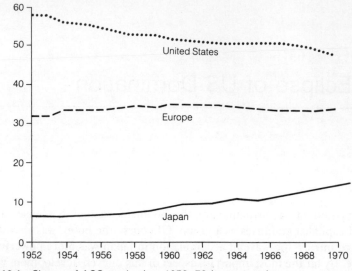

Figure 10.1   Shares of ACC production, 1952–70 (percentage).
Source: see Appendix.

55, France 46, Germany 37 and Italy 25. In coal mining US productivity was somewhere between four and five times greater than that in either the United Kingdom or Germany and about seven times as great as in France. In manufacturing the USA was over twice as productive per worker as Britain and over three times as productive as Germany; the differential was much greater in relation to Japan. In 1950 the USA produced seven times as many manufactures as Germany and over 20 times as many as Japan; in 1953 it exported five times as many manufactures as Germany and 17 times as many as Japan. In 1957 only seven non-US firms were in the biggest 50 in the world.

The dominance of US business was more overwhelming in the early fifties than the statistics for exports suggest. US exports were still constrained in Europe and Japan by a welter of trade and monetary restrictions, directed specifically at US products. Although the dismantling of these restrictions was a United States priority, enshrined in the IMF and GATT agreements, the debacles of the 1940s over premature opening up of trade and payments (chapter 4) dictated a more measured pace for liberalization linked to the export capacity of Europe and Japan. With free trade and payments in the early fifties, the United States would have tended to secure a far greater share of world trade. Balance could only have been achieved by further devaluation of European currencies against the dollar.

The growth of trade

The years of the boom saw a phenomenal explosion of trade. Between 1951–3 and 1969–71 the volume of world trade in manufactures grew by 349 per cent whereas the volume of output grew by 194 per cent. The ACCs expanded their exports of manufacturing by 480 per cent between 1950 and 1971. By far the fastest growing part of that enormous growth was in the form of trade between the various advanced countries (table 10.2); their exports to the underdeveloped countries and the Eastern bloc grew far more slowly.

Table 10.2 Exports of manufactures, 1950–71 ($ billion, 1955 prices)

	1950	1971
Within Europe	4.6	46.7
Within North America	2.5	11.7
Europe to and from North America	2.6	15.6
Japan to and from Europe and North America	0.3	13.7
Total among ACCs	10.0	87.8
To rest of world	14.3	53.2
Overall total	24.3	141.0

Source: Batchelor et al., 1980, table 2.4.

The effect of this explosion of trade between the advanced countries was to increase sharply the proportion of imported manufactured goods consumed inside these countries. Within Europe in particular, 'import penetration' rose far above the levels of the early fifties, which in turn were similar to the very low levels of the interwar period (table 10.3). The levels reached by 1971 exceeded even the considerable levels achieved before the First World War. In the United States, however, the rise in import penetration, all of which occurred in the 1960s, represented the first serious incursion this century by imported manufactured goods. Only Japan, of the major exporters, remained virtually impervious to import penetration – all the phenomenal growth of manufactured

Table 10.3 Import penetration by manufactures, 1913–71 (percentages)[a]

	1913	1937	1950	1963	1971
Europe[b]	13	6	6	11	17
USA	3	2	2	3	8
Japan	34	11	3	4	5

[a] Imports as a percentage of production of manufactures plus imports.
[b] Unweighted average of UK, France, Germany, Italy.

Sources: Maizels, 1980, table 6.4; Batchelor et al., 1980, table 3.3

exports being devoted to paying for the soaring import bill for materials (chapter 12).

For the industrial countries as a whole, around half the increase in imported manufactures between the years 1950 and 1963 represented greater import penetration of the domestic market and half reflected a larger market; between 1963 and 1971, when trade between the advanced countries grew by 156 per cent, almost two-thirds of the increase represented imports taking a greater share of the domestic market.

A major development encouraging trade between the advanced countries was tariff cuts. The reduction of tariff barriers after the formation of the EEC in 1958 increased trade by the order of 25–35 per cent. Within EFTA (the free trade zone formed by seven of the non-EEC European countries, including at that time the United Kingdom) lower barriers resulted in extra imports of around 10–15 per cent for the countries concerned. The Kennedy round of cuts in the later sixties saw the average level of tariffs on manufactures falling by one-third, and by half on machinery and vehicles. Very high rates of tariff covering about 7 per cent of goods in the United States and United Kingdom almost disappeared, and the proportion of trade (excluding agriculture and fuels) which attracted tariffs of 15 per cent or less rose from 54 per cent to 85 per cent in the USA, from 37 per cent to 85 per cent in the United Kingdom and from 71 per cent to 97 per cent for the EEC. Additional imports generated may have been around 15 per cent for the United Kingdom, rather less for the EEC but a good deal more for the United States.

Some of the rise in import penetration would undoubtedly have occurred anyway, especially in the fifties when non-tariff restrictions were dismantled and firms took advantage of falling transport costs and rapid growth of demand to break into new markets. But still tariff cuts in the sixties were certainly an important influence on the trade during the period. Only the Japanese market remained more or less impenetrable.

International oligopoly

This great expansion of trade and competition between the advanced capitalist countries outweighed the trend within each country or bloc towards more monopolization. The data are patchy, but indicate a steady, if unspectacular, rise in concentration. Data for the USA, EEC and Japan all point to an increase in the share of manufacturing output accounted for by the largest firms (figure 10.2).

Whatever impact this increased monopolization had in reducing the degree of competition in domestic markets was swamped in most instances by the greater challenge from imports. Indeed, much of the merger movement within countries was a reaction to the strengthening of overseas competition.

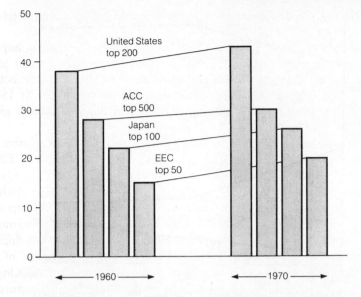

Figure 10.2   Share of manufacturing output produced by top firms, 1960, 1970 (percentage). *Sources*: Caves, 1980, pp. 511–12; Dunning and Pearce, 1981, tables 3.6, 4.28; Japanese Government, *Census of Manufactures*; Locksley and Ward, 1979, p. 96.

US business slips back

The United States orchestrated the great increase in trade in order to take advantage of its overwhelming postwar strength. Yet it was US business, together with its partner in decline, the United Kingdom, which of all the major ACCs gained least from the boom in trade (figure 10.3 and table 10.4).

Table 10.4 Growth of export volumes, 1953–71 (average annual percentage growth rates)

	1953–59	1959–71
USA	0.2	6.3
Germany	16.9	9.2
Japan	19.0	15.9

Source: Branson, 1980, table 3.14.

The fundamental problem faced by US business was that rivals in Europe and Japan were accumulating capital at a far faster rate (figure 10.4) and were doing so on the basis of far lower wage costs (table 10.5). Between 1955 and 1970 the capital stock in US manufacturing rose by 74 per cent; in the major European countries the rise was 115 per cent, and in Japan it was some 500 per cent. Taking into account the rise in employment, the rise in capital stock per

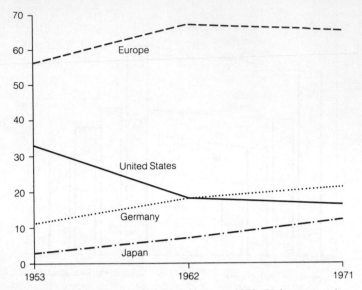

Figure 10.3 Shares of ACC exports of manufactures, 1953–71 (percentage).
Source: Branson, 1980, table 13.3.

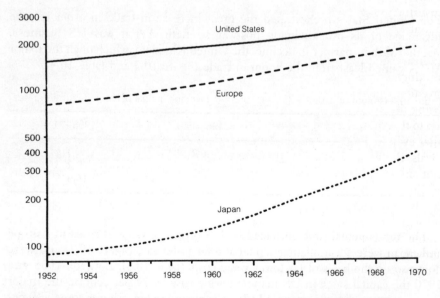

Figure 10.4 Business capital stock, 1952–70 ($ billion, 1980 prices, log scale).
Source: see Appendix.

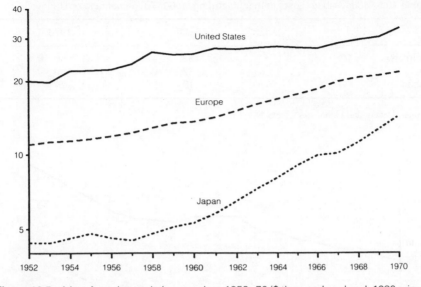

Figure 10.5   Manufacturing capital per worker, 1952–70 ($ thousand per head, 1980 prices, log scale).
Source: see Appendix.

head (an index of increased mechanization) was 51 per cent in the United States, 90 per cent in Europe, and 202 per cent in Japan (figure 10.5). New investment per employed worker in US manufacturing in 1955 was running at about 1.6 times the European level, and nearly five times that of Japan; by 1970 US manufacturing was investing about the same per worker as European industry and one-third less than Japanese. In the United States average productivity rose by about one-third between 1955 and 1970, in Japan it rose by five times and in Europe it doubled. But even this productivity explosion did not bring the average level of European and Japanese manufacturing productivity up to that of the United States (figure 10.6). The estimates in table 10.1 suggest that even in 1970 US manufacturing was still about twice as productive as its rivals. But the crucial point is that old plants in the USA, and in some industries not only the old plants, were increasingly faced with the challenge of new plants in Europe and Japan with techniques and labour productivity approaching US levels, but with far lower wage costs. In 1960 hourly manufacturing labour costs, including social security contributions, were around three times as high in the USA as in Europe, and ten times as high as in Japan. Even the far faster growth of money wages outside the USA in the years up to 1970 left capital in Europe and Japan with a huge advantage in terms of labour costs (table 10.5).

Table 10.5 Hourly labour costs in manufacturing, 1960–70 (percentage of US level)

	1960	1970
Germany	32	56
UK	32	36
Japan	10	24

Source: Hooper and Larrin, 1989, table 1.

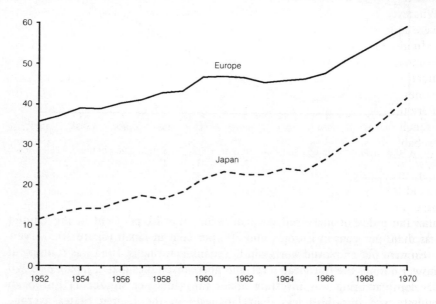

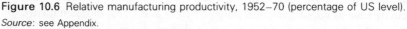

Figure 10.6 Relative manufacturing productivity, 1952–70 (percentage of US level).
Source: see Appendix.

Low accumulation at home

The low rate of accumulation in the United States is undoubtedly a crucial symptom of the declining relative strength of US business. But the explanation can hardly lie in low profits. In manufacturing industry where the US decline was sharpest, the rate of profit (before taxation) seems to have been significantly higher than in the rest of the ACCs (28 per cent over the years 1955–70 as against 23 per cent elsewhere). While high US labour costs and productivity appear to have had roughly offsetting effects, leaving the share of profits similar in the United States to elsewhere, the output-capital ratio was much higher in the USA, suggesting very efficient organization of production (including shift-working).

Taxation appears to have taken a higher fraction of profits in the United States than in some other countries (around one-half in the USA in 1960 as against about one-third in Japan). This did not reflect higher state spending. Over the period 1952–70 government spending on civil and military programmes comprised 26 per cent of GDP in both the United States and the rest of the major ACCs. Certainly the weight of military spending was much greater (9.4 per cent of GDP as against 3.9 per cent), but this was balanced by lower spending on civil programmes, especially social security transfers, which took 8.6 per cent of GDP in other countries and only 5.1 per cent in the USA. Whatever disadvantages US capital faced in terms of policing the 'free world' were more or less offset by lower state spending on welfare.

In any case, shortage of profits is quite implausible as an explanatory factor. Companies in the countries which were accumulating rapidly were investing much more than their retained profits – borrowing the rest from the banks or money market. Thus Japanese companies in the early sixties were financing more than 40 per cent of their investment by tapping external sources of funds; French firms borrowed one-third of the funds they needed and German firms probably did the same. But US companies only ploughed back into new investment a sum equal to their profits. They undoubtedly could have borrowed more and expanded their capital stock faster. If they had done so, the economy would have retained a much fuller utilization of capacity, which in turn would have increased the companies' profits (from 1957 to 1963 the capacity utilization rate in manufacturing averaged only 80.5 per cent, nearly 12 per cent less than the peak achieved in 1966).

So why did US companies fail to invest at a higher rate? Perhaps part of the answer lies in the fact that much of the new technology which had been developed before and during the war had already been incorporated into the capital stock. The existing technology may not have offered sufficient new opportunities, in contrast to Europe and Japan where the combination of backward technology and low wages offered great scope for profitable modernization. But even if the relative lack of profitable investment opportunities goes some way to explaining the poor investment rate, then if US business had felt itself under more pressure, it might have made greater efforts to improve technology. In the early sixties, the United States was spending roughly 2¾ per cent of GDP on research and development (R and D) as compared with 1.5–2 per cent in continental Europe and Japan. But about half of US R and D was financed by the federal government, 80 per cent of which went for space and military purposes. Indeed it was precisely the industries which most benefited from this R and D (aerospace, electronics) which maintained their world lead most effectively. Other sectors such as steel and cars were more complacent.

All this suggests that lack of competitive pressure felt by US business played an important role in the loss of its pre-eminent position The structure of domestic industry was probably dominated by fewer firms than in Japan or the EEC taken as a whole. But this is a crude indicator, at best, for how business behaves. Industries dominated by very few giant firms may be ferociously competitive; these few firms may invest at very high rates, as in Japan. The comparative stability of the oligopolistic structure in the United States may well have bred a complacency which Japanese and German capitalists, faced with rebuilding their position on world markets almost from scratch, could never afford.

Once US firms followed a path of low accumulation, there was a strong tendency for them to stay on it. Wages were only pulled up slowly, implying weak pressure to scrap old plant and replace it with new. By contrast, rapid accumulation, such as occurred in Japan, forces its logic on each individual firm. In that situation failure to accumulate in the face of rapidly rising real wage costs spells disaster. US business appears to have been locked into a pattern of low accumulation from which it proved difficult to escape even when the rising tide of competition began, in the sixties, to have a noticeable effect in the domestic US market.

Investment abroad

However sluggish it was in its domestic investment, US business did respond to the possibilities for profitable investment in Europe by a wave of overseas investment. The total book value of US direct investment overseas rose from $12 billion in 1950 to $78 billion in 1970. Manufacturing investment in Europe, to gain access to the cheaper labour and to escape the external tariff after the formation of the EEC in 1958, grew fastest, rising from $1 billion in 1950 to $14 billion in 1970.

Three aspects of this 'American Challenge', as it was called, need emphasizing. First, it never represented a major investment outlet for US business as a whole. Taking the years 1956–70, if all (net) US direct investment overseas had instead been invested in the United States, gross private investment there would have increased only by around 4 per cent. Second, this investment abroad was not financed out of domestic profits; over the same period US business received profits from its past investment overseas equivalent to around 1¼ times as much as it was sending overseas. While switching towards Europe (where 31 per cent of US direct investment was located in 1970 as compared to 15 per cent in 1955) from Latin America (where the share fell from 38 per cent to 19 per cent) and from mining and petroleum to manufacturing (32 per cent in 1950, 41 per cent in 1970), on average US overseas investment more than financed itself.

Third, while of modest significance for US business as a whole, overseas investment was much more important for the giant multinational enterprises. Over the period 1957–65 for US manufacturing, extra sales by overseas subsidiaries counted for an estimated 13 per cent of the total increase in production (additional exports accounted for only a trivial 2 per cent). For a sample of giant US firms, increased production by their subsidiaries overseas represented 29 per cent of additional sales. By 1966, 20 per cent of their total sales was accounted for by overseas subsidiaries. In 1972 an estimated 22.5 per cent of US multinationals' production took place overseas. In that year petroleum, office and photographic equipment multinationals (mainly American) reported overseas production ratios of 58 per cent, 41 per cent and 37 per cent respectively.

The fact that they tapped in to the rapidly expanding European market undoubtedly helped the giant US firms to offset some of the effects of slow domestic growth. Nevertheless, they still grew substantially more slowly than their rivals from the EEC and Japan, even in the crucial high-research-intensity sectors (table 10.6). This eroded the extent to which the giant US firms towered over the rest. In 1957, 74 out of the top 100 firms were from the United States; in 1972 the figure was 53. The sales of the largest 100 US firms were nearly double the sales of the largest 100 non-US firm in 1962; in 1972 they were only 40 per cent more. Since the US firms were usually the largest, their slower growth of sales led to a reduced concentration in the industries concerned – measured by the sales of the top three firms as a proportion of the top 20. In 11 out of 16 industries the concentration ratio declined, reflecting the greater degree of competition as European and Japanese firms began to match US firms for size. To take the case of cars, in 1962 the big three US producers accounted for 67.5 per cent of the sales of the top 20 producers; in 1972 the share was 58.1 per cent. In 1957 the biggest three US car firms sold 11.6 times as much as their three biggest rivals; in 1972 the difference was 4.2 times. In iron and steel the ratio fell from 4.7 times to 0.9.

As the case of cars suggests, the giant US firms, although squeezed, were by no means throttled. As late as 1977 the biggest five firms in aerospace, office equipment (including computers), scientific and photographic equipment were still American, as were the biggest four in paper and wood, the biggest three in vehicles, the biggest two in electronics and rubber, and three out of the biggest five in petroleum, industrial equipment and food.

Table 10.6 Growth of sales of giant firms, 1962–72 (percentage by which growth of EEC and Japanese firms exceeded that of US)

	EEC	Japan
High research intensity	29	71
e.g. electronics	19	50
Medium research intensity	27	158
e.g. motor vehicles	51	218
Low research intensity	7	68
e.g. textiles	11	57
All giant firms	26	106

Source: Dunning and Pearce, 1981, table 5.5

The boom, Bretton Woods and the dollar

The decline of the position of US capital was one of the most important developments of the boom. Just as the enthronement of the dollar at the centre of the world's monetary system symbolized US dominance at the end of the war, so the weakening of the dollar was to symbolize the erosion of that power.

The international financial system established, essentially by the United States, at Bretton Woods in 1944 (chapter 3) was not fully implemented immediately. Indeed, it was not until the late 1950s that full convertibility for trade purposes of most European currencies was achieved. Only then were businesses in Europe entirely free to use their domestic currencies to buy dollars in order to pay for imports; and controls on capital movements remained widespread. Nevertheless, the progressively more complete operation of the system of pegged exchange rates between convertible currencies undoubtedly assisted the massive expansion of trade which occurred. The heyday of the Bretton Woods system was short-lived, however. As the 1960s rolled on, fundamental weaknesses of the system were revealed, centring on the contradictory role of the dollar. Various attempts to patch up the system failed, and the final crisis phase of the boom (chapter 13) saw enormous financial turbulence and the abandonment of the Bretton Woods framework.

The general interest of US business and finance in the postwar period, perceived as such from 1947 onwards at least, was that the capitalist world as a whole should expand rapidly, with as open access as possible for US commodities and capital. Inasmuch as the Bretton Woods system contributed both as a framework for the expansion of the other capitalist countries and as a mechanism for granting US exports and capital access as soon as practicable, it can only be counted as a success. But a more subtle question concerns the terms on which the United States gained this access. The very operation of the system, while putting the dollar in a privileged position in certain respects, made it progressively more difficult for US business to take full advantage of the opportunities on offer.

The dollar was the lynchpin of the Bretton Woods system. Not only were the values of other currencies effectively pegged to the dollar (formally speaking, to gold) but dollars had to make up the greater part of the other countries' official holdings of reserves. This is because production of gold, at the fixed price of $35 an ounce, was insufficient to provide for both its industrial and monetary uses. But perhaps more importantly, other countries found dollars not just as good as gold, but better than gold, since they could earn interest on their dollar holdings. In the 1950s about three-fifths of total gold production found its way into official reserves. But this represented an increase in the stock of gold held as reserves of only 17 per cent. Over the same period the value of trade in goods and services, which these reserves were supposed to support, more than doubled. In the 1960s, out of a higher total level of gold production (which peaked in 1965) much less than 10 per cent reached the reserves, constituting an increase of a mere 3 per cent. In the 1950s most of the additional reserves which countries accumulated to support their burgeoning trade had to consist of dollars; in the 1960s gold's contribution was negligible.

US gains

This situation, in which other countries were relying on the United States to provide them with the dollars needed to boost their reserves, seemed to leave the USA in a highly privileged position, for the only way that other countries could accumulate reserves was if the USA provided them, by spending abroad more than it received. This is just what the United States did.

Its overall deficit was not the result of a trade deficit (merchandise trade showed a surplus of $70 billion over the years 1950–67). Receipts of interest and dividends netted a further $60 billion. But government expenditure abroad (on loans, grants and for military purposes) together with the outflow of capital exceeded these credit items and resulted in $30 billion of gold or dollars flowing into foreign central banks. Up to the late 1950s this inflow of dollars was generally welcome as it relieved the earlier shortages. However, the combination of rising amounts of dollars held abroad (dollar liabilities) and falling US gold stocks ($7½ billion over the eight years) meant that by 1968 the US gold stock could hardly have repaid 40 per cent of the dollars held abroad in reserves. As this ratio fell, the convertibility of dollars into gold became more and more fragile until it finally snapped (table 10.7).

Before considering how events developed, it is important to clarify in whose interests the system had been operating. At first sight, it seems clear that the United States was gaining. Could it not buy up businesses abroad ($45 billion over the whole period 1950–67), make loans and grants to foreign governments ($50 billion) or finance military expenditure abroad ($44 billion) simply by printing money? Was it not buying businesses and influence abroad with worthless pieces of paper?

Such a description, attractive to critics of the United States from de Gaulle leftwards, is an oversimplification. First of all, the US deficit was not financed literally with paper dollars; foreign central banks which received dollars invested in the New York money market at the going rate of interest. This meant that the USA was actually borrowing overseas, although admittedly paying rather a low rate of interest in *real* terms (after allowing for inflation, the real rate of interest on US Treasury bills was 1½ per cent per annum over the years 1960–6). The United States, or to be more precise, US capital, was clearly gaining if it could borrow at 1½ per cent and invest in setting up or buying businesses in Europe, which would earn a much greater rate of profit. But the reason that US business was investing so much in Europe and elsewhere was not that the United States could run a balance of payments deficit financed by borrowing from central banks overseas. Their investments were based on their

Table 10.7 US balance of payments, 1950–67 ($ billion)

	1950–59	1960–67
Merchandise trade	29.3	39.6
Services and remittances	−5.3	−8.5
Net military transactions	−23.1	−20.5
US government grants (ex. military)	−20.5	−14.8
Net interest and dividends received	25.5	36.5
Current account balance	6.0	32.3
Direct investment (net)	−17.2	−27.9
Investment in shares and bonds (net)	−3.7	−6.4
Government loans	−4.1	−10.6
Long-term capital	−25.0	−44.9
Balance on current and long-term capital	−19.0	−12.6
Dollars held abroad by private sector[a]	1.5[b]	−2.8
Financed by		
Dollars held abroad in official reserves	13.0[c]	8.1
Reduction in US reserves	4.5	6.7
(of which gold)	(5.1)	(7.4)

[a] Includes net short-term capital.
[b] US liquid liabilities to private foreigners are not included.
[c] Includes US liquid liabilities to private foreigners.
Source: US Government, Survey of Current Business, June 1975, October 1972

monopolistic position in world markets, their competitive edge in terms of
know-how, manufacturing techniques and products, which made investment to
capture overseas markets attractive. If the United States had not been able to
run a deficit to finance the investment abroad, one response could have been a
lower value of the dollar, more competitive exports and a sufficient trade
surplus to finance the overseas investment. As their resistance to a dollar
devaluation against their currencies showed, European and Japanese capital
stood to lose more if the United States financed its capital outflow through a
trade surplus. The real objection to the United States was in relation to US
activities abroad rather than to their financing. In short, claims that the United
States was abusing its financial position were a way of claiming that US
competition was 'unfair' rather than just effective.

The real European complaint was that US financial power attracted funds to
New York and that US industrial power was strong enough to allow it to
organize successfully a large volume of production overseas. What prevented
French or German firms borrowing on similar terms in Europe or the United
States to those faced by US firms, and using the money to buy up firms in

Europe or indeed the United States, was their financial and industrial weakness, not the state of Europe's balance of payments. The charge that the USA was abusing, rather than simply using, its position, only had weight to the extent that the United States was putting pressure on central banks abroad *not* to convert more of their dollars into gold. Such pressure began in a mild way in 1960 after some speculative activity in the gold market occurred, based on dawning fears that the dollar might not for ever be 'as good as gold' (i.e. fixed in terms of gold). The United States responded by informally requesting her partners to use restraint in exercising their right to convert dollars into gold. In the next year the United States and other major countries founded the 'Gold Pool' under which they would all, not just the USA, supply gold to stabilize the private gold market.

As the gold backing for the dollar crumbled in the 1960s, the United States increased its pressure on central banks not to join private speculators in demanding gold; in 1967 West Germany issued a formal declaration undertaking not to 'cash in' its dollars for gold, and most other countries, with the notable exception of France, apparently made unofficial statements to the same effect. Finally, in 1968, as the private speculative pressure mounted, the Gold Pool was dissolved (in reality it had been drained). The private market for gold was allowed to find its own level. Formally the United States still maintained the myth that it would convert official holdings of dollars into gold at the old price of $35, while informing other central banks that if they attempted to take advantage of this offer at all it would instantly be withdrawn.

Despite all this pressure to sustain the position of the dollar, it seems that the extent to which the USA was gaining by its ability to finance a deficit was limited. Such gains should show up in receipts of profits from the investments made abroad. But between 1960 and 1967 the amount of interest, profits and dividends received from abroad (net of payments) increased only from $3.4 to $5.3 billion. Most of this increase in any case represented the returns on the investments which the United States had 'earned' by investing the surplus earned from exports exceeding imports. The part of the increase due to its 'privileged' position of being able to borrow cheaply and invest profitably abroad must have been rather small, let alone the part which could be in any way attributed to direct pressure on foreign central banks to provide this finance.

Costs of maintaining the dollar

Furthermore, there were very considerable costs to the USA involved in maintaining the value of the dollar, not against gold, but against other currencies. In the 1960s the US balance on merchandise trade failed to grow, and then sank to virtually nothing in 1968, while the amount US business was investing abroad was rising steadily. In terms of relative costs, US competitiveness hardly changed over the sixties. But as European and Japanese business turned their attention to the US market their relatively low wage costs allowed them to make substantial inroads. At the same time these low wage costs and the expanding European market encouraged a growing level of US foreign investment. The United States began to buy more consumer goods from abroad than it exported in 1959; by 1969 the deficit was $4 billion; in 1968 the balance on cars became negative. Only in capital goods and chemicals was there a growing balance – the combined surplus rising from $5 to $11 billion between 1959 and 1969. A lower exchange rate would have tended to enhance the competitiveness and profitability of US exports and import substitutes. Workers' real wages would have been reduced, provided money wages did not rise. The billion-dollar question was whether a devaluation of the dollar would jeopardize New York's position as a financial centre. Certainly it was regarded as worthwhile to protect the dollar by limiting capital outflows. In 1963 an interest equalization tax was imposed to reduce purchases of foreign bonds and shares; in 1965 US bank lending to foreigners was curtailed. In 1968 US multinationals were required to raise the funds abroad to finance their overseas investments. How long the dollar could be defended and to what extent it was actually in the interests of US capital to do so were resolved by the crisis which followed. This radically changed both the function of the US dollar in the international monetary system, and its relationship with other currencies.

International monetary reform

Some rather fundamental reform of the international monetary system would have been inevitable even without the deterioration in the US balance of payments at the end of the 1960s. The basic contradiction was that the very process by which the rest of the world obtained international liquidity (piling up dollars) undermined the status of that liquidity (by reducing the gold backing of the dollar). Barring central banks from cashing in dollars for gold prevented the stocks in Fort Knox from declining, but left growing dollar liabilities. All the ingenious forms of longer-term borrowing undertaken by the United States from overseas monetary authorities merely changed the form of these liabilities, and could only be a stop-gap. The only way that the gold backing of the dollar could be increased would be by an increase in the price of gold. At a stroke the gold reserves in Fort Knox would be worth more dollars, thus improving backing for the dollar; gold reserves for other central banks would be worth more, encouraging them to accumulate further interest-earning dollar reserves; gold production would be stimulated and private demand reduced (as industry tried to economize and speculators took their profits), allowing countries to absorb additional gold into their reserves.

The immediate costs to the United States would have been political, the main gainers being the major gold producers – South Africa and the USSR – and those who had previously speculated against the dollar by demanding gold.

More fundamentally there was no guarantee that a once-and-for-all increase in the price of gold (a doubling was frequently suggested) would suffice. If the only problem was that the price of gold, fixed prewar at $35 an ounce, had to be adjusted for the wartime inflation in order to secure an adequate supply, then perhaps doubling the gold price would do the trick. Certainly US inflation subsequently had been extremely low; between 1952 and 1967 the US wholesale price index rose at only 0.8 per cent a year. With other currencies fixed to the dollar, this limited the inflation rates elsewhere, the average price of the exports of OECD countries rising by only 0.9 per cent a year. So the insufficiency of gold reserves resulted from higher volume of trade, not higher prices. But by the end of the sixties, the US boom, associated first with Keynesian measures and then with the Vietnam war, was seriously threatening US price stability. Between 1967 and 1970 US wholesale prices rose by 3.3 per cent a year. Continuation of inflation at this kind of rate would cause the whole problem to recur in that the value of gold stocks, at the new fixed-price, would be regarded as insufficient in relation to the rising value of trade, and speculation on a further gold price rise, against the dollar, would redouble (as it would have been proved so profitable the first time). Only a return to US price stability would allow a once-and-for-all rise in the gold price to work, and there was nothing in the act of raising the price of gold which would make that more likely (indeed, the improved gold backing for the dollar would relax such pressure as there was on the US government to maintain price stability in order to defend the dollar). Otherwise an increase in the price of gold seemed to guarantee a continued subservience for the position of the dollar in the international monetary system: always under threat of further humiliation by falling in value in relation to gold. It was for these reasons that the United States in the late 1960s consistently opposed an increase in the official price of gold.

It is highly likely that there was no possible adjustment to the gold price in the 1960s which would have ensured an adequate flow of gold into the reserves of the USA and other countries. The balance between industrial demand, speculation and monetary needs could probably never have been achieved in the inflationary context of the time. At the other extreme from attempting to stabilize the monetary system by an appropriate use of the price mechanism (the price of gold) there arose a multitude of plans for the conscious creation of international money which would certainly supplement, and perhaps do away with, the role of gold and even dollars as part of international reserves. The US government began to look favourably on such plans in the mid-sixties, presumably out of a realization that something more permanent than arm-twisting had to be done to protect the gold in Fort Knox. The system of special drawing rights (SDRs), agreed in 1968 and implemented in 1970, gave countries credits in the books of the IMF, fixed in value to gold and earning an interest rate of $1\frac{1}{2}$ per cent, which they could use to settle balance of payments deficits. This 'paper gold' was intended to take the heat off the dollar by increasing what was in effect the gold content of reserves. The supply of SDRs to be made available would not be disturbed by the vagaries of industrial demand, Russian gold sales or speculation. The initial allocations ($9½ billion spread over three years) were expected to provide for a reasonable growth of reserves in the context of a staunching of the flow of dollars. It seemed to be a triumph for international cooperation and reason. As we shall see, this triumph was short-lived (chapter 12). In the turmoil that ensued, it became apparent that US capital, while weakened, was by no means incapable of defending its interests.

11
Overaccumulation

The decline of the United States was not the only problem generated by the boom. The sheer pace of accumulation was itself a mixed blessing. It propelled capitalism up the longest and steepest economic incline in history, but at a cost. Towards the end, the engine of growth was overheating badly and the ride was increasingly bumpy. *Overaccumulation* had set in.

The basic idea of overaccumulation is that capitalism sometimes generates a higher rate of accumulation than can be sustained, and thus the rate of accumulation has eventually to fall. Towards the end of the postwar boom, an imbalance between accumulation and the labour supply led to increasingly severe labour shortage. The excess demand for labour generated a faster scrapping of old equipment. Real wages were pulled up and older machines rendered unprofitable, allowing a faster transfer of workers to the new machines. This could in principle have occurred smoothly: as profitability slid down, accumulation could have declined gently to a sustainable rate. But the capitalist system has no mechanism guaranteeing a smooth transition in such circumstances. In the late sixties the initial effect of overaccumulation was a period of feverish growth, with rapidly rising wages and prices and an enthusiasm for get-rich-quick schemes. These temporarily masked, but could not suppress, the deterioration in profitability. Confidence was undermined, investment collapsed and a spectacular crash occurred. Overaccumulation gave rise, not to a mild decline in the growth rate, but to a classic capitalist crisis.

This chapter and the following two examine this process. This one focuses on underlying developments in accumulation. The next two give a more blow-by-blow account of mounting economic difficulties.

Development of the working class

One way in which rapid accumulation undermines the conditions for its own existence is by creating a mass proletariat. Capitalism's hunger for additional workers creates a larger and larger class of waged workers. Their economic conditions are essentially similar – in that they are deprived of the wherewithal to produce on their own account and so must work under others for wages – and their interests are ultimately antagonistic to those of their employers.

Total employment rose, in line with population growth, by 30 per cent between 1950 and 1970. This would in itself have increased the size of the working class by almost a third. As it was, the proletariat grew considerably faster than total employment. While civilian employment in the ACCs rose by 46 million, the number of self-employed and 'family workers' fell by 20 million. In 1954, 31 per cent of those officially classified as in work were in this category. By 1973 the proportion had fallen to 17 per cent.

Outside agriculture the number of self-employed actually grew by 1 million, while falling substantially as a proportion of total employment. The growth of services, with many opportunities for small businesses, was the main reason for the growth in absolute numbers. In industry the self-employed were generally slowly squeezed by the superior performance of big business, although 15 per cent of those engaged in manufacturing in Italy and Japan were still self-employed in 1970.

So the story behind the statistical shift from self-employment to wage labour is one of an exodus from the land. For the individuals concerned the trek was often one away from the dreary world of the family farm towards the bright lights of the big city. For society as a whole it was a process of massive proletarianization.

A number of factors made this development possible. One was underemployment in the countryside. Many farms had more family workers than could be fully employed, and so migration to the cities could occur without loss of food output. In Japan, the United States, France and Germany the number of unpaid family workers fell by nearly 12 million, or 70 per cent. Mechanization in the countryside also reduced labour requirements. This was achieved partly through capitalist agriculture driving out family farms. The number of self-employed farmers in the United States, Japan, France and Germany fell by about 6 million, or 50 per cent.

Reduced underemployment, mechanization (spurred on in part by the exodus of family workers) and improved methods of cultivation allowed agricultural output to grow significantly and employment to fall substantially. Productivity grew faster in agriculture than in industry, both overall (table 11.1) and within every major country except Japan.

These developments within agriculture reflected the growth in demand for labour in other sectors. This proceeded at a faster pace in services than in industry. The annual average percentage growth rates of employment in the ACCs from 1955 to 1968 were (OECD, 1970):

Agriculture	−3.8 per cent
Industry	1.5 per cent
Services	2.0 per cent
Total	1.0 per cent

Table 11.1 ACC sector growth rates, 1955–68 (average annual percentage growth rates)

	Output	Productivity
Agriculture	1.8	5.6
Industry	5.7	4.2
Services	4.9	3.0

Sources: OECD, *The growth of output 1960–80*, tables 3 and 7; Ohkawa and Rosovsky, 1973, table 2.5

The pattern of demand – including the rise in the share of investment (chapter 8) – ensured that industrial production rose more quickly than the output of services. Nevertheless, employment grew faster in services as productivity rose more slowly (although the measurement of output and hence productivity in many services is difficult).

Some of the growth in service employment was in state provision outside the market, notably in the form of the welfare state (chapter 9). State employment rose from some 11½ per cent of total employment in 1960 to some 14½ per cent in 1974. (Nationalized industry employees are excluded; they produce commodities for the market and contribute directly to the pool of profits.) Some privately employed labour also works for non-profit-making bodies. In Japan, where state welfare provision is poor, this constitutes some 2 per cent of employment. None of these jobs represents work for capitalists. But they are wage labour, and those performing them are a part of the working class.

The switch to waged work of previously independent producers also increased union membership. In the ACCs membership grew from about 49 million in 1952 to 62 million in 1970. But the proportion of wage and salary earners in unions declined from 37 per cent in 1952 to 31 per cent in the late sixties. Much of the explanation for this lies in two interrelated trends: towards more white-collar jobs and towards more service jobs, both traditionally weakly organized. In both Britain and Germany the number of manual workers stayed virtually constant over the boom while white-collar employment rose by 50 per cent in the United Kingdom and doubled in Germany. Since unionization levels among white-collar workers are about half those for blue-collar in both countries, this shift worked to pull down the average level of unionization even though more white-collar workers started to join unions.

Overall membership figures are crude indicators of the development of unionization. They lump together the British miners, the American teamsters and Japanese 'company' unions. But, for Europe at least, certain generalizations can be made. They include the increasing importance of white-collar and public sector unions and the cementing, in the context of continuous growth in living standards, of the power of national trade union bureaucracies. These developments were to influence the form of workers' struggles once full employment was achieved (chapter 12).

The late 1960s: the problem of full employment

By the mid-sixties the enormous growth of waged jobs had effectively created full employment. The measured unemployment rate for the advanced capitalist countries had fallen below 3 per cent. It then fluctuated around that level until 1973, although rising quite sharply in the 1971–2 recession (chapter 12).

In full employment lay both the historic achievement of the boom and its undoing. The difficulties raised by full employment manifested themselves most obviously in accelerating inflation. A less noticeable but ultimately more crucial problem was a general decline in profitability. But perhaps the most fundamental difficulty was a threat to capitalist control on the shop floor. The Polish economist Kalecki, whose work had in other ways anticipated that of Keynes, had predicted just such a development a quarter of a century earlier:

> The *maintenance* of full employment would cause social and political changes which would give a new impetus to the opposition of the business leaders. Under a régime of permanent full employment, 'the sack' would cease to play its role as a disciplinary measure . . . 'discipline in the factories' and 'political stability' are more appreciated by business leaders than profits. Their class instinct tells them that lasting full employment is unsound from their point of view and that unemployment is an integral part of the normal capitalist system. (Kalecki, 1971, pp. 140–1).

Tight labour markets

Measured in terms of unemployment rates, the intensity of demand for labour appears to have subsided a little by 1970. But unemployment can be an unreliable indicator of the tightness of labour markets. Patterns of registration shift as regulations change, or as previously 'marginalized' groups, such as married women, become consolidated into the labour force. Rapid changes in the pattern of demand for labour (across regions or industries) can also leave a residual of 'structural' unemployment in a context of intense labour shortage. The speed of the upswing in 1972–3 generated bottlenecks and labour market 'mismatches'.

An alternative indicator of demand for labour is employers' notification of vacancies. Although open to misinterpretation, this at least in principle shows the extent to which employers were hunting for workers. Vacancy figures show intensity of demand reaching a peak in Germany in 1970 and in Japan in 1973 (figure 11.1). In the United Kingdom, vacancy figures show extremely tight labour markets in the early seventies.

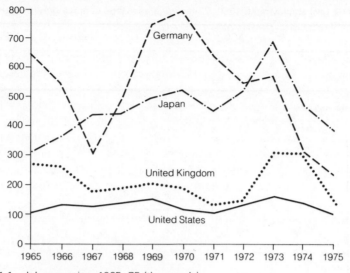

Figure 11.1 Job vacancies, 1965–75 (thousands).
Source: OECD, *Main Economic Indicators*.

Accumulation and the demand for labour

The very high level of demand for labour was maintained throughout the late sixties and early seventies by the trend of capital accumulation. The accumulation rate for the ACCs peaked in 1970–1 at just over 5½ per cent – an increase of over 1 percentage point relative to the early sixties. In Europe the rate of accumulation peaked first in the early 1960s, then a decade later at a slightly lower level. In the United States it peaked around 1966, but was still much higher in the early seventies than in the early sixties. In Japan the accumulation rate peaked at the end of the sixties and the increasing weight of the Japanese capital stock also contributed to the upward trend in the ACC accumulation rate over the 1960s as a whole (figures 11.2 and 11.3).

The impact of accumulation on demand for labour depends on its form as well as its extent. If accumulation in the boom had been based on an unchanged mass of machinery per worker then an extension of the capital stock would have required an equivalent increase in workers employed. But new means of production systematically embodied a higher degree of mechanization than their predecessors (chapter 8). So the rate of growth of employment was much less than the rate of accumulation (figure 11.3). But in the absence of an increase in the speed of mechanization in the early seventies, the peak rates of accumulation achieved at that time generated peak intensities of demand for labour. Since labour supply did not increase to meet this demand, the growth of civilian employment was only marginally higher in the late sixties and early seventies than in the first half of the sixties (table 11.2).

Table 11.2 Civil employment, 1960–73 (average annual percentage growth rates)

	ACC	USA	Japan	Europe
1960–66	1.1	1.7	1.4	0.3
1966–73	1.2	2.2	1.2	0.2

Source: see Appendix

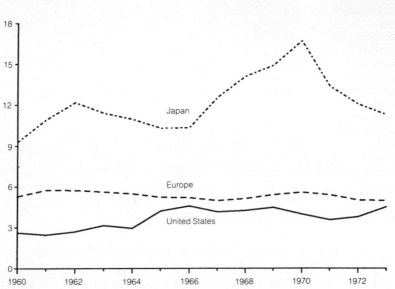
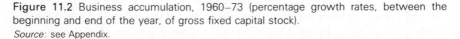

Figure 11.2 Business accumulation, 1960–73 (percentage growth rates, between the beginning and end of the year, of gross fixed capital stock).
Source: see Appendix.

For the capitalist countries as a whole, about half of the 1.7 per cent per year growth of the non-agricultural labour force between 1968 and 1973 resulted from a combination of a declining agricultural labour force and increasing female participation in non-agricultural labour (table 11.3). Immigration was much less important – contributing 0.1 per cent to the growth of the labour force each year. Given declining male participation rates (particularly because of earlier retirement and extended education), employment would have grown only half as fast without these sources of additional labour. Labour shortage would have been more intense.

Labour shortage could also have been relieved by longer hours of work. In fact, average hours worked per year generally fell faster in the early 1970s, according to the rather sketchy data available, as workers used their stronger bargaining position in tight labour markets to reduce time spent at work. However, shorter hours also reflected the growth of part-time work as more married women entered the labour force.

Table 11.3 Sources of labour, 1968–73 (average annual percentage growth rates)

	ACC	USA	Japan	Europe
Growth of 'home' population of working age	1.0	1.5	1.2	0.4
Effect of net migration	0.1	0.2	0.0	0.1
Growth of total population of working age	1.1	1.7	1.2	0.5
Effect of change in participation rates	0.2	0.3	0.3	0.1
Growth of labour force	1.3	2.0	1.5	0.6
Effect of decline in agricultural labour force	0.4	0.2	0.7	0.5
Growth of non-agricultural labour force	1.7	2.2	2.2	1.1
of which women	2.4	3.1	2.2	1.8

Sources: OECD, *Labour Force Statistics*; McCracken, 1977, table A11.

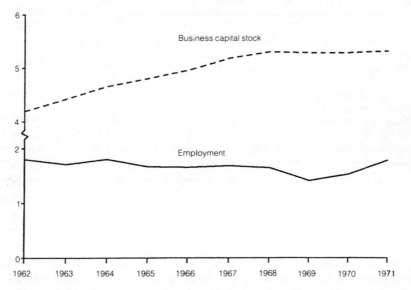

Figure 11.3 ACC business accumulation and employment, 1962–71 (percentage growth rate of five-year moving average centred on specified year – thus figures for 1962 include changes in 1960 and 1961, and figures for 1971 include changes in 1972 and 1973).
Source: see Appendix.

The profits squeeze

An increasing imbalance between accumulation and supplies of additional labour requires the faster scrapping of old plant to speed up the transfer of workers to new means of production. With little additional labour available, employers compete fiercely for labour to operate newly installed machinery. A faster increase in money wages results. Inflation may accelerate as well, but, if faster scrapping is to occur, not as fast as money wages. For it is the increase in product wages (the real cost to the employer of hiring workers) which makes the old machinery unprofitable and permits labour to be transferred to the new. This faster scrapping, and the faster growth of product wages which causes it, are signs that the rate of accumulation is excessive in relation to the available labour supply. A further sign of overaccumulation is a squeeze of profits.

Between 1965 and 1973 the share of profits in business output fell by about one-eighth (table 11.4). All the blocs experienced the squeeze, though with varying intensity. In Europe the profit share fell in the early sixties and again in the early seventies. A sharp decline began in the United States after 1965. In Japan profitability plummeted after 1970. Although the squeeze on profits occurred during very different time periods, the falls were quite similar: profit shares declined to around 80 per cent of peak levels almost everywhere.

Table 11.4 Profit shares, 1960–73 (percentages)

	ACC	USA	Europe	Japan
Business				
Peak year[a]	25.4	23.4	29.2	40.3
1973	22.1	17.2	24.5	32.9
1973/peak year	0.87	0.74	0.84	0.82
Manufacturing				
Peak year[a]	25.2	24.3	26.4	42.0
1973	22.1	18.7	20.7	34.9
1973/peak year	0.88	0.77	0.78	0.83

[a] The 'Peak year' is defined as the year before the sustained decline in profitability. It is 1965 for ACC and the USA, 1960 for Europe and 1970 for Japan. 1973/peak year shows the ratio of the 1973 figure to the peak value, e.g. 0.87 means that the 1973 level was 87 per cent of the peak value.

Source: see Appendix

In each bloc the decline in profit shares started at about the time that the accumulation rate peaked. This is no coincidence: accelerated accumulation, combined with labour shortage, was the basic cause of the profits squeeze.

It was not the only influence at work, however. The behaviour of both productivity and product wages do not conform precisely to the simplest description of overaccumulation. Productivity and product wages determine the course of the profit share and an account of their movements is given in the next two sections. Tracing the course of the profits squeeze is inevitably rather complicated and speculative because the various influences cannot be quantified.

Productivity growth

Faster scrapping of old plant as a result of insufficient labour should increase the rate of growth of labour productivity. With a faster rate of transfer of workers from old machines to new ones, the proportion of more modern, higher-productivity machines in use rises. Yet faster productivity growth did not occur in the early seventies. Despite a faster rate of accumulation in relation to the labour force (reflected in the capital–labour ratio growing 1 per cent per year faster), the growth of productivity was around 1 per cent slower in the early 1970s compared to the early 1960s (figure 11.4). The decline took place in the United States and Japan. In manufacturing industry, productivity growth slipped back in the early 1970s in Europe and Japan (table 11.5).

Table 11.5 Productivity and capital per worker, 1960–73 (average annual percentage growth rates)

	ACC	USA	Europe	Japan
Business				
Hourly productivity				
Early 1960s	5.2	3.5	4.8	9.0
Late 1960s	4.6	1.5	4.8	10.1
Early 1970s	4.0	1.4	4.8	7.6
Capital per worker				
Early 1960s	3.9	1.1	4.7	8.1
Late 1960s	4.5	2.0	4.8	8.9
Early 1970s	4.9	1.7	4.9	11.2
Manufacturing				
Hourly productivity				
Early 1960s	5.8	3.7	6.2	8.6
Late 1960s	5.7	1.2	6.2	11.4
Early 1970s	5.8	3.9	5.5	9.5
Capital per worker				
Early 1960s	5.2	0.9	5.6	11.9
Late 1960s	5.5	3.7	4.5	10.2
Early 1970s	6.2	4.0	5.1	11.9

Dates refer to successive cycles from peak to peak, with slightly varying patterns across different countries.

Source: see Appendix

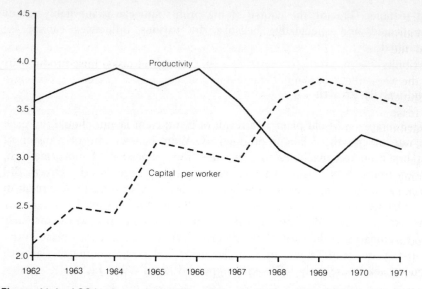

Figure 11.4   ACC business productivity and mechanization, 1962–71 (percentage growth rate of five-year moving average centred on specified year – see figure 11.3).
Source: see Appendix.

   Three factors probably contributed to the decline in productivity growth. The argument that faster scrapping leads to a faster growth of productivity assumes that mechanization – the installation of new machines – continues to yield the same increases in productivity. If mechanization was to yield less productivity gains however, then average productivity growth would slip back despite faster scrapping.

   It is plausible to suppose that the most productive increases in mechanization in Europe and Japan occurred in the fifties and sixties. A laggard in the technological race may take shortcuts to 'catch up'. Productivity growth would then decline as the frontier set by the United States was approached. But this cannot fully explain the slowdown. Europe and Japan still lagged far behind in the late sixties and seventies. In 1970 productivity in European manufacturing seems to have been around or perhaps a little over one-half of the US level, while in Japan it was only about 40 per cent of the US level. Moreover, catching up cannot explain the slowdown in US productivity which occurred outside the manufacturing sector and which can only partly be explained by the less intense expansion once the excess capacity of the early 1960s had been used up.

   Productivity growth does not depend solely on equipment – whether or not new, high-productivity machines replace old, low-productivity ones. Productivity on the whole range of plant, old and new, may be improved as experience in operating it breeds better methods of organization. Conceivably such gains were tailing off by the late sixties. Productivity is also affected by the extent to which the employers can maintain or increase the intensity of labour – the proportion of the working day during which the worker is literally working – and the speed of that work. Faster production lines and increased labour 'flexibility' (so that workers carry out a wider range of tasks) raise productivity on the whole range of plant. Tight labour markets and increased union strength at the end of the sixties may well have made it more difficult for employers to increase work intensity and carry out schemes of reorganization. This probably contributed to the slower growth in labour productivity at that time.

Two industries are particularly interesting in this respect – the car industry, which is the obvious archetype of 'Fordist' methods of work organization, and mining, always a barometer of class conflict. In both cases productivity growth slowed down in most countries, often sharply, in the late 1960s or early 1970s.

Product wages

As we have seen, a faster increase in product wages is the basic factor which forces a faster rate of scrapping when there is a growing discrepancy between accumulation and the available labour supply. The growth rate of product wages did peak in 1969, just when accumulation was reaching its peak, and it grew a little faster (about ½ per cent per year) between 1968 and 1973 than over the period 1960–8. This fairly small increase in product wage growth underestimates the increased pressures to scrap (and thus the extent of overaccumulation) for two reasons. A slowdown in the productivity gains on all plants (old and new) – gains which could be obtained from reorganization and more intensive work – meant that a given growth of product wages already implied faster scrapping. Some old plants which would otherwise have remained profitable as a result of faster or more effective working would have become unprofitable as a result of these productivity gains not being achieved. Secondly, the rising cost of raw materials (chapter 12) tended to increase scrapping by making old plants unprofitable even in the absence of a faster growth of product wages. The case of the United States illustrates this. Between 1960 and 1968 materials prices rose about ½ per cent per year and final goods prices by about 1 per cent. Between 1968 and 1973, by contrast, final goods prices rose by 4½ per cent per year while materials prices shot up by 11½ per cent per year. The effect of this rapid increase in the cost of materials, relative to the price at which final output was sold, was to make some old plants less profitable. Overaccumulation meant there was insufficient labour to keep old plants going, so they had to be scrapped. Faster materials price increases meant that this required only a small acceleration in product wage growth (figure 11.5).

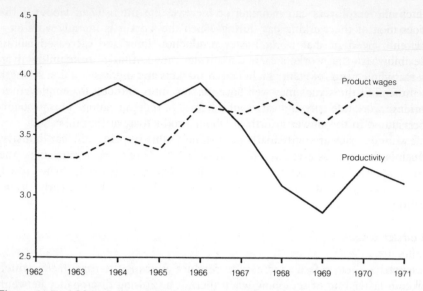

Figure 11.5   ACC business productivity and product wages, 1962–71 (percentage growth rate of five-year moving average centred on specified year – see figure 11.3).
Source: see Appendix.

International competition

As if all these factors, and their relationships, were not complex enough, there is another influence on the profit share which must be mentioned. Increased international competition almost certainly contributed to holding down profit margins. More trade and investment flows, based on the tendency towards an equalization of productivity levels, must have decreased the extent of monopoly power exercised by domestic producers. It certainly contributed to holding down inflation, so that the money wages generated by the high demand for labour were easily translated into product wage increases and the necessary scrapping rates achieved. The increased general level of international competition, which may have eroded profit margins in all the countries concerned, must be distinguished from sudden shifts in the relative competitiveness of individual countries. Such shifts may drastically worsen the profitability of the country suffering reduced competitiveness. An extreme example was the sharp decline in competitiveness of Japanese industry between 1970 and 1973 when a rising yen pushed up Japanese relative labour costs by one-third. This may have played some role in the big decline in the profitability of Japanese industry over the same period as Japanese exporters were forced to accept lower profit margins, but there will have been some compensating improvement in the profitability of import-competing industries in the United

States and Europe as Japanese exporters found themselves obliged to raise their prices to recoup some of the cost increases.

Even in this period in Japan, however, it is highly unlikely that the exchange rate movement was the dominating factor in declining profitability. For profitability appears to have fallen just as fast outside manufacturing, where the pressure of international competition must have been negligible. Forces working to equalize profit rates could hardly have transmitted the effects of international competition to these insulated sectors in such a short space of time. Labour shortage, by contrast, affected all sectors and is a much more plausible explanation for the profits squeeze.

Falling output–capital ratio

The rate of profit depends on the output–capital ratio as well as on the share of profits (chapter 8). A faster rate of scrapping would tend to reduce the measured output–capital ratio. Some part of the scrapped capital stock would still count in the statistics, since these are based on the assumption of a constant scrapping rate (a constant economic life). During the periods when the profit share declined, a definite fall in the output–capital ratio occurred. The fall in the output–capital ratio was around 5–10 per cent in both business and manufacturing for the ACCs as a whole (table 11.6). For the individual blocs the falling output–capital ratios were rather greater (10–20 per cent) and thus contributed significantly to falls in profitability.

Table 11.6 Output–capital ratios, 1960–73

	ACC	USA	Europe	Japan
Business				
Peak year[a]	0.76	0.85	0.70	0.86
1973	0.70	0.77	0.65	0.66
1973/peak year	0.92	0.91	0.93	0.77
Manufacturing				
Peak year[a]	1.16	1.50	0.81	1.25
1973	0.99	1.18	0.74	1.11
1973/peak year	0.85	0.79	0.91	0.89

[a] The 'peak year' is defined as the year before the sustained decline in profitability. It is 1965 for ACC and the USA, 1960 for Europe and 1970 for Japan.

Source: see Appendix

If faster scrapping was properly taken into account in the capital stock statistics it would show up in a higher figure for depreciation (and thus a lower profit share) rather than a falling output–capital ratio. But it seems likely that influences other than faster scrapping also contributed to the decline in the measured ratio of output to capital. All the factors discussed above which reduced the growth rate of labour productivity contributed to the fall. In addition, the relative price of capital goods stopped declining. In the early 1970s the price of investment goods rose slightly faster than the price of output, whereas in the 1960s the price of output had risen about 1 per cent faster than the price of investment goods. The explanation for the changed pattern of relative prices is not clear. Possibly the productivity slowdown was particularly marked in investment goods sectors (the US construction industry is an example frequently cited). In addition, the very high demand in the early seventies may well have pushed up investment goods prices especially fast. It is certainly the case that the rapid increase in materials prices would tend to push up investment goods prices (which include an imported materials element) faster than output prices (which are defined to exclude the impact of import prices). Finally, some part of the fall in the output–capital ratio in the United States after 1966 must have reflected the decreasing capacity utilization. While it is impossible to measure precisely the influence of these factors, they all probably contributed to the falling output–capital ratio and the consequent decline in the profit rate.

Falling rate of profit

Declining profit shares and falling output–capital ratios combined to push down the rate of profit (figures 11.6 and 11.7). Between 1968 and 1973 the profit rate

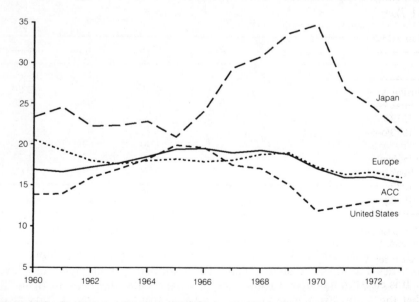

Figure 11.6   Business profit rates, 1960–73 (percentage).
Source: see Appendix.

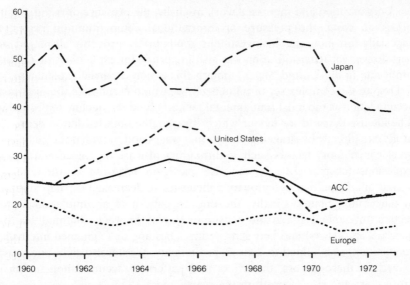

Figure 11.7 Manufacturing profit rates, 1960–73 (percentage).
Source: see Appendix.

for the ACCs as a whole fell in the business and manufacturing sectors by one-fifth. By 1973 the profit rate in business and manufacturing had fallen from its previous peak in each major bloc by about one-third. The fall began in Europe in 1960, in the United States in the mid-1960s, and in Japan in 1970 (table 11.7).

Table 11.7 Profit rates, 1960–73 (percentages)

	ACC	USA	Europe	Japan
Business				
Peak year[a]	19.4	19.9	20.5	34.8
1973	15.4	13.2	16.0	21.6
1973/peak year	0.79	0.66	0.78	0.62
Manufacturing				
Peak year[a]	29.1	36.4	21.5	52.7
1973	21.9	22.0	15.4	38.8
1973/peak year	0.75	0.60	0.72	0.74

[a] The 'peak year' is defined as the year before the sustained decline in profitability. It is 1965 for ACC and the USA, 1960 for Europe and 1970 for Japan.

Source: see Appendix

It is clear from our discussion of the profit share and the output–capital ratio that the profit rate was subject to a large number of influences. Decreasing productivity gains from mechanization, difficulties in obtaining more productive work organization and increased work intensity, the pressure of rising materials prices on costs, the pressure of international competition on prices, and especially fast increases in investment goods prices probably all played some part. Lower capacity utilization was also important for explaining the fall in the profit rate in the United States, though this is only a partial explanation.

Despite the complex set of influences, we would emphasize the high rate of accumulation as the most fundamental factor behind the decline in profitability. The intense demand for labour which it generated both tended to depress the profit rate directly by dragging up product wages and provided the backdrop to other contributory factors such as difficulties of work organization and wages explosions (chapter 12). It was also partly in response to the effects of overaccumulation that deflationary policies led to decreased capacity utilization in the United States. Finally, the uneven pattern of accumulation between sectors (investment goods and consumer goods), between commodities (basic materials and others) and between countries (leading to heightened international competition) also helped to depress profitability. Whatever weight one attaches to each of these factors, the extent and pattern of accumulation undeniably drove down the rate of profit in the years before 1973.

Post-tax profits

Although it is the profit rate before taxation which reflects the underlying economic forces of capital accumulation, labour supply and competitiveness, it is the profit rate *after* taxation which is of most direct concern to employers when they make investment decisions. Governments could have offset declining profitability by cutting taxes on profits or by increasing the generosity of tax allowances given for investment. Calculation of the impact of taxation on the profitability of new investment is extremely complex, but a detailed international study provides some valuable information on the levels and trends of corporate taxation in various countries (table 11.8).

Table 11.8 Tax rates on new manufacturing investment, 1960–70

	US	UK	Germany	Japan
1960	51	31	50	29
1970	51	4	47	23

Source: King and Fullerton, 1984, various tables

Table 11.8 (and other partial data for France and Italy) suggest that in general the burden of company taxation was not much reduced in the 1960s, so that the fall in profitability applied post-tax as well as pre-tax. The exception is the UK where taxation on corporate profits began to decline in the 1950s. By

1970 the generosity of tax concessions for new investment was such that they wiped out the effect of corporation tax and rendered the post-tax rate of profit virtually as high as the pre-tax rate. Accelerating inflation partially offset this trend in the early seventies as companies were being taxed on the inflated values of their stocks of materials and semi-finished goods, but the Labour Government of 1974–9 retrospectively removed taxation from increased stock values. In the UK, then, the impact of declining profitability was substantially cushioned by tax concessions for companies. This meant a shift in the burden of taxation towards workers, reducing the extent to which their take home pay benefited from their stronger bargaining position.

Did workers gain?

At first sight it might seem that workers clearly gained from the onset of overaccumulation. Full employment meant a more or less guaranteed job, shorter working hours, and perhaps reduced intensity of work and improved working conditions. Finally, the faster growth of product wages would seem to imply faster growth of living standards.

But the issue is more complex. Whether or not accelerated product wages lead to a faster increase in living standards depends on how the prices of the goods that workers consume move relative to those that they produce, and on any changes in the proportion of their incomes that workers pay in taxation which are not reflected in increased benefits or social services.

For the ACCs as a whole real take-home pay rose by nearly 1 per cent per year faster in the early 1970s than in the 1960s, despite the slowdown in productivity growth (table 11.9). The rising share of wages and more slowly growing tax burdens provide the explanation. There were rather diverse trends in the three blocs. In Europe workers also gained from a slower growth, relative to prices in general, of consumer prices; this may in part have reflected pressure on governments to increase subsidies or hold down nationalized industries prices. Japan provides the most dramatic case of a rising wage share maintaining the growth of take-home pay despite a major decline in productivity growth. In the USA a rising wage share after 1966 prevented total stagnation of take-home pay as productivity slowed, consumer prices rose relatively fast and taxes were increased.

Workers' living standards also depend on government services. Spending on these rose steadily in the sixties. There was a sharp twist towards civil spending. Military spending was drastically reduced in the United States, allowing a very rapid rise in civil expenditure. In Japan civil spending also increased sharply. In Europe, where the share of civil spending had risen steadily throughout the sixties, the pace was not maintained (Table 11.10).

Of the 2½ percentage points increase in the share of civil spending in total production about half is accounted for by services (health and education) and

Table 11.9 Business productivity, the wage share and real wages, 1960–73 (average annual percentage growth rates)

	(1) Productivity	(2) Relative consumer prices	(3) Real incomes	(4) Share of wages	(5) Real wage	(6) Tax effect	(7) Take-home pay
ACC							
1960–69	3.7	0.4	3.3	−0.1	3.2	0.6	2.6
1969–73	3.1	0.3	2.8	0.8	3.6	0.1	3.5
Europe							
1960–69	4.2	0.2	4.0	0.3	4.3	0.9	3.2
1969–73	3.7	−0.8	4.6	1.0	5.6	0.4	5.2
USA							
1960–66	3.2	0.2	3.0	−0.5	2.5	0.1	2.4
1966–73	1.2	0.6	0.6	0.8	1.4	0.6	0.8
Japan							
1960–70	9.2	1.9	7.3	−1.0	6.3	0.0	6.3
1970–73	5.9	1.4	4.4	4.0	8.4	0.7	7.7

Break points represent cyclical peaks.

(1) is non-agricultural business output per person employed.

(2) is the price of consumer goods relative to the price of business value added.

(3) = (1) − (2); this measures the purchasing power of business sector incomes in terms of consumer goods.

(4) is the share of wage income in business value added.

(5) = (3) + (4); this is the purchasing power of pre-tax wage incomes per head.

(6) is the effect of changing proportion of incomes taken in taxation.

(7) = (5) − (6); this is the purchasing power of post-tax wage incomes per head.

Sources: see Appendix plus IMF, *International Financial Statistics* and OECD, *Economic Outlook.*

Table 11.10 Public expenditure, 1960–73 (percentage of GDP)

	1960	1968	1973
ACC			
Civil[a]	19.2	21.9	24.2
Military	6.6	5.8	4.1
USA			
Civil[a]	16.8	19.4	22.5
Military	9.1	8.8	5.7
Europe			
Civil[a]	23.1	27.4	28.8
Military	4.4	3.7	3.4
Japan			
Civil[a]	15.2	16.0	18.7
Military	0.9	0.7	0.7

[a] Civil spending refers to 'programmes'; i.e. it excludes debt interest and subsidies (the effect of the latter is included in the discussion of taxation).

Source: see Appendix

half by transfers. Practically all the higher share of spending is accounted for by increases in the relative cost of providing them. So the 'quantity' of services provided (measured, for example, by the number of workers employed in providing them) rose no faster than output as a whole. The rise in the share of transfers (pensions, dole, etc.) also probably took the form (as it did over the period as a whole; see chapter 9) of an extension of coverage of schemes rather than of a growth in real value in excess of productivity. But the substantial cut in military spending which allowed accelerated expansion of welfare services without a correspondingly faster rise in the burden of taxation represented a gain for workers. It was another product of pressure for improved conditions.

Therefore, in the early 1970s the working class made substantial gains in take-home pay and public services, as well as in high employment, cuts in hours and probably improved conditions of work. For the moment, capital was bearing the costs of overaccumulation.

Inflation

Thus far the discussion has been conducted entirely in 'real' terms: the shares of incomes going to profits and wages, productivity, hours of work, and so on. The only prices discussed have been *relative*: investment goods in relation to consumer goods, imports relative to exports and so forth. Changes in the overall price level have been ignored.

Adjustment to full employment could in principle occur without any tendency towards inflation. Competition for labour would pull up money wages more rapidly. Higher inflation would enable old capital to stay competitive, but profitable capacity would then exceed market demand. So competition for markets from the cheaper products made on newly installed machinery would hold price increases down to the existing rate. The faster growth of money wages would mean a faster growth of product wages. Older vintages would be scrapped more quickly, making space for the new in both labour and product markets. Faster growth of product wages would mean faster growth of real wages. Consumption would rise as a share of production, and profits and investment decline. Steady extension of credit would allow the expanded production to be sold without any change in the rate of inflation.

But this is not what happened in the early seventies. Inflation rose steadily from the mid-1960s. In 1965 consumer prices rose on average by 3 per cent a year in the ACCs. By 1973 the average annual inflation rate had risen to 7.8 per cent. Prices accelerated for a number of interrelated reasons. Trade unions, strengthened by high demand for labour, secured money wage increases which, given the existing inflation rate, exceeded those required to generate sufficient extra scrapping. On occasions, wage pressure exploded in very sharp increases, especially where it had previously been compressed by incomes policies. Such wage increases tended to reduce profitability. This happened directly when employers were unable to raise prices sufficiently to offset 'excessive' wage increases because of growing international competition and fixed exchange rates. But international competition was not always binding. Governments sometimes responded by promptly devaluing the currency to offset the cost disadvantage of the wage increases.

Even where prices could be raised to offset the wage increases, aggregate profits would still fall eventually if credit was not extended fast enough to allow the sale of the same volume of commodities at the higher price level. So governments faced strong pressure to offset the adverse effects of wage explosions on profitability by facilitating a rapid expansion of credit. When they acquiesced, the result was higher inflation. Capitalists were also unwilling to accept the decline in accumulation implied by the falling rate of profit. Access to credit enabled capitalists to maintain the rate of accumulation by increasing the proportion of funds borrowed (largely workers' savings). In Germany and the United States in particular, business borrowing was higher in the early seventies than in the early and mid-sixties. Business borrowing in Japan and France also peaked in 1973 (table 11.11).

This additional borrowing, being routed in part through the banking system, ensured a faster growth of the money supply. The investment financed by this borrowing stoked up demand for commodities, permitting sales to be maintained at higher and higher prices.

Governments were not responsible for this expansion of credit in the sense of running larger deficits and printing money to finance them. There was no

Table 11.11 Business borrowing[a] as a percentage of fixed investment, 1962–73

	USA	Japan	France	Germany[b]	UK
1962–67	15.4	n.a.	32.3	31.9	n.a.
1968–72	27.2	29.4[c]	31.8	33.8	5.2
1973	36.1	39.2	40.8	41.2	8.3

[a] Business borrowing is the difference between saving (including transfers) and fixed investment. Refers to non-financial corporate and quasi-corporate sector.
[b] Includes unincorporated enterprises.
[c] 1970–2.

Source: OECD, *National Accounts*, 1981, Vol. II

upward trend in government borrowing (table 11.12). On average the advanced countries were in rough budget balance. But governments failed to prevent the expansion of credit. They allowed the banking system to respond to demands from capitalists for credit at rates of interest which failed to keep up with inflation (that is, at declining 'real' interest rates). This helped to maintain the return on shareholders' investment. Even though investments earned less overall, by financing an increasing proportion through borrowing at declining real interest rates, capitalists helped maintain the profitability of shareholders' funds. In the United Kingdom, for example, between 1965 and 1973, the fall in the pretax rate of profit to shareholders was one-seventh, while the return on all capital employed fell by more than one-quarter.

Table 11.12 Government surpluses, 1965–73 (percentages of GDP)

	ACC	USA	Europe	Japan
1965–67	−0.4	−0.2	−1.2	0.8
1968–70	0.3	0.4	−0.6	1.8
1971–73	−0.3	0.0	−1.5	1.3

Source: see Appendix

With inflation eroding the purchasing power of accumulated savings, workers were obliged to save more of their incomes if they were to rebuild the value of past savings. So the extra credit funnelled through the banks was ultimately provided by workers.

In the fifties and early sixties the cost of imports had risen much more slowly than prices inside the advanced countries. But in the early seventies the cost of imported raw materials accelerated rapidly (chapter 12).

With workers attempting to increase their real incomes by militant wage bargaining, and capitalists attempting to maintain accumulation through extended borrowing, these higher materials costs could not be absorbed without a struggle. Employers passed the burden on to workers via higher prices.

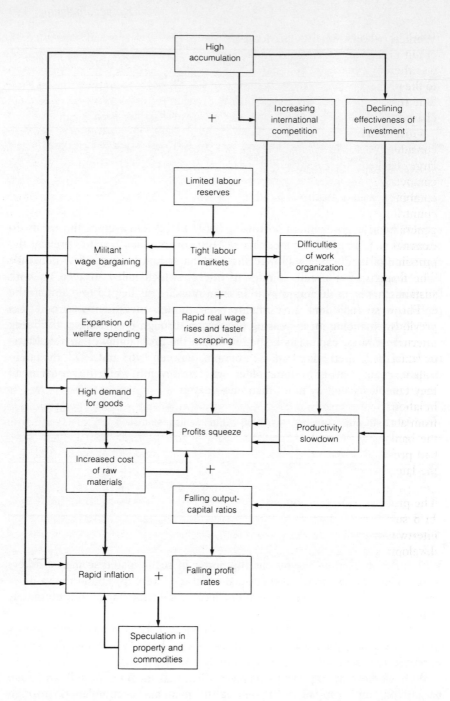

Figure 11.8 Overaccumulation.

Workers responded with higher wage demands. Governments permitted the credit expansion required to finance the higher price level. Part of the burden was thereby eventually eliminated as the prices of advanced countries' exports to the primary producers rose – reducing the deterioration in the terms of trade. The rest was shunted back and forth between capitalists and workers as wages chased prices and vice versa. The net result was further inflation.

Governments' credit policies were not constrained by international monetary considerations. The relative decline of US capital (chapter 10) was reflected in large balance of payments deficits as US goods became less and less competitive and war expenditures in Vietnam climbed. These deficits, combined with substantial outflows of capital, provided the other advanced countries with additional dollar reserves. So their credit policies were not generally held back by balance of payments considerations. And when the external account did pose a problem, governments often devalued rather than pursuing deflationary policies to the extent that would have been necessary. The floating of the pound in 1972 symbolized this turnaround in favour of sustaining expansion regardless of the inflationary cost.

The acceleration of US inflation relaxed the constraint on price rises, previously provided by the linking of other currencies to the dollar. And where internal inflationary pressures were stronger than in the United States, devaluation was used to push the constraint aside. Countries with lower inflation rates resisted revaluation as this would reduce export profitability. So they tended to have chronic balance of payments surpluses, which stoked up inflationary pressure by maintaining high demand for goods. This came both from abroad and from borrowers at home, who could easily obtain credit from the banking system which was flooded with foreign cash. The United States had provided a reasonably stable inflationary ceiling up to the mid-sixties. In the late sixties it furnished a steadily rising floor.

The process of overaccumulation described in this chapter is complex. Figure 11.8 summarizes the various forces at work. The story of the unfolding and intertwining of these forces and of their interaction with other, less fundamental, developments is the subject of the next chapter.

12

Overheating

In the late 1960s most economic commentators believed that the long boom was permanent. Keynesianism seemed to have banished mass unemployment for ever and wage rises seemed as natural and regular as the tides. In the mid-1970s, by contrast, the mood became one of gloom and despondency. This chapter and the next tell the story of the series of 'shocks' that undermined the earlier complacency.

Strike waves and wage explosions

A wave of strikes swept across Europe between 1968 and 1970. The May 1968 events in France triggered a three-week general strike. Next year Germany and the Netherlands were drenched by waves of wildcat strikes, and Italy sweated through a Hot Autumn of industrial unrest. In the United Kingdom the Wilson government's incomes policy broke down in 1969–70 in a 'winter of discontent'.

The strikers won big wage increases, around twice those of the preceding years (table 12.1). These gains were all spearheaded by settlements negotiated to conclude key strikes: the Grenelle agreements of May and June 1968 in France, the agreement between IG Metall and the iron and steel producers in September 1969 in Germany, the metal-working agreements of December 1969 in Italy, and the public sector settlements of winter 1969–70 in the United Kingdom.

The phenomenon was confined to Europe. The United States and Canada did experience more industrial unrest in the early seventies than in the fifties and sixties, and money wages rose faster. But the shift began earlier and was far more gradual. The number of strikes in Japan did not noticeably increase.

Within Europe the experience was remarkably uniform. The strike waves took place at around the same time and all won major wage increases. Many strikes were headed by groups of workers who had previously been fairly quiescent. Many were in white-collar jobs, often in the public sector. Often the

Table 12.1 The European wage explosions, 1965–70

	Strikes[a]	Money wage[b]	Real wage[b]
France			
1965–67	2,569	5.8	2.9
1968–69	76,000[c]	11.0	5.4
Germany			
1966–68	147	5.6	3.3
1969–70	171	12.0	9.2
Italy			
1966–68	10,761	6.9	4.3
1969–70	29,356	11.3	7.3
UK			
1967–69	4,774	6.9	2.4
1970–71	12,265	12.0	3.9

[a] Thousands of days occupied in strikes, annual averages.
[b] Average annual percentage change during the years shown.
[c] Kendall's estimate (1975, p. 365).
Source: Allsopp, 1975, table 3.4

workers were unorganized, or organized only weakly. The strikes were sparked off by the rank and file, most were unofficial, and often they were resisted at the outset by national trade union leaderships. So they should be seen essentially as a unified development.

They also marked a watershed in industrial relations, showing clearly that the consensus had failed to unite divergent class interests. Since 1968–70 there have been more strikes than in the fifties and sixties, and more of them have been unofficial. The wage explosions also had an immediate economic impact: by jacking up costs they squeezed profits further and boosted inflation.

So the industrial turbulence of these years is important. But why did it happen?

At first glance it looks like a straightforward consequence of overaccumulation (chapter 11). Europe as a whole was booming by the late sixties. As we saw, labour markets were tight. Accumulation could be maintained only if wages rose and scrapping accelerated. Otherwise there would be a shortage of workers to operate newly installed machines. So faster wage rises were needed if the system was to function smoothly.

The effective full employment also provided the mechanism to push up wages. By tilting bargaining power towards labour, it encouraged big pay claims. Capitalists resisted, which was an instinctive response, but also a rational one. Real wages had to rise somewhere if less efficient plant was to be scrapped and the labour shortage contained. But it was clearly to any one firm's advantage if somewhere was elsewhere. Workers backed up their claims with strike action. And they won, because employers could not find substitute labour and because, with demand for commodities high, they lost heavily from any interruptions of production. Capitalists were forced to concede the wage rises which for the system as a whole were needed to sustain accumulation.

Actually the situation was more complicated. The money wage increases which workers won exceeded those required to generate enough scrapping to ease labour shortage. The result was not only an increase in real wages but also a higher rate of inflation. And the strike waves did not all occur in particularly tight labour markets. Those in Germany, Italy and some smaller countries did, but those in France and the United Kingdom did not.

The wage explosions were certainly a product of overaccumulation in a general sense: more or less full, and rapidly expanding, employment during much of the long boom was a necessary backdrop. It bred a new generation of workers with no memory of mass unemployment. But to go beyond this general observation we must examine the pattern of accumulation since the late fifties.

Europe underwent a sustained boom from the mid-fifties through to the early sixties. Prices and wages accelerated upwards and wage explosions occurred in Germany in 1961–2 and in Italy and France in 1962–3. Balance of payments difficulties followed in Italy in 1963, France in 1964–5 and Germany in 1965–6. The profit share fell sharply from 1960.

As we argued in the previous chapter, this profits squeeze fundamentally reflected overaccumulation. Labour markets became very tight and money wages rose rapidly. Firms were unable to pass these increases on fully in prices because of international competition. The US economy was stagnant with fairly stable prices, and its export prices dominated those for world manufacturing. The formation of the EEC in 1958 also saw substantial tariff reductions by member countries which increased competitive pressure on their industries. The fact that unemployment did not result prior to deflationary policies suggests that real wage rises did not exceeed those required to adjust scrapping to the pace of accumulation and labour supply.

Governments responded to the profits squeeze and loss of competitiveness by deflation and incomes policies. The Bank of Italy clamped down on monetary policy in 1963, generating a major recession in 1964–5. Unemployment jumped from a low of 2.7 per cent to a high of 4.3 per cent in 1966. In France, Debré's 1963 Stabilization Plan embodied deflation. Unemployment rose slowly from 1.4 per cent in 1961–3 to 2.7 per cent in 1968. The Bundesbank tightened monetary policy sharply in 1965. By mid-1966 unemployment in Germany exceeded vacancies for the first time since 1959. Deflation in the United Kingdom began with the 'July measures' of 1966 aimed at staving off a devaluation of sterling. Unemployment rose from 2.3 per cent in 1965 to 3.8 per cent in 1967.

The French government tried to negotiate a voluntary incomes policy with the unions in 1964. When this 'dialogue of the deaf' broke down the authorities imposed limits on the public sector. In Germany the unions cooperated with the 'concerted action' programme initiated when the SPD entered the government in 1966. This involved long-term contracts and ceilings on increases. The Italian government did not attempt an incomes policy, but it did persuade the metal workers, whose settlement traditionally sets the pace for other sectors, to postpone the renegotiation of their three-year contract from 1965 to 1966. The British Labour government introduced a statutory incomes policy in 1966. A six-month freeze was followed by six months of 'severe restraint'. Further stages operated until 1969.

Incomes policies are often presented as a preferable alternative to deflation since inflation can be reduced without higher unemployment. But the real success of either policy depends, from the employers' perspective, on the extent to which real wages are held down and the potential profitability improved. Holding down money wage increases can reduce both inflation and real wage rises, as lower cost increases enable employers to raise profit margins where competition is weak. But in reality the two approaches more often go together. Incomes policies aim to persuade workers to accept lower money wage increases; deflation aims to weaken their bargaining position, and so offer them no choice. The threat of deflation as the only alternative to incomes policy is also more powerful when supported by a taste of the deflationary medicine.

Employers also launched an offensive on working practices and plant-level bargaining machinery. In Germany and Italy this shows clearly in cuts in plant-level wage supplements. In France it seems mainly to have taken the form of rationalization during a major merger boom. In Italy it also involved a major intensification of work. In the United Kingdom it took the form of productivity deals aimed at eroding shopfloor control over working practices.

These developments occurred against the background of a temporary relaxation of international competition. The US economy had moved into the Vietnam boom and its export prices had begun to rise significantly. This helped European capital to hold down real wages by raising prices. The policies were successful. The fall in both the share and rate of profit was reversed in 1966. Profitability then rose until 1969.

But resentment built up among workers. Deflation, incomes policies and attacks on plant bonuses held down wages. Incomes policies eroded differentials, and trade union action was limited by long-term contracts. The employers' offensive worsened job conditions and hamstrung plant-level union representatives.

The strike waves were the delayed expression of this resentment. In Germany and Italy better conditions for a fight back were provided by a tightening of labour markets in the boom of the late sixties. But British and French workers did not have to wait for an economic upturn.

The students' revolt provided the catalyst in France. The French working class also has a tradition of sudden quasi-general strikes. It struck in this way in 1953 and in 1936. Finally the workers who had suffered most were in the public sector, where incomes policy had held wage growth well below that of elsewhere. Most of the early strikers were state employees.

Public sector workers played a similar role in the United Kingdom. Incomes policy had been applied more rigorously in the state sector there too, and the winter of 1969–70 saw the novel spectacle of group after group of public sector workers rejecting settlements negotiated by their leaderships. The strength and traditions of the British labour movement are the other key factors. Shop stewards would lead unofficial disputes even in a downturn, confident that management would not dare attempt victimization.

The attacks of the mid-sixties also explain the wildcat nature of the strikes. Many trade union leaderships had become enmeshed in participation in incomes policies and arrangements for long-term contracts. The employers' offensive was also, almost by definition, at plant level. It was to be expected that resistance would begin here too.

There is also a rough correlation between the groups most hit by the austerity measures and those in the vanguard of the strikes. Public sector workers in France and the United Kingdom have already been mentioned. The other prominent group in the United Kingdom was motor industry workers, who had also borne the brunt of the attack on shopfloor organization and working practices. In Italy unskilled migrant workers from the centre and south both suffered most and fought back most tenaciously.

The wage explosions were the price of industrial peace. In France, they also bought political stability.

We have so far stressed the similarity of strike waves. But it is worth looking at two major examples in more detail to get a flavour of those heady days.

Italy's Hot Autumn

Italy is particularly interesting. The Hot Autumn marked a greater shift in the balance of power between labour and capital than occurred elsewhere. Before 1968 Italian unions were very weak. Their membership was low and they had failed to organize the immigrants from the centre and south who increasingly provided the majority of semi-skilled and unskilled labour in the industrial north. The unions had almost no influence on the factory floor and were ineffective in collective bargaining. They were divided politically into communist (CGIL) and non-communist (CSIL) federerations. But since the beginning of the seventies the semi-skilled became highly organized. Shopfloor bargaining became standard in large plants and effective national negotiations became the norm. The two federations have worked together fairly closely.

The Hot Autumn also marks a greater turning point in economic performance than occurred elsewhere. Only the United Kingdom economy performed as badly during the seventies and it has always been near the bottom of the league. Italy, on the other hand, underwent an 'economic miracle' during the fifties and sixties. The shift in the balance of forces reflected in the wage explosion of 1968–70 was almost certainly the chief factor behind Italy's worse performance in the 1970s. Indeed, the story of Italian economic policy in the seventies is largely one of attempts to adapt to or reverse this shift.

The Italian labour movement suffered enormous defeats in the late forties (chapter 6) and the trade unions remained ineffective throughout the fifties. Membership figures are unreliable but suggest that no more than 10–15 per cent of the work force was unionized. More reliable data for the metal workers, the most powerful sector, show only 20–25 per cent unionization. Almost all negotiations were at industry or national level, and ineffective. Agreements on conditions at work were either disregarded by employers (for example the 1950 national agreement on dismissals) or used to undermine links between trade union representatives and employees (for example the 1953 National Agreement on Works Councils which made these, and not union structures, the official plant representatives for employees). Industrial agreements on minimum wages were imposed by employers' confederations, dominated by small firms, which set them 'at rates which employers could afford to pay' (Kendall, 1975 p. 164).

Fiat allocated housing to employees on the basis of 'managerial judgements of the worker's union affiliation, politics and docility. . . . [For] some time Fiat systematically transferred all known members of FIOM, its CGIL metal workers union, to a particular plant which was shortly afterwards shut down. . . . If there are Communists in a man's family, he is not hired. . . . There are no doubt exceptions, but some such policy is commonly found throughout Italian industry' (Edelman and Fleming, quoted Flanagan, et al., 1983, p. 512). Tough measures were encouraged by the United States, which threatened to withdraw contracts from companies with CGIL majorities on works councils.

It is hardly surprising that real wages rose less rapidly than productivity and hence that profitability and competitiveness improved. Nor is it surprising that the accumulation of capital was accompanied by an accumulation of employee grievances.

An opportunity for some of this pressure to vent itself was provided in the early sixties. Italy shared in the European boom of the period and the consequent general tightening of labour markets. In the key northern industrial region of Lombardy official unemployment fell to 1.7 per cent in 1962 and 1963. This strengthened labour's hand. Workers could now press for improvements. The government could have clamped down at an early stage with tough deflationary policies. But it pursued accommodating policies at first and did not deflate until 1964.

The Chistian Democrats wanted an alliance with the Socialists. They had consistently failed to push through reforms when governing alone. They were also losing votes to the left: in 1948 the Christian Democrats received 49 per cent of the votes while the Communists and Socialists together polled 31 per cent; by 1963 the Christian Democrats' share had fallen to 38 per cent and the

Socialists and Communists' had risen to 39 per cent. Finally, the Socialists had become more acceptable to the Christian Democrats because they had begun to distance themselves from the Communists after 1956.

The Socialists' price for the deal was a redistribution to labour. The Christian Democrats paid up by accommodating the wage explosions. The governor of the Bank of Italy – a Christian Democrat and strong supporter of rapprochement with the Socialists – relaxed monetary policy during the strike wave to 'permit' the wage rises of 1962 and 1963.

The big wage increases were led – not for the last time – by the metal workers, who concluded a new agreement late in 1962. Manufacturing money wages skyrocketed, with national rates rising by 10.7 per cent in 1962 and 14.7 per cent in 1963, accompanied by significant wage drift.

Since manufacturing productivity rose by only 2.9 per cent a year between 1962 and 1964, this implied some combination of higher inflation and lower profitability. With world manufacturing prices growing at less than 1 per cent a year, international competition prevented much passing on of higher unit labour costs. So labour's share in the value of manufacturing output rose from 72 per cent in 1960 to 80 per cent in 1964. Profits and international competitiveness suffered accordingly. Neither the government nor the employers were prepared to accept redistribution on this scale. Both tried to reverse it.

The government deflated sharply in 1964 and unemployment began to rise steeply, reaching 5.4 per cent in 1965. This severely weakened the unions. Nationally, this can be seen most clearly in the poor settlement achieved by the metal workers. Their three-year agreement was due for renegotiation in 1965. But the employers persuaded them to hold off until 1966, when they settled for a mere 5 per cent rise over the three years to 1969. National no-strike agreements were also concluded for continuous process industries.

Weakness at plant level was reflected in sharply negative wage drift in 1964 and 1965. Employers also took the opportunity to launch an assault on working practices.

> If one reads the union press; if one follows case histories of individual factories, one obtains the impression of a general intensification of the work process, which came in different ways and used different methods: reduction in labour-time on a particular machine operation; supervision of an increased number of machines; increased assembly line speeds; spread of incentive payments systems; increase in heavy and onerous work loads. (M. Salvati, quoted Flanagan et al., 1983, p. 519).

These policies achieved quite a lot: 'By 1966 businesses had begun to re-establish profits through policies which aimed at reducing unit costs. The method most frequently applied was an increase in assembly line speeds unaccompanied in general by a proportional increase in wages. Similar changes were observed in almost all the factories studied' (M. Salvati, quoted Flanagan et al., 1983, p. 519). Unit labour costs fell by 2.3 per cent in 1965 and 1.9 per cent in 1966.

Labour's share of manufacturing output fell from 80 per cent in 1964 to 76 per cent in 1968. International competitiveness rose: between 1961 and 1963 Italian export prices rose by 1.2 per cent relative to the EEC export price index; between 1964 and 1968 they fell by 5.4 per cent. The key role played by intensification is indicated by the sharp increase in manufacturing productivity achieved during the downturn. Between 1962 and 1964 output per head rose by 5.8 per cent; between 1965 and 1967 it rose by 19.6 per cent, despite a lower rate of accumulation in the latter period.

This improvement in Italian business performance was once again only achieved at the expense of a powerful buildup of shopfloor grievances. As the general secretary of the CISL put it, 'In the years 1965–66, especially, a process of rationalization in the industries caused serious tensions to arise and was the cause of a new awareness of the problems of working life, this process having taken the form of a balance of forces highly unfavourable to the worker' (Reggio, quoted Flanagan et al., 1983, p. 520).

These grievances were to find expression in the strike wave that occurred once economic conditions improved. This happened in 1968. Italy shared in the general European boom of the late sixties and, as labour markets tightened, the balance of industrial power tilted towards the workers. Resistance began in spring 1968 but developed only slowly. Commentators spoke of Italy's 'creeping May'. It was to take a year and a half to build up the momentum for the Hot Autumn. A milestone on the way was the onset at Pirelli in the summer of 1968 of an avalanche of wildcat strikes. Another was a dispute at Fiat in spring 1969.

A number of important changes took place over the 18 months. One concerns the workers taking part. Grievances were felt particularly strongly by migrant workers who bore the brunt of the hardship because they were almost completely unorganized. They also suffered most from the centre-left government's failure to push through reforms – in particular, its failure to modernize the badly overstretched social infrastructure in the northern cities to which the migrants had flocked.

At the beginning the immigrants' lack of experience and poor organization hampered mobilization, and so other workers struck first. The spring 1968 strikes mainly involved older, skilled workers. The Pirelli strike was started by printers, and the Fiat dispute was led by skilled, indigenous northern workers. The young migrants first became heavily involved in the winter of 1968–9. Student activists and dissident trade union officials initially played an important role, formulating and popularizing demands. But by the autumn of 1969 the migrants dominated events.

Workers also developed new tactics. At first, industrial action took the form of short strikes – the unions' traditional weapon since the early fifties (although by the spring of 1968 the level of picketing and violence was unusually high). Later more imaginative tactics were adopted to try to achieve maximum disruption for a small loss of earnings. All-out strikes gave way to 'spot strikes', rolling strikes' and 'go slows'. Favourites were 'confetti strikes', where different workers struck for a set period at a time determined by the last digit or colour of their registration cards. Picketing gave way to marches through factories, when workers would chase blacklegs and occasionally kidnap managers. Public sector workers tried to hit at the state with minimum disruption of services to consumers. So ticket collectors would strike while train drivers worked normally.

Workers' relationships with the trade unions also changed. The unions were initially caught on the hop, because the disputes arose on the shop floor where few if any formal union representatives worked. The strike committees which mushroomed from the summer of 1968 did so outside whatever trade union structures existed (although individual union activists played a key role). The trade unions did not respond to events in a unified way until the summer of 1969.

When they did, they centred their national claims around the four basic demands coming from the shop floor. These were for higher wages, reduced differentials, greater workplace control and more shopfloor participation in bargaining. They also worked hard to channel shopfloor activity through new plant-level union structures. They demanded, and often won, access to factories for trade union officials. Workers would sometimes carry the officials, who had previously been barred from entry, shoulder-high through the gates The unions then organized massive workplace meetings to discuss national claims – something unknown since the immediate postwar period. Two or three thousand such meetings were held.

The metal workers' agreement of December 1969 was the key breakthrough on pay and conditions. It included a flat-rate increase of 65 lire an hour (nearly 10 per cent of average hourly earnings), a progressive reduction in weekly working hours to 40 by 1972, equal treatment of blue- and white-collar workers when sick, and overtime limits with compensation for lost earnings. It required for the first time, shopfloor ratification. It also broke the dam for other sectors.

Another crucial agreement was the 1970 Workers' Charter. This removed all obstacles to union activity at plant level and granted time and facilities. I formed the basis for the development of plant-level bargaining in the big factories, which was to characterize the Italian economy throughout the seventies.

May 1968

Unlike the steady build-up in Italy, the French general strike of May–June 1968 was wholly unexpected.

On 22 March 1968 students at Nanterre University formed the Mouvement du 22 Mars during an occupation over the state of higher education. This new organization united the previously fragmented student left. On 2 May the dean closed Nanterre indefinitely, saying, 'There is a strange climate in the faculty . . . a very real war psychosis' (quoted Posner, 1970, p. 64). Communist Party leader Marchais denounced the students in these words, 'The pseudo-revolutionaries of Nanterre and anywhere else labour in vain, they will change nothing of historical reality' (quoted Posner, 1970). The authorities evidently felt less sanguine. They ordered 500 riot police (CRS) to surround the building.

Next day the rector of the Sorbonne summoned police to a student protest against the closure of Nanterre. The CRS fired tear-gas canisters and arrested 600 students. The Sorbonne and science faculty were closed. The National Union of University Teachers called a protest strike.

On 6 May the CRS broke up a 60,000-strong demonstration by students and teachers in Paris. Over 700 demonstrators received treatment in hospital. Students erected barricades and strikes began to spread throughout the universities and high schools. The second largest trade union federation, the CFDT, supported the students. The largest, Communist Party federation, the CGT, did not. The next day the Communist Party denounced the demonstration as the act of pampered adventurists.

On 8 May a student demonstration in Marseilles was attended by a large number of workers. The next day the CGT in Dijon supported a student demonstration, against the instructions of head office.

On Friday 10 May students occupied the Latin quarter of Paris and built 60 barricades, which were violently attacked by the CRS. Twenty of the thirty Paris *lycées* were now on strike, and over 350 were occupied nationwide. The trade union federations called a general strike for 13 May to protest at government repression.

The strike was a major success. Demonstrations were the largest since the war. The CGT failed in its attempt to separate worker and student contingents. The CRS withdrew from the Sorbonne, and students occupied the building, decking it out with red flags and a barrier proclaiming 'Labourers and workers are invited to come and discuss their common problems with the university students'. It became the headquarters and shop window of the movement. Students' action committees began coordinating demonstrations and contacting workers' organizations. Immediate relations were established with workers at Renault, Citroën, Air-France, Rhône-Poulenc and the Paris metro.

On 14 May workers at Sud-Aviation in Nantes locked the director in his office and occupied the plant. Broadcasting workers voted to strike in protest at media coverage of events. By the end of the day almost all universities were occupied or on strike, as were many hospitals.

On 15 May CFDT leaders shared a platform with students at Sorbonne. Prime minister Georges Pompidou said that 'groups of enragés [roughly "rabid extremists" – the term used to describe the extreme left in the French revolution of 1789] are encouraging the spread of disorder with the aim of destroying society . . .'. Students adopted the slogan, 'Nous sommes de plus en plus enragés'. By then all the Renault plants had been occupied and students and workers held joint meetings to plan future action at Renault and Sud-Aviation. The CGT was rapidly losing control of even its most loyal factories.

By 17 May all air traffic had been halted and the Post Office workers had struck. Many occupied factories were organizing crèches and discussions for local residents. In the Loire-Atlantique region distribution had broken down entirely. Students, workers and peasants formed a joint committee to organize supplies. The police trade union warned that its members were close to striking. Students set out on a 'Long March' across Paris from the Sorbonne to the Renault works. Despite CGT opposition they were warmly received. By the next day the railways were paralysed and Paris bus stations, metro lines and post offices had been occupied. The actors' trade union demanded the right to decide democratically on what plays to perform. French film makers broke up the Cannes festival in solidarity. Radio journalists took control of news bulletins. The CFDT called for democratization of industry.

The government set up Committees for the Defence of the Republic. Extreme right-wing groups offered support in exchange for the release of imprisoned right-winger, General Salan. A public opinion poll showed 55 per cent support for the students and 60 per cent for a 'new society'.

On 19 May Socialist Party leader Mendès-France demanded the resignation of the government. De Gaulle announced, 'Les réformes oui, le chienlit [untranslatable army vulgarity] non!' Students adopted the slogan, 'Le chienlit, c'est lui!' Strikes now covered all transport, nationalized industries, metals, banking and public services.

Next day all mines and ports closed, Michelin and Peugeot workers struck and the non-union work force at Citroën occupied the plant. CGT secretary Séguy announced that he was not concerned with such 'vacuous ideas as workers' control, reform of society and other inventions'. Rather, 'going the whole hog means a general rise in wages, guaranteed employment, an earlier retirement age, reduction in working hours without loss of pay, and defence and extension of such trade union rights in the factory'. But the CGT technicians' section came out in support of the students for workers' control.

By 21 May 10 million workers were on strike. The employers association headquarters was occupied. Young magistrates formed a union and voted to establish an independent judicial system. The government withdrew facilities for independent radio stations.

On 24 May police stations were sacked and the stock exchange was set alight. Police attacked bystanders and Red Cross workers. The largest peasant demonstrations in French history took place. Workers at the right-wing newspaper *Le Figaro* refused to print an article by sociologist Raymond Aron unless he had 'more respect for the facts'.

Next day the government began negotiations with trade union leaders. The Socialist Party's François Mitterrand demanded elections. On 26 May the left made big gains in local elections in Dijon.

On 27 May the government, the employers and the CFDT and CGT concluded the 'Grenelle agreements', embodying a 10 per cent across-the-board wage rise, an increase in the minimum wage, a small cut in working hours and a marginal extension of trade union rights. Up and down the country factory meetings debated the agreements and rejected them overwhelmingly. The Loire-Atlantique CGT left the federation, declaring that 'the struggle is not economic but political'. The CFDT then refused to sign the agreements and called for intensification of the strike movement.

The government halted the distribution of petrol and the Committees for the Defence of the Republic began distributing arms. De Gaulle left the country for Baden-Baden to consult with French army commander General Massau, who agreed, in return for the release of General Salan, that the army would support any legal government but would not intervene openly unless the Communist Party called for insurrection. In reporting what little was known about these discussions at the time, the *Economist* warned of 'the danger that some as yet unknown army officer, drumming his fingers in some provincial headquarters, will decide that enough is enough' (1 June 1968).

Meanwhile the communists refused to support the left's call for a transitional government headed by Mendès-France on the grounds that he was too closely associated with the new movement. The national news agency and the major publishing houses struck. The strike movement had reached its peak.

On 30 May pro-Gaullists were supplied with petrol for carefully organized massive demonstrations (1 million in Paris alone). Slogans included 'Cohn-Bendit [a German Jewish student leader] to Dachau'. Right-wing groups fired on left-wing demonstrators. De Gaulle dissolved the National Assembly, announced elections for 23 June and 30 June and formed a new government of similar complexion to the old.

Negotiations began in most factories. The CGT promised to respect any agreements reached. A despondent Renault worker remarked, 'It seems to me that we came very close to something new.' Close, but not quite close enough. On 7 June the CRS occupied the Renault plant at Flins after pitched battle. Two days later the exiled leader of the extreme French settlers in Algeria, George Bidault, returned to France. Many foreign students and workers were deported. On 11 June two workers were killed at Peugeot and a student at Melun. Several left-wing organizations were banned. On 15 June Salan was released. On 16 June the CRS took the Sorbonne. Next day Renault returned to work. On 20 June Peugeot went back and the first sackings of trade union leaders occurred. On 23 June the Gaullists took a big lead in the first round of the elections. One million workers were still on strike. On 30 June the Gaullists completed their election victory. France had returned to work and to bourgeois normality.

The underlying cause of the French general strike was the same as that of the other strike waves. France, like Italy and Germany, had experienced a wage explosion in the European boom of the early sixties. In 1962 and 1963 private sector wages rose by 10.8 and 11.1 per cent respectively and those in the public sector by 17.0 and 14.6 per cent. With prices rising by only 4.8 per cent in each year, this implied considerable real wage increases and a sharp fall in profitability. Since French prices were rising considerably more rapidly than those in the United States and Germany, it also implied a loss of competitiveness.

The 1963 Stabilization Plan was designed to restore profits and competitiveness. These policies were incorporated into the Fifth Plan, formulated in 1964 and 1965, which aimed at an annual rate of growth of profits of 8.6 per cent between 1964 and 1970. Planned wage growth was restricted to 3.3 per cent a year. After abortive negotiations on a voluntary incomes policy between October 1963 and January 1964, the government adopted four major policies towards this end.

One was deflation. Registered unemployment rose from 1.4 per cent in 1961–3 to 2.7 per cent in 1968. Another policy was control of public sector wages. The Toutée procedure, adopted in May 1964, fixed an aggregate figure for wage increases in particular sectors, leaving the distribution of the overall increase to be negotiated between unions and management. A third device was the use of 'contract programme' agreements negotiated with major companies. These covered pricing policy and the principle was that companies were allowed to raise prices sufficiently to rebuild profit margins, providing they gave certain guarantees on employment, exports, investment and wages. The agreements were confidential and their content unknown to the work force. By 1969 some 85 per cent of industry was covered by them.

The final policy was the encouragement of a major merger drive to promote rationalization. This was part of de Gaulle's attempt to modernize an industrially backward France – 'to make her marry her century', as he put it.

The policies were fairly successful. The rate of growth of real wages in the private sector fell to 3.9 per cent a year in 1965 and 1966, and 3.4 per cent in 1967. Public sector wages were squeezed tighter still, and in four years fell 9 per cent behind the private sector. The annual value of mergers more than trebled from a fairly stable trend in 1966 and 1967.

French inflation slowed to a rate comparable with that in Germany and the United States. Deflation hit productivity growth which slowed down somewhat. The share of profits in both manufacturing and business showed little change, despite lower capacity utilization. As in most deflationary periods, profitability did not rise immediately. But the potential for profitable production did improve, as the post-May 1968 expansion demonstrated.

This modest success was bought at the expense of mounting employee grievances. These included the slow growth of real earnings overall and, for public sector workers, the deterioration in their position compared to the private sector. The dislocations resulting from rationalization were also important. A government report, issued shortly after the May events, summarized their causes as: 'a failure to comprehend the resistance to change, to prepare the groundwork for unprecedented dislocation resulting from mergers, combinations, business failures and dismissals, which accompanies modernization. The changes on the labour market had come with greater rapidity than anticipated, too much reliance had been placed on the automatic adjustments, the mobility, of the market mechanism' (quoted Flanagan et al., 1983, p. 605). In this sense May 1968 was the price de Gaulle paid for his attempt at a shotgun wedding between French industry and the twentieth century.

Two main differences, besides the obvious ones of speed, scale and aspirations, distinguish the French strike waves from the Italian. One is the fact that, while in Italy a tightening of the labour market played a key role, in France the strike occurred in the context of the highest levels of unemployment and excess capacity since 1960. The other difference is that the Hot Autumn significantly altered both industrial relations and economic performance in Italy, whereas the altogether more dramatic French experience brought no comparable long-term changes.

The students' revolt was clearly important to the timing of events in France. This was closely linked to the accumulated grievances of the workers, being also largely a product of de Gaulle's modernization strategy. In the fifties university student numbers had risen from 135,000 in 1949 to 220,000 in 1960. In the sixties the pace accelerated: 520,000 enrolled in the autumn of 1967. This growth far outstripped the provision of facilities. In the academic year 1967–8 there were 30,000 too many students in Paris alone.

The government's response was a plan to replace the baccalauréat system, which guaranteed places to those obtaining certain qualifications, with one of competitive selection. The occupation at Nanterre which gave birth to the 22 Mars movement was to protest against this proposal. The government's repressive response played a role in building sympathy for the students. Workers would probably have been less inclined to support them if their protests had met with reasoned discussion rather than tear gas.

Finally, the structure and traditions of the French labour movement were important. Collective bargaining hardly existed under de Gaulle. Union membership fell rapidly to around half of the immediate postwar level. In 1968 only around 15 per cent of the work force was unionized. This did not reflect a few well-organized sectors and a larger number of unorganized ones as was the case in the United States, for example, where the average level of unionization was similar. In the private sector printing was the only heavily unionized industry. Unionization was high in the public sector but union activity was restricted to dealing with individual grievances and the empty version of wage bargaining embodied in the Toutée procedures. So employers and the government could virtually ignore trade unions if they wished. Under de Gaulle they opted almost unanimously to do so.

The low level of unionization did not simply reflect apathy or a lack of militancy. All companies with more than 50 employees were required by law to have enterprise committees elected annually by the work force (their function being largely consultative, with some responsibility for health and safety). In 1967 and 1968 turnout for these elections was around 75 per cent, with 80–90 per cent of the vote going to union candidates.

But the low level of unionization did influence the form of industrial struggle. It meant that major strikes almost invariably began from the bottom up and were largely outside the control of the unions. As one commentator put it, the unions 'functioned as skilled surfboard riders'. Strikes were often imitative, a few key factories providing a 'signal'. In 1968 that initiating role was played largely by the Renault and Sud-Aviation plants.

The chief reason why the May events failed to transform the industrial relations structure – let alone society as a whole – is the behaviour of the CGT and the Communist Party. The CGT was far and away the most powerful union federation. It had around three times the membership of the CFDT and received about half of the votes cast in enterprise committee elections. The Communist Party was a major force in French politics. We have already seen the role that these organizations played at key stages of the struggle.

The *Economist* described the situation vividly: 'Whenever one hears somebody on the French radio vituperating against "adventurers" one can be sure that M. Cohn-Bendit or some other leftist student is the target. But one cannot guess the political colour of the speaker. It might be a Gaullist or it might be a Communist. On the other hand, if somebody talks about revolution, structural changes or socialist society, one is safe in assuming he is not a Communist' (25 May 1968).

It also provided an astute analysis:

> *A revolution set alight by students, snuffed out by communists*
> A modern revolution requires the coincidence of a revolutionary situation and a party or organization ready to seize power. As France comes virtually to a halt, the situation might look revolutionary. But the party which has always claimed the revolutionary role now shows no signs of fulfilling it. The Communists have climbed on the bandwagon, but only to put the brakes on. This is not because they want to preserve General de Gaulle's regime. It is because they are using a revolutionary weapon – general and unlimited strikes – in order to achieve a parliamentary aim, the formation of a popular front government (*Economist*, 25 May 1968).

No one can be certain what would have happened if the Communist Party had tried to lead a revolution in May 1968. Indeed such a question is virtually meaningless. The Communist Party's behaviour was no sudden aberration. Its attempts to strangle the revolutionary movement at birth during May 1968 were consistent with the approach taken over the previous 30 years, including the immediate postwar period (part I). Two things are clear, however. Its strategy was an abject failure on its own terms, for the Gaullists romped home in the June elections. Secondly, by denouncing the CFDT's demands for industrial democracy and restricting negotiations to the traditional issues of pay and hours, the CGT ensured that the May events would have little impact on the future structure of industrial relations.

Clampdown and the 1970–1 recession

For the ACCs as a whole, both monetary and fiscal policy swung sharply towards restriction between 1968 and 1969. This picture is dominated by developments in the United States, but a definite shift towards restriction is observable elsewhere, prompted by the acceleration of prices noted above and by growing economic and social unrest.

The effect of this shift was a highly synchronized but relatively mild recession. Idle capacity rose by about 3 percentage points between the second halves of 1969 and 1971; rather more in the United States and Japan and considerably less in Europe. From peak to trough, registered unemployment rose from 3.5 per cent to 6.0 per cent in the United States and from 1.8 per cent to 3.0 per cent in Europe. Inflation peaked at 5.8 per cent in the United States in 1970. As a result of the recession and price controls it fell to a trough of 3.3 per cent in 1972. In the wake of the wage explosions inflation rose more in Europe. It reached 6.5 per cent in 1971 and thereafter hardly fell back.

Policy-makers felt general disappointment with the stubbornness of prices in the face of rising unemployment. The term 'stagflation' became common parlance and increasing doubts were expressed about the effectiveness of Keynesian 'fine tuning'.

The break-up of Bretton Woods

We left the fortunes of the international financial system and of the dollar with the 1968 decision – implemented in 1970 – to issue special drawing rights (SDRs) on the IMF (chapter 10).

This might have shored up the dollar for a time had the US balance of payments improved as expected. But it did not. The current account deteriorated as the trade balance shrank; business investment overseas doubled between 1965 and 1970. The situation was concealed in 1968 and 1969 as short-term capital was attracted to US banks by high interest rates: $12 billion flowed in during those two years, more than covering the long-term capital outflow. Simultaneously, foreign central banks' dollar holdings fell. But this policy was drastically reversed in 1970 when monetary policy became extremely permissive. The US money supply was allowed to grow at 10 per cent per year or more for the next four years, having been virtually unchanged in 1969. Predictably, the $12 billion 'hot money' left US banks as interest rates fell. Added to an already heavy outflow of long-term capital, the flight of dollars became a rout. In 1970 foreign central banks acquired $17 billion and the

United States lost $2½ billion of reserves. Reserve backing for the dollar deteriorated more in 1970 than during the previous decade.

In May 1971 the publication of figures showing a marked worsening of the US current account coincided with a further reduction in interest rates. Money flowed out of the United States into almost all OECD countries, but especially those with strong currencies – Germany, Switzerland, Austria and the Netherlands. Germany alone received $9 billion in 1970 and $4 billion in the first five months of 1971.

The countries receiving the dollars were largely powerless to do anything about it, despite their fears that credit would expand and inflation rise. The sums involved made it difficult to prevent the inflows from boosting the money supply by selling bonds, and in any case, if this were attempted it would only prevent interest rates from falling and keep the currency attractive to those anxious to get out of dollars. Initially many central banks made the best of a bad job by loaning the dollars to borrowers in Europe via the so-called Euromarkets, where a premium over US interest rates could be obtained. This stimulated the growth of these 'offshore' markets for dollar loans. The funds were often borrowed by speculators who then reinvested them in strong currencies in the expectation of revaluations, a hideous spiral by which central banks were providing funds to speculators who stood to make a profit from them if the currency was revalued.

In March 1971 central banks agreed to freeze the deposit of reserves on the Euromarkets. But speculative pressure continued and high demand for Eurodollar loans pushed interest rates on the market well above the usual 0.5 per cent premium on US rates. This in turn led to further withdrawals of dollars from the United States for deposit on the Euromarkets. Between April and June 1971 speculation against the dollar ran at an annual rate of $14 billion. A number of foreign exchange markets closed temporarily and hasty exchange-rate adjustments were made, with strong currencies being revalued or, as in the case of the Deutschmark, floated. This proved to be only a warm-up.

Action began in earnest in the summer. United States trade figures for the second quarter of 1971 showed a deficit for the first time. Between July and September hot money flowed out of the dollar at an annual rate of $35 billion. During the first two weeks of August non-US central banks began welshing heavily on their agreement not to convert dollar reserves into gold, and US gold reserves fell alarmingly. President Nixon, whose grasp of such matters was immortalized on tape in 'Well, I don't give a [expletive deleted] about the lira' (quoted Williamson, 1977, p. 175), responded on 15 August 1971 by suspending indefinitely the convertibility of the dollar into gold. He also introduced a 10 per cent surcharge on imports. For the next four months all major currencies floated.

After some hard bargaining, in December 1971 the major OECD countries signed the Smithsonian Agreement which established a new system of fixed exchange rates. The United States accepted a cosmetic increase in the price of gold following European insistence that it must be seen to devalue. But nobody seriously proposed the convertibility of the dollar into gold. Indeed, it was out of the question given the dollar's enfeebled position. The events of that year, combining as they did an enormous outflow of dollars (the overall deficit for 1971 of $30 billion exceeded by 70 per cent the cumulative total for the previous ten years) with considerable 'cashing in' of dollars for gold in the weeks preceding the suspension of convertibility, reduced massively the extent of potential gold backing for the dollar. At the beginning of 1971 US gold reserves had been sufficient to cover 32 per cent of foreign dollar holdings. Twelve months later they could cover only 18 per cent.

The further diminution of the role of gold amounted, then, to little more than a recognition of the existing situation. The main benefit to the United States of the Smithsonian Agreement lay in the new exchange rates which embodied a 9 per cent devaluation of the dollar in relation to other currencies compared with the pre-August rates and thus increased US competitiveness. This devaluation was much smaller, though, than the United States had wanted. During the negotiations the United States indicated that it was seeking a rate for the dollar that would yield a $13 billion boost to the US current account. This would give a current account surplus of $9 billion a year, enough to finance a capital outflow of $6 billion a year and to improve confidence in the dollar by reducing liabilities to central banks by $3 billion a year.

The United States continued with its permissive monetary policies and dollar outflows began to mount again in the second half of 1972. The crunch came early in the next year. The events of 1971 assume the proportions of a small-town poker game in comparison to the speculation of February and March 1973. In February the Smithsonian Agreement was seriously breached when the yen was floated (sterling had already been floated in June 1972). The dollar was also devalued by a further 10 per cent in recognition that the Smithsonian Agreement, hailed by Nixon as 'the most significant monetary agreement in the history of the modern world' (quoted Gilbert, 1980, p. 164), was insufficient to restore US competitiveness. This had been demonstrated by the rise in US imports of manufactured goods, which rocketed by 27 per cent in 1972 following a 20 per cent rise in 1971: 'it was evident that industry abroad was making major adjustments and marketing efforts to enlarge its share of the US market' (Gilbert, 1980, p. 105). Even this further devaluation failed to restore confidence as the US treasury secretary announced that the United States would not intervene to support the dollar and intended to remove all controls on capital exports.

On the single day of 1 March 1973, Germany absorbed $2.7 billion, and in the first quarter of 1973 as a whole the US reserve position deteriorated by $10 billion.

On 19 March the major central banks renounced the commitment to maintain their exchange rates within a band of $\pm$ 2.25 per cent with respect to the dollar. This constituted the formal abandonment of the second and, since the suspension of dollar/gold convertibility in 1971, the only remaining basic principle of the Bretton Woods system which was thus now dead.

Dollar devaluation

The determination of the US authorities to secure a substantial devaluation of the dollar against other currencies and consequent improvement of the US trade balance is beyond doubt. Whether their monetary policy from as early as 1970 was designed to force such a devaluation is another question. On the one hand, driving interest rates down would predictably lead to a dollar outflow. It has been argued that the form the expansion took – monetary expansion rather than tax cuts – is proof of this intention. On the other hand, the United States carried out a series of crisis measures apparently aimed at shoring up the dollar. In the last week before convertibility was suspended in 1971, $2 billion was borrowed by the United States from other central banks to try to hold the line. The United States certainly pursued a policy of 'benign neglect' towards the dollar, expanding the economy for domestic reasons with little regard to the effect on the exchange rate. By early 1973 it was clear that they would do little or nothing to protect the exchange rate from the impact of domestic policies, and indeed increasingly resented the attempts of European and Japanese central banks to prevent the dollar rate from finding its own level.

Such a position would be quite incomprehensible if the main thrust of US policy was an attempt to run as large as possible a balance of payments deficit (on current and long-term capital account) in order to grab real resources from the rest of the world in exchange for paper dollars. On the contrary, given the heavy and increasing rate of capital exports, which was a major priority for many of the dominating US multinationals, it was far better from the United States' point of view that these capital exports should be mainly financed by a current account surplus rather than by endless piling up of US liabilities abroad to foreign central banks. The return paid on these liabilities was certainly low (the short-term interest rate in real terms averaged 0.4 per cent over the years 1968–74). But the onslaught of European and Japanese competition made it far more important to attempt to maintain the position of domestic manufacturing industry with a lower exchange rate. This would help domestic industry to maintain both its market share and its profitability, as European and Japanese firms would be obliged to increase their dollar prices to compensate for a fall in the dollar against their currencies. Indeed, the huge capital exports by US business provided a 'justification' for the United States running a current account surplus and were used as such during the Smithsonian discussions over the size of adjustment of the exchange rate. This argument was to be repeated in succeeding years during discussions over reform of the international monetary system, in which the United States consistently held that balance of payments targets should be defined in terms of current and capital account combined.

So the United States 'needed' a current account surplus to finance its capital exports. The United States could, and did, also claim that it actually required a greater surplus than this so that it could begin to chip away at the huge 'overhang' of dollar liabilities with a view to restoring convertibility of the dollar to the SDR (special drawing rights) once confidence had been restored. The basic negotiating position of the United States, presented to the IMF in November 1972, was that countries should peg their currencies to the SDR, but that they would be obliged to devalue or revalue if their reserves fell below or rose above certain predefined warning levels. This was directly aimed at the 'surplus countries', especially Japan and Germany, and was an attempt to bind them into a system where they could not pile up persistent surpluses.

The surplus countries

The 'reserve indicator plan', as it was called, described above was never a very serious possibility. Under it, major changes in reserves would have created an overwhelming presumption that a change in the exchange rate was around the corner, and thus encouraged speculation on what was in effect a certain bet. But the significant point is that it underlines the United States' determination to prevent the persistent undervaluation of the mark or the yen. Such a concern is explained by the fact that these countries had repeatedly demonstrated their willingness to go to enormous lengths (in effect taxing imports of capital, encouraging exports of capital and, even in the case of Japan, organizing plans for importing huge stockpiles of raw materials) in order to prevent an upward movement of their currencies. If these countries felt they were being exploited by having to run a surplus and thus provide finance for the US deficit, such behaviour would be quite incomprehensible. On the contrary, their exporting sectors, extremely powerful in both countries, had a very strong interest in maintaining the exchange rate at a low level in order to generate the maximum possible export surplus. This was not primarily due to some old-fashioned desire to pile up reserves, however comforting that might be for central bankers and useful when it came to securing influence by making loans to weaker countries. The fundamental concern was rather their export sectors' immediate interest in sales of, and profits on, exports. Revaluation, while cutting the cost of living for workers as the price of imported goods fell, would reduce their ability to compete profitably abroad, especially in the American market if the revaluation was with respect to the dollar.

Although the Europeans and Japanese firmly resisted the reserve indicator plan, which would apply heavy pressure on surplus countries, they insisted that the United States should in effect reinstitute convertibility. 'From the US standpoint, the demand for dollar convertibility was simply the demand for an exchange value guarantee on the fiduciary instruments [dollars] that financed their deficits, while surplus countries retained their freedom to allow their surpluses to pile up' (Gilbert, 1980, p. 185). What they were not prepared to countenance was that 'the United States should redeem its unwanted dollars in goods, by undervaluing the dollar and thereby running a large and persistent export surplus: such a treatment was wholly unacceptable to export interests in Europe which would suffer the increased US competition' (Tew, 1977, p. 192). Precisely the same fear of revaluation underlay the continual reluctance of the German and Japanese authorities to see their currencies held as reserves by other countries. Quite simply, such an additional demand for the currencies concerned would help keep them at a higher level, with a consequent reduction in their export surpluses. Whatever prestige and influence might be gained by being a reserve currency was wholly insufficient to compensate for export profits being lost by overvaluation.

US competitiveness and payments

The successive downward movements in the relative value of the dollar brought a marked improvement in US competitiveness. The dollar fell by 24 per cent against the yen and Deutschmark between 1970 and 1973; against currencies on average (weighted by their importance in US trade) the fall was 15 per cent. Moreover, since unit costs actually rose less in the United States than in competing countries over the same period, the improvement in US cost competitiveness was actually 27 per cent on average. In dollar terms, unit labour costs in manufacturing rose in the USA by 6 per cent, in Japan by 72 per cent and in Germany by 64 per cent.

This improvement in competitiveness undoubtedly contributed to arresting the deterioration in the US balance of payments. For several years after 1972 the level of net imports of consumer goods stabilized. Net exports of capital goods doubled between 1972 and 1974 (assisted by strong demand from the oil producers). As demand for food rose, the United States suddenly became a major exporter of agricultural goods, the surplus on that account rising from $1½ billion in 1972 to $10½ billion in 1974. A large surplus would have resulted but for the $20 billion rise in the cost of oil imports as the OPEC price increases coincided with – indeed, were encouraged by – rising US oil imports (chapter 13). Even though the current account was back in surplus in 1974, it was not nearly enough to cover the outflow of capital, and the result was that dollar liabilities rose by nearly $9 billion.

The story of the US balance of payments during the break-up of the old international monetary system is summarized in table 12.2.

Despite the huge amount of interest received (nearly $9 billion a year), there was on average over the period hardly any current account surplus. To the long-term capital outflow of $42 billion had to be added a new element, a short-term capital outflow of $22 billion, as foreign firms and individuals either withdrew their cash from US banks or increased their borrowing from them.

Table 12.2 US balance of payments, 1968–74 ($ billion)

Merchandise trade	−9.3
Services and remittances	−10.2
Net military transactions	−19.8
US government grants (ex. military)	−16.7
Net interest and dividends received	61.4
Current account balance	5.4
Direct investment (net)	−42.2
Investment in shares and bonds (net)	10.8
Government loans	−11.1
Long-term capital	−42.5
Balance on current and long-term capital	−37.1
Dollars held abroad by private sector[a]	−22.5
Financed by	
Dollars held abroad in official reserves	58.1
Reduction in US reserves	1.5
(of which gold)	(2.4)

[a] Includes net short-term capital.

Source: US Government, *Survey of Current Business*, June 1982.

The total outflow of some $60 billion was financed by increases in the reserves held by the central banks of the industrial countries.

Of course, no foreign central bank was compelled to hold a single additional dollar – indeed, they could have unloaded part of their existing holdings. When they could not get gold for their dollars after 1971 (the US gold stock fell by only $2½ billion over the whole period), they only acquired these dollars because they were prepared to sell their own currencies in order to prevent them rising further. The reason why they maintained these holdings in dollars, rather than selling them for some other currency, was that dollar investments in New York remained attractive despite the decline in the relative value of the dollar in the early seventies. In 1974 the reserves of the industrialized countries stopped growing, while simultaneously the reserves of the OPEC producers shot up by $31 billion. Most of these reserves were held in the Eurodollar market, which meant that rather than deposit them in New York the central banks of the oil producers deposited them in banks outside the United States. Many of these were the overseas branches of US banks which made a healthy margin in acting as the go-betweens between the OPEC members, who wanted to lend dollars, and the countries with balance of payments deficits which wanted to borrow them.

US capital undoubtedly benefited from its ability to borrow via foreign central banks' holdings of dollar securities. Between 1967 and 1974 net US receipts of profits and interest rose from $5.3 billion to $15.5 billion. In contrast to the preceding period, none of this rise can be attributed to the investment of current account surpluses. A substantial part of the increase certainly represented increased profits in money terms on the existing stock of US industrial investment abroad. But a substantial part must also have resulted from the new investment overseas which was now being wholly financed by borrowing overseas at a very low real rate of interest. Shorn of all element of compulsion, now that the United States was no longer even pretending that the dollar was convertible into gold, the rise in official holdings of dollars showed that dollars were the best asset to hold. The United States was reaping the benefit of its industrial and financial might without having to resort to any crude use of political power.

When the issue of international monetary reform had been seriously debated in 1972 the United States started from the position that 'the system should neither bar nor encourage official holdings of foreign exchange', suggesting that 'the United States still thought of the SDR as providing a substitute for gold rather than for the dollar' (Williamson, 1977, p. 176). Although the United States accepted the case for the dollar eventually being convertible into SDRs, in its view this had to result from the dollar being sufficiently competitive to generate enough capital and current account surpluses over a period to make convertibility a reality. The European (and Japanese) unwillingness to accept this is shown at a theoretical level by their refusal to accept proposals which would have required revaluations, and in practice by their preparedness to pile up dollar reserves.

The Europeans suggested that the IMF should convert their existing dollar holdings into SDRs. This would protect the holdings against a future decline of the dollar, but at the cost of pushing the risk on to the United States if it were required to compensate the IMF (which would take over these dollar holdings) for any losses. This was simply keeping their cake (dollars earned by running of vast surpluses through refusal to revalue) and eating it (obliging the United States to guarantee the value of the assets they accumulated via these surpluses). There has never been any reason why the United States should accept this type of proposal. Limiting the size of US deficits by forcing revaluations (as in the US proposals for a 'reserve indicator plan' in the context of fixed exchange rates) or making official statements that the dollar is too high (the 'open-mouth policy', subsequently implemented on occasion under floating exchange rates) is quite consistent with the dollar maintaining an international role. Such a role, which inevitably involves the dollar's use as a reserve currency, is the product of US industrial and financial power, and was hardly eroded by the end of dollar convertibility and of the fixed exchange rate system.

The 1972–3 mini-boom

1972 and early 1973 was a period of very rapid growth throughout the world capitalist system. Between the first halves of 1972 and 1973 output rose by 7 per cent and industrial production by 10 per cent. This 'mini-boom' had three distinctive features, which culminated in an unprecedented rise in commodity prices:

- It was highly synchronized, occurring in all major capitalist countries it about the same time.
- It was very rapid. Although the *level* of capacity utilization reached at the height of the upswing was lower than in the previous boom (and so the extent of 'overheating', as conventionally measured was less), the *rate* of expansion was faster than at any time since 1958–9. Moreover, capacity utilization was considerably lower when the previous upswing had begun than it was at the start of the mini-boom of 1972–3.
- It had a greater impact on prices than previous upswings of comparable magnitude. Inflation for the system as a whole, which had fallen to 4 per cent a year in the first half of 1972, rose to an annual rate of 7 per cent in the first half of 1973.

The reasons for these characteristics are complex and interrelated.

The *synchronization* happened when most governments simultaneously moved from a tight monetary and fiscal stance to expansion. US fiscal policy was expansionary in 1970 – it gave some tax relief and additional transfer payments to households – but this stimulus was subsequently eroded by rising tax bills. Elsewhere fiscal policy was generally expansionary in 1971 and 1972. This was enormously reinforced by monetary developments. The opening years of the 1970s were a period of easy money. In the ACCs, the money supply began to accelerate at the beginning of 1970. It grew by 12 per cent in 1971 and slightly more in 1972. Short-term interest rates halved between early 1970 and early 1972.

The expansionary policy of nearly all governments resulted from three main factors. First, the synchronized nature of the 1970–1 recession meant that governments found themselves simultaneously at a similar, recessionary phase of the cycle. Traditional Keynesian fine-tuning criteria for output and employment thus suggested expansionary policies for each country at around the same time. Second, the enormous increase in international liquidity generated by the exodus from the dollar (see above) meant that the countries which still had weak payments balances could borrow easily. Finally, an unusually large number of major elections took place in 1972. There was a presidential election in the United States, and elections for the principal legislative assemblies in Canada, Germany, Italy and Japan. Taken together, these economies produce about 70 per cent of OECD output. Electoral considerations prompted 'give-away' budgets and hence expansionary policies.

The *speed* of the upswing was largely the result of the scale of monetary and fiscal stimulus given to the system as a whole. This, in turn, was chiefly the result of two main factors. First, the high degree of synchronization. The fact that other economies are expanding adds an external stimulus to any internal impetus provided by reflation. The degree of reflation 'required' will therefore tend to be overestimated by governments in a synchronized upswing, if they rely on past experience derived from periods of less international synchronization of business cycles.

Second, the exodus from the dollar created more expansionary monetary conditions than would otherwise have been adopted by some governments. Here we can distinguish two broad groups of countries. One consists of those for whom the expansionary repercussions on domestic liquidity of balance of payments surpluses, resulting from dollar inflows, did not exceed the degree of stimulus felt desirable. The United Kingdom, Italy and, initially, France, fall into this category. For these countries, the *scale* of expansion was not affected by the dollar crisis (although the *form* may have been – the 'automatic' nature of the monetary expansion generated by dollar inflows may have bred a more monetary, and less fiscal, policy mixture than would otherwise have been adopted, and thus contributed to the easy money regime).

The other group consists of countries for whom the deterioration of the US payments balance and the inflow of speculative funds generated a faster rate of monetary expansion, and lower interest rates, than would have been adopted on purely domestic criteria. In Japan expansionary monetary policies were adopted in 1972 to offset the expected deflationary impact of the Smithsonian yen revaluation and, later, to reduce the still large payments surplus achieved under the short-lived Smithsonian regime. In Germany the maintenance of a fixed, and clearly unsustainable, exchange rate in the face of massive speculative inflows rendered domestic monetary management virtually impossible from the late 1960s to March 1973 when the Deutschmark was floated.

The rapid acceleration of prices was the result of the interaction of a number of developments. In contrast to the last fillip to inflation in Europe provided by the wage explosions at the close of the sixties, this price acceleration clearly began in goods, rather than labour, markets. Indeed, wages only began to catch up and threaten a widening wage/price spiral in 1973. The very speed of the upswing helped to push up prices because bottlenecks developed, the prices of those goods rose and 'feed-through' effects followed. But the major inflationary impetus was provided by the conjunction of two factors.

First, low profits (and their failure to rise during a rapid upswing) led to and combined with poor business confidence. Firms reacted to the expansion of demand by raising prices, as well as expanding output, in order to try and raise profit margins. Because low profits also militated against the use of available funds for productive investment, investors were encouraged to search for short-term speculative 'killings'.

Second, the existence of very slack monetary conditions (mainly because of the dollar crisis discussed above) led to negative real rates of interest. In principle, this made profitable the speculative holding of stocks of goods whose price rose only at the average rate. More significantly, in practice it encouraged speculation in the more traditional sense – on assets whose prices were expected to rise by considerably more than the overall price level (and would indeed do so if enough speculators made similar judgements). Initially, this speculative money found its way into fairly traditional havens. The London gold price rose two and a half times between early 1972 and the middle of 1973. New house prices rose by around 50 per cent in the United Kingdom between early 1972 and early 1973. The price of developed building land in Germany rose by more than one-third between 1970 and 1972.

If speculation had been restricted to these traditional fields then the effect on the overall price level would probably have been relatively insignificant, since the feed-through effects to other goods would have been modest. But it was not. The prices of another, broader category of goods began to rise faster than the general price level and attracted enormous sums of speculative funds. The result was the commodities boom and a major upward twist to inflation.

The commodities boom

Prices on the major US and UK commodity exchanges began to rise very rapidly in 1972 and maintained the pace through 1973. In 1973 and 1974 this price rise fed through to contracts between major producers and users. The magnitude of the increase was very similar, with both types of prices more or less doubling relative to the prices of manufactures. No rises of this scale had previously been recorded in peacetime.

There are a number of reasons why primary product prices should have begun to rise in real terms around this time. On the supply side, there had been underinvestment in many areas of primary production for some years. This was the result of the expectations of inadequate and wavering returns, because of gently deteriorating terms of trade between primary products and manufactures, and fear of investing in politically volatile, or potentially volatile, Third World countries. There had also been a long-term rundown of producer stock levels, especially of US grain buffer stocks. Finally, specific short-term shortages arose in the early 1970s, the most important being the 1972 crop failures (when grain output was down 3 per cent on the previous year, against a trend growth rate of 3 per cent a year). Anchovies – an important source of protein for animal feed – also mysteriously disappeared from the Peruvian coast around this time.

On the demand side, the effects of the rapidity of the synchronized upswing were reinforced by the materials processing sector responding less rapidly than others. User stock levels were also historically low as a result of steady improvements in stock control techniques and expectations of relative price falls (as a result of the previous trend deterioration in the terms of trade for primary products). Finally, materials stockpiling was encouraged by the Japanese government in 1972–3 in an attempt to hold down the yen exchange rate.

Taken together, these factors were sufficient to generate commodity price rises considerably in excess of the general rate of inflation. This attracted speculative funds. Many commodity markets are institutionally well suited to speculation, having developed facilities for buying crops before they are harvested (futures markets) for small down-payments (margin trading). This speculation pushed prices up further.

There is no way to measure the significance of speculation in the commodities boom. But it must have been considerable. The scale of price rises is quite out of line with that which could plausibly be required to balance 'real' supply and demand; and quite out of line with previous responses to fluctuations in industrial production.

We know that speculation was rife in this period, for example in currencies, gold and real estate, and a number of highly publicized incidents took place in commodities markets. The tendency of official commentators, such as the OECD, to play down the role of speculation is totally unconvincing.

The above discussion does not distinguish between different primary products or markets. This reflects the fact that the commodities boom was highly generalized, and therefore unlikely to have been a freak coincidence of very different developments in different markets. But it is nevertheless worth looking at one market in some detail – that for grains. This market is quantitatively the most important (after oil, which is discussed separately in chapter 13), and is well documented. Moreover, it was the acceleration of food prices – largely as a result of developments in the grain market – which, of any (non-oil) commodity price rise had the greatest overall effect on inflation.

The grain market

Grain is big business, in more senses than one. In 1975 around 160 million tons were traded internationally for about $50 billion. Before the war the volume of grain exported seldom exceeded 30 million tons a year. So growth of trade had been rapid. Production for the international market is concentrated in the most powerful capitalist state: the United States accounts for around 50 per cent of world grain exports. Finally, the trade is dominated by a handful of the world's largest – and most secretive – multinationals: Cargill, Continental, Louis Dreyfus, Bunge and Andre. Frank Church, chairman of the Senate Sub-committee on multinational corporations, has said of these companies, 'No one knows how they operate, what their profits are, what they pay in taxes and what effect they have on our foreign policy – or much of anything else about them' (quoted Morgan, 1979, p. ix). Cargill boasts in its company brochure that 'some of our best customers have never heard of us' (Morgan, 1979, p. 4).

During the Second World War, the United States operated a 'bare-shelves' policy towards grain stocks, fearing a repeat of the price crash which followed the First World War. But this approach was rapidly changed in the reconstruction period. Enormous bonuses and premiums were offered to farmers.

Between 1945 and 1949 the United States provided one-half of world wheat exports. Nevertheless persistent surpluses became a problem from 1948 onwards. The strength of the farm lobby prompted the US administration to operate a price support system. Internationally it entered into a *de facto* cartel agreement with Canada, whereby export prices were kept low enough to discourage new producers.

In the 1950s, the main way of disposing of the surpluses was as 'aid'. Public Law 480, passed in 1954, gave governments cheap credit when they bought US grain, initially repayable in domestic currencies. (The United States built up huge rupee balances which it eventually wrote off.) At first, one-quarter of US wheat exports and one-fifth of rice were financed under PL480. By 1959 four-fifths of wheat and nine-tenths of soya bean oil exports were paid for in this way.

In the 1960s policy moved away from PL480 towards boosting commercial exports. The United States broke the unofficial cartel with Canada and tried to shoulder her out of markets. From 1964 onwards US wheat prices were subsidized enough to undercut all comers on world markets.

In the late 1960s almost all major exporters began to cut back production, apparently believing that surpluses would otherwise become unsustainable. World food output had grown steadily in the fifties and sixties (except in 1965 and 1967, after Indian droughts). Prices were stable and stocks mounting. The prospects for the 'green revolution' appeared good. There was talk of India soon becoming a grain exporter and she discontinued PL480 shipments in 1971 because of shortage of storage capacity.

So the four big wheat producers (United States, Canada, Australia and Argentina) all offered large subsidies in return for acreage reductions. Their combined wheat production fell from 80 million tons in 1968 to 60 million in 1970.

In 1971, however, the USSR indicated to the United States that it was interested in regular grain purchases. The United States responded enthusiastically, offering credit (which the Russians had not asked for) and 14 million tons were sold, initially at heavy cost to US taxpayers who subsidized the export price.

Between 1971 and 1975 the global grain trade grew by nearly 50 per cent in volume, most of the increase coming from the United States. Their farm exports rose in value from $7.6 billion in 1971 to $17.6 billion in 1973, and grain stocks fell from 23.5 million tons in the middle of 1972 to 7 million tons one year later. The price rises wiped out the need for farm subsidies. The companies did particularly well. Cargill's after-tax profits rose from $19.4 million in fiscal year 1971–2 to $150 million in fiscal year 1972–3. Dreyfus paid its top trader a 'special bonus' of $1.2 million and two underlings $0.75 million each. The only losers in the United States were workers faced with higher food prices.

End of an era

The mini-boom marked the end of an era. It was the last upswing before the onset of slump, stagnation and mass unemployment. So we shall briefly stand back and assess its significance.

Many of its effects are fairly obvious and generally acknowledged. Most commentators agree that the rapid price acceleration played an important role in generating high inflationary expectations, which remained remarkably resilient even under later conditions of mass unemployment. It generated further disillusionment with fine tuning and, indeed, with Keynesianism in general. This contributed towards the shift in policies of the late 1970s and early 1980s. The easy money regime focused attention on monetary policy and contributed to the significance accorded to the money supply in later years. And high demand for basic inputs including oil provided an important condition for the 1973–4 oil crisis (chapter 13).

Conventional discussion of the breakup of the boom and its underlying causes are generally inadequate. The most influential view is that expressed by a report for the OECD, which sees the intensifying economic difficulties of these years as resulting from 'an unusual bunching of unfortunate disturbances unlikely to be repeated on the same scale, the impact of which was compounded by some avoidable errors in economic policy' (McCracken, 1977, p. 14). The 'unfortunate disturbances' are the breakup of the Bretton Woods system and the commodities boom, while the 'errors in economic policy' refer primarily to the 'all systems go' monetary policy which so many countries adopted in 1971 and which 'was the most important mishap in recent economic policy history' (McCracken, 1977, p. 51).

This account is at best naive and at worst apologetic for the behaviour of the Organization's largest member – the United States. For the 'unfortunate disturbances' were in no sense 'random shocks' and the easy money regime was only in part a policy preference. The break-up of the Bretton Woods system, at the time and in the form in which it occurred, to a large degree forced an easy money regime on the rest of the system, and thereby fuelled the speculation that in turn fuelled the commodities boom. The commodities boom also affected the major capitalist powers in different ways. Commodity exporters, including the United States, benefited from the boom. Major importers, most notably Japan, were worst hit. The most obvious manifestation of this was a substantial reduction in the US payments deficit, a corresponding reduction in the Japanese surplus, and an increase in the deficit of a number of European countries. As the next chapter shows, the subsequent oil price rises were also to hit Germany and Japan much more heavily than the United States.

13

Oil and the Crash of 1974

The mini-boom of 1972–3 proved to be the final and most feverish phase of the long postwar boom. The 'oil crisis' of winter 1973–4 and an international crash in the summer of 1974 brought the golden years to an abrupt and painful halt.

The oil crisis

In October 1973 war broke out in the Middle East. The conflict bred solidarity among Arab oil states and gave a new impetus to the Organization of Petroleum Exporting Countries (OPEC), a cartel of the major non-US oil producers which had previously been rendered ineffective by internal divisions.

In an attempt to reduce support for Israel, OPEC announced a 10 per cent across-the-board cut in oil exports (later briefly raised to 25 per cent) and a selective embargo, directed chiefly at the United States. The oil companies dutifully followed OPEC instructions to the letter.

> When they were told to cut production, they did so without quibble. When Aramco was told to cut production by 10 per cent and then, on top of that, shut in liftings equivalent to that which had been produced for ultimate sale to the USA in pre-embargo months, the company dutifully cut production back 23 per cent below September levels. When the Saudis insisted that Aramco impose tight control over the destination of its oil, the company got tanker captains to sign affidavits as to their destination and arranged to receive cabled acknowledgements of each ship's eventual arrival at the approved port or terminal. (Turner, 1983, pp. 135–6).

Exxon even acceded to a Saudi request to provide information on their supplies to US military bases worldwide.

The selective embargo, however, proved ineffective because the companies transhipped oil from one destination to another, spreading the cutbacks equally. Despite widespread fears to the contrary (see below), the cutback in supplies of some 5 million barrels a day, or 9 per cent of non-Eastern bloc output, caused few lasting problems. But its effect on spot oil prices – which skyrocketed – was used by the producers to justify a general price rise.

OPEC succeeded in imposing and maintaining a major increase: oil prices quadrupled during the winter of 1973–4, raising the oil producers' annual revenue by around $64 billion.

This price rise occurred in the context of restrictive policies, rapidly decelerating output and double-digit inflation. Restrictive policies were introduced in all major countries in 1973 in response to the price acceleration of the mini-boom and the large wage claims that were beginning to be submitted in its wake. The measures were largely monetary: the annual rate of growth of the ACCs' money supply fell from 14 per cent at the end of 1972 to 8 per cent at the end of 1973; short-term interest rates rose from 4 per cent in early 1972 to 10 per cent in mid-1973. Fiscal policy also moved towards restriction, with the important exception of the United States: in Europe and Japan, policy became more restrictive to the tune of around 1½ per cent of GDP.

ACC real GDP growth fell from an annual rate of 8 per cent in the first half of 1973 to one of 3 per cent in the second half of the year (though the latter figure was reduced by output losses resulting from the oil embargo). Unemployment began to rise in the autumn of 1973.

Materials and food prices began to drift downwards from the summer of 1973. But world inflation rose to an annual rate of 10 per cent in the second half of the year as previous materials price rises fed through to final goods markets.

The oil price rise worsened profitability and reduced demand. It raised input costs, thereby tending to reduce profitability and intensifying the pressure on industry to raise prices (much fixed capital could no longer be operated profitably at existing output prices). It also transferred, at a stroke, 1½ per cent of world purchasing power to OPEC. The recipients did not, and in the short run simply could not, spend the majority of their extra revenue. So world demand fell.

These pressures were intensified by the introduction of yet more restrictive policies: monetary conditions were further tightened in most economies in the spring of 1974. Nevertheless, inflation rose for some months, and production continued to grow in all major economies except the United States during the first half of 1974. In part this resulted from increased opportunities for exporting to the periphery. The commodities boom had increased many less developed countries' (LDC) export earnings, and imports rose with some lag. A number of non-oil-producing LDCs borrowed unspent OPEC reserves, channelled through the ACCs' banks.

The oil price rise reactivated the boom in commodity prices and boosted inflation, which reached an annual rate of 15 per cent in the spring of 1974.

Many accounts of the 1970s present the oil crisis as *the* key development. OPEC is often cast as a super-villain, holding the world economy to ransom for political motives and disrupting an otherwise smooth pattern of growth. It is true that the oil crisis dealt an important blow to the functioning of the system and had a major impact on the form and timing of the crisis – constituting a trigger for the crash which separates the period of overheating from the subsequent one of mass unemployment and stagnation. But this picture is nevertheless misleading in two important ways.

First, it seriously underplays the extent to which the system was in severe difficulties before the oil price rise. The basic problems – overaccumulation in relation to the labour supply and sharp decline in profitability – preceded the oil crisis and would not have evaporated in its absence. Nor is there any reason to assume that the system would have adjusted smoothly to the onset of overaccumulation had the oil crisis not occurred. The feverish character of the mini-boom hardly augured smooth adjustment.

Second, it ignores the extent to which the oil crisis had its roots in previous developments. The Middle East war which prompted the actions of OPEC was, of course, itself a product of the economic and political history of postwar capitalism. But there are more direct economic connections. For one thing, it is doubtful if OPEC could have successfully imposed the price increase at the time it did in the absence of the high levels of demand that accompanied the mini-boom. In addition, the dollar devaluations worked to encourage a price rise, because most oil was priced in dollars which were being eroded in value.

Furthermore, OPEC would almost certainly have been unable to sustain massively higher prices in the context of the subsequent crash had US policy towards oil imports not changed dramatically in the seventies. Throughout the sixties the United States limited imports of oil and petroleum products by law (the legislation was enacted in 1959 to bolster the dollar). Until 1970 the United States was 90 per cent self-sufficient in energy. The policy was then radically reversed. In 1971 price controls on domestic production were imposed and the legislation limiting imports was repealed. Oil imports soared in 1972. In August 1973 a two-tier pricing system was introduced: the price of oil from wells already functioning in 1972 was fixed at a maximum of $4.35 per barrel; oil from wells begun in 1973 or later and oil imports were exempted from the price ceiling. Following the OPEC price rise, the oil companies preferred not to work pre-1973 wells very intensely. This preference was reinforced by the announcement that the controls were temporary. In 1976 the imposition of price controls on natural gas led to further substitution of oil imports for domestic energy sources.

The net result was that the United States moved during the 1970s from being 90 per cent self-sufficient in energy to importing 50 per cent of its needs. By the end of the decade it was importing 8–9 million barrels per day, or about 30 per cent of OPEC output. This cost some $40 billion a year before the 1979 oil price rises. Although the United States is the single largest exporter to OPEC (supplying about 15 per cent of its foreign purchases), its deficit with those countries largely accounted for its overall trade deficit in the second half of the seventies.

Finally, the price rise was a product of the boom in a more general and fundamental sense. The tremendous increase in oil consumption which accompanied the great burst of accumulation threatened to deplete reserves: by the early seventies considerable disquiet was expressed about the possibility of the 'depletion horizon' of known reserves being reduced below the conventional level of 25 years' supply. These worries were reinforced by the influential Club of Rome's 1972 report *Limits to Growth*, which popularized the notion that the world was running out of essential materials and fuels, including oil. BP's exploration manager argued that oil production would peak in the early 1980s and that demand would outstrip supply by 1978. Within the industry it became a commonplace to point out that the discovery of 'a Libya a year' would be required to maintain the depletion horizon. A major price adjustment was needed to encourage both energy-saving and exploration.

The above account of the effects of the oil price rise applies to the system as a whole. But the impact varied considerably across industries and countries.

The most important division between industries is that between the oil companies and the rest. Whereas the bulk of industry faced higher costs and a squeeze on profits, the oil majors had a profit bonanza. Returns on their operations rose from $3.9 billion in 1972 to $12.1 billion in 1974. Those on investments in OPEC increased from $2.6 billion to $6.1 billion over the same period. Chase Manhattan estimated that the worldwide rate of profit for leading oil companies rose from 9.7 per cent in 1972 to 19.2 per cent in 1974 and 24.0 per cent in 1979.

When viewed in the context of other changes in the industry, however, the oil price rise appears more of a mixed blessing for the seven major oil companies. The rise of OPEC brought changes in ownership and operation as well as in price. Direct exports by OPEC national oil companies rose from a negligible proportion of production within the area to some 50–55 per cent over the course of the 1970s. Host government ownership of oil production in OPEC rose from some 2 per cent in 1970 to 60 per cent in 1974 and 80–90 per cent in 1980. By the end of the decade the majors had secure ownership rights to crude oil only within the OECD area.

Despite the boost given by the price rise to exploration and production, OECD oil output rose only from 5 million barrels a day in 1973 to 6.3 million in 1980, providing only 35 per cent of the seven majors' refining needs. Furthermore, OECD governments also began to demand an ownership stake in production. The share of world refining accounted for by the majors fell from 51 per cent in 1973 to 38 per cent in 1980.

The differing impact of the price rise on consumer countries is exemplified by comparing Japan with the United States.

Japan is almost entirely dependent on oil imports for all its basic energy requirements, having no fossil fuel deposits. So the oil price rise enormously increased its import bill. The additional exports required to earn the extra foreign exchange constituted a drain from domestic incomes. Since this deduction would have to come from either wages or profits, it worked to intensify distributional struggle and to reduce the rate of accumulation. In addition, the larger cost in foreign exchange worked to increase balance of payments constraints and hence to reduce the room for manoeuvre over domestic economic policies. For Japan, then, the 'oil shock' was a major blow without mitigating benefits.

The United States fared differently. For a start, the oil companies are predominantly US-owned. Furthermore, the USA's large oil reserves allowed it, unlike its major rivals Germany and Japan, to be self-sufficient in oil. In addition, the two-tier pricing system allowed US domestic industry to purchase oil well below world market prices (some 40 per cent below in the first half of 1979). This obviously gave it a competitive advantage. Finally, in a longer-term perspective, the United States possesses enormous energy reserves in the form of shale oil and bituminous schists. The development of these was not remotely economically viable at pre-1974 oil prices. The 1979 round of oil price rises made extraction more or less economically feasible. Shale extraction could make the United States self-sufficient in oil for the foreseeable future, thus eliminating dependence on foreign supplies, which has increasingly worried the Pentagon.

So, while the oil crisis caused major difficulties for the system as a whole, its impact – like that of the commodities boom and the dollar crisis – was uneven. The United States suffered less than its major rivals.

The crash

A major crash began in the summer of 1974. ACC industrial production fell by 10 per cent between July 1974 and April 1975. In the first half of 1975, ACC output was 3½ per cent down on the level of a year earlier, and international trade was 13 per cent lower. For 1975 as a whole, output was marginally lower than in 1973 (1½ per cent lower in the United States and some 1½ per cent higher in Japan). The previous worst postwar two-year period ended in 1958, with output 4½ per cent higher than in 1956. The crash of 1974 was far and away the biggest since 1929.

Most economic crashes are kicked off by a collapse in investment, especially in inventories, and this one was no exception. So any explanation of why it started must focus on the collapse in investment. In the long run, investment is closely tied to profits. So the underlying cause of the fall in investment is the decline in profitability. But that does not explain the precise timing. Profits had been falling for some years; investment collapsed suddenly in summer 1974.

Capitalists invest because they hope to make profits. So the level of investment depends on expectations about future profitability. These expectations will usually be heavily influenced by past profits, but they are not the only consideration. A host of factors shape capitalists' confidence in the future. The loss of confidence in the mid-1970s is usually put down solely to the oil crisis. Although this was an important factor, accounts which focus on it too narrowly are unsatisfactory.

Confidence is in one sense a delicate psychological state. Once it has been shattered, it is hard to re-establish, as we tried to show when discussing the origins of the boom. But confidence, like trust, is also fairly robust. Once firmly established, it tends to justify itself, as we tried to show in the section on the strength of the boom. It then takes a major blow to fracture it. The oil crisis alone could not have shattered the confidence which capitalists felt during most of the golden years. The blow was so crippling because confidence had already taken quite a few knocks. And even then, it did not produce an immediate crash.

Over the previous few years capitalists had been hit by the European wage explosions and a general worsening of industrial relations. They had experienced the break-up of the Bretton Woods system and increasing international financial uncertainty. Inflation had accelerated and commodity prices had gone through the roof. Profitability had fallen by one-third and the fast and highly synchronized boom of the previous couple of years had failed to restore it.

Worsening expectations had not yet led to a collapse in investment, however. They had brought a modest decline in the face of extreme boom conditions, but no collapse. Their most obvious effect had been a massive increase in speculation as more capitalists tried to make money by wheeling and dealing rather than by productive investment: hence the huge foreign exchange dealings and the booms in share prices, gold, land, real estate and commodities. The acceleration of inflation, the soft monetary stance of the authorities and the commodities boom all worked to boost stockbuilding.

The oil crisis undermined confidence further. Initially, worries centred on securing supplies in the face of the cutback and selective embargo. Most governments, having projected a fall in supplies of around one-fifth for 1974, rushed through emergency legislation to economize on the use of oil. In December 1973 the oil companies claimed that OPEC had cut supplies by 17½ per cent.

There was a run on all major stock exchanges. Prices on Wall Street fell by 5 per cent a week in November. The gold price soared again, shooting up by nearly one-fifth in the first week of 1974. The *Economist* commented, 'For years the gold enthusiasts have been regarded as barbarians. Now that it is fashionable to talk of the imminent collapse of civilization, their day has come on Wall Street' (16 February 1974). It described the mood in Japan as one of 'considerable panic'.

From January 1974 the oil once more began to flow freely. There was a mild stockbuilding boom, probably to make up for dislocations over the winter, and commodity prices took off again. Worries now shifted to the higher prices and to what became known as the 'recycling problem'.

It was clear that OPEC would be unable to spend much of its new revenues and would lend massively on international financial markets. Many countries would also need to borrow heavily to pay for oil imports. The problem was that OPEC was likely to lend mainly in US markets whereas the potential borrowers were concentrated in Europe and the Third World. There was widespread scepticism about whether private financial institutions could successfully channel funds from lenders to borrowers, and general agreement that the IMF should play a major role.

Italy soon found difficulties in borrowing, as the *Economist* described:

Another sign of possible 1929-style international financial crisis is upon us. Eurobankers are beginning to be chary of lending to the nationalized industries and state authorities of even big countries in balance of payments deficits. Italy seems to be coming close to that point of no return; it is rapidly exhausting its reserves of international goodwill as well as its reserves of foreign currency. Where Italy is being given a cold shoulder today, could other deficit countries with particular political problems – a Mitterrand France, a Wilson Britain, a post-Franco Spain, a Denmark with a parliament of all-sorts – be jilted tomorrow? (20 April 1974).

The chances of the IMF organizing a major recycling programme were poor. At the time of the Smithsonian Agreement the Group of Ten – the leading central bankers – had announced that discussions would begin promptly on a new long-term monetary reform. After US obstruction, a Committee of the Board of Governors of the IMF was eventually set up for this purpose late in 1972. It had 20 members. British finance minister Barber remarked that reaching an agreement would only be twice as difficult in the new forum as in the old. Little was achieved.

Revelations of the Watergate affair, which dominated the world's media in spring 1974, did not help. The country with the largest single vote in the IMF, the largest recipient of OPEC funds and the key issuer of international money was being run by a president whose attentions were more and more focused on saving his own skin. Meanwhile doubts about the private banks' ability to cope caused mounting worries.

While recycling dominated economic discussions, developments elsewhere were hardly comforting. Output was decelerating, inflation rising, and governments everywhere (except the United Kingdom) deflating sharply. Commodity prices tumbled in May 1974, led by copper and given a push by official Japanese encouragement to firms to sell stocks to improve liquidity. A crash in share prices, which was to prove greater than that of 1929, was well underway: between September 1973 and September 1974 they were to fall by between 23 per cent in Japan and 55 per cent in the United Kingdom. With consumer prices rising by some 15 per cent over the period, the fall in the real value of the shares was considerably greater. Real share prices in the United Kingdom fell to the level of the wartime blitz.

The international banking system began to crack. On 26 June Germany's largest private bank, the Herstatt, collapsed as a result of speculative foreign exchange losses. US banks, which also lost heavily, were furious with the Bundesbank for refusing to compensate them. The German commercial and central banks refused to bail out Herstatt and many depositors lost money.

The ramifications were enormous. The international banking community was so nervous that for a while no forward foreign exchange markets operated properly anywhere. The lion's share of all foreign exchange dealing was restricted to a few New York banks, who refused to deal with many smaller banks and with most French and Italian ones. The volume of foreign exchange transactions plummeted (figure 13.1). Money was moved out of small banks all over the world. The *Economist*'s assessment of the mood six weeks later was that 'the first whiff of even a false rumour is liable to cause a run' (3 August 1974). But by then the crash had already started.

It is hard to explain why confidence broke precisely when it did. Searching for the elusive final straw is not a very fruitful activity. So it would be a mistake to place too much emphasis on any one event, such as the Herstatt collapse. All that can sensibly be said is that, given everything capitalism had gone through over the previous few years, a collapse of confidence was to be expected at some point.

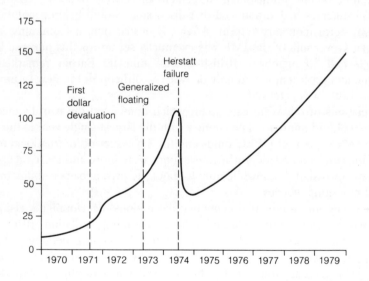

Figure 13.1 World foreign exchange trading volume, 1970–9 ($ billion per day). *Source*: UNCTAD, 1981, *Trade and Development Report*, chart 14.

The resulting slump left a considerable proportion of productive capacity idle. By the autumn of 1975 around 11 per cent of fixed capital was gathering dust. Registered unemployment in the ACCs rose from around 8 million at the end of the mini-boom to about 15 million in the spring of 1975. Even this increase is a severe underestimate of real job loss: participation rates fell sharply, underemployment rose and the number of migrant workers in Europe fell by over a million.

Two other developments generated concern at the time. One was the maintenance of high inflation rates despite the collapse of output. Minerals and metals prices fell by 30 per cent between May 1974 and the end of the year. Food prices fell by 33 per cent between November 1974 and June 1975. But, while inflation slowed from the summer of 1974, prices as a whole continued to rise at an annual rate of 10 per cent during the depths of the slump. Inflationary expectations and processes had become extremely stubborn.

The other development which caused consternation was the beginning of large public sector deficits. Government revenues fell as the slump reduced taxation yields, while public spending rose as unemployment benefit payments rocketed. If governments had not run such deficits then the slump would have been far deeper, since the deficits worked partially to offset the collapse in demand which resulted from the big increase in OPEC savings and fall in investment. Nevertheless, obsession with the size of public sector borrowing requirements began at this time.

The most important effect of the crash, however, received less attention at the time – a further collapse in profits. In the two years 1974 and 1975 the profit rate fell by as much as in the previous five (table 13.1). By 1975 it was only 60 per cent of the 1968 level. The fall was significantly smaller in the United States, where capital was hit less hard by the oil price rise. In manufacturing industry by 1975 the profit rate had fallen to only half of its 1968 level (table 13.2).

Table 13.1 Business profit rates, 1968–75 (percentages)

	ACC	USA	Europe	Japan
1968	19.3	17.1	18.8	30.8
1973	15.4	13.2	16.0	21.6
1975	11.7	11.0	11.4	14.5

Source: see Appendix

Table 13.2 Manufacturing profit rates, 1968–75 (percentages)

	ACC	USA	Europe	Japan
1968	26.8	28.8	17.4	52.8
1973	21.9	22.0	15.4	38.8
1975	13.1	16.2	8.8	15.2

Source: see Appendix

The large increase in the price of oil – an important input into production – and the sharpness of the subsequent crash made inevitable an immediate fall in the rate of profit. The worsening of the terms of trade for the ACCs, largely as a result of the oil price rise, reduced the resources available for profits and wages by around ½ per cent of output per year. The crash also brought a slight decline in productivity. A prerequisite for the profit share being maintained was a fall in real wages of about 1 per cent a year between 1973 and 1975. In the event, high inflation and sharply rising unemployment worked to halve the rate of growth of real wages in comparison to the previous five-year period (the effect was particularly marked in the manufacturing sector in Europe and Japan). But real wages were not cut. So the profit share fell. The crash also pushed down the output-capital ratio, by an average of one tenth, as excess capacity mounted. The combined result was a sharp decline in the profit rate.

This further sharp decline in profitability, following on that of earlier years, and taking profits to levels well below those which had come to be expected during the boom, is the key to the sustained sluggishness of accumulation in the latter half of the 1970s and the early 1980s. This sluggishness is in turn the key to the mounting unemployment of those years.

PART III

Coping with the Slowdown, 1974–

14

The Great Slowdown

The outstanding feature of the period since the postwar boom collapsed in the ACCs in 1974 has been the slowdown in the growth of production. This final part of the book is concerned with describing and analysing the reasons for and implications of the great slowdown. This chapter outlines the facts of the slowdown and examines the general stagnation of productivity and rising unemployment, especially in Europe, together with the phenomenon of de-industrialization. It shows that just as the overaccumulation which precipitated the slowdown was the product of a sustained period of rapid growth and high demand for labour, so it took some ten years or so of slow growth to twist the balance of power back to capital. Even then the recovery of profitability was uneven and the response of investment was hesitant, especially in the manufacturing sector most exposed to the increasingly harsh and decreasingly predictable pressures of international competition. Moreover, the period of slow growth and reduced opportunities for productive investment led to an increasingly fragile financial system. Governments borrowed more to maintain demand, consumers increased their indebtedness to keep living standards rising despite stagnant real incomes, and banks and industrial corporations engaged in ever more sophisticated financial manipulations in order to try to generate rising profits for shareholders.

The basic figures for the slowdown are set out in table 14.1. Over the whole period since 1973 growth in the ACCs has been at hardly more than half the rate of the sixties and early seventies. The slowdown was greatest (absolutely and relatively) in Japan and least in the USA. If the OECD economies had grown as fast after 1973 as in the previous period then their output in 1989 would have been nearly 40 per cent higher. The extra goods and services available would have been roughly equal to the entire output of the USA. An important focus of this and subsequent chapters is the question of who has borne the impact of this slower growth.

The period since 1973 comprises two cycles of recession and recovery. In response to the crash, governments in the major countries introduced

Table 14.1 The growth slowdown 1960–89 (average annual percentage growth rates of total output (GDP))

	1960–73	1973–89	1973–75	1975–79	1979–82	1982–89
USA	4.0	2.6	−0.8	4.1	−0.1	4.0
Europe	4.7	2.2	0.7	3.4	0.9	2.7
Japan	9.6	3.9	0.7	5.1	3.7	4.3
OECD	4.8	2.7	0.1	3.9	0.8	3.6

Source: OECD, *Historical Statistics* and *Economic Outlook*

expansionary tax cuts and spending increases early in 1975. But the recovery that developed was (except in the USA) slower than the *average* growth rate of the sixties. The further doubling of oil prices in 1979 was met by restrictive policies, especially monetary policy, and outside Japan output stagnated for three years.

A long period of expansion initiated by tax cuts and spending increases in the USA continued from early 1983 to 1989; the spectacular stock market crash of October 1987 was shrugged off with little impact on economic growth. But even during this recovery the growth rate was well below that of the golden age. The experiences of the three main blocks have been rather different in the years since 1982. Growth rates around 4 per cent per year represented a continuation of golden age growth in the USA but a very drastic slowing in Japan. Europe's growth, at less than 3 per cent per year in this period of recovery, was little more than half the average of good and bad periods in the golden age.

Why growth has slowed

A slowdown in the growth of production over an extended period of time inevitably involves slower growth both of demand and of productive potential. Capital accumulation holds the key to both these intermingled developments, as we argue in the next sections. Beginning with the more immediate question of demand, we examine first which types of expenditure have particularly contributed to the slowdown (table 14.2).

Consumers to blame . . .

Since household expenditure (on consumption and housebuilding) is the largest portion of aggregate demand it is no surprise that it accounts for about one-half of the slowdown of expenditure. But workers as consumers play an essentially passive role (chapter 8). The markets provided by other types of spending – business investment, exports and government spending – largely shape the growth of the wage bill. This, together with changes in tax rates and

Table 14.2 Contributions to ACC demand 1960–89

	1960–73	1973–89	1973–75	1975–79	1979–82	1982–89
Total GDP	5.5	2.7	−0.7	4.3	0.7	3.6
Accounted for by						
Household consumption and housing	3.5	1.9	0.3	2.7	0.5	2.4
Government expenditure	0.9	0.4	0.4	0.5	0.2	0.4
Business sector						
Fixed investment	1.0	0.4	−0.9	0.7	0.1	0.8
Stocks	0.1	0.0	−1.2	0.4	−0.6	0.2
Net exports	0.0	0.1	0.6	0.0	0.4	−0.2

Figures show the extent to which each element of expenditure accounts (in percentages of GDP) for the average annual percentage growth of total output. Government expenditure refers to current and capital spending on goods and services (i.e. excluding transfers). Revisions to data mean that figures for growth in total GDP do not correspond precisely to the most recent estimates shown in table 14.1. Rounding means that total growth may diverge slightly from sum of components.
Source: OECD, 1989, *Economic Outlook*, June, table 31 and earlier issues

in government transfer payments, determines the growth of disposable incomes. Households' discretion is thus limited to fluctuations in the proportion of income saved.

Betweeen 1960 and 1973 the proportion of household income saved increased from 8.2 per cent to 13.2 per cent, as more had to be set aside from consumption to offset the erosion by inflation of the real value of past savings. About half of these increased savings was absorbed in increased investment in housing. The savings ratio wobbled from 1973 until the early eighties, after which it fell very sharply in all the major ACCs except Japan and Germany. In the rest the fall in the savings ratio contributed around 1 per cent per year to the growth of consumption; in France, Italy and the UK this represented one-third to one-half of the rapid rise in consumption which was an important feature of the recovery. Housebuilding also expanded sharply in 1987 and 1988 after declining between 1973 and the mid-1980s.

Consumers reacted to the stagnation of their real incomes by increasing their borrowing from financial institutions flushed with cash and newly liberated by financial deregulation. This helped to bolster expenditure growth in the middle and late 1980s and played a notable and unprecedented role in such recovery as occurred at that time. But spread over the whole period of stagnation, household expenditure has been relatively passive, constrained by the growth of incomes.

. . . Or foreigners . . .

The reduction in purchasing power within the ACCs implied by the two rises in oil prices has been a favoured scapegoat for slow growth. But such direct effects of commodity price increases can be exaggerated. The deterioration in the terms of trade which resulted reduced spending power in the ACCs by a little less than 1 per cent per year between 1973 and 1975 and by about half as much during 1979–82. But as table 14.2 shows, this effect was substantially offset by the rise in net exports as the recipients of higher oil price revenues increased their imports from the ACCs (or lent such revenues to the less developed countries (LDCs) who did likewise – see chapter 16). After 1982 the ACCs' terms of trade improved substantially but the beneficial effect this had on spending power was offset by the decline in net exports as the oil producers and particularly the heavily indebted LDCs were forced to cut back drastically on their import bills. Thus while the cost of imports into the ACCs, and possibilities of exporting, played a very important role in the alternation of severe recessions and recoveries since 1973, they were not important in shaping the pattern of demand over the period as a whole.

. . . Or governments?

In the 1960s and early 1970s increased state spending on goods and services provided markets for nearly a 1 per cent per year growth of output (table 14.2). After 1973 the direct impetus for growth provided by government spending was only half as strong. As discussed in chapter 17, current civil spending on health, education and other social welfare programmes has grown more slowly, and many capital programmes, such as housebuilding and road construction, have been sharply cut back.

State budgets moved from balance in the early seventies to a deficit of 4 per cent of GDP in 1975. Since then the average deficit has fluctuated cyclically in the range 2–4 per cent of GDP. The slow growth of output and therefore real incomes depressed the rise in tax revenues. On the other side of the account, rising unemployment jacked up the cost of state benefits while larger numbers of pensioners eligible for benefits helped to keep the share of transfers rising rapidly until 1979. Moreover, accumulated deficits and higher interest rates increased interest payments on the national debt.

Economies would have been even more depressed since 1973 had governments not run up these deficits. But it was only in 1975, and to a lesser extent in 1978, that there were substantial deliberate increases in government deficits aimed at sustaining demand. The early eighties saw a prolonged fiscal expansion in the USA, but this was counterbalanced by austerity policies, especially in Germany and Japan (see chapter 17).

In sum, the deceleration of state spending contributed significantly to the slowdown of markets. After 1979 deliberate increases in government expenditure and in state deficits played little role in halting the stagnation. The limitations of such Keynesian policies in the face of fundamental weaknesses in the growth process were graphically revealed, and as explained in chapter 17 these policies were abandoned. It is to the more fundamental problems that we now turn.

Investment

After 1973 the growth of business fixed investment directly contributed the equivalent of 0.4 per cent of GDP a year to the growth of overall spending, less than one half of the impetus it exerted in the sixties (table 14.2). The collapse in the investment rate was concentrated in 1974–5 (chapter 13), with a further sharp rundown of stocks in 1980–2. But even in the recovery periods the growth of fixed investment was below that of the sixties; for example, in the long expansion after 1982, when there was much talk of an investment boom, the contribution of investment to expanding demand was distinctly lower than during the average of recessions and recoveries in the sixties.

The stagnation of investment not only inhibited market growth, it also steadily undermined the rate of accumulation, and thus the growth of productive potential. While one year of flat investment causes no more than a hiccup in the accumulation process, a decade or more of slowly growing investment brings about a significant loss of momentum. A stagnant level of investment adds less each year to the capital stock. Since the stock is still growing, in each succeeding year more of the investment is needed simply to replace what has been scrapped. The decade after 1973, therefore, saw a substantial decline in the rate of accumulation. The growth rate of the business capital stock averaged 5.3 per cent per year between 1965 and 1973. By 1983 it had fallen to 3.2 per cent per year.

Just as the accumulation rate takes a while to subside, a recovery in investment takes a long time to lever up the growth of the capital stock. As we have seen, the expansion of investment after 1982 did not reach the increase in the golden age. By 1989 the rate of growth of the capital stock averaged 4.6 per cent and was still below the peak rate of 5.6 per cent reached in 1970. Here, however, there were very important differences between the major blocks, and between manufacturing and the rest of the economy (figures 14.1 and 14.2 and table 14.3).

In the USA the business accumulation rate over the whole period 1973–89 was very similar to that of the 1960s; the rate at the end of the 1980s was somewhat below that of the early seventies but the extent of the weakening of accumulation was relatively slight. In Japan the accumulation rate dipped severely after 1973, indeed as already discussed (chapter 11) the weakening of Japanese accumulation began in the early 1970s with the onset of overaccumulation. By 1983 the accumulation rate was well below half of the peak rate at the beginning

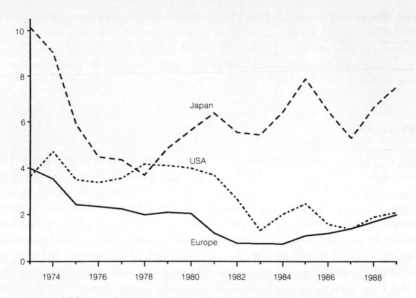

Figure 14.1 ACC manufacturing accumulation, 1973–89 (growth rates, between the beginning and end of the year, of gross fixed capital stock, percentage change).
Source: see Appendix.

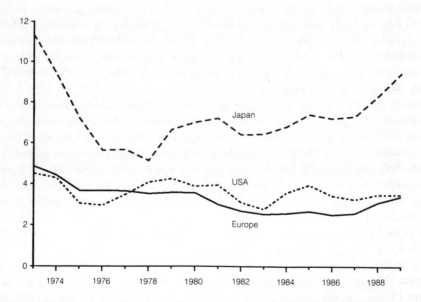

Figure 14.2 ACC business accumulation, 1973–89 (growth rates, between the beginning and end of the year, of gross fixed capital stock, percentage change).
Source: see Appendix.

Table 14.3 The accumulation rate 1960–89 (average annual percentage growth rates of capital stock)

	Business					Manufacturing				
	1960–73	1973–89	1973	1983	1989	1960–73	1973–89	1973	1983	1989
USA	3.7	3.6	4.5	2.8	3.5	4.0	2.9	3.6	1.3	2.1
Europe	5.2	3.2	5.0	2.6	3.4	5.1	1.7	4.0	0.8	2.0
Japan	12.4	7.0	11.3	6.5	9.4	14.0	6.0	10.1	5.4	7.6
ACC	5.0	3.9	5.4	3.2	4.6	5.5	3.0	4.9	1.9	3.2

Source: see Appendix

of the 1970s. Subsequently, however, there has been another phenomenal investment boom in Japan, levering the accumulation rate back nearly into double figures. By 1989 the business capital stock in Japan was moving up towards its 1973 growth. Judged by this crucial indicator at least the crisis of accumulation seems to have been substantially surmounted in Japan by the end of the 1980s. In Europe the story is rather different: Europe's accumulation rate was the weakest of the three blocs with capital stock growth declining steadily from the peak rate of 5½ per cent in 1970 to 2½ per cent in the mid-1980s. By 1989 the investment 'boom' had only pushed it back up to 3½ per cent.

An important general feature of the pattern of accumulation has been the much weaker capital stock growth in manufacturing than in total business. In both Europe and Japan the accumulation rate in manufacturing after 1973 has averaged under half the pre-1973 rate. In the USA the accumulation rate in manufacturing in 1989 was half the pre-1973 rate. In Japan the recovery in manufacturing accumulation has been a little weaker than in business, although this has still left the capital stock growing around three times as fast as in Europe and twice as fast as in the USA. Before 1973 the accumulation rate in manufacturing was similar to or greater than the accumulation rate elsewhere; after 1973 it was slower and usually a lot slower. The relative lack of dynamism in manufacturing, the most important component of international trade, especially between the ACCs, has been a major feature of the years of stagnation; the reasons for and implications of this will be a recurrent theme in this final section of the book. One striking result is that the upswing of the later 1980s brought capacity utilization in manufacturing practically back in 1989 to its peak level of 1973–4; in the major European economies it was actually rather higher.

The major slackening in the rate of accumulation and subsequent failure to regain the growth of capital achieved in the sixties is central to the stagnation after 1973, especially in Europe. It is to the key manifestations of this stagnation that we now turn, before examining the reasons for the weakness of investment since 1973.

Stagnation of productivity and rising unemployment

As a matter of accounting, a slower growth of output must be reflected in a slower growth of employment, a slower growth of productivity or some combination of the two. A slower growth of employment must imply rising unemployment unless the growth of the labour force declines in parallel. A slower growth of productivity is inevitably translated into more slowly growing living standards and/or public services. One way or another the mass of the population must obviously suffer as a result of slower growth. Moreover, *given* the slower growth of output, there is a 'trade-off' between these different forms of deteriorating performance. The better employment is maintained the more productivity growth suffers, with probable consequences for take-home pay. The better the social services are maintained, for a given slowdown in productivity, the more the brunt is taken by workers' take-home pay. First we examine the extent to which a slower growth of output has been divided up between employment and productivity (table 14.4).

Table 14.4 Output, productivity and employment, 1960–89 (average annual percentage growth rates)

		Europe	USA	Japan	OECD
GDP	1960–73	4.7	4.0	9.6	4.8
	1973–89	2.2	2.6	3.9	2.7
	Change	−2.5	−1.4	−5.7	−2.1
Productivity	1960–73	4.3	2.1	8.2	3.7
	1973–89	1.8	0.6	3.0	1.6
	Change	−2.5	−1.5	−5.2	−2.1
Employment	1960–73	0.4	1.9	1.3	1.1
	1973–89	0.4	2.0	0.9	1.1
	Change	0.0	0.1	−0.4	0.0

Source: OECD, *Historical Statistics, Economic Outlook*

The most striking feature of table 14.4 is that, for the ACCs as a whole, *all* the slowdown in output growth has been reflected in a decline in productivity growth. Employment growth has continued at the same rate as before 1973. Employment growth slowed notably in Japan, but not at all in Europe, and actually accelerated a little in the USA. How this can be reconciled with the emergence of mass unemployment is the topic of the next section but one. The immediate task is to examine the massive slowdown in productivity growth.

The productivity crisis

All the blocs achieved much slower productivity growth after 1973 (table 14.5). The one exception is the manufacturing sector of the USA, where

Table 14.5 Productivity, 1960–88 (average annual percentage growth rates)

	ACC	USA	Europe	Japan
Business				
Hourly productivity				
1960–73	4.2	2.5	4.8	9.6
1973–79	2.2	0.4	3.5	3.6
1979–87	1.9	0.6	2.7	3.8
Manufacturing				
Hourly productivity				
1960–73	5.1	3.2	5.9	10.5
1973–79	3.2	1.2	3.7	5.7
1979–87	3.9	3.4	3.4	5.8

Source: see Appendix

productivity rebounded after 1979. But a substantial part of the rapid growth there represented the expansion of the electronics industry (as the output of computing power rose enormously), while in many other manufacturing industries quite heavy investment and rationalization efforts yielded modest results (see chapter 15). The decline in productivity growth was particularly large in Japan (5–6 per cent per year slowdown in both business and manufacturing) and rather less elsewhere (about 2 per cent per year in Europe and US business). The usual pattern was for productivity growth to slow down as much as, and usually rather more than, the rate of growth of fixed capital per worker (see figure 14.3). So while the general factor behind the productivity slowdown was the decline in accumulation, even the investment that did take place yielded smaller productivity gains. This was despite severe rationalization under the pressure of rising unemployment which afflicted the traditional heavy industries in most of the advanced countries.

The effects of productivity slowdown have been felt above all in a drastic slowdown in the growth of living standards financed out of earnings from work and in the growth of social expenditure. Figure 14.4 shows that workers' living standards have been growing by only around 1 per cent per year since 1973; this is true even of Japan where productivity growth has continued at a respectable rate (in comparison with long-run growth in the ACCs if not with Japan's golden age performance). The growth of social expenditure (health, education, pensions etc.) also declined after 1973 and over the whole period social expenditure recorded less than half its previous growth; since 1980 the growth rate has been little more than one-third that of the golden age.

One important issue in respect of the productivity slowdown is whether capital goods production was equally affected. In fact the price of investment goods in the OECD appears to have risen nearly 1 per cent more slowly than consumer goods after 1973 (as compared to ½ per cent more quickly between

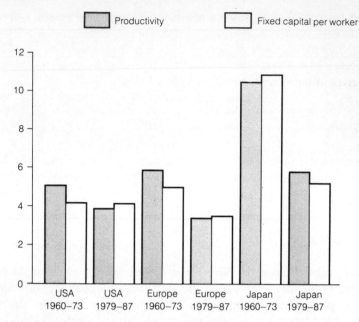

Figure 14.3 Manufacturing productivity, 1960–87 (average annual percentage growth rates).
Source: see Appendix.

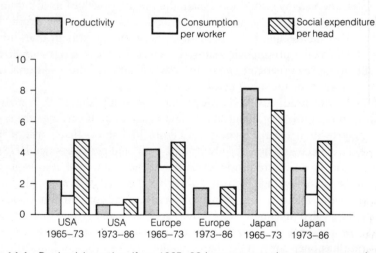

Figure 14.4 Productivity and welfare, 1965–86 (average annual percentage growth rates). Consumption per worker is consumption out of earned income (see Glyn, 1991). Social expenditure (health, education, transfers etc.) is expressed per head of the population of working age.
Source: see Appendix; also OECD, 1988, *The Future of Social Protection*; Glyn, 1991.

1960 and 1973). This suggests that the rate of introduction of new technology may have been better maintained in the capital goods sectors. This has contributed to the recovery of profitability, since it reduces the cost of capital goods relative to the value of the output produced with them, and helped to prevent rises in the output–capital ratio (see below).

The rise in unemployment

The rise in unemployment has certainly been the most visible expression of the stagnation of output (figure 14.5). And yet, as described above, there has not been any fall off in the growth of employment. Where then have the unemployed sprung from? The essential facts are presented in Table 14.6.

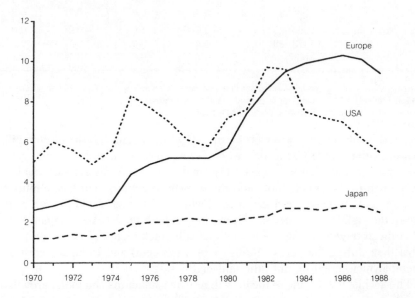

Figure 14.5   Unemployment rates, 1970–88 (percentage).
Source: OECD, *Economic Outlook*.

The missing link in the explanation for the rise in unemployment is the behaviour of the supply of labour. Even a constant growth of employment will imply a rise in unemployment if the labour force expands faster. This is exactly what has happened in the ACCs taken as a whole since 1973. Europe, where practically all the rise in OECD unemployment has been concentrated, typifies this pattern. There a combination of a faster growth of population of working age and a slower decrease in the proportion of the population who are registered as in the labour force (the 'participation rate') combined to secure a doubling of the growth rate of the labour force. Such a change would have

Table 14.6 Employment, labour force and unemployment 1960–89 (average annual percentage growth rates)

		Europe	USA	Japan	OECD
Employment	1960–73	0.4	1.9	1.3	1.1
	1973–89	0.4	2.0	0.9	1.1
	Change	0.0	0.1	−0.4	0.0
Population of working age	1960–73	0.7	1.7	1.7	1.2
	1973–89	0.9	1.3	0.9	1.0
	Change	0.2	−0.4	−0.8	−0.2
Participation rate	1960–73	−0.3	0.3	−0.5	−0.2
	1973–89	−0.1	0.7	0.1	0.3
	Change	0.2	0.4	0.6	0.5
Labour force	1960–73	0.4	2.0	1.2	1.0
	1973–89	0.8	2.0	1.0	1.3
	Change	0.4	0.0	−0.2	0.3
Unemployment	1960–73[a]	0.0	0.0	0.0	0.0
	1973–89[a]	0.4	0.0	0.1	0.2
	Change	0.4	0.0	0.1	0.2

[a] These statistics refer to the annual increase in the percentage unemployment rate (i.e. first difference); all other statistics in this table refer to proportionate growth rates.
Sources: OECD *Historical Statistics, Economic Outlook*

required employment to grow faster after 1973 than before, if the more rapidly growing labour force was to find work. As we have seen, employment growth was simply maintained; the apparently small percentage discrepancy between the growth of the labour force and the growth of employment has cumulated over 16 years to generate mass unemployment. Although rapid growth at the end of the eighties tightened labour markets in both the USA and Japan, in the USA the average unemployment rate was still much higher (7.1 per cent) after 1973 than during the period 1960–73 (4.8 per cent) and in Japan registered unemployment crept up until the mid-eighties.

Thus, while the decline in the growth of living standards and in the growth of social services was a pervasive feature of the period of slower growth, continuous mass unemployment was specifically a European phenomenon. Moreover, our analysis has shown the importance of the development of the labour supply in the rise in unemployment. It is to this, and the related question of changes in the structure of available jobs, that we next turn.

De-industrialization and structural change

While the growth of employment in total has been maintained since 1973, the structure of employment has been changing rapidly, giving rise to much discussion of de-industrialization. Indeed employment in the industrial sector has grown 2 per cent per year more slowly than services employment in both the USA and Japan since 1973. Here, however, we focus on the case of Europe, where the extent of this de-industrialization has been even more severe and (as table 14.7 shows) has been associated with an overall decline in the number of industrial jobs.

Table 14.7 OECD–Europe: sectoral output, productivity and employment 1960–87 (average annual percentage growth rates)

	1960–73	1973–87	Change
Output			
Agriculture	1.7	1.7	0.0
Industry	5.1	1.3	−3.8
Services	4.7	2.7	−2.0
GDP	4.7	2.1	−2.6
Productivity			
Agriculture	4.7	3.4	−1.3
Industry	4.5	2.5	−2.0
Services	2.8	0.8	−2.0
Total	4.3	1.9	−2.4
Employment			
Agriculture	−3.0	−1.7	1.3
Industry	0.6	−1.2	−1.8
Services	2.0	1.8	−0.2
Total	0.4	0.2	−0.2

Source: OECD *Historical Statistics 1960–87*

A slower growth of industrial employment than of services was already a feature of the golden age. Then it was a reflection of the faster growth of productivity in industry than in services, for the volume of output of the two sectors was growing at the same speed. The share of industrial employment in total employment still grew slightly, because of the very rapid rundown of employment in agriculture (a product of both slow output growth and rapid productivity growth).

After 1973 the situation changed in important ways. First, the rundown in agricultural employment eased to about half the golden age rate. When job markets slackened, the rate at which labour was drawn out of the countryside slowed down (see chapter 11). Productivity growth slackened by an equal amount in both industry and services. There was, however, a much bigger slowdown in output growth in industry – after 1973 it grew only half as fast as services output. The result was that industrial employment fell by nearly 2 per cent per year. So de-industrialization, in its true sense of declining share of employment in industry, became a reality.

As argued above, the decline in the number of industrial jobs in Europe after 1973 was a reflection of its particularly slow growth of industrial output. One explanation might be a decline in net exports of manufactures as European producers faced increasing competition from Japan and the newly industrializing countries (see chapter 16). A familiar story in Europe has been of factory closures as a response to rising imports. While this has been important for some European economies, like the UK, such direct loss of markets has not applied to Europe as a whole. Net exports of manufactures from the EEC rose from $35 billion in 1973 to $97 billion in 1987. These net exports represented a constant (7 per cent) share of manufacturing production and thus cannot directly explain the slow growth of industrial output in Europe. One important factor was the slow growth of investment, which we have stressed in other connections. Since expenditure on investment is disproportionately concentrated on industrial products (machinery and buildings), a slow growth of investment will hold back industrial output growth. It may also be that consumers are finally shifting towards the consumption of relatively more services (in addition to having to pay more for them as productivity grew slowly leading to relatively fast cost and price increases). However, one study for the UK suggests that this has not yet happened to a substantial degree, although as a low income country in OECD terms the UK case may not be typical.

Whatever the precise reason for the weakness of industrial output in Europe the loss of industrial jobs has had a major influence on the extent of unemployment increase. In both Japan and the USA, where major increases in unemployment were avoided, total industrial employment was higher in 1987 than in 1973; in Europe with mass unemployment it was more than 15 per cent lower. Moreover, within Europe it was in those countries with the severest loss of industrial jobs (Spain, UK, Belgium, Ireland, Netherlands and France) that the rise in unemployment was greatest. In some of these countries (such as the UK and Netherlands) unemployment rose despite the fact that there was no fall in services employment growth at all. Why should the loss of industrial jobs have proved so decisive?

The great majority of industrial workers are full-time. Their skills are often specific to industrial work and not transferable to other sectors of the economy. Moreover, industrial employment is often geographically concentrated in particular areas. When there is a major decline in industrial employment this cannot be achieved through natural wastage as workers retire, but only through large-scale redundancies and plant closures which throw large numbers of middle-aged workers on to the local labour market.

In principle a decline in industrial employment can be offset by increasing employment in services. However, if the industrial decline is deep, this is unlikely. Most service employment, in health, education, restaurants and shops, is population-based and spread relatively uniformly around the economy or dependent on incomes so that it grows less in areas of falling industrial employment. It therefore has limited potential for offsetting geographically concentrated job losses in industry. Moreover, many of the new service jobs are part-time, and are frequently occupied by married women drawn back into the labour force. It is for these reasons that loss of industrial jobs has played such an important role in the rise in unemployment. Moreover, since men are more dependent on industrial jobs than women, the decline in industrial employment had a particularly large effect on male employment.

Women's and men's employment

Since 1973 women's employment has been growing much faster than men's. Similar trends also applied during the golden age (though not in Japan where the massive rundown of agriculture reduced women's measured participation in the labour force), but the discrepancy increased after 1973, as the case of Europe illustrates particularly sharply (table 14.8). The reason was that services employment continued to increase rapidly while industrial employment collapsed. Since around two-thirds of women's non-agricultural employment was in services in 1973, while a slight majority of men were in industry, the collapse in industrial employment hit men much harder.

So men's employment fell after 1973, while women's actually rose at 1 per cent per year, which was *faster* than before 1973. Despite this, women's unemployment rose faster than men's. The explanation is that women entered

Table 14.8 OECD–Europe: women's and men's employment 1960–87 (average annual percentage growth rates)

		Women	Men
Participation rate	1960–73	0.2	−0.6
	1973–87	1.1	−0.7
	Change	0.9	−0.1
Labour force	1960–73	0.8	0.3
	1973–87	1.6	0.3
	Change	0.8	0.0
Employment	1960–73	0.7	0.3
	1973–87	1.0	−0.1
	Change	0.3	−0.4
Industrial employment	1964–73	−0.2	−0.3
	1973–87	−1.7	−1.5
	Change	−1.5	−1.2
Services employment	1964–73	2.0	0.9
	1973–87	1.6	1.2
	Change	−0.4	0.3
Unemployment	1964–73	0.1	0.0
	1973–87	0.6	0.4

Data for unemployment refer to average annual change in percentage rate; data for industrial and services employment cover only five countries. Data for total employment include agriculture.
Source: OECD, *Historical Statistics*

the labour force much faster after 1973. So while women's measured unemployment rose very considerably, there was also a substantial fall in 'hidden unemployment' as many more women took paid work. For men the position was starker – a rise in open unemployment and probably some increase in hidden unemployment as redundant male industrial workers took early retirement.

Profits

The course of profitability after 1973 broadly followed the phases of recession and expansion already described. After the nose-dive of the profit rate during 1974–5 (see chapter 13), there was some modest recovery by 1979, another, though much less severe, fall during the recession surrounding the second OPEC price increase, followed by another period of recovery. For the ACCs as a whole the business profit rate in 1987 had still not regained its 1973 level, and the manufacturing profit rate was still one-quarter below. Some clues as to the pressures involved can be gleaned from the analysis in table 14.9, which shows how changes in the pattern of growth of productivity, real wages and the output–capital ratio have contributed to the shifts in business profitability.

Table 14.9 Factors behind ACC business profitability 1965–87 (average annual percentage growth rates)

	1965–73	1973–87	1973–75	1975–79	1979–82	1982–87
(1) Labour productivity	3.2	1.5	−0.7	2.5	0.4	2.3
(2) Relative consumer prices	0.3	0.5	0.2	0.2	1.1	0.6
(3) Real incomes (1) − (2)	3.0	1.0	−0.9	2.3	−0.7	1.6
(4) Real wages	3.5	0.9	1.0	2.0	−0.2	0.8
(5) Wage share (4) − (3)	0.5	−0.1	1.8	−0.4	0.5	−0.9
(6) Profit share	−1.7	0.2	−6.8	1.5	−1.8	3.4
(change in percentage points p.a)	−0.41	0.05	−1.5	0.3	−0.4	0.7
(7) Real output–capital ratio	−0.6	−1.3	−6.0	0.8	−3.7	0.5
(8) Relative capital costs	0.5	−0.2	0.5	0.4	0.2	−1.2
(9) Output–capital (current prices) (7) − (8)	−1.1	−1.1	−6.5	0.3	−3.8	1.7
(10) Profit rate (6) + (9)	−2.8	−0.9	−12.8	1.9	−5.6	5.1
(change in percentage points p.a.)	−0.50	−0.13	−1.9	0.2	−0.7	0.6

Source and explanation: see Appendix, p. 351

The first two columns of the table compare the pre-1973 period of profit squeeze with the post-1973 years as a whole. The profit rate fell much less rapidly in the second period, by around 0.1 percentage point per year. Although the output–capital ratio fell at the same rate over the two periods, the sharp profit squeeze of the first period was halted and slightly reversed after 1973. Before 1973 the wage share rose steadily as real wages grew faster than 'real incomes', that is labour productivity adjusted for the relative rise of consumer prices. After 1973 real wages grew sufficiently more slowly for the wage share to fall slightly and the profit share to edge upwards. But they did not rise sufficiently slowly to maintain the profit rate as the trend in the real output–capital ratio deteriorated.

Within the whole period since 1973 there have been important changes in profit trends. The fall in profitability during the 1974–5 recession was much more severe than during 1979–82. This was both because the profit squeeze was more severe in the former period and because the output–capital ratio deteriorated more. The main reason for the less intense profit squeeze was that real wages fell after 1979 but kept rising after 1973. In neither situation was there 'room' for real wage increases without squeezing profitability. This was because productivity stagnated (after 1979 especially) and because there were rapid increases in the relative price of consumer goods. The fall in the output–capital ratio was sharper after 1973 as stagnant output coincided with a very high rate of accumulation. Excess capacity built up at a much faster rate than after 1979 by which time accumulation was proceeding more warily. Figure 14.6 illustrates the relaxation of pressure on the profit share after 1979 in Europe as real wage increases slowed down.

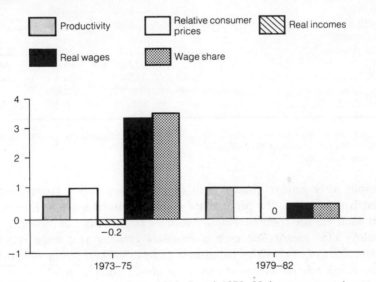

Figure 14.6 European wage share, 1973–5 and 1979–82 (average annual percentage growth rates).
Source: see Appendix.

Just as the fall in profitability was less after 1979, so the rise in profitability was greater in the expansion after 1982 than during the recovery after 1975. Again the main explanation is the considerably slower growth of real wages after 1982, growing at less than 1 per cent per year or half the pace of the 1975–9 period. An additional factor was that the price of capital goods grew relatively slowly after 1982 which allowed the output-capital ratio to rise strongly and thus contribute to the recovery in profitability.

This pattern for the ACCs as a whole was the product of different and rather surprising trends in the different blocs. As table 14.10 shows, in Europe the profit rate in both business and manufacturing had regained the 1973 level. The rate was certainly well below the peak levels of the early sixties, but at least the additional sharp falls in 1974–5 and 1979–82 had been entirely reversed (figure 14.7). The situation in Japan was quite different. The rate of profit had fallen much more sharply there after 1970, and there has been virtually no recovery since then.

Table 14.10 Profit rates, 1960–87 (percentages)

	ACC	USA	Europe	Japan
Business				
Peak year[a]	19.5	19.9	20.5	34.8
1973	15.4	13.2	16.0	24.6
1987	13.6	11.2	16.3	15.7
1987/peak	0.70	0.56	0.80	0.45
1987/1973	0.88	0.85	1.02	0.64
Manufacturing				
Peak year[a]	29.1	36.4	21.5	53.6
1973	21.9	22.0	15.4	38.8
1987	15.9	15.4	14.8	14.6
1987/peak	0.55	0.42	0.69	0.27
1987/1973	0.73	0.70	0.96	0.38

[a] The 'peak year' is defined as the year before the sustained decline in profitability; it is 1965 for the ACCs and USA, 1960 for Europe and 1970 for Japan.
Source: see Appendix

Despite very similar growth rates of real wages and a faster growth of productivity in Japan, the profit share recovered much more in Europe. The explanation was the continued rapid rise in the relative price of consumer goods in Japan. This meant that even a modestly growing real wage required a constant share of value added in business going to workers if they were to afford rapidly rising relative prices of consumer goods, such as food and rent, not subject to the intense competitive pressures which helped especially to keep down the prices of manufactured goods. A further influence on the profit rate was a continued fall in the amount of output produced per unit of capital in Japan as the accumulation rate stayed high. The pattern in the USA is closer to that of Europe. In this case a fall in real wages after 1982 allowed a sharp rise in the profit share and the output–capital ratio also improved as excess capacity was taken back into use.

It seems certain that a major contributory factor to the profit recovery in Europe has been the impact of mass unemployment in undermining workers'

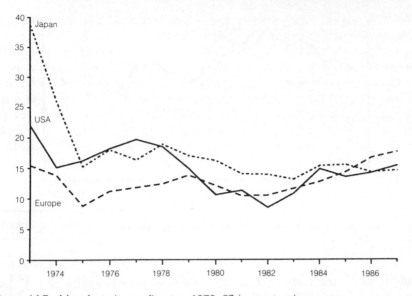

Figure 14.7 Manufacturing profit rates, 1973–87 (percentage).
Source: see Appendix.

bargaining position – precisely the function of the 'reserve army of labour' explained by Marx. What is more surprising is the failure of profitability to recover in Japan. Despite the slower rate of accumulation and growth of output than before 1973, the demand for labour has been maintained at a very high rate in Japan. In the middle of 1989 the ratio of job offers to vacancies exceeded 1 for the first time since 1974. There was a slightly slower growth rate of the population of working age than in the 1960s (see table 14.6) and the reserves of labour which could be drawn out of agriculture were much diminished. Despite increases in women's participation in paid work the labour market was very tight and real wages continued to rise. Business was also severely hampered by factors such as agricultural protection and housing shortage, which pushed the cost of consumer goods up and increased the money wage increases necessary for workers to keep their purchasing power growing.

Profitability and accumulation

In broad terms there is a parallel downward shift in accumulation and profitability for both manufacturing and the whole business sector (figures 14.8 and 14.9) Putting together the patterns for profitability with those for accumulation for the individual blocs earlier yields an immediate paradox. In Japan, where the rate of profit fell most and recovered least, the rate of accumulation has recovered most and is not very far below the 1973 rate. In

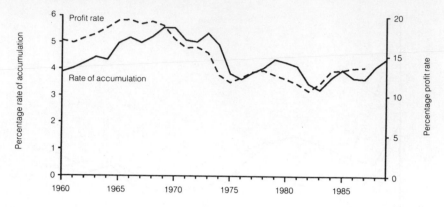

Figure 14.8   ACC business accumulation and profit rates, 1960–89.
Source: see Appendix.

Europe, where the years of stagnation and mass unemployment have by and large restored profitability, the recovery of accumulation has been very tentative (figures 14.10, 14.11 and 14.12).

Part of the explanation for this probably lies in the fact that, despite its sharp fall, the profit rate in Japan appears still to have been higher than elsewhere (though conclusions must be tentative because of the difficulty of making comparisons of profitability across countries where methods of calculation differ). Since 1973 the average rate in business has been higher than in the other major countries with the most comparable estimates (16 per cent in Japan as compared to 11 per cent in Germany and the USA and 6 per cent in the UK). Moreover, the profit rate has been much more stable in Japan than in

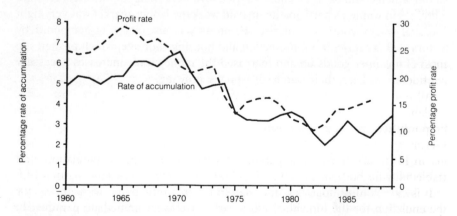

Figure 14.9   ACC manufacturing accumulation and profit rates, 1960–89.
Source: see Appendix.

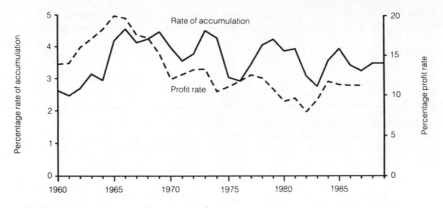

Figure 14.10 United States business accumulation and profit rates, 1960–89.
Source: see Appendix.

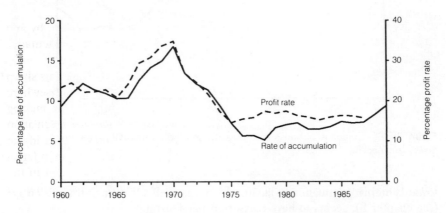

Figure 14.11 Japanese business accumulation and profit rates, 1960–89.
Source: see Appendix.

most of the other countries, which is an important factor in stabilizing capitalist confidence (see figure 14.7).

All our data are for pre-tax profits, but taxation of profits certainly cannot explain the disparate behaviour of accumulation. It is true that the rate of corporate taxation seems to have been lower in Japan than in the USA and Germany, but not than in the UK. Moreover, there were no cuts in corporate tax in Japan which could help to explain the upswing in accumulation there (table 14.11).

It is clear that the powerful upswing in the rate of accumulation in Japan at the end of the 1980s – at about three times the rate in the USA or Europe (see table 14.3) – cannot be wholly explained by the behaviour of profitability. After a breathing space in the later 1970s and early 1980s the strong tendency

Table 14.11 Tax rates on new manufacturing investment, 1970–86 (percentages)

	USA	UK	Germany	Japan
1970	51	4	47	23
1980	44	−1	44	29
1986	44	n.a.	44	29

Figures for Germany and Japan for 1986 are rough guesses based on there having been no major changes in the tax system up to that time. In the UK the tax rate in 1986 was probably positive, but fairly low. *Source*: King and Fullerton, 1984, various tables, OECD, *Economies in Transition*, tables 5.13, 5.14.

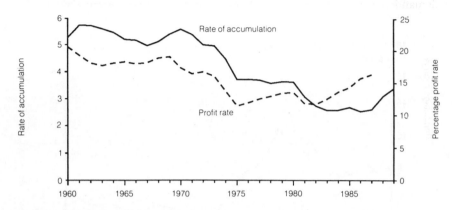

Figure 14.12   European business accumulation and profit rates, 1960–89.
Source: see Appendix.

towards high accumulation in Japan, which was such a feature of the golden age (see chapter 8), seems to have reasserted itself strongly.

Inflation and unemployment

Our analysis of inflation (chapters 11 and 12) was centred on the idea that the upsurge in inflation in the later 1960s and early 1970s reflected workers' attempts to increase their real wages when their bargaining position was strengthened by tight labour markets. This took place in the context of increasing commodity prices and lax credit policies. The years since 1979 have seen a winding down of inflation because of the weaker bargaining position of workers (see chapter 15) and the reversal of the commodity price explosion (see chapter 16). The first inflationary peak in the ACCs was in 1974 when on average consumer prices were rising by 13 per cent. By 1976 the combination of falling commodity prices and weaker bargaining pushed the inflation rate down to 8 per cent, but workers resisted the further cut in wage claims which would have been necessary to drive inflation down further (figure 14.13). The second round of oil price increases took the inflation rate back up to 13 per cent, in 1980, after which it fell steadily to around 2 per cent in 1986. Commodity prices fell by about 30 per cent between 1980 and 1986 and petroleum prices by nearly 60 per cent. But behind the continued decline in inflation also lay the weaker bargaining position of labour in both Europe and the USA, where mass unemployment was taking its toll (figure 14.5) and there was a parallel slide down in wage increases and inflation. But after falling to below 3 per cent in 1986 inflation crept up again as the upswing began to reduce unemployment and commodity prices responded to the higher level of demand.

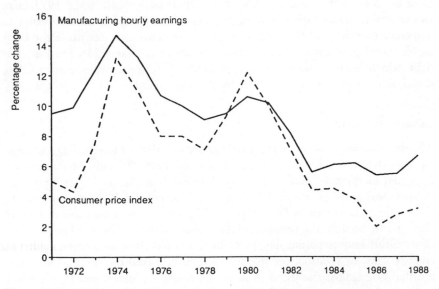

Figure 14.13 ACC hourly earnings and prices, 1971–88 (percentage change).
Source: OECD, *Historical Statistics* and *Economic Outlook*.

Finance and the legacy of overaccumulation

The middle and later 1980s saw an improvement in profitability in Europe and to some extent in the USA, a rise in the accumulation rate in Japan and to some extent in the USA and Europe, and growth in the OECD as a whole averaging a rather steady 4 per cent per year. This occurred in the context of inflation that was very modest in relation to the previous 20 years. While distinct recovery from the worst of the slowdown is clear, the legacy of overaccumulation has not been wiped out. As we argued in chapter 11 the overaccumulation encountered by the ACCs at the end of the sixties reflected an imbalance between the growth of capital and the availability of labour. A slowdown in the rate of accumulation was inevitable under these circumstances. But the form that overaccumulation took, with intensified struggle over wages and profits, compounded by sharp increases in input prices, led to a much more severe slowdown in accumulation and output growth than was implied by the shifting balance between demand and supply of labour. The result has been much slower growth of productivity in all the ACCs and mass unemployment in Europe. The remainder of the book is devoted to exploring how the period of slower growth has affected relations between labour and capital (chapter 15), international economic relations (chapter 16) and the economic policies pursued by governments of right and left (chapters 17 and 18). But before exploring these further ramifications of overaccumulation there is one more, specifically macroeconomic, legacy which must be dealt with – the fragility of the financial system. Since 1973 large amounts of financial capital have been accumulated in the form of government and consumer debt, with no counterpart in productive investment. In the USA an increased proportion of productive investment is financed by fixed interest debt, which leads to increased vulnerability of the enterprises concerned to deteriorations, even relatively short-lived, in profitability.

Government debt

The government deficits of the 1970s and early 1980s increased the value of national debt outstanding. Between 1973 and 1986 the ratio of government debt (net of financial assets) to GDP doubled from 16 to 33 per cent. The increase was much greater in Germany and Japan (some 30 percentage points) than in the famous case of the US (some 12 points). The latter caused so much alarm partly because the very size of the US economy makes small percentages of its GDP into awesome figures of billions of dollars for commentators to conjure with. In addition, the rise in US debt occurred during the 1980s (see chapter 17), against the trend in many European countries and Japan, which had halted or even reversed the rise in their outstanding debt.

The fundamental problem generated by the general increase in government debt is that it implies a rising burden of interest payments which in turn has to be paid for at some stage by higher taxation. Such higher taxation exacerbates distributional conflict as workers resist the impact on their living standards. Within financial markets the increased value of government debt provides a potential source of instability. If fears of inflation increased, for whatever reason, attempts by holders of government debt to unload their holdings in favour of real assets would provoke very large falls in bond prices and risk dislocating the financial system. This would force the government to support the debt market by pumping in extra cash, or to allow interest rates to rise sharply, threatening inflation or recession.

Government deficits fell in the late 1980s, and debt ratios stabilized (except in Italy and a few smaller countries). But a combination of the costs to the US government of the Savings and Loans crisis (see below), of the costs to the German government of reconstructing what was East Germany and of pressure on the Japanese government to expand made a sustained reduction in outstanding government debt unlikely. This left a potentially dangerous overhang from the period of slower growth.

Consumer debt

As pointed out above in the discussion of consumption, the 1980s saw a rapid increase in many countries in consumer borrowing to finance purchase of houses and consumer durables. While nothing significant of this sort seems to have occurred in Germany and Italy, in the rest of the major countries, and a number of smaller ones such as Australia and Sweden, there has been a very large increase in outstanding consumer debt (see figure 14.14).

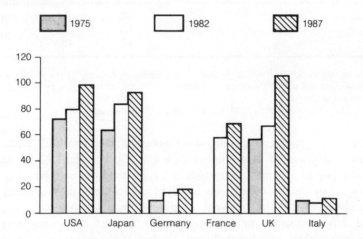

Figure 14.14   Consumer borrowing, 1975–87 (debt as percentage of disposable incomes). *Source*: OECD, December 1988, *Economic Outlook*.

Where the rise in borrowing has been substantial it has combined with higher interest rates to push up sharply the proportion of workers' incomes paid out in debt interest. If borrowers' incomes fall, or even fail to rise as anticipated, then expenditure on new consumer goods has to be cut back as people struggle to meet their repayments of loans and interest. For example, in the UK, where, as figure 14.14 shows, the increase in household borrowing has been fastest and has proceeded furthest, the proportion of household disposable incomes paid out in debt interest rose from 4.1 per cent in 1978 to 7.4 per cent in 1988. When interest rates were further raised in 1989–90 many borrowers were unable to meet their commitments despite cutting their other spending to the bone and repossession of houses by lenders reached record levels. While the rise in consumer debt helped to finance the recovery in the later 1980s, its longer-term cost for the economy as a whole was increased vulnerability to economic fluctuations.

Financing productive investment

Accumulation declined alongside the fall in profitability. This allowed corporations to continue financing a high proportion of their investments from internal funds. Even in 1982, at the trough for profitability, internal funds were maintaining their share; by 1987 the self-financing ratio was higher than it had been in 1973 (see table 14.12).

Table 14.12 Internal funds as a percentage of real investment, 1973–87

	1973	1982	1987
USA	75	95	94
Japan	63	64	78
Europe	66	68	102

Data refer to non-financial companies; Europe is unweighted average of France, Germany and UK. Internal funds are net retained earnings plus capital consumption; real investment refers to fixed investment and stocks.
Source: OECD, *National Accounts*, 1987, Vol. II, table 13, and earlier issues

Despite the maintenance of self-financing, the financial position of companies deteriorated in a number of countries. For the UK the Bank of England reported a record proportion of profits paid out as interest in 1989. Encouraged by the tax concession for debt interest, the development of the 'junk bonds' market in high-risk, high-yielding, fixed-interest securities enabled US companies to substitute fixed interest borrowing for funds previously supplied by shareholders. Within the average rise in interest payments of one-half in the USA, there were much larger increases for those companies using the junk bond market most aggressively. When the market collapsed in early 1990, it left many companies in a situation where a sharp downturn in their profits would leave them unable to meet their interest payments, making bankruptcy likely.

A careful assessment of the corporate financing position in the USA raised the following possible scenario:

> Bankruptcies or financial distress amongst some major firms could contribute to a liquidity crisis in several ways. Perhaps most important would be the effect of such news on . . . fragile confidence. . . . More directly the legal proceedings initiated by bankruptcy would freeze the liabilities of the failing firms, converting assets that the firms' creditors may have previously considered to be fairly liquid into illiquid assets and worsening the illiquidity problem of the creditors. Similarly, major bankruptcies might contribute to cash-flow problems of the firms' suppliers

and customers. As the liquidity crisis of the 1930s seriously disrupted the ability of the banks to function, a corporate liquidity crisis could disrupt the production and investment activities of firms. In such a situation, the liquidity of nonfinancial firms and banks would be closely intertwined (Bernanke and Campbell, 1988, p. 96)

The fragility of US corporate financing is compounded by a potentially more menacing situation in the financial sector itself. The US Savings and Loans Institutions (the 'thrifts') have incurred enormous losses as a result of speculative investments encouraged by financial deregulation (see chapter 17). A very detailed analysis in early 1989 of the losses likely in this sector reached a figure of almost $150 billion, with the costs being borne 85 per cent by the taxpayer (because of state guarantees to depositors). Subsequent press reports have suggested figures for the costs of more than $300 billion (equivalent to the GDP of Belgium and Austria). The analysis of the cost of resolving the 'thrift crisis' also concluded gloomily that, 'the problems among thrifts have obscured from public view a taxpayer obligation for failed banks that in other times would be highly unsettling' (Brumbaugh et al., 1989, p. 283). The authors explain that 'given the large number and asset size of weak banks, [and] the extent to which . . . accounting techniques hide market value losses, it is possible that losses in the commercial banking industry could eclipse those in the thrift industry, (especially if the economy enters a recession) before the weak capitalization of many banks is corrected' (Brumbaugh et al., 1989, p. 250). These losses stem from agriculture, real estate and the oil industry within the USA and from lending to the LDCs (see chapter 16). Despite much publicized write-offs of LDC debt, it was calculated that these loan loss reserves of the major banks represent only half the market estimates of the losses incurred on these loans. More plausible estimates of the losses would reduce the capital of Bank of America, Chemical Bank and Manufacturers to a perilously low level, with the Bank of America 'realistically at or near market value insolvency' (Brumbaugh et al., 1989, p. 257).

Such specific financial strains seem most pronounced in the USA. However, there is evidence of extreme speculative activity in the Japanese financial market as well. The general level of share prices can be assessed by comparing them with the cost of the underlying assets (see figure 14.15).

Share prices tended to slip down in the seventies and early eighties and by 1982 they were everywhere at around half of the 1973 level and one-quarter of the 1960 level. The 1980s saw a substantial recovery which took share prices in Europe back to the 1973 level. The biggest rise was in Japan, which took the rate well above the 1973 level, even though the underlying profit rate in Japan was far below that of the early 1970s. The powerful upturn in real accumulation was mirrored by euphoria in the financial markets. Confidence in the prospects of Japanese manufacturing has been based on the combination of technological leadership in some sectors and successful innovations in the

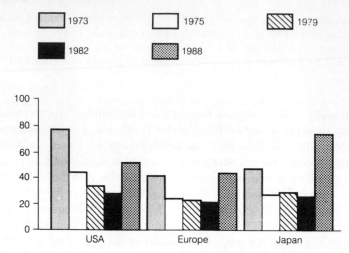

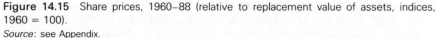

Figure 14.15   Share prices, 1960–88 (relative to replacement value of assets, indices, 1960 = 100).
Source: see Appendix.

organization of production (see chapter 15). But outside manufacturing, where the rate of accumulation is even higher despite moderate growth in the home market, it seems likely that the boom in real investment has a substantially speculative character (property investment and so on). With a much lower rate of profit from productive activity than previously, in manufacturing and services, the explanation for high share prices is expectations of large capital gains on the assets held by companies, such as office blocks in central Tokyo. A fall in share prices in Tokyo of some 30 per cent in the first quarter of 1990 suggests that this particular bubble may have burst.

The Economist (18 August 1990) emphasized the significance of shaky property and share markets:

Japan's huge commercial banks are caught in the spiral. If property and shares fall, so might they. . . . A Japanese crash could become a global one, as and when it either forces local banks to cut their lending or, heaven forbid, if banks start to go bust. Eight of the world's ten biggest banks are Japanese; they account for almost 40% of all cross-border bank loans and a sizeable chunk of domestic lending in America and Britain. The sudden loss of that would be disastrous.

To many, Japan's commercial banks look impregnable. But they have made 20% of their outstanding loans directly to domestic property and construction, and around 30% if indirect exposure is included. Worse, their ability to maintain credit lines depends on the stockmarket. In a scandalous compromise when international capital-adequacy rules were agreed under the Bank for International Settlements in Basle, Japanese banks are allowed to count 45% of unrealised gains on share investments as capital. Every time the Nikkei's fall makes those gains smaller, the banks' capital shrinks and so must their lending.

Is there a link between these rather diverse indicators of financial vulnerability – higher government debt ratios, increased consumer borrowing, weaker corporate balance sheets, troubled financial institutions, real investment distorted by speculative considerations? The common thread is that they all developed, although certainly to a different extent in different countries, in a situation where the existing profitability of productive investment had fallen, and confidence in the sustained growth necessary to maintain and increase that profitability had been eroded. In this sense the turbulence of the 15 or so years prior to the recovery of the later 1980s, the reflection of the basic forces of overaccumulation, has left a deep imprint on the financial structures of the ACCs.

15

Workers and the Organization of Production

Our analysis of the break-up of the long boom placed the relations between labour and capital at the centre of the story. This chapter addresses the consequential question of whether the long period of slowdown has decisively weakened the power of labour and thus restored one of the conditions for a new period of smooth growth. We then turn to the related issue of whether the much vaunted Japanese system of work organization and industrial relations represents a model for a new, renewed pattern of capital accumulation.

It should be stated clearly at the outset that unions have been forced on to the defensive by mass unemployment in Europe and, in the early 1980s, in the USA. Together with the other very important trend towards an intensification of international competition this has made preservation of work rules especially difficult. The recognition by some employers of the value to them of the firm-specific skills built up by sections of their labour force has led to widespread attempts to cement these workers to the firm, through individualized payment systems and to elicit their active involvement in solving production problems. Alongside these developments have gone attempts to turn unions into the company-type institution typical of Japan.

Unions and strikes

Assessing the organizational strength of trade unions from statistics on numbers of union members is hazardous. After all, the increased power of unions during the sixties coincided with a declining proportion of workers in trade unions, as fewer jobs were for manual workers in industry, the traditional union stronghold. Moreover, aggregate strike statistics have to be interpreted carefully – there may be a shift towards more defensive strikes, for example. Despite these limitations trends in union membership and strikes since the slowdown are important.

In the USA and Japan the proportion of wage and salary earners who were union members declined steadily throughout the 1970s and early 1980s. The most dramatic case was the USA, where by 1985 the proportion was only 18 per cent, down from 31 per cent in 1970. In Europe the story was quite different. The 1970s saw almost universal increases in unionization. The most dramatic examples were in some Scandinavian countries where density reached almost 90 per cent, but even in Italy union coverage rose by almost one-third to exceed 50 per cent. Increased unionization among public sector employees, whose numbers grew especially fast early in the period, accounted for some of this increase. The period from 1979 to 1985 saw a much more diverse pattern – declines in unionization of around 1 per cent per year in Italy and the UK, constancy in France (at a very low level) and Germany and continued increases in the small north European countries (apparently reaching 98 per cent in Denmark). Only in the USA do these patterns represent anything approaching the collapse of trade unionism which ocurred in the interwar period in most European countries. At that time union membership fell by one-half or more from the early twenties to the early thirties.

Workers did not accept the effects of stagnation on jobs and living standards willingly or easily. Strike rates remained high throughout the seventies, but then declined in the early and mid-eighties under the pressure of mounting unemployment (table 15.1). Particularly significant were a number of key confrontations between employers and unions, the outcomes of which both exemplified the shift in the balance of power towards capital and encouraged other unions to make concessions over issues of wage bargaining, redundancies and work rules. We discuss briefly the Fiat strike in Italy, the air traffic controllers' dispute in the USA and the miners' strike in the UK, all of which were rather decisive victories for the employers. Finally in this section we look at the less clear-cut result of the struggles of IG Metall in Germany.

Table 15.1 Days occupied in strikes, 1953–87[a]

	1953–61	1962–66	1967–71	1972–76	1977–81	1982–87
USA	113	79	165	105	90	28
Japan	45	25	19	21	5	2
France	41	32	350	34	23	13
Germany	7	3	8	3	8	9
Italy	64	134	161	200	151	93
UK	28	23	60	97	112	88

[a] Average number of days per year occupied in strikes per 100 workers in industry and transport.
Source: *Employment Gazette*, October 1963, October 1972, March 1983, March 1984 and June 1989.

From 1976 to 1979 the Italian Communist Party (PCI) cooperated with the Christian Democrat government in an attempt to realize its 'historic compromise'. One facet involved the unions holding back on pay and accepting redundancies. The communist secretary-general of the main union confederation, the CGIL, said that pay 'will have to be very restricted' and that 'we can no longer force firms to keep on a number of workers which is superfluous to their productive possibilities'. He called for 'sacrifices, not marginal but substantial sacrifices' (quoted Flanagan et al., 1983, p. 555).

Electoral reverses forced the PCI back into opposition. The employers then moved on to the offensive, with what was described as a new sense of identity and cooperation. In the autumn of 1979 Fiat fired 61 workers for misconduct (alleged intimidation, insults to foremen and sabotage) and union officials failed to win support for strike action. A British observer noted that 'Fiat's action has already produced a marked change on the factory floor: the general attitude to foremen has changed, and there has been an end to the insults to which they were previously subjected. It is clear that the Fiat episode has also made a strong impression on workers in some other large companies such as Pirelli, Alfa Romeo and Italsider' (Incomes Data Services, November 1979).

In September 1980 the Fiat unions were forced, after a 33-day strike, to accept 23,000 lay-offs and the transfer of surplus labour to other jobs in the area. The decisive event was a march of foremen and plant managers opposing the strike, at which some 3000 were expected. This turned into the 'march of the 40,000', with many rank-and-file workers demonstrating opposition to the union line. The *Economist* reported that 'Because of Fiat's size and symbolic importance in Italy, the outcome is already being described as the "hot autumn in reverse"' (25 October 1980).

In October 1980 Ronald Reagan – soon to become the first US president to have been a trade union leader – wrote to the president of one of the few unions to endorse his candidature: 'You can rest assured that if I am elected President, I will take whatever steps are necessary to provide [your members] with the most modern equipment available and to adjust staff levels and work days so that they are commensurate with achieving a maximum degree of public safety.... I pledge to you that my administration will work very closely with you to bring about a spirit of co-operation between the President and [your members]' (quoted Ackerman, 1982, p. 110). The union was PATCO, the Professional Air Traffic Controllers' Organization. Ten months later, on 3 August 1981, Reagan fired the entire 11,000 membership. Union leaders were hustled to jail in chains.

A crucial flight reduction plan eased the pressure on traffic control. It also enabled the major airlines, suffering from around 50 per cent excess capacity and furious competition from the newly deregulated cut-price operators (see chapter 17), to cut down on their losses. After the strike was defeated, new air traffic controllers had to sign an agreement not to engage in industrial action.

The treatment handed out to PATCO intimidated other state sector workers and encouraged some private sector employers to try to break their unions. In the private sector, workers had been forced to make major concessions to management in the form of wage cuts, wage freezes, premature renegotiations of existing contracts and easing of work rules. Major wage concessions took place in the trucking industry in 1982: no general wage increases were granted, and cost-of-living adjustments both covered a smaller proportion of inflation (70 per cent) than previously and were to be paid less frequently. Automobile workers accepted a deal with no general wage increases and a delay in the cost-of-living adjustments (which in this case gave 90 per cent protection). Probably of more long-term significance, important changes in work rules have been accepted – speeding up a process already underway. *Business Week* reported many examples – from steel, autos, railroads, meat-packing, rubber, airlines, construction and other industries – of jobs being 'enlarged' by the addition of duties or combination of crafts, and management being granted greater flexibility to schedule hours of work and to change staffing after the introduction of new technology. One observer remarked: 'You can go back to almost any recession and find examples of unionized companies going more aggressively after work rules. But you have to go back to the Depression to find as much of it as is going on now' (*Business Week*, 16 May 1983).

The British miners' strike of 1984–5 exemplified the difficulties faced by workers in resisting unemployment. The immediate occasion for the strike was the announcement of the closure of five loss-making collieries; in the background was a much longer-term threat to jobs represented by heavy investment in new mining technology and a sluggish market for coal. The government's case followed the market logic that the nationalized British Coal (BC) should close pits which made a financial loss. It disregarded the costs of closure (redundancy pay, loss of tax receipts and so forth), which were much less than the subsidies required to keep such pits open; it ignored the reduction of coal reserves if pits closed; and it paid no heed to the social devastation in communities largely dependent on the industry. BC promised no compulsory redundancies, with transfers to other pits for those who did not take the substantial available redundancy money. So jobs for individual miners were not at stake; the issue was rather the continuing availability of jobs for communities in areas of very high unemployment.

The strike was fatally weakened by the fact that substantial numbers of miners kept working, especially in the Nottingham coalfield, which felt less threatened by the closure plans. As well as providing coal to the power stations this hampered attempts to gain support from workers in other industries. The Conservative government, remembering the two humiliations inflicted by the National Union of Miners (NUM) on its predecessors in the early seventies, had prepared carefully by building up coal stocks and adapting coal-fired power stations so that they could burn oil. The police were used in unprecedented numbers (up to 8000 a day) to prevent effective picketing and more than 11,000 miners were arrested. The government's new employment laws were also deployed to seize the union's assets.

The union eventually led a return to work without a settlement after nearly a year on strike. The aftermath in the industry was devastating. A breakaway union, based in Nottinghamshire, severely weakened the bargaining position of the NUM. In the four years after the strike half the pits were closed, 115,000 jobs were lost and productivity nearly doubled as old work practices were scrapped and new technology was implemented. A decline in the world price of coal and the threat from the to-be-privatized electricity industry to import large quantities kept the industry under continual pressure. As an example of savage rationalization, in the wake of an industrial confrontation, the British coal industry is probably unequalled. But many other countries saw employment in basic industries slashed in similar ways from the early 1980s on, with disastrous effects on the dole queues.

In 1977 the German unions pulled out of the so-called concerted action sessions in which guidelines for wage increases were discussed with the government and employers. The president of the German union federation, the DGB, complained that 'the honeymoon is over' and said that 'if the social market economy isn't capable of re-establishing full employment one must wonder whether such a system will remain defensible in the future' (quoted Flanagan et al., 1983, p. 285). A strike wave, major by German standards, followed in 1978 and early 1979 as unions resisted new technology (in printing) and downgrading of jobs (engineering), and fought for better pay (engineering) and a 35 hour working week (steel). The employers retaliated by locking out vast numbers of workers. In engineering alone nearly 200,000 workers were locked out, three times as many as were on strike. In steel, where the strike lasted six weeks, the employers reacted to strikes in plants supplying the car industry by locking out the rest of the work force. The resulting financial pressure helped to force the workers back on substantially the employers' terms. In the printing industry reporters were to be allowed to type directly to computers. In engineering, technologically displaced workers were to be transferred or retrained. In steel the working week remaining intact. Fewer than half the strikers voted for the settlement and this was widely regarded as a vote of no confidence in the union leadership. The steel and engineering union was forced in 1979 to accept a moratorium on all non-wage issues until 1983.

Despite this setback, 1984 saw the 'longest and toughest industrial dispute in the history of the Federal Republic of Germany' (*German Tribune*, 1 July 1984) when seven weeks of selective strikes in the engineering industry led to 400,000 workers without work. Ironically, Toyota-type production systems in the German car industry, with minimal stocks (see below), increased employers' vulnerability and some workers who were laid off were denied social insurance (with the law being subsequently changed to exclude from benefits workers laid off in a dispute from which they stood to gain). IG Metall did not achieve the 35-hour week it was seeking, but it succeeded in reducing average hours within plants to 38.5 per week with some flexibility between groups of workers and over periods of time, so that the operating time of machinery did not suffer. Three years later another agreement, negotiated without strike action, cut average hours to 37 but with some increase in flexibility provisions, and in 1990 a further agreement brought the 35-hour week into sight for the mid-1990s. These developments took place in the context of the high levels of unemployment (averaging around 8 per cent in Germany) which have generally tilted the balance of power at the bargaining table.

Relocating production

One response from the employers to the development of effective workplace organization in the 1960s and 1970s has been to disperse production geographically. Even during the boom, management often opted to spawn new plants on fresh sites rather than to enlarge existing ones. In the United Kingdom the share of net manufacturing output contributed by the 100 largest plants only crept up from 9 to 11 per cent during the fifties and sixties, while that contributed by the 100 largest firms jumped up from 22 to 41 per cent. One factor inhibiting growth of plant size was the difficulty in controlling labour. A crude indicator of such difficulty is the incidence of strikes. In the United Kingdom in 1971–3 plants with between 11 and 24 employees had strikes which occupied 15 days per thousand employees; strikes in those employing more than 5000 occupied 3708 days per thousand employees. It is unlikely that this difference arises solely from plant size. Some of the most repetitive and alienating jobs are housed in giant plants. But labour control problems have undoubtedly encouraged firms to limit their plant size.

Some of the new technology can be used very effectively on a small scale – a report in the *Engineer* magazine quotes the case of a Japanese man with a plastics factory in his back garden in which the mouldings are handled by robot arms leaving him with the tasks of filling the hopper with raw materials and replacing the boxes for mouldings to fall into. Work has been 'put out' to such small subcontractors. In Italy management embraced 'decentralized production' as a conscious antidote to working-class strength, especially after the 'Hot Autumn' (chapter 12). Small factories could often avoid union control, state measures to protect workers, and taxes and social security contributions. In the Modena area of Italy the number of small workshops quadrupled between 1963 and 1975. Ironically, many were set up by union militants victimized in the fifties. One account of this 'high-technology cottage industry' has described these firms:

> Most of the shops and factories in these areas employ from 5 to 50 workers, a few as many as 100, and a very few 250 or more. Some recall turn-of-the-century sweatshops: the three or four workers are children scarcely fifteen years old, supervised by an adult or two, perhaps their parents; the tools are simple, the product crude, the hours long, the air full of dust and fumes. But many of the others are spotless; the workers extremely skilled and the distinction between them and their supervisors almost imperceptible; the tools the most advanced numerically controlled equipment of its type; the products, designed in the shop, sophisticated and distinctive enough to capture monopolies in world markets. If you had thought so long about Rousseau's artisan clockmakers at Neuchâtel or

> Marx's idea of labour as joyful, self-creative association that you had begun to doubt their possibility, then, you might, watching these craftsmen at work, forgive yourself the sudden conviction that something more utopian than the present factory system is practical after all. (Sabel, 1982, p. 220)

Even this enthusiast admits that artisan-type creativity is limited to the top stratum of skilled workers. The firms are reluctant to train unskilled workers, because 'once they possess the generally applicable skills that innovative work requires, nothing prevents the newly minted craftsmen from moving to another firm or going into business for themselves' (Sabel, 1982, p. 228).

In Japan subcontracting is more extensive and tightly organized than elsewhere. The average manufacturing firm employing more than a thousand people has 160 subcontractors. Even those employing less than four workers have on average three subcontractors. Subcontracting gives parent firms great flexibility. In downturns it is more difficult to cut staff and overheads in the parent than to cancel orders from subcontractors. A further advantage is steep wage differentials by firm size. In 1981 the average manufacturing wage in firms employing between five and twenty-nine people was only 57 per cent of that in firms employing more than 500.

According to the chairman of one substantial subcontractor:

> There is no such thing as labor–management relations in his company, as they are all people working together. . . . From December to March the company becomes very busy, and the employees have to work late-night overtime. Late-night overtime generally lasts from 10 p.m. to 4 a.m. When workers participating in this late-night overtime finish work at 4 in the morning, they sleep for about 3 hours in the dormitory on the grounds of the factory (in order to avoid loss of time through commuting) and report for work next day at 8 a.m. The owners of the company understand very well that this procedure is against the Labor Standards Law, but the work accumulates and there is no labor union in the company to monitor compliance with the law, so workers tend to co-operate with management in this respect. (Anasz et al., 1986, pp. 47–8)

The relationship between Japanese subcontractors and parent companies is often very close, and is becoming more so: 70 per cent or more of parent companies specify daily deliveries from their subcontractors. In 1982 a reported 10 per cent were even designating delivery by the 'hour'. Parent companies are also heavily, and increasingly, involved in keeping subcontractors' technical standards up to scratch. After the 'oil shock', an electronic condenser manufacturer developed an automatic assembly machine and insisted that its subcontractors installed it. 'The parent company set forth a policy that subcontractors not investing 5 million yen per worker ($25,000) would cease to receive orders' (Ikeda, 1979, p. 68). This in turn radically reduced the subcontractors' use of home workers from neighbouring farms. The Toyota company is famous for its highly organized and sophisticated system of subcontracting. Technical levels and quality controls are closely monitored and many firms in other countries are following this facet of Toyotaism (see below).

In Japan subcontracting of work takes place inside the core plants as well. Data are hard to come by. But one-quarter of the workers in one Toshiba factory are reportedly employed through subcontractors or as part-timers, with very low wages and no union protection, and 9.5 per cent of non-agricultural workers are classified as casual workers or day labourers.

There is evidence that employment in small firms has been of increasing importance. In the USA the share of employment in establishments employing less than 100 workers rose from 49.5 per cent in 1970 to 55.9 per cent in 1985, in Japan from 71.5 per cent in 1972 to 77.1 per cent in 1981, and in Germany from 47.0 per cent in 1977 to 49.6 per cent in 1985. Around one-half of such increases represents shifts in the employment structure towards services where smaller establishments dominate.

Trends towards small plant employment have been identified within manufacturing as well. The most dramatic case of this is the UK, where the share of small plants rose from 19.7 per cent in 1974–5 to 26.2 per cent in 1983, with the very largest plants showing a large fall in their share of employment. It has been suggested that such trends reflect a decisive shift in competitive advantage back to small firms, because new technologies or the development of much more variegated consumer markets have reduced the economies of scale from mass production. But it is far too early to draw such a conclusion. In the first place the share of employment in large *firms* has declined much less than the share of large *plants*, as giant firms now span increasingly large numbers of separate plants. Moreover, large firms may have been more affected by the periods of severe recession and may have pruned their labour force more effectively in response. It is particularly striking that the share of small firm employment in Japanese manufacturing *fell* in the early eighties having increased in the seventies. That this should happen in by far the most advanced manufacturing sector in terms of work organization (see below) strongly suggests that it is far too soon to suggest that the historical trend to giant firms (figure 10.2) has been reversed.

Within the advanced countries, capital has migrated away from areas with strong traditions of industrial militancy. In the United Kingdom, a shift away from conurbations to smaller towns began in the sixties. Labour relations almost certainly played a part. In the United States manufacturing has been attracted to the southern 'Sunbelt' states where labour organization is weak.

From Fordism to Toyotaism

Throughout the history of capitalism a central problem for management has always been how to make workers work hard enough. What employers buy on the market with a wage is an employee's capacity to work. Work of requisite quality and intensity has to be ensured through a system of work organization. In the mid-1980s an authoritative article in the *Harvard Business Review* proclaimed that 'in factory after factory there is a revolution under way in the management of work' (Walton, 1985, p. 77). The author explained as follows:

> The traditional – or control-oriented – approach to work-force management took shape during the early part of this century in response to the division of work into small, fixed jobs for which individuals could be held accountable. The actual definition of jobs, as of acceptable standards of performance rested on 'lowest common denominator' assumptions about workers' skill and motivations. To monitor and control effort of this assumed caliber, management organized its own responsibilities into a hierarchy of specialized roles buttressed by a top-down allocation of authority and by status symbols attached to positions in the hierarchy. . . . At the heart of this traditional model is the wish to establish order, exercise control and achieve efficiency in the application of the work force. . . . The model's real father is Frederick W. Taylor, the turn-of-the-century 'father of scientific management'. (Walton, 1985, p. 78)

The production line, immortalized in Chaplin's *Modern Times*, tried to achieve the necessary degree of control over the work process by allocating each worker a limited task and allowing a certain time in which it had to be performed before the product-in-process was whisked off to the next work station. Such a mechanized system of producing standardized commodities, in which individual workers carried out limited and repetitive tasks, has acquired the nickname of Fordism and, spreading out from the USA, was regarded as the leading system of production during the great boom. But as the *Harvard Business Review* went on to explain, the Fordist system of production encountered increasing difficulties:

> Recently, however, changing expectations among workers have prompted a growing disillusionment with the apparatus of control. At the same time, of course, an intensified challenge from abroad has made the competitive obsolescence of this strategy clear. . . . Especially in a high-wage country like the United States, market success depends on a superior level of performance, a level that, in turn, requires the deep commitment, not merely the obedience – if you can obtain it – of workers. And as painful experience shows, this commitment cannot flourish in a workplace dominated by the familiar model of control. (Walton, 1985, pp. 78–9)

Opposition from workers to the production-line system of work organization grew as labour reserves dried up towards the end of the sixties (chapter 11). The difficulties were signalled in a 1970 article in *Fortune* magazine headlined 'Blue Collar Blues'. A notorious 'revolt' at General Motors' Lordstown plant in 1972 highlighted the problems, which took their most extreme form in the Fiat workers' struggles for control over work organization in the late sixties and early seventies. Yet if pressure from workers had been the main factor pushing for the transformation of work organization it is hard to imagine that the trend would have survived the onset of mass unemployment. Undoubtedly the decisive influence was the perceived superiority of Japanese methods of work organization demonstrated in the struggle for world market shares. According to the business journals Toyotaism was increasingly displacing Fordism as the best practice system for organizing work.

The distinctive feature of Toyota's system was that it was directed towards producing numerous different, but related, models in relatively short runs rather than the huge runs of standardized cars typical of Fordism. In the early postwar years this was the result of Toyota's limited market, but the techniques which it evolved proved to be highly effective as its production expanded in a market for cars which was becoming more and more variegated.

> Modern assembly lines of passenger cars specifically designed for the production of a particular model turn out thousands of varieties of cars, distinguished by different combinations of engine and transmission, color, body type, options and so on. At the assembly factory of one Japanese manufacturer, 32,100 varieties of cars were produced in 1978, and the average amount of output per variety was 11 in a three month period. (This factory only produced 500 varieties in the mid-1960s.) (Aoki, 1988, p. 20)

In terms of work on the production line, Ono, the designer of Toyota's system, began with old-fashioned 'speed-up':

> One of the ideas Ono had was to redistribute worker motions and cycle times to eliminate idle time for a series of workers, and then either remove one or more of them or have the last person on a line take over some of the tasks of his neighbor, and so on down the line. While American engineers invented this technique along with time and motion studies, Ono applied it with much more rigour. He was determined to eliminate all unnecessary movements and to allow no idle time, for machines or workers. . . . When demand was low he dropped line speeds, cut out workers, and tightened job routines and cycle times. He made employees work even faster when there were many orders. (Cusumano, 1985, pp. 272–3)

Exactly the same principles were applied to machine operators.

> Another of Ono's 'rationalizations', and a key reason for the rise in productivity in Toyota during the 1950s, was his decision to make a distinction between the operating time of a machine and the working time of its operator, and then to have each worker operate more than one machine. Toyota had followed the American system prior to Ono's arrival in the machine shop: Workers at distinct stations specialized in operations such as lathe processing, milling, boring, or welding. Americans even established different unions and job specifications for dozens of specialties, making it difficult for management to adapt their workforce to changing production requirements. It was obvious that, with so many single-functioned machines and operators, production volumes had to be huge to pay the

costs of equipment and personnel. Yet it also seemed to Ono that, in times of slow demand or low production, specialization resulted in idle time that could be eliminated if machinery and workers did more than one job each. Nor did all machines require constant attention when running, though employees considered themselves to be working while they waited for machines to finish. (Cusumano, 1985, p. 273)

Accordingly workers were made to operate three or four machines rather than just one.

Such techniques for speeding up the work process, which were still essentially Fordist, were complemented by what were ultimately more far-reaching changes. Toyota, along with leading companies in the steel and other industries, practised job rotation whereby individual workers were assigned by the foremen to a dozen or more positions on the assembly line over a period of time or worked with the whole range of machinery in the workshop. This allowed workers to be substituted into any job contributing 'greatly to the efficiency of the auto production line. Daily changes occur very frequently in an assembly line workshop. Along the same line are assembled cars with various specifications, such as two or four doors or with an air conditioner. Although these changes are of a minor nature, they require adjustments in the deployment of the workforce in order to maintain a high speed of production. . . . To cope with such changes in conditions a flexible labour force is required' (Koike, 1988, pp. 140–1). At Toyota, after the worker was rotated and trained in each job, 'the final step is scheduling the workers through job rotation at a frequency of several times a day' (quoted Aoki, 1988, p. 14).

Arguably more important than the direct benefits of flexibility is the potential which rotation develops in the workforce to cope with non-routine circumstances, such as machine malfunction or product defects. Such capacity was particularly important in Toyota, whose most distinctive innovation was the 'just-in-time' approach to the supply of components. Stocks were kept at a minimum (by the early sixties its inventories were one-quarter to one-third of the US level) and the pattern of production was adjusted rapidly to fluctuations in the model mix ordered by dealers. The danger was that the benefits of low inventory would be swallowed up by interruptions to the production process. To overcome this workers were required to check for defects as they fetched the parts they needed; they were also required to rectify minor problems with the machinery. Job rotation was supposed to enhance workers' capacities to undertake this work by increasing their understanding of the production process.

The drive to improve quality also involved large scale participation of workers in 'quality circles' (QCs) in which small groups of workers discussed improvements to productivity, quality, safety and maintenance. By 1970 Toyota claimed to have about 2000 of these quality circles; in the early eighties Nissan, initially lagging behind Toyota in QC activity, claimed that 99 per cent of its employees were in QCs and that savings resulting from QC activities were running at $20 million per year. The car companies also ran individual suggestion schemes: in 1982 Toyota claimed 1.9 million suggestions, more than one per fortnight per worker (double the rate at its arch-rival Nissan), with a remarkable 95 per cent being adopted by the company. These extraordinary claims (and what looks from the statistics like a battle to be the first car company to reach one million suggestions a year) suggest a great deal of company manipulation. Indeed, 'Nissan and Toyota officials also conceded that QC circles functioned primarily to increase employee participation in company operations and to boost employee morale by allowing employees to work in groups to solve problems' (Cusumano, 1985, p. 334).

However inflated the claims for QCs the success of Toyota and other Japanese companies in achieving high quality is not in doubt and there is a consensus that the system for the multi-skilling of workers through job rotation contributed importantly to this as well as to raising direct productivity. Making workers responsible for quality and machine maintenance reduced the number of quality control, maintenance and supervisory staff. A comparison between a Japanese and an American car assembly plant of similar size in 1980 found 50 per cent fewer production workers in Japan, 60 per cent fewer quality control workers, 60 per cent fewer maintenance workers and 75 per cent fewer management staff.

In total, productivity at Toyota appears to have been some 50 per cent above the US level by 1965; by 1979 it was estimated that it took only one-third as much working time to produce a car at Toyota as at an average US producer. While the contribution to productivity of the extremely high rate of investment in Japan should be recognized, it is not surprising that attempts to import the Japanese system of work organization have followed hard on the heels of the flood of Japanese manufactures. But devising improved methods for utilizing workers' capacity is only one side of the problem. It is also necessary to ensure that such capacity is exerted to the full. In this respect too, Japan has excelled in developing payment and promotion systems which guarantee maximum 'commitment' from workers, free from trade union challenge.

Japanese labour practices in large companies have long been characterized as 'seniority wages plus lifetime employment'. This is a serious oversimplification. In the first place 'lifetime employment' is an inaccurate description of a situation where, for every two workers joining large firms, one has left by the end of the first year. No doubt the pace and intensity of work plays an important part in explaining this. While turnover decreases sharply as length of job tenure increases, the proportion of manufacturing workers with more than 10 years' work in the same large company is not extraordinarily higher in Japan than in EC countries. Moreover, when redundancies do occur, those who lose their jobs are disproportionately aged over 45 in Japan (the opposite of a 'last in first out' principle).

The average blue-collar worker in a large Japanese company certainly experiences much more steeply rising earnings if he stays with the company than his counterpart in Europe or the USA. Since similar patterns are observed for male white-collar workers outside Japan this has been dubbed the ' "white-collarization" of the blue-collar wage system' (Koike, 1988, p. 53). The fact that rising wages are based on 'seniority' in the firm, and not age as such, implies that middle-aged Japanese workers would lose a great deal if they shifted to another firm. The 'cost-of-job-loss' for such workers is therefore tremendous, even assuming they could get another comparable job:

> If a Japanese male employee works for a large firm for 27 years, his earnings are likely to be almost three and a half times his initial earnings in real terms. But if he changes jobs at that time and his tenure at the original firm is not counted, his earnings would be a little less than half of what he currently gets. If the American employee works for one large firm for 30 years, on the other hand, his earnings would only be doubled; however if he separates from the firm at that point, only a quarter of his earnin s would be sacrificed. (Aoki, 1988, p. 59)

It should not be concluded from such figures that progression up the 'seniority wage scale' is automatic and relatively independent of the worker's performance. Both the speed with which a worker proceeds to a higher rank or grade and the payment within the grade depend very heavily on the foreman's assessment of the worker's performance (which includes of course ability to master a range of tasks). For example, it appears that at Hitachi maximum pay rates for a particular grade of production worker are double (or more) the minimum rates and that the top grade of production worker earns on average more than double the bottom grade. This suggests that the best paid production workers can earn around four times what the worst paid earn. The foreman's 'merit assessment' even covers the part of the wage nominally dependent on evaluation of the job, for this is 'in practice the disguised evaluation of personal attributes' (Aoki, 1988, p. 97). At Hitachi even the twice-yearly bonus is heavily dependent on 'merit assessment'. Progress up to the top grades of production workers can take as short a time as 15 years or as long as 35 years.

The less-than-cooperative worker may be 'dispatched' by the parent firm to subsidiaries or related firms where wages are lower (on average some 20 per cent lower in the main subsidiaries of Toyota and Nissan, for example). Toyota, operating in a rural area, even enlisted family pressure:

> Management staff compiled the aptitude evaluation to judge an employee's suitability for a particular job or promotions by soliciting formal opinions from supervisors and co-workers. Employees then had to file an individual report at the end of each year that stated their objectives for the coming year, how well they met those of the past year, and whether or not their current positions were suitable. The company sent these reports along with comments on the behaviour and attitudes of the workers to their families. In Japan, especially in a rural area where people were highly sensitive to public criticism, managers found that involving the

family made employees conform more readily to company policy. (Cusumano, 1985, p. 182)

It may be concluded that large Japanese companies have instituted a wages and employment system where the 'incentives' to cooperate fully with management in reorganizations of the production process are extremely powerful. Nor do Japanese unions provide a serious counterweight to these pressures. We have already seen (chapters 4, 6 and 8) how early postwar radicalism in the trade union was defeated and 'second' or company unions were installed. Encouraged by the Japan Productivity Centre, management introduced processes of consultations at firm and shopfloor level to cover matters such as investment, improvement in methods of production as well as working conditions, safety and so forth. This acted as 'a kind of buffer system to evade the real growth of trade union control of the shop floor' by inducing the expectation among workers that 'their complaints or discontent will be "democratically" dealt with by the consultation bodies. . . . [Management] conceded that the concrete measures for "rationalization" as well as all problems arising from "rationalization" should be matters for consultation provided the trade union accept the "managerial prerogative". It seems that they wanted to widen the sphere for consultation so as to restrict the sphere for collective bargaining' (Totsuka, pp. 3 and 9). Such consultation extended to wage issues so that by the time that collective bargaining began, an agreement on how the negotiations should proceed had been struck between the union officials and the personnel department. Not surprisingly, 'collective bargaining has a ceremonial function designed to mobilize the union members rather than constituting a meaningful negotiation' (Saga, p. 4) and repeatedly unions would receive 100 per cent of their wage 'demands'.

Frequently the union functioned as little more than an offshoot of the personnel department, with graduates receiving training in the personnel department, then moving over to become full-time union officials before returning to the company as personnel managers. By 1978 ex-managers of the company trade union executive committee comprised one-quarter of the board members in major companies.

The wearing of two hats is also common at lower levels. Rank-and-file workers are often represented by their immediate superiors:

In most cases the shop stewards of big enterprise unions in the private sector are foremen with the remainder comprised primarily of charge-hands who are soon to be appointed foremen. In other words, in the consultation body on the shop floor, usually the management side is represented by a superintendent and the union side is represented by foremen or charge-hands. Such a consultation between a superintendent and foreman might be expected to work smoothly without any serious friction. (Totsuka, p. 10)

Some commentators describe this as simply confirming very different cultural attitudes from those in the West. But, as described in chapters 6 and 8, the unions were only captured by their companies after a long struggle. Moreover, in the public sector a tradition of independent trade unionism was maintained. The most notable example was the National Railways Union, which fought off a managerial onslaught on work rules in the early seventies despite widespread victimization. Breaking up this union and implementing redundancies was a major motivation behind the privatization and splitting up of the National Railways. This and other privatizations contributed to the weakening of the Sohyo union federation, and then its absorption into Rengo. This body had covered the main private sector unions, with demands generally closely tailored to the competitive requirements of the employers. In these unions disagreement with the pro-management line is supressed. Elections in the Nissan workers' union, for example, suggest an amazing unanimity of opinion. In 1978, 218 candidates stood for 218 seats and won an average 99.7 per cent of votes cast on a 99.96 per cent turnout.

Two Nissan workers explain:

> When we vote, we are asked to gather around the supervisor's desk in a group of several at a time, and write out our voting slips right on the spot, on the desk, in front of everybody. The desk is an ordinary office desk of about 1 metre in width. And standing beside the desk are the election administrators, I mean, the assistant manager and the shop steward, who watch closely to see if we write down the right name. . . . If blank votes or invalid votes are found, the shop steward is forced to submit a written apology to the top union leaders. That is why he keeps an eye on how we fill in the voting slips. He even fills out the ballots for new employees, saying that they mis-wrote the characters or that they may not know who the candidates are. (Quoted Yamamoto, 1980–1, p. 30)

The union leadership justifies this surveillance on the ground that votes critical of the existing leadership would 'reveal disunity in the union to the management'.

At Toyota, too, most shop stewards are foremen or 'team chiefs', and members of the union committee are supervisory staff, in effect company appointees. In 1971 a rank-and-file member with the temerity to stand against the union's president secured a fifth of the votes. The union responded by changing its rules. In future candidates must be nominated by 50 workers: 'As it now stands, you can't run for chief executive unless you find fifty supporters who have the courage to openly oppose the union, which emphasizes cooperation with the management' (Kamata, 1982, p. 183). Such a stand would endanger promotion. The unsuccessful candidate for president found himself stuck at the bottom of the wage scale.

Dissent from the union's line is not tolerated, as the following report from Toshiba shows:

When Mr Ueno, a 25-year-old press operator in a section making console boxes for computers, took issue with the authoritarianism of the shop union system, he found himself branded as a dangerous subversive. One day last spring Mr Ueno handed out a single handbill to a colleague. It expressed criticism of the low wage demand made by the company union. The union's reaction to this 'challenge' was swift and heavy handed. First Mr Ueno's supervisor ordered the spiky-haired young man to sign an apology: 'I realize I was wrong to hand out a pamphlet without permission. . . . In case I ever repeat such a thing I am ready to accept any punishment.' He refused. Then he was summoned to the union office, threatened with ejection from the union (and thus from the firm) and told he would be placed under surveillance by shop stewards. (*Guardian*, 11 May 1982)

Physical and psychological harassment followed.

The Nissan union seems to have been second to none in the ferocity with which it suppressed any dissent in its ranks and in the autocratic style with which 'Emperor Shioji' ran the union. It does seem to have been quite exceptional in the extent to which the union represented a power base in the company, using a powerful shopfloor organization controlled by the foremen to limit managerial prerogatives which were untramelled virtually everywhere else in Japan's private sector. It 'was able to influence staff promotions at Nissan through a recommendation system that evaluated a candidate's activities in the union and standing in the hierarchy of union officials. While management usually approved only about half the recommendations that the [union's] executive committee submitted for positions as shop foremen, the company treated a negative appraisal from the union as a veto' (Cusumano, 1985, p. 172). This was an important method for ensuring rank-and-file loyalty to the union. But the union's influence was not limited to promotion:

It is the plant-level consultation meetings on the operating schedules of production that discuss and set the details of monthly production schedules – concerning such matters as the number of automobiles to be manufactured, the manning level (including changes in duties) and working hours (including the schedules for holiday work and overtime work). In practice, the operating schedules proposed by management would not be put into effect without the union's consent . . . which is very close to a 'veto' power. . . . We may surmise that many of the management's proposals for reducing the manning levels and for shortening production time seem to have actually been withdrawn in the face of union refusal. (Tabata, 1988, p. 66)

At the particular Nissan plant under investigation an example was found of the union blocking the introduction of some new equipment on the ground that it fulfilled neither of its requirements for agreement – the elimination of dirty or stressful work and the maintenance of jobs. Another academic concluded that 'union opposition was a major reason why Nissan did not try to compress cycle times, raise line speeds or use overtime to the same extent as Toyota, even though these techniques contributed to Toyota's higher productivity and operating profits' (Cusumano, 1985, p. 382). The designer of Toyota's production system 'was able to control the Toyota union, partly because management threatened to fire dissident workers, which it did in 1950, and partly because he was personally close to the union leaders' (Cusumano, 1985, p. 307). He later explained that he 'still considered his success in controlling the union to have been the most important advantage Toyota gained over its domestic and foreign competitors' (Cusumano, 1985, p. 307).

This picture of union power in Nissan should be seen in the context of a productivity level that, by the early eighties, was estimated to be well above the US level. Nevertheless, it was markedly lower than that of Toyota, to whom Nissan was losing market share. In 1982 the union withdrew from the '3-P' movement (productivity, participation and prosperity) on the grounds that the management meant by 'participation' commitment to the company, whereas the union understood more thoroughgoing consultation with the union. Opposition to the union's line originated with the sub-managers and foremen and then with the white-collar staff at head office (reminiscent of the 1953 coup against the 'first' union – see chapter 6). In 1986 the old leadership was voted out and under the slogan, 'The company should behave exactly as a company is supposed to and the union as the union is supposed to', a comprehensive agreement was signed with the company under which all matters subject to consultation (including production and employment) could be decided unilaterally by the management.

The effect at the shopfloor level was remarkable. The system was transformed into one resembling Toyota's manufacture of:

> Cars of the exact models and varieties, and in the exact quantities, as ordered daily by the customers. Such a production system would call for timely and flexible adjustment of manpower allocation and working hours to the shops . . . manning levels were reduced by 20 to 30 per cent in many of its production lines . . . working hours grew phenomenally longer. . . . In March 1987, [the] Company drastically revised its wage system, adopting one primarily based on the principle of payment according to ability. Under the new personnel system, the degree to which an individual worker's wage and promotion are determined in accordance with his performance and ability evaluation became far greater than before . . . [enticing] not only veteran workers of the foreman class – traditionally the main pillars of [the union] . . . but also rank and file workers into believing that loyalty to the company would be far more rewarding to them than loyalty to the union or solidarity with their fellow workers. (Tabata, 1988, pp. 78–80)

Nissan had clearly succeeded in overcoming its somewhat unusual labour relations, and has instituted the combination of flexible work practices, 'merit' payment systems and cooperative unions that has provided the internal context in which the large Japanese companies have accumulated capital and dominated world markets.

In the myriad of subcontractors supplying the big companies, and among the temporary and subcontract employees working alongside 'regular' workers in the big plants, wages and other conditions are worse, multi-skilling is less prevalent and in general a more Taylorist system of work organization dominates (see p. 268). Moreover, Japanese industries vary very widely in their efficiency.

> The Japanese labor productivity advantage is enormous in high volume assembly processes where hundreds, even thousands, of interdependent steps must be co-ordinated. In simpler processes, such as foundry, where perhaps thirty operational steps are required, the Japanese productivity advantage is slight, and sometimes non-existent. In process industries, such as paper, chemicals and metal refining, Japanese labor productivity in comparable plants is no better than can be found in western plants. The same is true of other simpler manufacturing. (Abeglenn and Stalk, 1986, p. 61)

Indeed in textiles and food processing Japanese productivity is very low. Nevertheless, the spectacular success of Japan in industries such as cars and electronic goods has stimulated widespread attempts to copy their methods of work. The following descriptions of General Motors factories has a familiar ring.

In Chevrolet's gear plant in Detroit, 'while a worker might have stood in one place all day tightening bolts on a rear brake assembly, he is now responsible with other team members for the production and quality of an entire brake system'. At another plant

> production workers can learn all of the jobs in one section, giving management flexibility in assigning work and filling in for absent workers. Workers are paid according to the skills they acquire, giving them an incentive to learn new ones. . . . The plant, which cranks out 1200 engines a day, is divided into 15 departments that are in turn subdivided into business teams of 10 to 20 workers each, consisting of production workers who assemble the engines and perform nonskilled maintenance duties. The engines are still produced on an assembly line, but the employees have varied routines and participate in decision-making. . . . The teams meet weekly on company time to discuss issues such as safety and housekeeping. They decide when to award raises and rotate jobs, and they may even suggest redesigning the work flow. . . . The 23 members of [one] team rotate among 12 or 13 jobs on the line, 6 engine-repair jobs, and 4 or 5 housekeeping and inspection jobs. In the old Detroit plant, there were 45 job classifications, each with its own wage rate. In Livonia, there are four wage levels for experienced workers, ranging from $9.63 an hour to a maximum of $10.08 for a 'job setter' – a worker who sets up and changes tooling on the line. A worker reaches the top rate after learning all the skills on two business teams. (*Business Week*, 16 May 1983)

Quality circles (QCs) also became a vogue Japanese import in the late seventies. But, as an American trade unionist pointed out, QCs give workers 'no real transfer of power over their work environment'. *Management Today*'s correspondent noted that 'it is precisely this feature which explains the noisy QC bandwagon' (March 1982).

Together with all these 'innovations' in the organization of work, there has been the much older weapon of speed-up, imposed under the pressure from mass unemployment. British Leyland was a classic example. The *Sunday Times* (21 March 1982) described as a 'miracle' the transformation at Longbridge where 'a marriage of men and machines has dramatically improved the productivity of BL'. One Longbridge worker – transferred to five different departments in one year, and ten different jobs in one department in three months – described the 'miracle' as follows:

> In the past management couldn't shift you without the agreement of the union; now it's done without consultation . . . it means that you never get to know any of the blokes, it breaks up any unity. . . . In the old days the target was set by timing the operator, now the target is based on the gross potential of the machine, that means they set the machine as fast as possible, the only limit being quality, and you have to keep up with it. They give you targets you can't reach. The gaffer comes to check your counter every hour; blokes have been suspended for failing to have an adequate explanation of why they haven't reached their target. (*Militant*, 23 April 1982)

All the enthusiasm for Japanese methods of work organization should not obscure their fundamental objective, which is to maximize the amount of work performed. A report on the performance of Japanese car plants in the USA (the 'transplants') noted dissatisfaction from workers:

> Partly because of health problems stemming from what critics call 'speedup'. . . . It's not so much that the transplants' assembly lines run faster than the Big Three's. Rather, the Japanese insist on a higher work intensity. They use the *kaizen* concept that calls for assemblers to make continuous improvements in performing their tasks, both to improve quality and to eliminate unneeded motion. There is continuing pressure to produce cars at the same line speed with fewer people . . . at GM's modern Linden (N.J.) plant, workers work 48 seconds out of every minute. At NUMMI (the joint Toyota/GM factory in California), they work 55 seconds a minute. Isamu Nobuto, president of Mazda's Flat Rock plant, doesn't deny that workers have little free time. 'People should be employed doing work that has value. It is not respecting the employee if we have them doing work which is wasteful'. (*Business Week*, 14 August 1989)

Conclusion

The labour movement has suffered many setbacks since the mid-1970s. The reassertion of managerial control, especially over all aspects of the production process, has been the overwhelming preoccupation of employers, and workers have been forced to make many concessions. Yet over matters like hours of work, victories have been gained in France through legislation and in the UK and especially Germany through industrial action. Even though 'flexibility' has often been conceded these represent real gains. The most serious threat seems to be the fragmentation of unions through the trend to bargaining at the company level, as the examples of Toyota and Nissan cited in this chapter illustrate. In the Japanese car industry competition eroded trade union strength (even in the strange form it took in Nissan) as weak labour movements 'drive out' the strong. Exactly the same is reflected at the international level, where pressure from Japanese (or South Korean) competition forces previously strong unions to make concessions. The pressure can be imported even more directly, as in the USA where some of the ten manufacturing plants set up by Japanese car manufacturers have succeeded in keeping out the Auto Workers union.

16

International Relations

The mould of international relations set in the immediate postwar period showed few cracks during the boom. The cold war thawed a little, but neither Eastern Europe nor China became a significant market for exports of the capitalist economies. Many colonial countries achieved independence, but this seldom jeopardized economic relations with the advanced countries. Growth was uneven between the advanced countries, but with rapid expansion overall, such divergences could be accommodated. The turbulent period of over-accumulation around the early 1970s; and the subsequent period of slower growth, saw more disruptive swings in these various relationships.

The Eastern bloc

Despite a marked deterioration in political relations and the onset of the 'second cold war' in the early 1980s, economic relationships between the West and the USSR, Eastern Europe and China changed little. In the first half of the 1970s there was a brief burst of trade and the share of ACC exports destined for Eastern Europe and the Soviet Union (the 'East') rose by one-half to reach some 6 per cent in 1975. In certain sectors the eastern market was more important: in 1976 it took around one-fifth of the machine tool exports of Germany, France, Italy and Belgium.

Lack of competitive exports resulted in the East's hard currency deficit on the balance of payments reaching $10 billion in 1975, largely financed by borrowing from Western banks. Although import growth was sharply cut back, and deficits were eliminated by 1982, the debts of the eastern bloc (net of hard currency assets) had risen to $81 billion. Poland was the most dramatic example. It had incurred one-third of the East's debt and its debt-service ratio (interest and capital repayments as a percentage of exports) exceeded 100 per cent in 1982. A major rescheduling of debt repayments had to be carried out, and the East European countries found it practically impossible to borrow. The problem was the East's inability to export enough to cover the repayment of interest and eventual repayment of principal. Lenders will only increase the value of outstanding loans if they bear a 'safe' ratio to foreign exchange earnings. Loans and interest payments can grow rapidly without problem only if exports grow in parallel.

The Soviet Union suffered a catastrophic deterioration of nearly one-half in the terms of trade between 1985 and 1988 as a result of the fall in the world price of its oil exports. Domestic pressures ruled out its usual response of cutting imports and instead the widening trade deficit was financed by gold sales and an estimated rise of $10 billion in its net debt, to over $35 billion. Even so its ratio of debt-service to hard currency earnings was only 21 per cent. Of the East European economies Poland incurred most debt ($35 billion), while Hungary was the most indebted relative to population (some $1800 per head). In the second half of the 1980s net interest on the accumulated debt of the East was running at $6–8 billion per year, forcing further restraint on imports. By 1988 the share of ACC exports directed to the East had halved to a mere 3 per cent (equally split between Eastern Europe and the Soviet Union).

The 1970s saw a spattering of direct investments from the West to the East. For example, Citroën and Fiat signed major contracts to produce cars in Romania and Poland respectively, exports of which to the West were to cover the cost of imported machinery and know-how. The rapid acceleration of the pace of political and economic reform in 1989 quickened interest in investment possibilities, dramatized by the much-publicized opening of Macdonald's in Moscow. At the end of that year the United Nations noted, 'Both Poland and Hungary offer important attractions to international business. Both countries are close to major markets, are integrated into Europe's transport infrastructure, possess a skilled labour force and offer very low wage rates, competitive even with certain East Asian countries' (UNECE, 1990, pp. 55–6). Although 1000 joint ventures with western companies were recorded in the two countries by the autumn of 1989 the total capital invested was only about $1 billion. The UN report noted fears about future developments of exchange rates and 'difficulties of implanting direct investment into transforming economies (e.g. problems of supply linkages, lack of supporting services, especially of an adequate telecommunications infrastructure, commercial information etc.)'. In the Soviet Union only a tenth or so of the 1200 registered joint ventures were operational at the beginning of 1990, many of these being 'simply legalised import–export operations' (*Financial Times*, 12 March 1990) and foreign companies' capital contribution was put at $1.6 billion. The tiny scale of these investments is illustrated by the fact that total direct investment overseas by the ACCs into each others' economies, the LDCs and the East amounted to a total of $562 billion over the period 1981–8.

In East Germany the prospect of early unification with the Federal Republic had encouraged the signing of 600 joint venture agreements in the first four months of 1990. But the *Financial Times* reported that 'after early euphoria about opportunities in the East, West German business is acting cautiously . . .

apart from the car industry there has been little definite commitment on the part of manufacturers to take over and renovate the Kombinate [East German industrial groups]' (23 April 1990). The report noted that the East German IG Metall engineering union, with the backing of its Western counterpart, was proposing that 75 per cent of the capital of state-owned enterprises should be transferred to the workers, giving them a veto over management decisions. 'This may not catch on, but West German business is beginning to worry, none the less, that the West German unions are belatedly moving in to support their East German counterparts, and in some cases effectively taking them over. There is concern that this may have an effect on wage levels. . . . The unions in both Germanys will also do their best to block pro-business reform of the East German trade union law which bans lock-outs and gives unions more power than in the West.' According to a poll taken early in 1990 most West German business outside the retail sector had no intention of changing strategies on account of the prospect of German unification. But after monetary union in July 1990 there is a need for substantial modernization of East German industry if massive unemployment and levels of subsidization are to be avoided.

Given the likelihood that the East, apart from the special case of East Germany, will receive relatively little private direct investment from the West, it will be forced to rely heavily on official loans. By the beginning of 1990 some $30 billion in loans from international institutions (the European Bank for Reconstruction and Development, the Group of 24 countries and less definitely the World Bank) seemed in prospect for Eastern Europe. Although this seems an impressive sum, any idea that it would finance a bonanza of capital goods exports from the West should be discounted. Spread over, say, a five-year period it would no more than pay the interest on the East's debt. Even if compressed into a three-year period, and translated into a higher level of imports into the East than could otherwise be afforded, this would add 0.5 per cent to the exports of the ACCs – the equivalent of one month's growth at average rates. Only if Eastern Europe, and especially the Soviet Union, were to generate very rapid expansion of their own production, and in commodities competitive on world markets, could they provide substantial markets for the ACCs (especially Western Europe).

The less developed countries

Some commentators have suggested that developments in the LDCs contributed significantly to the economic fluctuations in production and employment in the advanced economies. This argument is sometimes used to excuse economic failures in the advanced countries. Although there is, of course, some influence in this direction because the LDCs are part of the same world economy, the argument at least up to 1982 was in general quite wrong. During the 1970s the LDCs (especially Asia and Latin America), by maintaining relatively rapid rates of growth of income, investment and imports actually helped to alleviate the slump in the advanced countries. The failure of the LDCs to continue playing this role after 1982 showed the limited degree to which they could expand more quickly than the ACC markets on which they relied.

There are obvious parallels between the role of the LDCs and that of the Eastern bloc but there are also two important differences. One is that the West's economic relations with the South were on a far larger scale. By the early 1980s, for example, Brazil and Mexico each owed as much to international banks as did the entire Eastern bloc. The other important difference is that, until 1990 at least, the West's relations with the South changed more radically than those with the East.

During the sixties accumulation proceeded roughly in parallel in the advanced and less developed countries. Between 1960 and 1973 investment grew by 6.2 and 7.6 per cent a year respectively. After 1973 the pattern was transformed for the rest of the seventies: in the advanced countries investment growth levelled off, whereas in the LDCs it bounded ahead – by 10.7 per cent a year between 1973 and 1979. The share of world capitalist investment carried out in the LDCs rose from 16.5 per cent in 1973 to 23.3 per cent in 1979. In the early seventies accumulation in the LDCs was close to the 5¼ per cent rate achieved in the advanced countries. By the end of the seventies it was running at about twice the 4 per cent a year to which the advanced countries had slipped. There was much variation within this high overall figure. The fastest accumulation took place in the oil producing countries and in a few (mostly Asian) countries with successful export manufacturing sectors.

Then, during the eighties, came a dramatic reversal. Very high rates of investment growth were maintained in the Asian export manufacturing countries and in China. But nearly everywhere else, because of the collapse of the price of oil and other primary products and the enormous burden of debt, the rate of accumulation fell sharply. Between 1980 and 1987 the annual growth of investment was 3.1 per cent in the advanced countries and 3.0 per cent in the LDCs as a whole. The latter average conceals enormous differences: over 12 per cent for East Asia, *minus* 4.5 per cent for Latin America and the Caribbean and *minus* 8.3 per cent for Africa.

For the two decades after 1960 the overall rate of growth of production and income in the LDCs as a whole did not vary much. But there were major shifts in the distribution of the growth, producing an enormous economic polarization between the fast growth of the oil producers and the manufacturing exporters and the much slower growth or even decline of many of the least developed countries. In the 1980s the overall growth rate of the LDCs fell sharply and the polarization became even more intense. (see table 16.1.)

The relative performance of the LDCs was crucially affected by the availability of foreign exchange, and the key sources of foreign exchange during the three decades were exports and foreign loans. Commodity prices held up in the wake of the first oil crisis and many LDCs began to borrow OPEC

Table 16.1 Growth rates of the less developed countries, 1960–87 (average annual percentage growth rates)

	1960–70	1970–80	1980–87
GDP			
Total developing countries	5.8	5.5	2.2
Manufacturing exporters	5.7	6.4	3.5
Oil exporters	7.2	6.0	−0.3
Least developed countries	3.4	3.2	2.4
GDP per head			
Total developing countries	3.2	3.0	−0.2
Manufacturing exporters	3.3	4.3	1.6
Oil exporters	4.3	2.9	−2.9
Least developed countries	1.0	0.5	−0.2
America	2.5	2.9	−0.9
Africa	3.2	1.1	−1.7
West Asia	4.7	3.2	−3.2
Other Asia	2.7	3.8	3.3

Source: UNCTAD, *Statistical Pocket Book*

surpluses channelled through Western banks. For a time their high import demand provided much-needed markets for Western exports. But developments in the ACCs prevented this situation from lasting. Commodity prices remained at more or less 1974 levels for the remainder of the decade, and by 1980 were three times higher than in 1970. But inflation in the advanced countries meant that primary product prices relative to manufactures were no higher in 1980 than in 1970. Then the recession of the early 1980s triggered a general relative decline in commodity prices which, along with the increasing obligations to service the debt, very sharply tightened the foreign exchange constraint. In the 1970s the non-oil producing countries had suffered from the oil price rises. In the 1980s it was the oil producing countries that experienced the worst fall in their terms of trade and in the purchasing power of their exports.

The terms of trade of developing countries as a whole fell by 17 per cent between 1980 and 1987. Within this aggregate the fate of various groups varied a great deal. For the oil producing countries the fall was 39 per cent; at the other extreme the East Asian manufacturing exporters' terms of trade rose by about 4 per cent. This deterioration in the terms of trade meant a decline in the purchasing power of Third World exports which was severely accentuated by the service of the debt eating up an increasing amount of export receipts. Hence during the period 1980–7 the real value of the imports of both Sub-Saharan Africa and the Latin American countries fell at around 6 per cent per year. For both groups this became a pressing issue during the 1980s. In the LDCs the decline in imports was associated with declines in both consumption and investment; in the advanced countries the cut in exports hit many manufacturing firms and, as we shall see below, created differences of opinion about how to deal with the debt crisis.

The oil producers

The economic fortunes of the oil producing countries ricocheted wildly during the seventies and eighties. Rapidly declining terms of trade in the early years of the 1970s led to the decision by the cartel OPEC to raise the price of petroleum.

The oil price rises of 1974 and 1979 pushed up the oil producers' real incomes. Between 1970 and 1980 the purchasing power of the major oil exporters' exports grew by 400 per cent, despite a stagnation of export volume caused by slow growth and energy-saving measures in the advanced countries. Between 1973 and 1980 the oil exporters' share of non-Eastern bloc incomes doubled, reaching 12 per cent. Most of these extra oil revenues accrued to governments, either as profits or as taxes on foreign oil companies. The share of profit incomes in Saudi Arabian GDP rose from 82 per cent in 1972 to 90 per cent in 1974.

Oil exporting governments embarked on huge schemes of economic and social development. The ratio of domestic investment to GDP rose from 21.4 per cent in 1970–3 to 28.0 per cent in 1979–80. With investment growing at 20 per cent per year, about one-third of the extra income generated by the oil price rise was invested. The burst of growth initially provided welcome relief in the advanced countries for industries hard pressed by the recession. ACC exports to OPEC grew in volume terms by a phenomenal 14 per cent a year. OPEC's share of the total rose from 4 to 8 per cent. The OPEC market was particularly important for the engineering industries. By 1980 it absorbed over 10 per cent of US and EEC exports of machinery and 13 per cent of Japanese. Western companies also provided much vital and profitable know-how for OPEC investment programmes. Imports of such private services as civil engineering rose ten-fold in value during the seventies.

For the advanced countries the ideal form of 'accumulation' by OPEC countries was apparently a build-up of military hardware. This should have provided export markets, created no problems of competitive capacity and eased the burden of 'policing' the region. But the oil producers could remain free from political turmoil only if they harnessed oil wealth to development schemes capable of meeting popular aspirations. Events in Iran – the centrepiece of Western strategy in the Middle East in the 1970s – showed that even the most expensive and elaborate techniques of repression could only delay, and thus render the more ferocious, explosive opposition to rotten dictatorships. The fall of the Shah raised the spectre of profitable arms exports being deployed against their suppliers, a threat soon dissipated by the war between Iran and Iraq.

Political stability was not the only problem in the early eighties. Much OPEC investment was concentrated in heavy industry. In the late seventies about one-fifth of investment by five major oil producers went into petroleum refining, petrochemicals, fertilizers, basic metals and cement. While plant sales boosted badly depleted Western order books, the end result was bound to cause further difficulty. Saudi Arabia alone aimed to corner 4–5 per cent of the world petrochemical market by the 1990s. Such additions to world capacity could have been absorbed without much difficulty had markets grown rapidly. But stagnation meant that even marginal increments to capacity – especially when backed by assured access to inputs – posed serious problems for industries in the advanced countries.

After 1984 the movie was run backwards. Major economies in fuel use in the advanced countries in addition to the coming on line of oil production facilities in non-OPEC countries (for instance the North Sea and Alaska) rapidly altered the market situation of petroleum and the price began to fall almost as quickly as it had risen during the seventies. The results were very dramatic. In the first place the problems of oil importers were relieved a little, thus in principle permitting an expansion of demand for other goods and perhaps a higher level of investment. By the time the oil price fell, however, a number of major importers among the LDCs were already embroiled in the aftermath of the debt crisis, whose effects dwarfed those of any change in the oil price (see the section on debt below).

The newly industrializing countries

The other major pole of accumulation in the LDCs was in the so-called newly industrializing countries (NICs). These countries began to present problems for the West well before OPEC heavy industry came on stream. Within OPEC rapid accumulation was a product of enormously increased export earnings. The NICs, in contrast, boosted exports through rapid accumulation (table 16.2). Their success seemed to rival Japan's, with export growth of 11 per cent a year between 1970 and 1980. In contrast to the experience of many of the

Table 16.2 Investment growth in newly industrializing countries, 1960–88 (average annual percentage growth rates)

	1960–73	1973–79	1979–88
South Korea	20.4	18.9	7.3
Hong Kong	4.6[a]	10.8	5.3
Singapore	16.6	4.6	6.4
Taiwan	14.2	5.0[c]	n.a.
Brazil	12.4[b]	6.5	−2.3
Mexico	9.3	4.1	−1.8

[a] 1968–73. [b] 1965–73. [c] 1973–7.

Sources: UN, *Yearbook of National Accounts Statistics*, 1980, Vol. II, table 6A; World Bank, *World Tables*

LDCs, both export and investment growth were maintained (especially in the East Asian NICs) after 1980. From 1980 to 1987 investment in East Asia grew by 12.1 per cent a year and the volume of exports by 10.1 per cent. The countries also, therefore, maintained a high rate of growth of imports from the advanced countries, though their demand was highly concentrated in Japan.

The NICs were originally considered to be a select group of countries in Asia and Latin America, although more recently the term has been used more for the four Asian countries of South Korea, Taiwan, Hong Kong and Singapore. These four together account for 46 per cent of all manufactured exports from the LDCs, with China adding a further 8 per cent. The share of Mexico and Brazil fell during the eighties and by 1987 was 3 per cent in each case. The share of manufactures in LDC exports rose rapidly during the seventies and eighties – from less than a fifth in 1965 to more than a third in 1978 to almost 60 per cent in 1987. In 1987, 18 per cent of manufactures imports into the advanced countries came from the Third World, as compared with 4.5 per cent in 1970.

Despite the rapid advance of manufactured exports from the LDCs as a whole, they remained during the seventies large net importers of manufactures. In 1980 they imported $175 billion more manufactured goods from OECD countries than they exported to them (these imports representing almost 20 per cent of the OECD's total exports of manufactures). Even the NICs were only in surplus on manufacturing trade to the tune of $10 billion. In 1980 the ACCs sold 31 times as many vehicles to the LDCs as they bought from them, nine times as many chemical products, seven times as much steel and six times as much engineering output. This net balance was substantially reduced during the 1980s to $82 billion by 1987 – a result of the decline in oil prices, the debt crisis and its resultant austerity programmes, and the other sources of economic crisis in Africa. The severe decline in the imports of many LDCs especially hit imports of manufactured goods from the advanced countries.

The progress of the Asian NICs continued and by 1988 their surplus on manufactures was nearly $50 billion. Their competitive success caused major problems for a number of sectors of industry in the ACCs. In the first stage the sectors in which the NICs began to win a large market share at the expense of the ACCs were labour-intensive products such as textiles, leather goods and footwear. In Korea, for example, in 1973 wage costs were only 5 per cent of those in the USA. Later the NICs began to break into many other areas, including high technology sectors such as computers and electronics and heavy industries such as shipbuilding. The Asian NICs developed a pattern of trade in which they had large surpluses with the USA and Western Europe and equivalent deficits with Japan.

The problem was not initially so much that the NICs were selling much more to the advanced countries than they were buying from them, but rather that they were selling consumer goods to the EEC and, especially, the United States, while buying capital goods from Japan. The LDCs as a whole imported $83 billion more machinery from the advanced countries than they exported to them, but in clothing the net flow was in the other direction to the tune of $37 billion. So friction between the advanced countries and the NICs was partly a reflection of friction between Japan on the one hand and the United States and EC on the other. Substantial portions of the export sectors of some NICs were owned by transnational companies: almost 90 per cent in the case of Singapore, 70 per cent in Mexico, 32 per cent in Brazil, about 25 per cent in South Korea and Taiwan, and 16 per cent in Hong Kong. A significant proportion of the Asian NICs' exports to the USA were by Japanese companies.

The competitive challenge posed by the NICs is underestimated by the above data by an amount equal to the extent that imports from them have been held down in the ACCs by special measures which restrain import volumes directly or indirectly to prevent imports from undercutting domestic producers (see below). The coverage of such controls in 1983 was 26 per cent for labour-intensive commodities (typically exported by LDCs) and only 9 per cent for capital- and technology-intensive products (typically exported by the advanced countries). Around 9 per cent of products in the EC face price controls, and around 15 per cent of volume controls are specified in terms of a country of origin, which usually means one of the NICs. Apart from foodstuffs and armaments, these controls are most widespread in clothing and textiles (nearly 80 per cent of such products being covered in the EC) and in footwear (70 per cent coverage in the United States).

Among the LDCs, only the NICs maintained really dynamic accumulation in the 1970s. And in the 1980s, while many other LDCs, especially in Latin America and Africa, began to experience severe economic recession and decline, the Asian NICs continued to expand their exports, investment and income, although in some cases the rate of expansion declined. Joining the NICs in rapid expansion in the 1980s was mainland China, which introduced liberalizing economic reforms following the change of leadership in 1978 and encouraged a great inflow of foreign investment. Between 1980 and 1987 remarkable rates of growth were attained – 11.7 per cent for exports, 19 per cent for investment and 10 per cent for GDP.

The debt crisis

To finance their rapid growth South Korea in particular, but also Taiwan and mainland China, borrowed heavily. But because the borrowing led to investment in productive capacity and exports expanded, the debt could be serviced. The Latin American NICs, on the other hand – the second division export manufacturers – had found by the early 1980s that the combination of rising interest rates, recession in the ACCs and the rise in the value of the US dollar (in which their debts were denominated) brought them to breaking point. Bankers who a few years earlier had regarded them as dream clients have, since the moment when in August 1982 Mexico abandoned the effort to pay what it owed and asked for rescheduling, come to find their LDC clients a source of nightmares.

Between the first oil shock of 1973 and the Mexican debt crisis of 1982 there was an enormous increase in lending from the advanced countries to the LDCs. The total outstanding debt of all the LDCs stood at $160 billion in 1975; by 1982 it had risen to $540 billion. Thereafter growth was slower but the figure still reached $877 billion by 1988 (table 16.3). Of this total, $378 billion was the debt of countries in Latin America and the Caribbean, $325 billion of Asia and $174 billion of Africa.

Table 16.3 Indicators of developing countries' indebtedness, 1975–87

	1975	1982	1987
Total disbursed long-term debt ($billion)	160.5	539.6	876.9
Average interest paid (%)	6.0	9.6	5.6
Ratio of debt service to exports (%)	9.1	15.1	16.3
America	18.5	31.9	26.8
Africa	9.2	20.8	27.1
West Asia	4.3	6.8	11.0
Other Asia	7.7	9.1	11.4
Ratio of debt service to GDP (%)	1.4	4.4	4.5

Source: UNCTAD, *Statistical Pocket Book*, 1989

The largest individual debtors are Brazil and Mexico, which together account for about one-quarter of the debt. The largest debtors, however, are not necessarily the most indebted in relation to gross national product. So a number of small highly indebted countries (such as Nicaragua, Somalia and Zambia) owe several times the value of their GNP while Brazil's debt is equivalent to 37 per cent of GNP and Mexico's to 54 per cent.

The debt of different countries is also heterogeneous in relation to the nature of the creditors. In Latin America and South-East and East Asia the accumulation of debts in the seventies was largely to the banks of the USA, Western Europe and Japan. In Africa and South Asia the new debts are largely to government agencies in the advanced countries (individual states or multilateral agencies).

The rapid accumulation of debt resulted from a combination of circumstances. The most often cited cause was the need of the LDCs to finance higher cost oil imports. The debt incurred was, however, much larger than the rise in imported oil costs and in any case there was little correlation between the rise in debt and the increase in the oil bill. Indeed, some oil producers (Mexico, Venezuela and Nigeria for instance) became major debtors on the security of their oil exports.

There were many other reasons why the rulers of the LDCs wanted to maintain a large inflow of funds, not least in order to afford them the foreign exchange which they would use to ship out their own personal assets. During the years of mounting debt there was also a huge outflow of liquid capital from the LDCs into Western banks. In some cases this has been calculated by the Bank of International Settlements to be in excess of the inflow of new loans. Countries owing the most to Western banks are not therefore always highly indebted in an overall sense. Rather, the vast debts of their central governments are offset by large foreign assets held by their privileged classes. This, however, is not available to repay the debt, whose burden must consequently be borne largely by the middle classes and the poor who have been afflicted with constant austerity and adjustment programmes.

In addition to the rise in demand for loans in the LDCs during the 1970s there was a strong move on the part of the banks, awash with the new petrodollars, to find clients to lend to profitably. The post-1973 slump in the ACCs led to a decline in demand for loanable investment funds, although the banks did manage to build up their very profitable consumer credit businesses through the universalization of 'plastic' as a means of payment. They were also anxious, however, to find suitable sovereign clients. With some encouragement from the US government, anxious to bolster friendly regimes in times of potential economic trouble, and hopeful perhaps that lending to clients with close economic links to the US economy would bolster the US balance of payments during the crisis, the banks found a dozen or so states (mostly in Latin America and Asia) who seemed to be suitable clients. These, during the 1970s, became the 'highly indebted countries', and the banks continued to lend to them in 1980 and 1981 despite drastically deteriorating prospects. In Latin America and some Asian countries the build-up of debt undoubtedly allowed positive rates of growth of output and accumulation to be maintained above the level that the international recession might otherwise have imposed. This also helped to maintain the level of imports which these highly indebted countries took from the ACCs. Among other things this situation led to a community of interest between financial and industrial capital in the ACCs.

In Africa and some smaller Latin America countries the crisis hit hard from the beginning of the 1970s. While in that decade Latin America and Asia as a whole showed quite fast rates of growth of GDP, Africa began a long and as yet unfinished process of economic decline. Total production fell in many countries and production per head fell almost everywhere on the continent. African countries, desperate just to maintain spending levels with declining resources, also got heavily into debt. For obvious reasons their debt was not commercial but was incurred as the result of official 'aid' programmes from the World Bank, the European Community or the former colonial powers. This debt, which is often a much higher proportion of national production than in the 'highly indebted countries', in part, therefore, reflects the unwillingness of Africa's aid donors to supply resources in the form of grants. The debt has helped to create a new kind of state-to-state colonialism. An increasing portion of the state loans have been tied to exports of the 'donor' country and so can in part be seen as a measure designed to help industry in these countries. The total volume of exports which the loans support, however, has been declining. The economy of Africa has been becoming increasingly marginalized in relation to the economies of the ACCs.

Latin American debtors did not maintain their relatively good economic performance for long into the 1980s. In August 1982, Mexico created a rapidly followed precedent by declaring that it could not afford any longer to service its debt without a major rescheduling. This started the debt crisis, which has continued ever since. The major debtors, especially in Latin America but also in other areas, are quite unable fully to service their debts and are in an almost continual state of renegotiation, moratorium or practical default.

The debt crisis suddenly hit in 1982 for a variety of reasons: the new slump in international demand for primary exports; the rise in the value of the US dollar, in which nearly all debts were denominated; the rise in interest rates (most of the new bank loans had been incurred at variable rates); and the drying up of new supplies of credit which could be used to roll over old loans. It should be noted that these developments had a good deal to do with the radical new economic policies adopted after 1980 by the Reagan administration (higher military spending, tax cuts and government deficit combined with severe monetary controls – see chapter 17). Once again the Third World was in crisis not only because of economic events in the ACCs but more specifically because of the aggressively selfish policies of the US administration.

Ironically, one of the consequences of the debt crisis was a crisis for many of the major banks which had participated in the rush for Third World sovereign borrowers. At times the obviously non-functioning nature of many of the loans led to alarm that one of the most exposed major banks would collapse as a result, or at least require a major government rescue package. In the event, the debt has in practice been slowly written down and transformed by the banks to the point that it no longer looks as if any sudden banking crisis is likely for this reason alone. The smaller US banks have sold their loans to the larger ones; and the larger ones have sold some to European banks who were originally less exposed but who now hold a larger share of the Third World debt than the American banks. And reserves have been laid down against possible non-payment of a high proportion of the outstanding debts.

None the less, the banks and their allies, such as the IMF, continue to devote an enormous quantity of resources to making sure that the number of formal defaults is as low as possible and that as much of the due debt as possible is paid. Numerous general and particular consolidation and rescheduling schemes have been devised (such as the much vaunted Baker and Brady plans). None of these has succeeded in making any basic change in the situation, which continues to be that a vast and unpayable debt exists. The amount (less than that due) which the LDCs have been obliged to pay during the 1980s has represented a catastrophe for their economies and large sections of their peoples. Latin American countries have been obliged as part of rescheduling agreements to deflate, open up and privatize their economies in stabilization and adjustment schemes. These have had the effect of lowering imports so as to produce a balance of payments surplus out of which the debt interest and principal can be paid. The net transfer of funds from Latin America's debtors to the creditor countries was running in the late 1980s at around $30 billion a year, or about 5–6 per cent of their national incomes (see table 16.4). As a first consequence the debtor countries have also reduced their rates of economic growth and of accumulation by a very large percentage. This is why, as a continent, Latin America in the 1980s joined Africa in showing on average significant declines in the level of income per head.

Table 16.4 LDC debt and debt service: the transfer of resources 1981–7 ($ billion)

Year	Net new loans	Debt service	Net transfer
1981	124	89	35
1982	114	99	18
1983	99	82	7
1984	92	100	−7
1985	89	110	−21
1986	86	116	−31
1987	90	119	−29

Source: World Bank, *World Debt Tables 1989*

This 'solution' to the debt crisis may have been the best the banks could have obtained in the circumstances. It has, however, led to a marked decline in the exports of producers in the ACCs to the debtor countries. This particularly affects US exports to South America. The debt crisis, therefore, disrupts the community of interest of banking and industrial capital which existed in the 1970s. The unsatisfactory solutions cooked up by the US Treasury probably reflect a vain effort to straddle this major divergence of interest between two important sections of US capital.

In 1990 the situation was that the LDCs were by universal consent unable to pay all which they juridically if not morally owed; but they were in fact paying much more than they could afford in relation to their longer-term stability and development. The debt crisis, therefore, remained as a major centre of conflict between competing interests among ACC capitalists and as a potential source of instability in the world economy. If it no longer threatened to topple banks, a series of major defaults could none the less trigger some very major economic and financial upheavals.

The advanced countries

Since 1973 accumulation and output growth slowed down far less in the USA than in Europe, let alone Japan (tables 14.1 and 14.3). But the USA has still lagged badly in productivity performance. After 1973 hourly productivity in manufacturing grew about 5½ per cent per year in Japan, around 3½ per cent per year in Europe and only 2½ per cent per year in the USA (table 14.5). It seems that this still left average productivity in Europe and Japan around one-third below the US level (see table 16.5), but in important industries (electrical goods and cars) Japan definitely had the productivity advantage.

Table 16.5 Relative productivity and wage costs, 1965–87 (ratios to US level in year in question)

	Japan	Germany	UK/France/Italy
Hourly productivity in manufacturing			
1965	0.21	0.51	0.43
1973	0.42	0.65	0.57
1979	0.53	0.77	0.64
1987	0.63	0.72	0.61
Hourly wage costs in manufacturing			
1965	0.15	0.45	0.38
1973	0.42	0.89	0.54
1979	0.61	1.25	0.75
1987	0.84	1.25	0.84

Productivity comparisons across countries are notoriously approximate. UK/France/Italy is simple average for the three countries.
Source: Hooper and Larin, 1989, tables 1 and 4 with their data adjusted for self-employment.

In the mid-1960s Japanese and European wages were so far below the American level that not even the massively higher US productivity left its manufacturing industry with a cost advantage. But wages grew more rapidly outside the USA (when measured in dollars) and caught up the US level more rapidly than did productivity. So by the early 1970s it appears that US labour costs per unit of output were competitive with those of Europe and Japan. This seems surprising in the light of the disastrous trade performance of the USA. But a recent intensive investigation of US industrial performance emphasized that:

> Productivity is only one of the factors that affect the performance of a company. Success may depend as much or more on the quality of a firm's products and on the service it provides to customers both before and after the sale. Competitiveness may hinge on the speed at which new concepts are converted into manufacturable products and brought to the market, on the flexibility with which the firm can shift

from one product line to another in response to changing market conditions, or on the time it takes to deliver a product after the customer places an order. (Dertouzos et al., 1989, p. 32)

US industry was found wanting in these respects. The changing competitiveness, understood in this broad sense, of the USA and the other ACCs has had crucial influences on their trade and financial relations.

Trade

The growth of world trade slowed down sharply after 1973, growing at an average 3.8 per cent a year over the period 1973–88, compared to 8.7 per cent per year during the previous decade. World trade in manufactures, the arena of sharpest competition, grew at 5.3 per cent a year, just under half the rate of growth during the boom. With markets growing more slowly competition intensified. The general trend was for the EEC and the USA to lose out in terms of export market share to Japan and the Asian NICs (table 16.6); even Germany's share of world trade in manufactures declined from 16.8 per cent to 14.0 per cent. Remarkably, the NICs increased their share of exports much more sharply than Japan in the 1980s.

Table 16.6 Manufacturing exports and imports, 1973–88

	USA	EEC	Japan	Asian NICs
Share of world exports (percentages)				
1973	12.9	44.7	9.9	3.6
1980	13.1	42.5	11.1	5.4
1988	11.3	37.5	12.5	9.7
Exports less imports ($ billion)				
1973	2.9	44.7	24.7	1.0
1980	20.8	103.2	96.7	10.2
1988	−119.4	99.6	180.2	47.9

EEC is sum of Germany, France, UK, Italy, Belgium/Luxembourg and Netherlands; NICs is South Korea, Hong Kong, Taiwan, Singapore; export data for Hong Kong and Singapore include 'substantial re-exports'.
Source: GATT, *International Trade 1988–89*, Volume II, tables IV.3, IV.4

The trade balance in manufactures depends on imports as much as on exports; the drastic deterioration in the US balance is more a reflection of its rising import bill than decline in export share. Despite the EEC's loss of export share its moderate growth rate left its imports growing quite slowly and so it maintained a substantial surplus on manufactures. The huge build-up of Japan's manufactures surplus reflected very slow growth of imports into the notoriously impenetrable Japanese market as well as export success. A more complete picture of trade patterns requires an examination of merchandise trade as a whole (including fuel and materials as well as manufactures) and of net flows between the various groups of countries (table 16.7).

In 1979 all the ACC blocs incurred substantial deficits with the Middle East as a result of payments for oil; the USA and Japan covered these with exports elsewhere, especially to the LDCs and to Western Europe, which was left with a large deficit. By 1988 the USA had run into huge deficits with both Japan and the NICs (included in table 16.7 in South and East Asia). Japan ran enormous surpluses in finished goods with North America, Europe and the NICs, with the fall in oil and commodity prices reducing its deficits with producers of these inputs. Europe compensated for a very large deficit with Japan and a modest one with the NICs with surpluses elsewhere, including North America. The major source of trade disequilibrium was obviously between Japan and the USA; the NICs exacerbated the problem by their surpluses and particularly by the triangular pattern of their trade – importing from Japan and exporting to North America.

The strength of Japanese exports meant that protectionist measures were not confined to the NICs. By the mid-1980s an estimated 22 per cent of imports into OECD countries were subject to 'non-tariff barriers' of some sort. Japan, despite its reputation as an impenetrable market, comes out with less than half the average coverage of barriers, and the USA is below the average in respect of manufactures. The early 1980s saw a steady upward trend in the extent of these barriers, especially in Europe. The IMF noted at the end of the 1980s that 'in

Table 16.7 Net flows of merchandise trade, 1973–88 ($ billion)

			Destination			
Origin	North America	Japan	Western Europe	South and East Asia	Middle East	Total
North America						
1973		−0.4	3.3	−0.4	1.4	6.5
1979		−2.2	15.1	−6.4	−8.6	18.4
1988		−51.4	−14.1	−40.3	0.4	−102.6
Japan						
1973	0.4		2.7	1.9	−3.4	2.4
1979	2.2		8.3	3.1	−17.3	7.6
1988	51.4		31.9	20.0	−9.2	99.6
Western Europe						
1973	−3.3	−2.7		−0.1	−5.9	−10.1
1979	−15.1	−8.3		−1.9	−24.0	−38.6
1988	14.1	−31.8		−7.3	14.4	0.5
South and East Asia						
1973	0.4	−1.9	0.1		−1.7	−4.2
1979	6.4	−3.1	1.9		−6.1	−5.8
1988	40.3	−20.0	7.3		−3.3	21.1

Source: GATT, *International Trade*, 1988–89, Vol. II table A3

recent years there has been a dangerous tendency towards an intensification of non-tariff restrictions – including "voluntary" export restraints and bilateral trade agreements – and a growing inclination to use trade measures to counter perceived unfair trade practices that are presently not covered by multilateral trade rules' (IMF, 1989, p. 38). An article in the *Economist*, written in 1983 but symptomatic of the whole of the 1980s, described what had been involved in graphic terms:

> Because of existing agreements, in any year only 11 out of every 100 British car buyers (and only three in 100 French) can choose a new Japanese car. America sins too. Despite its free-enterprise, free-trade bombast, the Reagan administration prevents Americans from buying more than 1.68 million cars from Japan in a year (a limit that was extended this month for a third year).
>
> Europe's latest agreement goes further than America's. It extends protectionism far beyond the old geriatric wards of textiles, steel, shipbuilding and cars into the maternity wards. The Japanese have been coerced into promising 'moderation' over a product range that extends from quartz watches to fork-lift trucks to machine tools (where they 'will pay special attention to the French market'). It imposes limits on the number of Japanese video tape recorders (VTRs) sold in the common market and guarantees a minimum share to Europe's own producers. (*Economist*, 19 February 1983)

Not surprisingly, the sharpest trade conflicts are between the USA and Japan:

> At the insistence of Congress, the Administration is battling Tokyo on goods ranging from logs to satellites. Washington is demanding that the Japanese government buy American supercomputers, construction services and communications satellites, that Japanese companies buy finished wood products rather than raw logs, and that Tokyo makes good on a promise to give U.S. companies greater access to their cellular telephone market.
>
> The most ambitious U.S. effort, however, is the so-called structural impediment initiative plan (SII), a Bush Administration plan to break down deeply embedded Japanese practices that keep US imports out. Targets include Japan's complex distribution system, the keiretsu interlocking groups of commercial consumers and suppliers, and government land-use and tax policies that discourage consumption. So far the Japanese, who only reluctantly agreed to the SII talks, have offered few meaningful concessions. Instead, Tokyo has returned the fire by bringing up the U.S. problems that reduce American competitiveness and increase imports: the budget deficit, the low savings rate, and a deficient education system. (*Business Week*, 22 January 1990)

1992

In contrast to the trade frictions between Japan, the USA and Europe the trend within Europe appears relatively harmonious, epitomized by the proposals to complete the EC internal market by 1992. The poor performance of the European economies, in terms of investment, output and productivity growth, was emphasized in chapter 14. One implication was that EC producers barely maintained their position in each other's markets. Despite the advantages of zero tariffs, EC exporters of industrial goods increased their shares of EC markets by only one-quarter after 1973 to reach 18 per cent in 1985, while non-EC sources increased their share by one-third to 13 per cent. Since around 1980 the share of EC producers in EC imports fell by almost as much as it had increased since the early sixties, and the position was acute in office and data-processing machinery and in electrical equipment and electronics, sectors where European productivity levels were especially low.

These facts were underlined in the EC Commission's lengthy analysis of the economic effects of its programme for 1992. This programme involved abolishing a list of non-tariff barriers to trade, in particular frontier formalities, differences in technical regulations, restrictions on competition for public contracts and restrictions on freedom to engage in certain service activities, notably financial and transport services. Despite the modest nature of many of these barriers (eliminating border formalities would save 1.5–2 per cent of the cost of visible trade), the Commission argued that the total effect on productivity of the restructuring which should flow from the competitive forces unleashed by these proposals could reach as much as 4–5 per cent for the EC economy as a whole. Output was expected to increase even more as a result of the diversion of demand to the EC's producers and of an investment boom encouraged in part by cheaper credit resulting from financial liberalization (put at only ½ per cent off interest rates, however). This would guarantee that none of the productivity increase resulted in unemployment, and indeed a rise in employment of nearly 2 per cent was expected.

These estimates seemed extremely optimistic, especially in relation to the difficulty in discerning such dynamic effects from the much more dramatic cuts in tariffs at the formation of the EEC. Apart from excessive optimism about the effects on productivity a fundamental weakness of the whole enterprise lies in the EC's bland remark that 'undoubtedly it is only a matter of time before such resources [released in rationalization] are effectively re-employed' (Emerson, 1988, p. 201). This is an astounding statement in the context of the mass unemployment of industrial workers in Europe over the previous 15 years. It allows the EC to gloss over the fact that some countries, and especially regions, would inevitably continue to suffer very severely from increased rationalization and concentration of production. Moreover, such rationalization would be occurring in the context of further development of the European Monetary System, leading towards monetary union. This would rule out the use of exchange rate depreciation by countries particularly disadvantaged by the extra competition.

Already, the EMS with adjustable rates has presided over an enormous rise in German trade surplus with the rest of the EC (over $40 billion in 1988). So the quite healthy position of European trade as a whole (table 16.6) conceals a very serious disequilibrium within Europe. With increasingly fixed exchange rates, the prospect of monetary union, and easier access to other EC markets provided by 1992, further rationalization (expected by the EC to be particularly large in the engineering, vehicles and chemicals industries, where Germany is especially strong) could only further increase German economic hegemony within Europe. A 1977 EEC report calculated that to reduce regional inequalities among the then EEC members by the amount achieved in existing federal states such as Australia, Canada and the USA would require a budget of 7 per cent of GDP. Thus the proposed doubling of the EC's regional funds to a mere ¼ per cent of the EC GDP would be wholly insufficient to prevent increased regional disparities. Growing strains between the EC partners seem inevitable.

Foreign investment

Protectionism was an important factor behind an upsurge in direct investment in manufacturing and other facilities overseas undertaken by companies whose export growth was threatened by trade imbalances. By 1987–8 inward direct investment into major OECD economies was running at an annual rate of some $70 billion, more than three times the 1970s rate (approaching double the rate in real terms). The USA was the recipient of well over half this investment, with the UK receiving twice as much as France or Italy and six times as much as Germany. Japan's foreign direct investment overseas exploded after 1985, rising from $6 to $34 billion in 1988. The UK and USA were the next biggest investors overseas at the end of the 1980s, investing at well over double the pace of Germany.

In the 1960s the USA undertook 60 per cent of the direct investment overseas by OECD countries and European capital was trying to resist the 'Defi Americain'. Over the period 1981–8, however, the USA was carrying out only 22 per cent of the total, was receiving nearly twice as much direct investment as it was undertaking abroad and was becoming alarmed about foreign control of its assets. This only amounted to some 4–5 per cent in total, but included approximately a fifth of banking assets, half the consumer electronics and cement industries and nearly half the commercial property in downtown Los Angeles. Nevertheless, the stock of US direct investment overseas was estimated to be worth around $1000 billion, or half as much again as overseas holdings in the USA. A further fear was that manufacturing investment, by Japanese companies in particular, would displace domestic production rather than imports. By the end of 1989 there were ten operational Japanese auto plants in North America (four of which were joint ventures with domestic producers). Their planned capacity was over two million cars and it was estimated that for every three they made only one would displace imports, with the other two reducing the market for domestic carmakers.

International money

The collapse of the fixed exchange rate system in 1973 (chapter 12) did not have the disastrous consequences for international trade sometimes predicted. Exchange rates between the major currencies have fluctuated considerably on a day-to-day basis, despite government intervention to smooth out 'disorderly' markets, but studies suggest that this has had little effect on the volume of overseas trade. Much more serious have been the trends in exchange rates from year to year. Floating rates 'should' balance out inflation rate differences, preserving real competitiveness. As figure 16.1 shows, up to the end of the 1970s the fluctuations in competitiveness were relatively limited. The balances on the current accounts of the payments balances of the USA, Japan and Germany all fluctuated from year to year in the range plus or minus $10–15 billion. Moreover, the fluctuations roughly balanced out. Between 1974 and 1981 the USA averaged a current account surplus of $¼ billion a year, Japan had a surplus of $1¼ billion a year and Germany was in balance.

The situation changed completely in the 1980s (see figure 16.1). The rapidly rising value of the dollar made US industry extremely uncompetitive by the middle of the decade. Between 1980 and 1985 unit costs in the US had risen by 38 per cent relative to those of its competitors (see figure 16.2). The US merchandise deficit, which had averaged $21 billion per year during the years 1975–81, leapt to an average of $133 billion per year during the period 1984–8

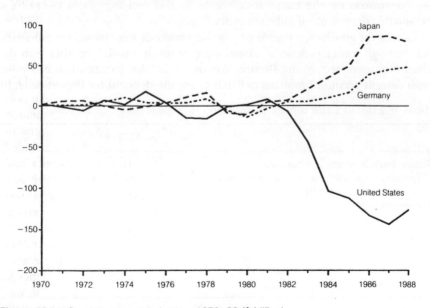

Figure 16.1   Current account balances, 1970–88 ($ billion).
Source: OECD, *Economic Outlook.*

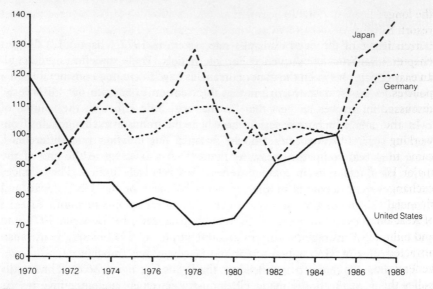

Figure 16.2   Real effective exchange rates, 1970–88 (index numbers, 1985 = 100).
Source: IMF, *International Financial Statistics*.

(see table 16.8). While the deterioration of US competitiveness was less than
that suffered by the UK between 1978 and 1980 (46 per cent), the importance
of the US economy and the size of the accompanying deficit focused attention
on the reasons for the manifest failure of flexible exchange rates to ensure a
reasonable degree of equilibrium in trading.

During the golden age the major way that countries were joined economically
was through trade, as flows of capital were relatively small. Together with the
fixed exchange rates of the Bretton Woods system this ensured that countries
with current account problems deflated to cut the demand for imports and, in

Table 16.8 United States balance of payments, 1975–88 ($ billion, annual averages)

	1975–81	1984–88
Private trade in goods and services	−16.0	−123.1
Government transactions (and private transfers)	−7.1	−19.1
Net interest and dividends	23.3	18.1
Current account balance	0.2	−124.1
Direct investment (net)	−5.1	15.0
Other private investment (net)	−17.1	77.9
Financed by		
Dollars held abroad in official reserves	15.1	24.3
US reserves and government assets	−13.8	−8.3

Statistical discrepancy averaged −13.8 and −8.3 billion dollars respectively.
Source: *Survey of Current Business*, June 1989, pp. 62–3

the longer term, to hold down inflation. Devaluation tended to be used as a last resort. Surplus countries had an interest in expanding demand to prevent their currencies being forced upward with adverse effects on export profitability (see chapter 10). With the collapse of Bretton Woods, depreciation appeared to be an easy option for dealing with payments deficits without the need for restrictive policies. This contributed to the rapid and speculative boom of 1972–3, as discussed in chapter 13.

In the 1980s, however, there was a crucial further modification to the working of the international system – financial flows, rather than trade flows, came to dominate foreign exchange markets. It was estimated by one of the major US banks that an average of $420 billion crossed the world's foreign exchanges each day in 1987, of which more than 90 per cent represented financial transactions unrelated to trade or investment. The particular pattern of Reaganomics (see chapter 17) took the form of an expansion through tax cuts and military spending increases while interest rates were kept high. Funds were attracted into the USA and pushed up the exchange rate. Because of the general view that the Federal Reserve Bank would stick to its tight monetary policy this led to expectations of further increases in the exchange rate so that investors in dollar financial assets stood to gain not only the high nominal interest rate, but a real capital gain in relation to their own currencies as the dollar was expected to increase further. The trade deficit which resulted from the combination of rising demand in the USA and the increasingly uncompetitive dollar helped to maintain demand and production in the rest of the world. In the absence of sufficiently strong productive accumulation in the rest of the world in the early 1980s it was the US government deficit which provided the financial assets for the rest of the world to accumulate.

Like all speculative surges, the rise of the dollar had to come to an end. The bubble burst in mid-1985 and two years later it had fallen by 30 per cent. In February 1987 the Group of Seven agreed, under the Louvre Accord, to defend the dollar at around the current rate, and then spent, according to the IMF, upwards of $150 billion doing so. Purchases of dollars implied that central banks had to sell to private holders of dollars an equivalent amount of their own currencies. This contributed to the growth of money and credit, part of which found its way into speculative investments on stock markets. In response governments outside the USA started to raise interest rates, in turn forcing rates up in the USA. The Bank for International Settlements reported that 'The upward spiralling of interest rates between the surplus countries and the United States was clearly against the spirit of the Louvre Accord and undermined its credibility. By giving rise to grave doubts about the future development of the world economy, it undoubtedly influenced the timing of the dramatic turn-round on the stock markets and contributed to renewed exchange market unrest which, despite co-ordinated intervention, could only be contained after permitting another substantial dollar depreciation' (BIS, 1988, p. 176).

In the short term, exchange rate depreciations have little, or even a perverse, effect on trade balances as import costs rise; this tends to reinforce speculative pressure. After 1987 the US trade balance began to decline but only very slowly.

The deep disruption caused by the huge exchange rate swings of the 1980s put the supporters of financial deregulation on the defensive. The Bank for International Settlements noted in response to criticism of destabilizing financial flows:

> A given change in balance of payments flow that affects, for example, the Deutsche Mark/dollar exchange rate will tend to give rise to a multiple of exchange market transactions associated with the maintenance of a consistent equilibrium pattern of exchange rates. It is these continuous arbitrage, balancing and market-making activities of the banks which explain why commercial transactions directly account only for a minor proportion of total exchange market turnover. This does not, however, mean that the bulk of exchange market transactions and short-term capital flows represent simply 'noise and nuisance'. On the contrary, they are essential for a smooth functioning of the markets.
>
> This is not to deny that short-term capital flows, including transactions in long-term assets for short-term speculative purposes, may at times have a strong destabilising impact on the exchange market. Moreover, it is certainly true that, as a result of the increasing global integration of national markets, these destabilising capital flows can assume vast proportions. The answer, however, is not new controls and impediments which would also curtail the stabilising capital flows and exchange rate transactions, but more stable national economic policies and their better international co-ordination. (BIS, 1988, p. 178).

The bank noted that the continued US deficit implied that 'the cumulative amount of position-taking in favour of the dollar necessary to finance this deficit will be very large. Even marginal attempts to reduce these huge open positions [holdings] in dollars could entail major exchange market pressures' (BIS, 1988, p. 179). Combined with the fragility of the US financial system in the face of the kind of interest rate increases that could be necessary to stave off a dollar collapse, this threat to the dollar represents a major source of instability in the international system.

17
Reversing the Consensus

During the boom a broad consensus was established. Major parties of both left and right generally accepted the notion of a 'mixed economy' – that is, a capitalist economy with some state enterprise. They also recognized rights for workers as workers, notably the right to free trade unions. In addition, they accepted responsibilities as governments, particularly the responsibility to provide various welfare services and to maintain more or less full employment. Workers could bargain for wages to rise in line with productivity, but managers retained the right to control production and allocate capital. The precise parameters of this consensus varied from country to country and shifted a little over time, and they were contested at the margin. Nevertheless, broad agreement existed across the major political parties; in Britain the consensus was labelled 'Butskellism' after a leading Tory, Butler, and the Labour leader, Gaitskell.

By the end of the seventies strains were evident because the economy was no longer delivering to order the jobs, living standards and welfare services. The dominant trend in policy-making became the reduction of the role of the state and of trade unions, both seen as interfering with the free and efficient working of the market mechanism. In this chapter we look at attempts by governments to reverse the old consensus, paying particular attention to the governments of Reagan and Thatcher, which espoused the new ideas most forcefully. The next chapter examines the attempts by governments and parties of the left to stand against this new orthodoxy, and the increasing problems such attempts faced.

The turn to free market economics had both macro- and microeconomic components. In the macroeconomic sphere, inflation was blamed on the attempts of governments to achieve 'overfull' employment, below the 'natural rate of unemployment' in Friedman's terminology. Expansionary demand management policies would lead to rising inflation and higher unemployment in the long run. According to Hayek, the leading thinker of the New Right, this 'passes the buck in an irresponsible manner, on to our successors. We are of course in this respect already reaping the harvest of the man [Keynes] who set this fashion since we are already in the long run in which he knew we would be dead' (Hayek, 1972, p. 109). The prescription was to run a tight monetary policy.

There is an equally important microeconomic component to the new orthodoxy, which is that government interference with free market forces should be greatly reduced. State expenditure should be whittled down to minimum proportions, increasing the dependence of the bulk of the population on paid work. People would be forced into taking any work that was available and as a result the minimum achievable, or 'natural', rate of unemployment would be cut. Cuts in taxes, and shifting the onus to provide for old age from state to private provision, would also increase the incentive for people to work harder and save more. Nationalized industries should be privatized and subject to free market competition in order to increase their efficiency. Regulations constraining the market should be withdrawn or softened. The result would be pressure to cut costs and produce as cheaply as possible, combined with greater dynamism in investment decisions, leading to faster long-term growth. Above all the political and industrial power of labour to constrain the free play of market forces should be broken. Hayek was explicit on this latter point:

> Public policy concerning labour unions has, in little more than a century, moved from one extreme to the other. From a state in which little the unions could do was legal if they were not prohibited altogether, we have now reached a state where they have become uniquely privileged institutions to which the general rules of law do not apply. They have become the only important instance in which governments signally fail in their prime function – the prevention of coercion and violence. . . . The whole basis of our free society is threatened by the powers arrogated by the unions. (Hayek 1972, pp. 66–8)

This approach constituted a coherent, and very radical, attempt to resolve the economic difficulties of the 1970s on capitalism's terms. It sought to cope with major problems generated by the end of the boom years – workers' increased ability to secure improvements in wages, state services and working conditions – by shifting fundamentally the parameters previously accepted by all parties. In other words, it was an attempt to return relations between capital and labour to how they were before the Second World War. Again, Hayek is very clear about what is involved.

> This path is still blocked, however, by the most fatuous of all fashionable arguments, namely, that 'we cannot turn the clock back'. One cannot help wondering whether those who habitually use this cliché are aware that it expresses the fatalistic belief that we cannot learn from our mistakes. . . . Nothing less than a rededication of current policy to principles already abandoned will enable us to avert the threatening danger to freedom. (Hayek, 1972, pp. 87–8)

Restrictive monetary and fiscal policy

In the early days of the Thatcher government it was fashionable to suggest that tight money would reduce inflation without affecting anything else. The idea was that the simple announcement of a tough target for the growth of the money supply would, through creating expectations of slower inflation, be enough to hold down wage and price increases. The leading theoretician of monetarism, Milton Friedman, talking of Britain, asserted in 1980 that 'only a modest reduction in output and employment will be a side effect of reducing inflation to single figures by 1982' (quoted Stewart, 1983, p. 172). This proved ludicrously optimistic. Tight monetary policy operates to weaken unions by creating mass unemployment.

If the government holds the growth of credit below the prevailing rate of inflation then interest rates tend to rise. This reduces the returns from business investment, makes hire purchase and mortgages more expensive, and encourages firms to sell off stocks which are now dearer to finance. The strength of these effects has been disputed for years, but a really sharp credit squeeze undoubtedly reduces spending. This deflationary impetus has been bolstered by floating exchange rates. High interest rates tend to attract foreign funds which push up the value of the currency. This makes exports uncompetitive and imports more attractive. Sales of domestically produced output fall further. The impact is greater on a country like the United Kingdom, where foreign trade is large in relation to production, than on a less open economy, such as the United States.

The purpose of engineering a slump is to sacrifice short-term profits in order to restore the profitability of production and investment in the longer term. Its success depends not simply on the extent to which wage *and* price increases are reduced by the slump (reducing inflation), but the extent to which wage increases are reduced *more* than price increases (squeezing real wages and raising profits). The effect the slump may have in increasing productivity is equally important.

In a recession, the weakest firms, with lowest productivity, tend to go bust first. Their demise raises average productivity. Tough deflation also puts pressure on management to force through changes in working practices – to reduce operating levels, impose speed-up and so on. The mechanism is fear. Managers rightly believe that the firm's survival may be at stake. Most importantly, deflation weakens workers' resistance to such changes. Again, fear is the key. Workers rightly believe that opposition may lead to redundancies or closure, and that it may be impossible to get another job. Pay rises are held down, it is hoped below the rate of price increases, by the same pressures.

A major difficulty with the approach is how to win electoral support for a programme of squeezing the economy. This is where academic doctrines like monetarism come in. They serve as a rationale for abandoning a fundamental feature of the postwar consensus – governments' responsibility to maintain full employment. J.S. Fforde, an adviser to the governor of the Bank of England, outlined the strategy:

> It would have been possible to initiate such a strategy with a familiar 'Keynesian' exposition about managing demand downwards, and with greater concentration on ultimate objectives than on intermediate targets. But this would have meant disclosing objectives for, *inter alia*, output and employment. This would have been a very hazardous exercise, and the objectives would either have been unacceptable to public opinion or else inadequate to ensure a substantial reduction in the rate of inflation, or both. Use of strong intermediate targets, for money supply and government borrowing, enabled the authorities to stand back from output and employment as such and to stress the vital part to be played in respect of these by the trend of industrial costs. In short, whatever the subsequent difficulties of working with intermediate targets, they were vitally important at the outset in order to signal a decisive break with the past and enable the authorities to set out with presentational confidence upon a relatively uncharted sea. (Fforde, 1983, p. 207)

The early years of the Thatcher government certainly saw savage monetary deflation. Long-term interest rates soared from 3 per cent less than inflation in 1979 to 4 per cent above in 1982. This increase was greater than in most countries (despite the fact that the monetary targets were far exceeded partly because the severity of the recession generated 'distress borrowing'). It hit sales opportunities, and hence production and employment, in various ways. The high cost of borrowing discouraged fixed investment, which fell by the equivalent of 1½ per cent of output between the second quarter of 1979 and 1981. The strain imposed on companies' cash position led to a massive rundown of stocks, which fell by 3½ per cent of output over the same period. High interest rates, combined with confidence in sterling engendered by its new status as a petro-currency, sharply reversed the previous decline in the value of the pound. The competitiveness of UK manufacturing industry deteriorated by a staggering 50 per cent. This hit exports, which fell by 2 per cent of output over the two years. Imports also rose by 2½ per cent of output, displacing domestic production.

Just as important as tight monetary policy was a ferocious budgetary squeeze which directly reduced demand in the economy by 5 per cent of GDP between 1979 and 1981. Increasing taxation and a cutback on public spending programmes reduced disposable incomes and held down consumption. Indeed the severity of the fiscal squeeze marks out British policy more distinctly from that of other countries over this period than does the tightening of monetary policy. The 1981 Budget was especially significant as it maintained the deflationary pressure in a situation where the economy was clearly in a recession, provoking a letter from 364 economists complaining that it would 'deepen the depression, erode the industrial base of the economy and threaten its social and political stability' (quoted Maynard, 1988, p. 68). Particularly important was the introduction of a system which fixed public expenditure in monetary terms, so the faster was inflation the more would spending in real terms be eroded.

The effects were dramatic. Output fell by more than in any other downturn for 60 years, including the crash of 1929–32. Official unemployment doubled, reaching 12 per cent of the labour force by the spring of 1981. By 1982 company liquidations were running at 12,000 a year, 2½ times the 1979 rate. The industrial sector was hardest hit. Manufacturing output fell by a colossal 15 per cent in 12 months from December 1979. This compares with a maximum fall in any single year during the 1930s of 5.5 per cent. By the beginning of 1983 imports of manufactures were 24 per cent higher than in 1979, while production stayed 16 per cent lower. The concentration of the crash in industry, and especially manufacturing, is important. These sectors are most subject to international competition. They must experience the pressures most strongly, and respond to them most positively, if the strategy is to succeed.

The US recession of 1982 was sharper than the United Kingdom's recession of 1980–1. But, being less prolonged, it reduced total output by about 3.0 per cent as compared to 3.7 per cent in the United Kingdom. Interest rates were pushed up to exceed 5 per cent in real terms – quite unprecedented for the United States. As in the United Kingdom, the rundown of stocks was the most important factor in the recession, reducing output by over 1 per cent. Private investment also fell sharply. The competitiveness of US industry was reduced by 20 per cent as the dollar rose, contributing to a sharp fall in exports. As in the United Kingdom, public expenditure on goods or services grew a little, and transfers a lot, helping to moderate the impact on consumption of the fall in incomes. Industry was worst hit. Industrial production fell by 8 per cent in 1982. Unemployment rose to over 10 per cent.

Following the recessions of the early eighties, both the Thatcher and Reagan governments achieved periods of sustained growth. Under Reagan the impetus came from expansionary budgets: taxes were cut (see below) and military spending increased. Over the five years 1982–6 this amounted to a direct injection of demand worth some 3.5 per cent of GDP. Output as a whole grew by nearly 4 per cent per year over the period 1982–9, considerably faster than in Europe, and unemployment fell to 5.4 per cent. This occurred despite very high real interest rates (7–8 per cent in 1983–5 when the expansion got under way).

In the UK, by contrast, the avowedly 'monetarist' Thatcher government presided over a phenomenal growth of credit as financial deregulation encouraged an explosion of borrowing. With the single exception of 1985, the OECD's measure of credit to the economy expanded at more than 20 per cent per year every year after 1980, financing a huge consumer and housing boom, and bringing the proportion of personal income saved down by two-thirds. Fiscal policy, after an initial boost around the time of the 1983 election, moved in a contractionary direction and this, together with the rise in tax receipts as consumption expanded, pushed the budget into surplus (some 2 per cent of GDP by 1989). GDP grew by 3.4 per cent per year between 1982 and 1989, sufficient to halve the unemployment rate to 6.5 per cent.

Germany and Japan have followed more consistently restrained policies than the USA and UK. Japan has kept the growth of credit to around 10 per cent per year since 1982, while steadily reducing the underlying budget deficit by around 4 per cent of GDP. In Germany the attempts at the end of the seventies to use tax cuts and public spending increases to boost growth and push unemployment down had been judged not only failures, but even counter-productive. Expectations, it was suggested, would turn on its head the traditional Keynesian multiplier effect of budgetary expansion: 'Just as adverse expectations may prevent a fiscal stimulus from raising overall demand, a gradual reduction of the fiscal impulse may be expected to stimulate private demand if indeed such a policy is in line with the preferences of the private sector' (quoted Carlin and Jacob, 1989, p. 24). So if financial markets are persuaded that a Keynesian expansion will collapse in accelerating inflation, then interest rates will rise immediately and prevent the expansion happening in the first place. Such arguments provided justification for reducing budget deficits; the Bundesbank believed that, in the early eighties, 'The policy of budgetary consolidation had a positive effect on the financial markets and thus eased the pressure on the financial accounts of enterprises, which stepped up investment activity in the course of the year' (quoted Carlin and Jacob, 1989, p. 24). The German government has in fact kept up a less consistent budgetary squeeze than Japan or the UK, with the financial markets being satisfied with the Bundesbank's fierce grip on monetary policy which has kept credit expanding at a little over 5 per cent per year. This has made Germany the anti-inflationary cornerstone of the European Monetary System. It has meant, however, growth at less than 3 per cent per year since 1982, and left unemployment above 7 per cent in 1990.

Cutting down the state

The 1980s saw a reversal of the inexorable rise in the share of the state in total spending. Figure 17.1 shows that after rising sharply in the recession of the early eighties (though not as fast as in 1974–5) the share of government spending stabilized. Total social expenditure grew in real terms by 2.6 per cent per year in the early eighties, down from 4.2 per cent during 1975–80 and 6.5 per cent per year in the years up to 1975. Social security transfers stabilized as a share of GDP in the mid-1980s, after comprising much of the increase in public spending earlier. The decline of two percentage points in the OECD unemployment rate helped, but much more significant was the tendency for the real value of benefits to be curtailed. In Belgium, for example, the real value of

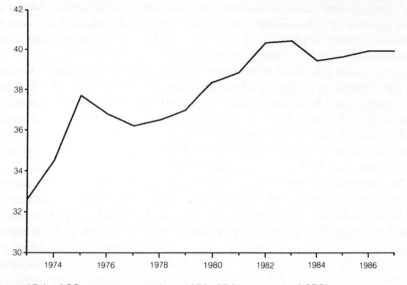

Figure 17.1   ACC government outlays, 1973–87 (percentage of GDP).
Source: OECD, *Economic Outlook.*

state pensions fell by 0.8 per cent per year in the 1980s, and the value of family allowances by 3 per cent per year. The ratio of unemployment benefit to earnings has tended to be reduced (in the UK earnings-related benefit was abolished) and eligibility criteria have been tightened. An extreme case is the spread of 'workfare programmes' in the USA, where people are obliged to spend up to 40 hours a week in 'job-clubs' filling in job applications or have to work for the state for enough hours at minimum rates to 'earn' the money they receive in benefits. A very significant shift implemented by Thatcher was abolition of the linking of state benefits to earnings and its replacement with a link with inflation. No longer was it regarded as fair that those dependent on the state should share in general prosperity, only that their minimum level of support should be protected against inflation. Between 1979 and 1989 the level of state pensions for a couple fell from 43 to 34 per cent of average earnings – a fall in relative value of more than 20 per cent. The relative value of income support for those without other means fell by more than one-quarter.

Direct public expenditure on welfare programmes has also been restrained. Government investment has been particularly hard hit, but the rise in current spending on health and welfare has also been held back. The objective of cutting the proportion of those working for the government has not been achieved in Europe (partly because private sector employment has grown so slowly). But heavy pressure has been exerted on public sector pay as a way of holding down the cost of public services. Despite their slow productivity growth (see chapter 14) the cost of public services grew no faster than the costs of the goods and services bought by consumers in the 1980s; at the end of the 1960s it was growing more than 2 per cent per year faster as the inherent difficulty of increasing productivity in this sector pushed up its relative cost of production. Core provision of public services has proved very difficult to erode, so cuts have tended to be marginal in their impact on total spending (though devastating for particular groups of recipients). Typical of this are the problems the Thatcher government faced in cutting health service expenditure in the face of rising costs of existing treatment, of expensive medical advances and of rising numbers of the elderly who require more treatment. This has meant dramatic pressure on some vulnerable items – medical prescriptions charged to patients rose in price over 1000 per cent under Thatcher.

The biggest exception to the squeeze on public spending was the military – between 1980 and 1986 military expenditure rose in real terms by nearly one-half in the USA and reached 6.4 per cent of GDP. Under Thatcher the rise was much less (some 16 per cent in real terms) up to 1984, after which there were cuts.

Tax cuts

Reagan's campaign promised a dramatic 30 per cent across the board cut in personal income taxes. He said he would institute 'an equal reduction in everybody's tax rates', not a 'shift of wealth between different sets of taxpayers'. What actually emerged was not only a smaller cut, 23 per cent over three years, but one which benefited the rich quite disproportionately. One calculation showed that families on $10,000 a year in 1980 paid more in tax, whereas those on $250,000 a year received increases in their post-tax incomes of about one-fifth.

Reagan's budget director, David Stockman, was very candid:

> The hard part of the supply-side tax cut is dropping the top rate from 70 to 50 per cent – the rest of it is a secondary matter. The original argument was that the top bracket was too high, and that's having the most devastating effect on the economy. Then, the general argument was that, in order to make this palatable as a political matter, you had to bring down all the brackets. But, I mean, Kemp-Roth [the original cuts proposal] was always a Trojan horse to bring down the top rate. (Quoted Ackerman, 1982, pp. 43–4)

The Trojan horse, it will be remembered, was not sugar to sweeten a bitter pill but an exercise in deceit.

New loopholes were opened up for particular groups. David Stockman summed up the lobbying for tax cuts by special interest groups as follows: 'Do you realize the greed that came to the forefront? The hogs were really feeding. The greed level, the level of opportunism, just got out of control' (quoted Ackerman, 1982, p. 50).

The 1986 Tax Reform Act further reduced the top rate of tax (so that it had declined from 70 to 33 per cent under Reagan), but balanced this by eliminating a host of tax exemptions. The OECD contrived to describe the overall effect as 'progressive' since it raised 'the slope of the effective rate schedule in the lower half of the income scale more than it lowered it in the upper half' (OECD, 1989, p. 178).

The Thatcher government reduced the top rate of income tax from 83 to 40 per cent; for those lower down the income scale cuts in the basic rate of income tax from 33 to 25 per cent were counterbalanced by increases in VAT from 8 to 15 per cent and increases in national insurance contributions from 6.5 to 9 per cent. The benefits of these tax 'reforms' have gone overwhelmingly to the better off. People in the bottom half of the income scale have benefited on average from tax and benefit changes to the tune of a pound or two a week and some quarter of them are actually worse off. Households in the top 10 per cent have gained by an average of £30 per week; in the 1988 budget alone the very richest 5 per cent of households gained around £1500 per year.

While such redistributions to the rich have been most blatant in the USA and UK they have extended much wider. As a simple indicator of the general tax burden, the ratio of government receipts (mainly taxes) rose from 33 per cent of GDP in 1975 in the OECD countries to 37.5 per cent in 1988 (Germany and the UK are the two major cases where the burden hardly rose). While the average burden of taxation was rising, the top rate of income tax (the simplest single indicator of the progressivity of the tax system) fell everywhere – the average fall being some 14 percentage points. The OECD noted a tendency for top rates to be aligned at around 50 per cent, and this meant much smaller cuts in the top rates in countries like France and Germany, where top rates were already around that level. The tax system has also become more regressive through increased reliance on consumption taxes, although political opposition prevented the introduction of broad sales taxes in Australia and Japan. Corporation taxes have been substantially reduced in many countries, notably in the UK from 52 to 35 per cent and in the USA from 46 to 34 per cent, favouring unearned income (see also chapter 14).

Much of the pressure for tax cuts has been special pleading from the highly paid and the wealthy. As J.K. Galbraith has pointed out, it was a most convenient theory that suggested that the way to improve incentives was to make the rich richer and the poor poorer. General tax cuts would have an economic logic in terms of buying wage moderation from workers whose take-home pay would be increased; more slowly increasing labour costs would tend to increase competitiveness and profitability. But short of an attack on the welfare state far greater than anything which has proved politically possible, major cuts in the overall burden of taxation are ruled out because of their effect on budget deficits.

Privatization

Publicly owned enterprises producing goods and services for sale are not counted as part of government spending; however, they are very obviously part of the public sector. The privatization of these enterprises has certainly been the most radical policy of the Thatcher government. The UK government reported in 1989 that 'The state sector of industry accounted for 11 per cent of GDP in 1979. The Government's privatization programme has reduced its size by just under half since then. 29 major businesses have been privatized, transferring nearly 800,000 jobs to the private sector (UK Government, 1989, para 5.32).

There have been privatization measures in other countries (railways and telecommunications in Japan, some of the industrial companies nationalized in the early eighties in France and odd companies elsewhere). But Thatcher's programme has been by far the most extensive and is widely seen as the model. Underlying the privatization programme have been the general arguments in favour of obliging these enterprises to operate as independent entities in the market. This would free them from minsterial interference and, much more importantly, force them to be more efficient by cutting them off from the 'soft budget constraint' provided by access to public funds. Ironically the idea that government enterprises cannot be efficient, according to the market's criterion of financial results, has been undermined most effectively by the Thatcher government itself. In the case of the steel industry (privatized in 1988) and British Coal (regarded as the 'ultimate privatization' of the future), the government has forced through the most ferocious policies of rationalization, which in both cases saw labour productivity doubling in five or six years (see chapter 15). The government was prepared to spend huge sums to defeat the industry's union (£3 billion of losses were sustained by the nationalized industries in the case of coal). It then slapped on draconian requirements for deficit reductions and these nationalized industries then outdid the private sector in the speed with which their finances were restored (at very heavy cost to the workers involved, who lost their jobs).

Extremely important in commending privatization to Thatcher's government was its effect on the public sector borrowing requirement (PSBR), the reduction of which was the cornerstone of the government's Medium Term Financial Strategy. By a quirk of accountancy, the sale by the government of shares in British Telecom did not contribute to the PSBR, and thus confirmed to the City the orthodoxy of the government's financial stance, while the sale of government bonds increased it. So financing part of public spending with the proceeds of the privatization programme and especially using them to 'finance' politically popular cuts in taxation was extremely attractive (see above). Over the years 1979–89 receipts amounted to some £27 billion (with a further £15 billion coming from the sale of council houses); privatization was expected to continue to yield around £5 billion per year for the following couple of years as receipts from water and electricity privatization were gathered in. Such financial 'benefits' from privatization are wholly bogus: selling off an asset whose value reflects the stream of returns it is expected to earn can never 'finance' any current spending. It was simply a means of cutting taxation without increasing the measured amount of government borrowing, but at the cost of decreasing the government's assets and future income.

The central argument for privatization rested on the benefits to economic efficiency which would result if the privatized enterprises were subjected to greater competition. But the desire to raise maximum sums of money had important effects on the form the privatizations took. In order to be attractive to the stock market, profits had to be assured. Combining privatization with increased market competition would threaten those profits. So would the institution of severe government regulation over the pricing policies of those privatized industries that were monopolies. So in the case of the monopoly public utilities, there was a structural incentive for the government to ensure their future profitability. In the instance of water privatization, it was in the government's interest to minimize the environmental restrictions placed on the water companies. Nuclear power was taken out of electricity privatization because the City would not subscribe to an industry with unknown future obligations in respect of costs of closing down nuclear reactors. In the case of electricity the desire to maximize receipts from selling off the industry took the form of huge price increases to raise profitability prior to privatization. The losers were the consumers forced to pay more for the output of the industry to be privatized. In effect they financed the taxpayers (concentrated at the top end of the scale – see above) who received the tax cuts. Post-privatization restrictions on price increases were generous.

Most fundamentally of all, there has been strong pressure to restrict the degree of competition to which the newly privatized firms would be subject. British Gas was not split up at all and was left as a 'horizontally and vertically integrated monopoly [which] has very few competitive threats to contend with, and is regulated with a remarkably light touch' (Kay and Vickers, 1988, p. 337). Even in the case of the electricity industry, which was split up into area boards and two private generating companies, the degree of competition allowed in supplying power was heavily circumscribed.

The inconsistency between maximizing the proceeds from privatization and inducing competition was not the only conflict. Maximizing proceeds also conflicted with the government's wish to foster widespread holdings of shares. In order to make shareholding seem attractive to the average person unacquainted with the mysteries (and expenses) of the business, a guarantee of immediate capital gains was desirable; this could be ensured by pitching the asking price for the shares below the likely market valuation. In the event market prices of the shares were frequently as much as one-third higher on the first day of trading than the issue price; up to the middle of 1987 these undervaluations presented those who applied for the shares with capital gains of some £3.5 billion. The most outrageous case concerned the Trustee Savings Bank, whose ownership was in doubt between the depositors and the government. The government actually gave the proceeds of the privatization back to the bank – subscribers to the share issue in effect got both the original assets of the bank *and* the money they subscribed. Through large numbers of people having subscribed to share issues the total number of shareholders is estimated to have risen by one-third to 11 million in the second half of the eighties. This has not, however, interrupted the long-term decline in the proportion of shares held by individuals (down from 33 per cent in 1978 to 18 per cent in 1989), as the proportion held by financial institutions grew (from 51 to 63 per cent). Many individuals were tempted by the promise of immediate capital gains to purchase the privatization issues of shares and then sold them on to the financial institutions.

The City institutions who organize the privatizations have also been enthusiastic supporters. The costs of privatization, including fees to merchant banks, underwriting costs, advertising budgets and so forth, have been huge – £190 million for British Telecom and well over £1 billion for the privatization programme as a whole.

A subsidiary form of privatization has been the 'contracting-out' of part of the operations of the public sector (laundry in the UK National Health Service for example). Despite a great deal of pressure on UK public bodies, results have been limited. The *Financial Times* (6 February 1990) reported:

> When the government mooted the idea of competitive tendering it was heralded as a potential cure-all that would save money, improve services and provide businesses with lucrative contracts. Contracting out, particularly cleaning work, is certainly saving money – about £42 million per year according to recent estimates – but the quality of service is hotly contested. . . . Many local authorities have imposed penalty clauses on private contractors for allegedly failing to fulfil contractual obligations or failing to maintain standards and some have cancelled contracts altogether.

It is too early to assess the performance of the privatized industries in the UK. Over the years 1983–8 British Telecom increased its productivity by some 2.5 per cent per year, which is slower than many nationalized industries, including the much-derided Post Office. Privatization can only assist capital accumulation if it reduces costs in the industry concerned, and thus increases the amount of surplus available. Fear of the sack under the new regime may intimidate workers into accepting lower wages or more intensive work patterns, and it is they who pay for the improved profitability. If privatization galvanizes management into cutting out loss-making services carried out for social reasons, then the increase in profits is at the expense of the consumers. The only case where privatization could bring general benefits is where the organization of the industry improves, or where access to private capital allows new technology to be introduced faster, *and* the resulting rationalization takes place in a situation where the workers who lose their jobs as a result can find comparable work elsewhere.

Deregulation

The removal of government regulations over the operation of industry (deregulating matters such as safety, environmental protection etc.) has been a strong trend in the 1980s. The philosophy was rather aptly expressed in 1980 in a report, the co-author of which was to become chair of the US Federal Trade Commission: 'Avoiding defects is not costless. Those who have low aversion to risk – relative to money – will be most likely to purchase cheap, unrealiable products. Agency action to impose quality standards interferes with the free expression of consumer preferences' (quoted Ackerman, 1982, p. 119).

The most extensive policies of deregulation have taken the form of changes in the competitive structure of industries by removing government constraints on competition between enterprises. Transport, telecommunications and the financial sector have been prime targets. Deregulation of air transport in the USA has been reported by OECD as saving air passengers $11 billion per year. But ten years after deregulation, under a cover story headlined 'The Frenzied Skies', *Business Week* (19 December 1988) reported 'Jammed runways, geriatric jets, a few giant carriers dominating the skies – this can't be what the fathers of deregulation had in mind. Capping the noble experiment's first decade are sky-high fare hikes'. The story reported that the biggest five airlines controlled some 70 per cent of passenger traffic as compared to 60 per cent before deregulation; they had succeeded in driving out the 'upstarts' in a vicious price war.

Particularly spectacular forms of deregulation have occurred in the financial sector, and again the UK is a good example. First, exchange controls were abolished soon after the Thatcher government came to power. Sir Geoffrey Howe, Chancellor at the time, recalled, 'We decided that there was nowhere to go but over the cliff. It was the only decision of my political life that has ever given me a sleepless night' (*Financial Times*, 23 October 1989). Its most important effects have been to allow a massive outflow of portfolio capital from the UK – financial institutions in the UK have increased their holdings of shares and bonds overseas by £75 billion in the nine years after abolition. At the same time it has ensured that any tendency for interest rates to diverge from what the financial markets believed is warranted by the future behaviour of the exchange rate provokes an immediate inflow or outflow of capital of unmanageable proportions.

The abolition of exchange controls also contributed to the pressure deriving from falling costs of communication and information towards the international-ization of financial markets. This forced the ending of certain restrictions to competition in UK financial markets (such as fixed commissions on share dealings and limitations on outside ownership of members of the Stock

Exchange) – the so-called Big Bang. A very important side-effect of the increased competition was the explosion of credit (see chapter 14) as financial institutions vied with one another to persuade consumers and housebuyers to borrow. The collapse of the housing and consumer credit boom in 1988 and 1989, following the Stock Market crash of October 1987, revealed just how extensive the overinvestment in all aspects of financial services had been (investment in offices and equipment in the financial sector rose by some 125 per cent betwen 1979 and 1988, while investment in manufacturing rose by 0.6 per cent).

The most spectacular effect of financial deregulation has been on the Savings and Loans (S & L) institutions in the USA. These institutions have their deposits guaranteed up to $100,000 by the government, and were deregulated just at the time they began to encounter severe difficulties as a result of having lent long term on fixed interest at rates far below those prevailing in the early eighties. In search of quick profits to balance their books, and freed from regulations on the type of business they could transact, they engaged in more and more speculative operations. One tiny S & L was persuaded that its way out was to 'finance trading in Treasury securities with profits from reverse repos [repurchase agreements] and to hedge the S & L's assets with offsetting positions in the interest-rate futures markets' (*Business Week*, 31 October 1988). Not surprisingly, it lost more than half its assets in six months. Apparently 80 per cent of S & L insolvencies involved 'wrongdoing' or negligence. In what has been described as 'a bailout that could dwarf the Marshall Plan', the taxpayer may be liable for more than $300 billion (see chapter 14). A contributory factor to the S & L crisis was deregulation by neglect when the body charged with oversight of the industry was refused funds to increase its examination staff. Similar reductions in staff to oversee pollution, health and safety or low pay have also been a notable feature in the UK.

Government subsidies to industry (whether private or public sector) have been a favourite target of free market rhetoric, but reductions have been small. An EC survey revealed state aid running at some 3 per cent of GDP. 'About half the total aid granted goes to the subsidy-hungry sectors of agriculture, railways and coal. The rest is in manufacturing sectors, especially in steel and shipbuilding where it amounts to one third of value added' (*Financial Times* 20 November 1989). Even in the rest of manufacturing, aid was as high as 16 per cent of value added in Italy ('a prodigious provider of subsidies on almost all fronts'), five times the UK and German levels. Available data suggest rather little fall in levels of subsidies in the 1980s.

Deregulation of the labour market

In addition to the general weakening of the position of labour implied by high levels of unemployment, governments have used a variety of legislative and regulatory changes to help tip the balance of power further away from trade unions. It was hoped that many of these changes would not be easily reversed by a tighter labour market. Here again the Thatcher government has led the way.

Drawing on the lesson of the Conservative government of the early seventies, whose radical industrial relations legislation was defeated by union opposition, Thatcher proceeded slowly to weaken unions in a series of Employment Acts. A list of the measures taken gives an indication of the scale of the changes. Picketing was limited, the establishment of closed shops was made more difficult, immunity for secondary industrial action (blacking and sympathetic industrial action) was restricted, unions were made liable for illegal acts performed by their representatives unless such acts were repudiated, commercial contracts stipulating the use of union labour were outlawed, inter-union and political disputes were no longer regarded as trades disputes, trade union officials had to be elected regularly by secret ballot, strike action had to be supported by a majority of union members in a secret ballot and unions could only maintain a political fund if this was supported by a majority of members.

Many of these provisions were used against unions in the course of industrial disputes, for example during the miners' strike and subsequent disputes on the English Channel ferries, in the printing industry and on the docks. While unions have clearly been constrained in taking industrial action by these changes in the law, there have been some paradoxical effects. It has been widely reported, for example, that the bargaining positions of unions before disputes, and their authority in the course of them, have actually been increased by their having secured (often very large) majorities for strike action. Very large majorities (averaging 84 per cent) voted in favour of their unions maintaining political funds, and in some unions they were set up for the first time.

Outside the UK, legal and administrative changes have been infrequent. Changes in German law over rights of strikers of social security (see p. 266) are one example. Administrative procedures whereby firms in France had to seek official permission for any dismissal were dropped in 1986. In Germany restrictions on the employment of temporary workers were eased.

Pressure on unemployed workers to seek work has been increased by reductions in the generosity of benefits relative to earnings in the USA, UK, Germany and Japan — of the larger countries only Italy and France have maintained stable replacement ratios. Minimum wages have been reduced relative to earnings in a number of countries, including the USA, Canada and Netherlands; France is the one country with both high and stable minimum wages. In the UK the minimum wage covering a number of low wage industries was abolished along with wages councils which set them, and young people were removed from coverage by those councils that survived.

Has it worked?

There is no straightforward way to draw a balance sheet for the ten-year turn to free market policies. What can be attempted first is some assessment of whether the policies have worked in their own terms.

We have repeatedly used the profit rate as our central indicator of the state of the capitalist economy. The data presented in chapter 14 show that there has been a marked recovery in profitability in Europe since 1982, which brought the profit rate in business and manufacturing back to 1973 levels. But the main factor underlying the recovery was the slowing down in real wages growth, rather than an improving trend in labour productivity. In the USA the recovery in profitability has been less and in Japan it has been non-existent despite its huge fall between 1970 and 1975.

The pattern for accumulation presented in chapter 14 is similarly mixed. Despite level profitability the growth of the capital stock has accelerated sharply in Japan in the later 1980s and is now very high, especially outside manufacturing. In the USA accumulation over the whole period since 1973 has been at a similar rate to that of the pre-1973 period, though with less impact on productivity. In Europe in particular the recovery in accumulation was very limited.

The picture is one of partial recovery at best. The UK, where the implementation of pro-market policies has been most thoroughgoing, illustrates this. There has been much talk of a productivity 'miracle'; indeed, in manufacturing output per hour worked has grown by 4.7 per cent per year since 1979. This is very fast compared to the rate achieved under the previous Labour government (1.2 per cent per year between 1973 and 1979) and faster even than before 1973 (4.2 per cent per year over the period 1960–73). But the recovery in manufacturing productivity growth in the UK was not the result of high investment – the growth of the manufacturing capital stock since 1979 has averaged a paltry 0.8 per cent – it was the result of the intense rationalization carried out under the pressure of the recession. Moreover, despite the setbacks suffered by the trade unions (see chapter 15) the employers were unable to drive money wage increases below 8 per cent per year. By the end of the decade wage increases were accelerating further and the engineering unions were winning a stubborn battle to cut hours of work to 37 per week. The investment boom which has occurred in the UK has been concentrated in mainly non-trade services sectors. In distribution and finance capital stock growth in the 1980s exceeded 4 and 7 per cent per year respectively, largely linked to the consumer boom. The disastrous consequences of this distorted pattern of accumulation were reflected in a mounting current account deficit on the balance of payments, which reached 4 per cent of GDP in 1989.

If the UK exemplifies the very partial nature of the recovery based on free market policies, it also exemplifies the strongly inegalitarian effects. This chapter has already shown that redistributions from the unemployed and from benefit recipients to top taxpayers were typical in other countries as well. In the UK the inequality of earnings from employment also increased, probably reflecting the combination of the reduction in well-paid manual jobs in manufacturing, which comprised much of the middle of the income distribution, together with the rise in employment in high-paying business services and in poorly paying other services. Unearned income (rent, dividends and interest) in real terms grew by one-half, around three times as fast as average earnings from work. Similar patterns occurred in all other major countries. Capital gains were also very large during the 1980s, reflecting the improvement in profitability. In the UK real capital gains on personal wealth were running at 4–5 per cent per year in the mid-1980s. In the USA and Europe stock market prices doubled between 1982 and 1988 (see figure 14.15) and in Japan they tripled.

The main achievement of the new economic policies has been the sharp rationalization of some important industries, under the pressure of mass unemployment, import competition and the prospect of privatization. In the context of slow growth and a withdrawal of the state from policies that temper the effects of rationalization, such as retraining and relocation of industry, it has had a markedly unegalitarian impact as its costs are born predominantly by the unemployed. This is an example of a more general phenomenon under right-wing regimes of the 1980s: that much of the apparent prosperity represents redistribution from sections of the population (notably the unemployed and benefit recipients) rather than a general rise in living standards. As shown above, tax and welfare policy has strongly contributed to such a pattern. In both the UK and the USA this impression of increasing affluence has been stoked up by the expansion of consumer credit, partially financed from overseas. The limits to a yuppie prosperity, based on squeezing the poor and expanding consumer credit, were felt most forcefully by the Thatcher government in 1990. The deterioration in the balance of payments, an upward move in wage claims and pressure on sterling forced higher interest rates and this combined with the extremely regressive poll tax to compound the government's unpopularity. But revulsion against the excesses of right-wing policies does not constitute a positive programme for the left. As the next chapter shows, left governments have encountered formidable problems in standing against the tide of pro-market trends.

18

Against the Tide

The answer of parties of the right to the slowdown in growth since the mid-1970s has been to set about unravelling the postwar consensus by the combination of deflationary macroeconomic and market-enhancing microeconomic policies described in the previous chapter. Here we consider the experience of three governments of the left since 1973. The 1974–9 UK Labour government and the French Socialist government of 1981–6 exemplify the problems encountered by governments proposing radical policies to reverse the slowdown. The experience of Sweden, mainly under the Social Democrats, represent a rather different policy thrust, concentrating more on ensuring that the costs of the economic slowdown were shared in an egalitarian manner than on escaping from it.

Attempts at expanding demand

The right aimed to cut the welfare state and reduce the power of organized labour to create the preconditions for a 'natural', that is market-based, recovery: higher profits would encourage competitiveness, employment and investment. As we saw in chapter 17, these policies have been more successful in redistributing income towards the better-off than in generating upswings. In the UK and the USA, where they were pursued most vigorously, the recoveries of the middle and late 1980s were the result of traditional demand expansions, leading to the equally familiar problems of budget deficits (USA), inflation above competitor countries (UK) and balance of payments deficits (both countries). Governments of the left, in pursuit of their top priority, full employment, have unsurprisingly met exactly the same difficulties. The financial markets, however, have shown far less tolerance towards them. So their attempts at expansion have been shorter-lived than those of the right.

The Labour party's election manifesto in the spring of 1974 pledged it to 'increase social equality by giving far greater importance to full employment'. Faced with the oil crisis, and having been bequeathed by the Conservative government the largest budget deficit of any OECD country other than Italy and Ireland, Labour contrived to hold out against severe deflation until 1976. Nevertheless, output grew more slowly in the UK in 1974 and 1975 than in any European country except Switzerland and Portugal (which was experiencing a revolution). Unemployment grew as quickly as the European average.

Slow growth, a declining balance of payments deficit and a slowing down of inflation (but from a higher level in 1975 than in other major OECD countries) did not prevent a spectacular sterling crisis in 1976. This was focused on the size of the budget deficit. It forced the government to apply for an IMF loan when the major central banks refused to extend credits further. Arthur Burns, chairman of the US Federal Reserve Bank, explained the bankers' view: 'I had my doubts whether the British could correct the fault in their economic management on their own. You must remember that I'm a neanderthal conservative, and naturally suspicious of a Labour Government. I thought it was a profligate government' (*Sunday Times*, 28 May 1978). The government agreed to cut spending by £3 billion over two years in return for the loan; the City was delighted to have such policies 'externally imposed'. As a result even the modest public spending increases announced earlier were not achieved. For example, by 1978 housing spending had grown only half as quickly as planned, and spending on education not at all.

Unemployment rose almost twice as quickly between 1975 and 1977 in the UK as in the EEC as a whole, to reach 6 per cent. Prime Minister Callaghan summed up his conclusions at the 1976 Labour Party Conference: 'We used to think that you could spend your way out of a recession and increase employment by cutting taxes and boosting government spending. I tell you in all candour that that option no longer exists and that insofar as it ever did exist, it only worked on each occasion since the war by injecting a bigger dose of inflation into the economy, followed by a higher level of unemployment at the next step'. This renunciation did not prevent his government introducing a substantial budgetary expansion in 1978, which pushed unemployment down a little. However, it proved incompatible with the government's attempt to cut inflation further through a reduced norm for wage increases (5 per cent when inflation was running at 8 per cent). The policy collapsed, and the government was defeated by Thatcher at the ensuing election after a series of bitter strikes, especially in the public sector.

The Mitterrand government also intended to rely partly on Keynesian policies to reduce what was already a high level of unemployment. Initially it boosted consumption by raising minimum wages and transfer payments, increasing public investment and expanding employment in the public sector. It was hoped that the economy would grow by 3 per cent in 1982, a modest 1 per cent faster than without the reflationary package, and that unemployment would begin to fall in 1983.

The first major blow to the plans for expansion came in June 1982, just a year into the government's term of office, when rapidly increasing imports and faster inflation than in the rest of the EEC fuelled speculation against the franc. A devaluation of 6 per cent was forced on the government, and followed on the heels of a 3½ per cent devaluation the previous autumn. Social security contributions were increased and the duration of some unemployment benefits was reduced. The government announced its intention of stabilizing its deficit and reduced its growth targets for 1982 and 1983 to 2 per cent. In March 1983 a further squeeze accompanied the third devaluation of 8 per cent against the mark. The deflationary package, including tax increases and reductions in public investment, reduced demand by around 1.5 per cent of GDP in 1984 and 1985, more or less exactly offsetting the expansion of 1981–82. Employment, which stabilized in 1982 (compared to falls of around 2 per cent in both Germany and the UK), began to fall in 1983. By 1985 unemployment had exceeded 10 per cent; the increase as compared to 1980 (some four percentage points) was a little less than the EEC average (around five percentage points), but was still edging up when the government was defeated early in 1986.

Market forces and the problems of expansion

The summary discussion above of the experience in the UK and France illustrates many of the difficulties encountered in engineering a successful expansion of demand and maintaining employment under the circumstances of slower OECD growth. First, especially in conditions of low profitability, an expansion of demand, via tax cuts and public spending increases, tends to generate inflation. Employers take advantage of higher demand to rebuild squeezed profit margins. Some need to raise prices to make profitable additional production on old, less efficient machinery and would lay off or not take on workers without such price increases. These price increases tend to reduce real wages at a time when workers' bargaining strength is increased by falling unemployment and their confidence is boosted by the election of 'their' government. Forceful wage bargaining, feeding into a price–wage–price spiral, is very probable.

Such a sequence is close to what happened in the early months of the Labour government. Encouraged by the success of the miners in their pay battle with the Conservative government and the abandonment of that government's statutory pay policy, wage increases accelerated sharply and coincided with the inflationary effect of the oil price increase. By the second quarter of 1975 wage increases were running at 27 per cent and during that quarter retail prices were rising at an annual rate of 38 per cent (nearly four times that of competitors). The inflation rate inherited by the Mitterrand government was also above the EEC average, and far above that of Germany, to whose currency the franc was pegged in the European Exchange Rate Mechanism and which was in the throes of its deepest postwar recession. This differential persisted over the period 1981–3. The sharp rise in the minimum wage contributed to confident wage bargaining and in 1982 hourly wages rose by 15 per cent, 5 per cent in excess of the official target.

A reduction of unemployment improves the budgetary position by reducing the dole and increasing tax receipts. If an initial budget deficit really 'primes the pump' of expansion, with the momentum taken up by private investment, then the deficit would be short-lived as expanding production increases tax revenues. With a weaker response from investment, and a strong propensity for the demand to leak into overseas markets, the deficit will remain. Indeed, the budget deficit increased by 3 per cent of GDP in France between 1980 and 1982 and by 2 per cent in the UK between 1973 and 1975 as the slowdown resulting from the oil crisis reduced tax revenues.

The idea that a greater deficit will automatically crowd out private investment is only correct when the economy is at full capacity and cannot expand further. Yet there is a more general concern that the expansion induced by the deficits will contribute to future inflation, for the reasons described above. For these reasons the likely reaction of financial markets to rising budget deficits will be a rise in interest rates. This occurs as domestic holders of government securities require higher rates to prevent them moving into shares and other assets that give a hedge against inflation, and as overseas holders require compensation for the likely effect of higher inflation on the future value of the exchange rate. Thus, in the UK long-term interest rates rose over the period 1974–6 to a level well above that of other major countries. Such a rise in interest rates certainly discourages investment; profits which can be retained for reinvestment are reduced by higher debt-service costs, and this is especially serious in the context of low profitability.

Maintaining the growth of demand out of step with trading partners also threatens the balance of payments. Part of the rise in consumption as more people are employed will be devoted to imported goods. Even a highly competitive consumer goods industry supplying most of the home market would require additional imports of raw materials and, probably, within-company imports of manufactured components from overseas plants. Borrowing overseas for a time may be a possible way of financing the deficit on the balance of payments, but at the cost of high and probably increasing interest rates as international markets fear a future depreciation of the currency. If the exchange rate is forced down, making competitive the additional exports required to finance the import bill, this just pushes the problem back on to wages. For the lower exchange rate means higher import prices and a reduction in the real wage. Thus the 20 per cent fall in the exchange rate in the UK between 1974 and 1976 and the 13 per cent fall in France between 1981 and 1984 contributed to the pressure on real wages.

Finally, even if all these immediate problems of inflation, government deficit and balance of payments deficit could be held at bay, the expansion could only be maintained if it was accompanied by an adequate level of investment. This is necessary anyway, from a domestic point of view, to generate the increases in labour productivity that can allow continued increases in production and living standards. But international competition imposes the need for competitive levels of investment in new products and processes if the economy is even to stand still.

Simply expanding demand and increasing the pressure on existing capacity does not automatically generate the desired increase in investment. Low initial profitability was a major problem faced both in the UK, where the manufacturing profit rate fell from 9 per cent in 1973 to 2.4 per cent in 1975, and in France, where it had fallen by one-third between 1979 and 1981. With the prospects for sustaining expansion in doubt for all the reasons already outlined, the necessary degree of 'confidence' on the part of the employers contemplating investment was likely to be lacking. Doubts by employers about the containability of real wage demands, about the sustainability of the expansion and about control in the factories are likely to curb investment. In both the UK in 1974–5 and France in 1981–2 private investment fell despite the expansionary stance of the government; in neither case were the falls as large as in countries which were acting in a deliberately deflationary fashion at the same time, but they still illustrate the difficulty of securing the rising level of investment necessary to sustain expansion.

So there are formidable problems with a Keynesian expansion in a situation of low profitability, militant workers, weak overseas demand and cautious employers and investors. The immediacy of these problems is likely to be compounded because financial markets tend to be particularly jittery when left governments are elected. Their very anticipation of problems with inflation and the exchange rate exacerbates the difficulties faced. Governments of the left are reckoned, partly on the basis of prejudice in the financial markets but also on the basis of their past experience, to be more inflationary as a result of their attempts to maintain demand. Expectations of the inflation to come will tend to lead to *immediate* rises in interest rates and falls in the exchange rates as operators in the financial markets position themselves to avoid bearing any of the costs of the higher inflation. Share prices may also be hit as a result of fear of measures such as price controls, which would reduce profitability, or legislation over employment issues, which would reduce the employers' freedom to declare redundancies. During the early time of the Mitterrand government real share prices fell by 40 per cent, confirming the 'plausibility of the story which links adverse expectations in financial circles to a fall in stock prices and thus a depressing effect on investment spending' (Sachs and Wyplosz, 1986, p. 293). The financial markets act as a transmission mechanism telescoping into the present problems which might occur in the future. The speculative pressure faced by sterling in the mid-1970s, and by the franc in the early 1980s, was also partly of this character: it represented anxieties that present trends would deteriorate, rather than simply reflecting current patterns of payments imbalances, inflation differentials, budget deficits and so forth.

Radical measures to curb market forces

Recognizing the likely market responses to attempts to expand under unfavourable conditions led the left to propose countermeasures. These involved increased government interference with market forces in a number of crucial areas. Inflation could be met by controls over prices; the balance of payments could be contained by import controls; and investment weakness could be overcome by increased state control over productive industry. Finally, the power of financial markets to pressurize the government through capital flight out of government securities and out of the currency could be met by controls over the freedom of financial institutions to allocate financial capital domestically and overseas. All these measures were proposed in the UK or in France or in both. Some of them foundered on the opposition of the employers and were never implemented; some were implemented but did not amount to a coherent set of solutions to the problems at hand.

Inflation and wages

Price controls seem an ideal way of reducing inflation since they guarantee workers' real earnings. The problem is that if they reduce profits (or fail to allow them to rise from existing low levels) this discourages the employment of workers in marginal enterprises and inhibits investment. Thus although price controls were used by Labour and the Socialists, both were forced to take a relatively relaxed view of the extent to which cost increases could be passed on as price increases. The latter years of both the left governments saw considerable increases in profitability. The manufacturing profit rate more than doubled in the UK from a perilously low level in 1975 and rose by one-third in the later years of the French Socialist government.

In the attempt to hold down inflation heavier pressure was exerted on wages. In the UK in particular there was a highly successful round of wage restraint agreed with the TUC. This saw wage rises of 14 per cent in the year beginning mid-1975; this implied a quite extraordinary degree of restraint in the face of inflation which had been running at an annual rate of 26 per cent. Further deceleration of earnings took place in 1977, the real level of pay falling by 6 per cent. Attempts to screw the going rate of wage increases down further provoked the pay explosion described above.

After the June 1982 devaluation the French government suspended wage indexation agreements and introduced a four-month wage freeze. This was the first suspension of free collective bargaining in France since 1950. The government then proposed that wages should rise in line with their forecast for inflation (which turned out to be consistently 1–2 per cent below the rates that occurred). By 1984 wages had slowed down to the actual inflation rate, and taking increased social security contributions into account, real take-home pay fell by 2 per cent in that year. Research suggests that in both the UK and France the deceleration of wage and price increases was greater than would have occurred anyway simply because of the rising unemployment.

The balance of payments and speculation

Neither Labour nor the Socialists had coherent proposals to deal directly with balance of payments difficulties. Labour had been scarred by international reaction in the mid-1960s to a mild import deposit scheme, which they had been forced to abandon after a couple of years. Despite campaign talk of 'reconquering the domestic market', the French Socialists explicitly rejected protectionism (apart from some temporary petty regulations, such as requiring all imported video recorders to pass through an obscure customs post at Poitiers). Mauroy, the Prime Minister, explained: 'Reconquering is a slogan which was needed in the election campaign. But we have to adapt it because you can't use the phrase in the same way once you have governmental responsibilities' (*Financial Times*, 6 June 1982). Both governments were left with no alternatives to the orthodox policies of devaluation and deflation when the balance of payments deteriorated (or failed to improve quickly enough in the case of the UK).

The UK and France both had rather extensive systems of exchange controls in place when the left gained power, and the French controls were tightened in the face of speculative pressures. While they have been shown to have some effects in limiting flights of capital (financial institutions, for example, were not allowed to increase overall portfolio investments abroad), neither system involved the degree of monitoring of commercial payments required to limit capital flight through 'leads and lags'. It is difficult enough to secure sufficient control over the transactions of domestic residents, but neither system of controls confronted the even trickier problem (politically) of limiting the extent to which overseas holders of the domestic currency could withdraw their funds. This has become an increasingly important problem as the holding of overseas bank deposits and other overseas assets has grown in the seventies and eighties. A study of the French experience concluded that 'we observe massive outflows in 1981 until the first devaluation in October, a reflux delayed until the second devaluation of June 1982, quickly reversed by the crisis in the first quarter of 1983 which led to the third and last devaluation in March' (Sachs and Wyplosz, 1986, p. 294). Such speculation, even when it simply reflects the underlying problems in international trade, eliminates the breathing space necessary to reorganize industry.

Industrial policy

Improving industrial performance, which in the longer run would help the balance of payments and inflation, was supposed to be the centrepiece of both

British Labour and French Socialist strategies. A radical 'remixing' of the balance of power between capital and the state was proposed, using the latter's increased control to promote investment and modernization. In the British case the policies to increase state control were never carried out; in France the radical measures of control were implemented but with different outcomes from those envisaged.

Labour's policy had two main strands. One was to nationalize at least one leading, profitable manufacturing company in each industry and then to direct its operations through a National Enterprise Board (NEB). The idea was that these newly nationalized companies would undertake major investment programmes and innovations. The architect of these proposals, Stuart Holland, argued that they would exert a 'pull effect on other big firms' based on: 'oligopoly leadership, or the situation in which one of the new firms at the top end of an industry breaks from the pack and pioneers a new product or technique on a major scale. While the remaining leading firms might otherwise have hung around and delayed introducing a similar product or process, they cannot any longer afford to do so without risk or losing sales, profits and market share to the pioneer firm' (Holland, 1975, p. 185).

Planning agreements constituted the other main strand of the new industrial policy. The government would require all major firms to present corporate plans, detailing proposed levels of output, employment, investment and so on. It would then amend the plans to fit in with overall economic objectives, while leaving firms free to decide how to carry them out. This was supposed to provide the government with sufficient leverage to plan the economy without having to resort to the traditional socialist device of nationalizing the 'commanding heights'.

In April 1973 the Labour opposition proposed that the next Labour government take powers to impose compulsory planning agreements and talked of nationalizing between 20 and 25 of the largest 100 manufacturing companies, accounting for around one-third of manufacturing output, with or without their consent. The 1973 Party Conference approved this position. The *Guardian* described the policy as 'little short of an industrial and financial revolution' (quoted Forester, 1975, p. 74). But, at the leadership's insistence, the word 'compulsory' was omitted from the section on planning agreements in the February 1974 election manifesto, as was any indication of the scale of NEB operations.

After the election the new Minister of Industry, Tony Benn, was greeted by his senior civil servant with the words, 'I presume, Secretary of State, that you don't intend to implement the industrial strategy in the Labour Party's programme' (quoted Coventry Trades Council, 1980, p. 33). The *Financial Times* reported that 'the CBI told Mr Wilson [the Prime Minister] that there was absolutely no room for compromise or negotiation about further state intervention in industry and further nationalization' (16 September 1974).

After the June 1974 referendum on EEC membership Benn was removed on the excuse that his anti-EEC views made his position untenable. The industrial policy plans published in August 1974 represented a victory for business pressure. Planning agreements were to be purely voluntary, and the NEB's powers were severely restricted by the clause that 'holdings in companies . . . should be acquired by agreement'. Its funds were limited to £1 billion over a five-year period.

The government transferred eight publicly owned companies to the NEB. Most had been acquired because they were close to bankruptcy. Two, British Leyland (BL) and Rolls Royce, accounted for 90 per cent of the Board's operations. It cut operating levels savagely in an attempt to restore profitability. In the Board's first two years of operation 19,000 jobs were lost at BL and 5600 at Rolls Royce. The NEB's other activities, lending money to small companies at commercial interest rates, were peripheral.

The only company to sign a planning agreement was Chrysler UK, in spring 1976. The US parent company had offered the government £35 million to take its loss-making subsidiary off its hands, thereby avoiding redundancy payments and other closure costs. Unwilling to see the loss of some 60,000 direct and indirect jobs or to nationalize the company, the government opted to provide a £55 million loan for investment and to guarantee a proportion of operating losses for three years, up to a ceiling of £72.5 million. In return Chrysler agreed to sign a planning agreement. Its trivial significance was shown when Chrysler Europe was taken over; the Labour government learned of it through the press.

The core of Mitterrand's industrial policy was a major extension of the public sector. The proportion of industrial sales undertaken by the public sector almost doubled to 30 per cent (see table 18.1). State ownership was concentrated in large enterprises, and most significant was the extension of public ownership in competitive sectors of manufacturing (rather than the monopoly utilities which constituted most of the state sectors of the ACCs). Five major industrial groups in electrical and electronic engineering and chemicals were taken over, together with the two largest steel groups (already effectively controlled by the government since 1978), 39 banks (taking the share

Table 18.1 French nationalization, 1982 (percentage of industry in nationalized firms)

	Before	After
Sales	17.2	29.4
Employment	11.0	22.2
Investment	43.5	51.9
Industrial employment		
Firms with >2000 employees		47.7
Firms with 500–2000 employees		15.4
Firms with <500 employees		2.7

Source: OECD, 1983, *Economic Survey of France*, March 1983, table 18

of banking in state hands from 60 to 90 per cent), two important financial holding companies and a major firm in each of aircraft, computers, telecommunications and pharmaceuticals. While they were very radical in scope, the nationalizations were by no means confiscatory. Shareholders in the 'big five' groups received 'far too much compensation' according to the *Financial Times*, given the losses they were making.

The 'Interim Plan' for 1982–3 called for the expanded state sector to increase research, development and innovation, providing a lead for the private sector in the necessary restructuring of the economy. Within five-year 'plan contracts' with the governments, management was to act independently; Mitterrand said that 'their autonomy of decision and action will be total' (*Financial Times*, 18 February 1982). This inevitably limited the impact of another innovation, the statutory rights for workers to have one-third representation on boards of management of these state-owned firms (see chapter 9). Apparently because of objections from management over his interventionist stance, Chevenement was replaced as Minister of Industry by the aptly named Fabius (the Roman Emperor Fabius was called The Delayer, the avoider of head-on battles, after whom the Fabian Society was named). Fabius said, soon after the March 1983 devaluation which marked the decisive move towards austerity, that 'the state must not substitute itself in the role of enterprises and of entrepreneurs, that politics must be kept out of industry, and the main effort in job creation, innovation and development should come from (largely private) medium and small companies' (*Financial Times*, 13 April 1983).

One theme of the Interim Plan was that the public sector would be able to take a long-term view of national economic needs, unconstrained by short-term profitability. A number of the newly nationalized groups were making heavy losses – in iron and steel alone these rose from 7 billion francs in 1981 to 10 billion in 1983. Subsequently, however, fierce rationalization took place in many of these industries. By 1985 losses in the newly nationalized industries had been reduced in total to 8 billion francs, less than half the average of the previous four years.

As the OECD pointed out, attempting to draw a balance sheet for the impact of the nationalizations is difficult,

> since the performance of the enterprises in question was far more dependent on the situation in that sector and the general state of the economy than on institutional factors. Nonetheless, it is noteworthy that the growth of investment was higher in the new public industrial concerns than in industry as a whole over the period 1981–84 (44 per cent and 26 per cent respectively in nominal terms) and the job losses were on a smaller scale (4.0 per cent and 7.5 per cent respectively). (OECD, 1987, p. 33)

One important result of the nationalizations was a major restructuring of the firms concerned, with parts of previously conglomerate groups being rationalized into more logical firms. This restructuring took place at the initiative either of the government or of the firms concerned; 'in all cases however, it was the supply of public funds which allowed the balancing of accounts, the necessary precondition for these transfers' (Stoffaes, 1985, p. 165). The chairman of the nationalized computer firm, Honeywell-Bull, said 'One of the main justifications for the nationalizations is that it was the only means of organizing the transfer to the companies of the funds needed to make them internationally competitive' (*Financial Times*, 17 March 1983).

The Socialists' restructuring served to facilitate the privatizations implemented by Chirac's right wing administration which came to power in March 1986. Its plans extended beyond the firms nationalized by the Socialists to some taken over in 1945, but excluded the state monopolies (railways, electricity, telephone) and some major loss-makers (Renault and the steel companies). Their ambitions exceeded the time available to them for they lost office in two years, with less than half their privatization plan carried through. Nevertheless, major enterprises such as Saint-Gobain, Paribas and the Société Générale were sold off, a faster rate of privatization (in terms of the funds raised) than that achieved by Thatcher. Moreover, the Socialist Party's hopes for nationalization have evaporated: since being returned to power they have not attempted further extensions to the public sector. Mitterrand committed the new government to 'neither nationalization nor privatization'.

The French nationalizations, and associated measures of restructuring, contributed to productivity growth in French manufacturing of 2.4 per cent per year over the period 1981–6, the same rate as in Germany. In France, however, this was achieved with no growth in output whatever, implying a corresponding fall in employment, and contributing substantially to the rise in the unemployment rate. In Germany output at least crept up, by more than 1 per cent per year, so that a similar rate of productivity growth to that in France implied a smaller rate of job loss. While improved productivity was certainly one of the Socialists' objectives, it was envisaged as being part of a process of expansion rather than as leading solely to job loss.

Distributing the results of slower growth

The radical policies of nationalization put into practice by the Socialists in France could not surmount the pressures preventing rapid expansion of production and employment. The very success of the nationalizations in promoting restructuring, which appears to have been considerable, did nothing to help employment in the short, or even medium, run. On the contrary, rationalization under the Socialists looked depressingly similar in its effects to that undertaken under Thatcher.

Acceptance of the constraints on the growth rate imposed by the general slowdown in the advanced economies does not imply the implementation of the full-blown pro-market policies discussed in chapter 17. It is possible within the context of slow growth to stick to solidaristic principles of egalitarianism and income redistribution. Central to the inegalitarian thrust of the right has been the use of mass unemployment as a weapon against the labour movement, with effects stretching well beyond the unemployed themselves. But slower growth of production of goods and services for sale by the market sector of the economy does not necessarily condemn the economy to rising unemployment. It is evident from table 14.4 that the decline in employment growth in Japan was tiny in relation to the output slowdown. This points to a more general phenomenon: there is no strong correlation within the advanced countries as a whole between the extent to which output growth slowed down after 1973 and the extent to which employment growth declined. In effect then, countries have distributed the impact of slower growth in very different ways: in some (notably members of the EC) the costs have been born disproportionately by the large numbers of workers made unemployed, in others employment growth has been maintained and the costs spread much more widely.

We take the experience of Sweden as exemplifying the policies of employment maintenance. Among European countries Sweden's unemployment performance (an average rate since 1973 of 2.2 per cent on the OECD's 'standardized definitions', with a maximum of 3.5 per cent in 1983) has only been more or less matched by Austria, Switzerland and Norway. Norway's position has been greatly eased by the fortuitous development of North Sea oil, which allowed that country to grow just as fast after 1973 as before. Sweden's performance is moreover far superior to both Austria and Switzerland in terms of employment. These latter two countries contrived to hold down registered unemployment by reducing the recorded labour force. Large numbers of foreign workers were effectively made unemployed and sent home (especially from Switzerland) and women workers were discouraged from entering the labour force. While the general trend has been towards increased participation of women in paid employment (see chapter 14), in Austria and Switzerland the female participation rate declined after 1973. In both countries, then, something approaching full employment has been maintained for male nationals, but substantially at the expense of other groups. Sweden, by contrast, achieved an extraordinary increase in employment after 1973. The 'employment rate', the proportion of people of working age (15–64) who have paid employment, rose by 8.9 per cent between 1973 and 1985 in Sweden (Germany and France registered declines of 10–12 per cent over the same period).

In the context of slow growth of production a number of policies may be implemented to maintain employment. On the one hand deliberate policies to subsidize marginal jobs may be implemented in order to hold back factory closures and the rationalization of production. In the later 1970s and early 1980s very large sums were paid out in industrial subsidies in Sweden; they tripled to nearly 4 per cent of GDP between 1970 and 1978. Aid was especially concentrated in steel and shipbuilding, which accounted for more than two-thirds of the subsidies. A sceptical account by US economists recorded that 'the magnitude of that support reached staggering proportions. Between 1977 and 1979 Swedish shipyards received subsidies equal to 120 per cent of their wage bill' (Lawrence and Bosworth, 1987, p. 71). Ironically the policy of subsidization was at its height during the period of conservative government in 1976–82, testimony to the right's fear of being labelled the party of unemployment. When the social democrats were re-elected the subsidies were radically reduced. Indeed, OECD figures show that between 1975 and 1985 employment in shipbuilding (of major importance in Sweden) fell by more than in any other country, by 89 per cent, and employment in steel fell by one-third, a similar proportion to Germany and Belgium.

For policies of subsidization to play a positive role they do not have to continue indefinitely. The innovative aspect of Swedish intervention has been the so-called 'active labour market policy', which includes expenditure on the employment services, youth measures, direct job creation and measures for the disabled. But generally regarded as especially important have been the large sums spent on retraining adults, running at 0.5 per cent of GDP in Sweden in the late 1980s, around double the typical EC figure, and five times the expenditure in the UK. On the one hand by slowing the rate of run-down in declining sectors, and on the other hand by retraining workers who lose their jobs, Swedish policy has helped to avoid the concentrated waves of redundancies of industrial workers with inappropriate skills which have swelled the dole queues in the EC (see chapter 14).

The second central aspect of Swedish employment experience, complementing policies to maintain the availability of work in the market sector, has been the very rapid growth of employment by the state. Sweden already had the highest share of government employment of any OECD country in 1973 (23.8 per cent); by 1987 the figure had reached 33 per cent. This has permitted a major extension of welfare services, a famous component of the 'Swedish model'. Such an expansion has played an important role in the enormous rise in the employment of women (whose employment rate rose from 61 per cent in 1973 to 78 per cent in 1987). Not only have many women found work in the state sector, but the provision of child care in particular has facilitated women taking jobs.

Finally the available work in the state and market sectors has been spread more widely through reductions in average hours worked. These have taken the form of both a shorter working week and increased employment of part-timers (frequently women working in the welfare services).

Table 18.2 shows how employment has been maintained in Sweden relative to an average of five EEC countries for which comparable data are available. Sweden only achieved slightly faster growth of market sector output, that is excluding the government, than the EEC countries (though after 1979 its performance was substantially better than in the EEC). But productivity grew distinctly more slowly in Sweden, partly as a result of the policies aimed at curbing headlong rationalization. This meant that the availability of work in the

Table 18.2 EEC and Swedish employment patterns, 1973–86 (average annual percentage growth rates)

	EEC	Sweden
(1) Market output per head of population	1.1	1.3
(2) less productivity	3.1	2.4
(3) = Hours in market sector/population	−2.0	−1.1
(4) plus share of state employment	0.4	0.9
(5) plus fall in average hours worked	0.5	0.4
(6) plus share of part-time workers	0.2	0.3
(7) = Employment/population (3)+(4)+(5)+(6)	−0.9	0.5

Source: Glyn, 1991

market sector declined only half as quickly in Sweden as in the EEC countries. The growth of state employment was about twice as fast as in the EEC countries. With hours cut and increases in part-time employment occurring at similar rates, it was slow productivity growth maintaining work in the market sector, together with faster expansion of state employment, which accounted for the enormous difference in employment performance. In the EEC countries the employment rate fell at almost 1 per cent per year, whereas in Sweden it grew by 0.5 per cent per year.

These methods of employment spreading have by no means been unique to Sweden. In the UK, Labour introduced the Temporary Employment Subsidy, which paid £20 per week for a year to an employer who would retain a worker who would otherwise have been made redundant. Mitterrand's government deliberately increased state employment by 200,000 and introduced cuts in the working week (from 40 to 39 hours) and longer holidays (from four to five weeks). But there was doubt as to the extent that the TES actually increased total employment, rather than parcelling it out in a different way between competing firms. Estimates also suggest that the employment effects of hours reductions in France may have been quite limited since they increased labour costs and caused firms to rationalize elsewhere.

What is common to all these methods of 'employment spreading' is that they have to be paid for. If more people are to be employed for a given output level each of them must exercise less consuming power. In the short run resources may be borrowed from overseas by running a balance of payments deficit and this can temporarily boost consumption levels. For example, in Sweden over the period 1973–6 net exports fell in real terms by nearly 6 per cent of marketed output, and the current account of the balance of payments deteriorated by 5 per cent of GDP. Resources may be borrowed 'from the future' by cutting down investment. In France during 1980–2 real investment (including holdings of stocks) fell sharply, again allowing consumption to grow faster than total production. A certain amount of redistribution from the richest sections in society can be achieved, thus maintaining the growth of consumption for the average wage and salary earner. In the UK over the period 1973–5 the share of consumption out of property incomes fell by 1 per cent of marketed output a year as dividends were held down and the value of interest receipts was eroded by very rapid inflation.

The 'raiding', whether deliberate or fortuitous, of these other categories of expenditure is an inherently limited, and usually short run, expedient. Investment has to be maintained for the reasons described earlier. Balance of payments deficits cannot be sustained, especially by left governments, as we have already seen. Too substantial cuts in consumption out of property incomes cannot be made without hitting small savers or risking further erosions of 'confidence', on which rising investment and the prevention of capital flight depend.

Thus, in the long run, employment can only be spread widely in the context of slow growth if many (or most) of those who would have been employed anyway accept static or slowly growing take-home pay. A substantial degree of redistribution within the working class is essential. Certainly those workers accepting restraint on pay increases will gain from improved leisure if hours of work fall; they or their families will tend to gain from improvements in the provision of public services as a result of increased employment; some families will gain through greater possibilities for a second family member to find a job. But the maintenance of full employment has a cost to them in terms of reduced consumption out of their pay packets (as taxation reduces the hourly take-home pay or as hours of work fall). In general the benefits are received by broader sections of the population than contribute to their financing. Espousing and initiating such policies demands, therefore, a high degree of social solidarity on the part of those with secure jobs.

If it requires social solidarity to espouse and initiate such policies, it also requires strong collective self-discipline on the part of the labour movement to prevent 'free-riding'. This would happen if individual groups of workers, who may be bargaining with their employers at a firm or industry level, seek pay increases to maintain (the growth rate of) their take-home pay in a situation where restraint is necessary for consumption spreading to work. Such pay increases would lead to faster rationalization and labour shedding elsewhere in the market sector. Indeed the situation may be even worse, to the extent that the higher real cost of labour reduces market sector output (as marginal exporters close, for example). Cuts in working time provoke similar effects if hourly earnings are increased to maintain weekly wages. So in addition to social solidarity the labour movement has to show strong collective discipline if employment spreading is to be successful.

Similar remarks apply to state benefits (pensions, for example) which also spread consumption beyond those currently in paid work. Maintaining the generosity of state benefits ensures that the costs of slower growth are not met disproportionately by those dependent on them. In Sweden, for example, the share of transfers in marketed output has grown by well over one-half since

1973. But again it is necessary that there should be collective discipline among the employed to accept their share of the costs. In the short run the problem may be concealed by rising state deficits, as occurred in Sweden in the late 1970s and early 1980s. But eventually tax rates have to rise, and if the implied cut in (the growth of) living standards is not accepted, the inevitable result is that the costs are pushed on to those made unemployed. Again both social solidarity and collective discipline are necessary if an egalitarian sharing of the costs of slower growth is to be a durable pattern.

In Sweden the sense of social solidarity and egalitarianism has been very strong and the trade unions have had very wide coverage of employment. They are organized into three national confederations (blue-collar, white-collar and state) which have considerable authority over their members. The pressures on the social solidarity and the discipline imposed by this pattern of spreading employment and consumption have been extraordinarily sharp. Over the whole period 1973–86 the amount that the average employed worker could consume out of her or his earnings (after taxation and social security) actually *declined* by more than 1 per cent per year, despite a growth of hourly productivity in the market sector of more than 2 per cent per year. That is, *all and more* of the growth of productivity since 1973 has been diverted to improvements in the welfare state (including transfers and employment in the public services) and cuts in average hours worked, leaving the average worker consuming less out of her or his pay packet than to begin with. While many families' consumption has benefited from there being a second earner, and living standards have been enhanced by improved welfare services and shorter working hours, this is still a very striking pattern for a capitalist economy subject to all the normal pressures through advertising to make personal expenditures on consumer goods the sole object of esteem. Moreover, 'solidaristic wages policy' has continued to reduce wage differentials both between men and women and within each category, leading to one of the most egalitarian wage structures in the world, but also leading to tensions between the union confederations.

These developments have all produced reactions and pressures for at least a relaxation of the 'model'. Tax rates have reached extremely high levels – the share of government receipts in Sweden reached 62 per cent of GDP in 1987 as the Social Democrats eliminated the huge budget deficit left them by the conservatives (7 per cent of GDP in 1982), but top rates of tax have been reduced from 86 to 72 per cent with further cuts promised. The growth of state employment has been held in check since 1986 and the growth of the cost of state services held down to below that of private expenditure through holding back public sector pay (before 1979 public sector expenditure was growing around 2 per cent per year more quickly than private consumption). Transfers have been cut by 1 per cent of GDP since 1983, but without major cuts in welfare benefits (apart from the fall in the real level of pensions after the devaluation of 1982). The combination of very low unemployment and the slow growth of living standards led at the beginning of 1990 to such wage pressure that the Social Democratic government called for a wages freeze and proposed, but was forced to withdraw, a ban on strikes.

Not only have the (very real) achievements of labour in Sweden been subject to severe strain but they have been broadly limited to the issues of employment and distribution. Important as these obviously are, labour's ambitions in the early seventies extended to securing a measure of control over industry. In 1975, the trade unions proposed a scheme for 'wage-earner funds' which would operate as follows:

> Firms above a certain size (fifty or a hundred employees) should be required to issue new stocks corresponding to twenty per cent of their annual profits, and . . . these stocks should be owned by funds representing wage-earners as a collective group. The shareholder voting rights of these funds were to be exercised partly by union-appointed boards and partly by direct representatives of the firm's employees. Such a reform, the committee argued, would facilitate the implementation of a solidaristic wages policy – on the assumption that highly paid workers in profitable firms would be more open to wage restraint if the 'excess profits' so generated were reinvested in the firm and translated into worker-owned capital. It would also counteract the tendency towards increased concentration of wealth and complement industrial democracy legislation by providing employees with ownership-based influence over corporate management. Under this scheme the higher the rate of profit, the more quickly collectivization would occur. The committee calculated that it would take thirty-five years for the wage-earner collective to acquire forty-nine per cent of stocks in a firm operating at a ten per cent average profit rate. (Pontusson, 1987, p. 13)

Rudolph Meidner, the chair of the committee, said in an interview: 'we want to deprive the capitalists of the power that they exercise by virtue of ownership. All experience shows that it is not enough to have influence and control. Ownership plays a decisive role.' Referring to Marx, he continued, 'we cannot fundamentally change society without changing its ownership structure' (quoted Pontusson, 1987, p. 14).

What finally emerged after bitter opposition from employers was a much scaled-down scheme, to run from 1984 to 1990, which would place funds from a 0.2 per cent payroll tax plus a 20 per cent profits tax on excess profits into five regional funds. These would buy shares in the market and channel the returns into the national pensions fund. Even combined, the funds could never acquire the majority of a firm's shares (even if shareholders were willing to sell them) and it was estimated that by 1990 they might constitute 5 per cent of the value of Swedish shares and 3 per cent of the value of pension funds. A US observer reported that 'The Wage Earner Fund legislation has become something of a full-employment act for Swedish accountants. In 1985, one of the most profitable years in Swedish industry, Volvo and many other major firms paid no profit-sharing tax into the funds. . . . In practice the Wage Earner Fund legislation has become little more than another increase in payroll taxes' (Flanagan, 1987, p. 171).

1990 saw the employers going more broadly on the offensive with a 'radical plan to transform social democratic Sweden into a robust free market economy' aiming 'to destroy the famed Swedish economic model with its collectivist values of equality and solidarity' (*Financial Times*, November 11, 1990). The employers proposed a halving of the share of the public sector, privatizations, introduction of market forces into the welfare state, ending national wage agreements and placing emphasis on linking pay with productivity and the abolition of wage earner funds.

Conclusions

The 1970s and 1980s saw a handful of attempts to translate the increased power of labour which was the product of the long boom into greater state control over the functioning of the economy. These were not full-blown socialist systems for substituting planning for market forces, however such systems might be conceived. They represented, rather, attempts to curb and shape those market forces. What has resulted has been the use of state funds mainly to lean against the wind of these market forces, reducing social and economic costs by spreading restructuring out over time, and sometimes to blow with them where rationalization dictated by market forces was being blocked by lack of funds or the opposition of specific groups. No systematic conception of an alternative set of criteria for organizing the economy has developed, let alone an idea of how it would function within one country in an increasingly interdependent economic system.

Maintaining full employment, and ensuring that the costs of economic slowdown are broadly spread, has been a very difficult target since the mid-1970s. It is only exceptionally that the labour movement has maintained sufficient power and authority as a legacy from the long boom to maintain these very important, if limited, objectives.

19

Capitalism Triumphant?

The fall of the communist regimes of Eastern Europe in 1989, and the decay of the system in the Soviet Union, have been widely hailed as the decisive defeat of socialism and victory for capitalism. The bankruptcy of the system of social and economic organization in the East is beyond dispute. But it in no way follows from this that collective, egalitarian and democratic forms of organizing the economy are off the agenda, and that giving the freest rein to market forces has been vindicated as the natural system of social organization. Comparisons of the relatively affluent lifestyles of the West with the everyday drudgery of life in the East contributed to the build-up of dissatisfaction with its bureaucratic and authoritarian regimes. But the regimes of Eastern Europe may yet be seen as having been as much a barrier to socialism as to capitalism and proclamations of the 'triumph' of capitalism had a distinctly hollow ring as the 1990s began. As part III of this book has shown, the performance of the advanced capitalist countries in the 1980s has been far from spectacular. On the contrary the 1980s emphasized that the most successful countries have systematically tempered the free play of market forces with a range of state interventions in the spheres of both production and distribution. Unfettered market forces still produce a capitalist system containing strong tendencies towards stagnation, conflict and the systematic exaggeration of inequalities.

First of all, growth even in the advanced countries has been weak. Productivity growth at around 2 per cent per year could generate improved living standards and public services but in Europe in particular much of this productivity growth has occurred through the rationalization of production and the creation of a large pool of unemployed workers. This kind of productivity growth has a strongly unegalitarian character. The same level of production involves less workers. Those who maintain their jobs and those receiving the benefits of lower production costs (shareholders or consumers) gain. But their gain is simply at the expense of those who lose their jobs. Without policies to ensure that displaced workers receive appropriate training to enhance their skills, and that work is brought to the areas where they live, such productivity gains systematically worsen the conditions of a section of the population. This type of rationalization, which is the market's intrinsic method of dealing with an outdated structure of production, is precisely what is being impressed on Eastern Europe by international organizations like the IMF.

The 1980s saw an important trend in the ACCs towards the systematic creation of inequality, justified as a means of increasing incentives. The progressive nature of the tax system, already full of loopholes for property owners in particular, has been sharply curtailed. The role of the benefit system and public services in maintaining decent standards for all in society has been whittled down. This has succeeded mainly in reducing the living standards of the most disadvantaged sections of the population, with the pressure of job insecurity and fear of unemployment acting as the real market 'incentive' for the mass of workers. Luxurious consumption at the other end of the income scale has contributed to an exaggerated appearance of prosperity. The countries of Eastern Europe are already under pressure to follow this route, including the creation of mass unemployment as a central part of restoring incentives.

In the sphere of international economic relations the 1980s have seen the continuing decline of the power of governments in the face of the world's financial markets, a process widely bewailed when exchange rates fluctuate but deliberately engendered through the rush to financial liberalization. These fluctuations in exchange rates have had disastrous effects in destroying sections of exporting or import-competing industries at times and stoking up unnecessary inflationary pressures at others. Such is the international financial 'non-system' from which the East is supposed to benefit.

The great triumph of the international financial markets in the 1980s was the channelling of lending to the LDCs. Frequently the loans were misused and found their way into the overseas bank accounts of powerful individuals. But even where productive capacity was expanded the indebted countries were unable to find outlets in the slowly growing markets of the ACCs for the exports necessary to finance debt repayment. The pressures to repay debt which have brought impoverishment to millions in the LDCs are a blight on the economic record of capitalism in the 1980s. A number of the regimes of Eastern Europe have already incurred huge debts to Western banks and have begun to suffer from the problems of repayment.

With the days of easy credit for poor countries long gone, and official loans likely to be very limited, can Eastern Europe rely on vast amounts of direct investment by Western companies to provide them with the technology to make products competitive on world markets? Again the experience of direct investment in the past decade is hardly impressive. A larger and larger proportion of it is directed within the charmed circle of the advanced countries, leaving a trickle for a few select newcomers with sufficiently authoritarian regimes. The lack of development of large areas of Southern Europe, to look no further, with unemployment rates that rose sharply in the 1980s, stands as an ominous warning for the East.

After the first flush of enthusiasm for the countries returning to the capitalist fold fades, they may well be largely left to their own devices, to sink or swim with the swings in market forces. Because of their weight in the world economy, and especially in international trade, the decisive element in these swings is developments in the ACCs.

This book has argued that although the advanced countries were profoundly transformed by the boom, they continued to be driven by the logic of capitalism. Their motive force remained the accumulation of capital in which the technical aspect of productivity has to be underpinned by particular relationships between the classes – employers must be able to exercise sufficient control over employees to ensure smooth production and profits. For full advantage to be taken of such conditions, relations between the competing countries must also be orderly.

On two occasions in the past 45 years the stability of the capitalist system was severely shaken and its prospects were distinctly problematic. Postwar radicalism, which was frequently explicitly anti-capitalist, had to be contained and this was achieved in the late forties and early fifties by a determined campaign under US leadership. From the late sixties to the early seventies the system faced another severe buffeting from a working class strengthened by the boom. These problems were exacerbated by the disorganization of the international system caused by the declining power of the USA and to increased independence of suppliers of inputs. The subsequent period of slower growth and higher unemployment has contained rather than eliminated these problems.

In terms of relations between capital and labour the dominant strategy of the employers has become one of divide and rule. Recognition of the value to them of a skilled and cooperative workforce for certain core operations has generated moves towards individualizing payment systems and delegating detailed control over work processes. Meanwhile, more routine low-paid jobs, in services as well as manufacturing, are still to be carried out under the pressure of the more traditional hierarchical systems of control of work. In both cases the purpose is increasing the effectiveness of the work done, in terms of quality and flexibility in the first case and in terms of sheer intensity in the second. The long-term problem of the first strategy is how to reserve workers' involvement and control to matters of the detailed organization of work, once concessions have been made to the principle of managerial prerogative over everything that happens in the factory. In relation to the mass of workers still performing unskilled and routinized work the fundamental problem remains that of controlling wages and other demands should the balance of bargaining advantage tilt back towards workers. While trade unions have faced huge problems in organizing the service sector and small-scale industry, the central lesson for employers of the experience of the 1960s and 1970s is the functional role under capitalism of the reserve army of labour. This understanding acts as a fundamental deflationary bias in the ACCs.

The other main source of instability for the ACCs has derived from the international system. Here the most important locus of vulnerability is undoubtedly the international financial system, which is out of the control of the monetary authorities. The international organizations claim self-righteously that such instability simply reflects the failure of governments adequately to coordinate their policies. Indeed international financial integration is a most effective means of disciplining individual governments, especially of the left, against policies disapproved of by the financial markets. But it still seems most unlikely, especially between the major blocks of ACCs, that sufficient coordination will develop to guarantee financial stability. Herein lies the most plausible cause of an uncontainable credit crisis which would spread to the productive sector and trigger a major recession as high cost of credit forced firms to cut their stocks and rein in their investment. Market forces would be revealed at their most destructive.

Barring a major crisis of this kind, which is definitely possible but the probability of which can never be quantified from past experience, the likelihood is of a continuation of moderate accumulation and growth, well short of 'golden age' rates but unlikely to tumble into major recession. In the background lies a threat which has grown in prominence at the end of the 1980s – environmental disaster. This has played no role in our story so far because the destruction of the environment has *yet* hardly acted as a constraint on the course of accumulation. Thus far the costs of pollution control, of the order of 1 or 2 per cent of GDP, have been resented by those paying but have paled into insignificance compared to other causes of the growth slowdown.

It is possible that this situation will change by the end of the century and that it will become apparent that environmental considerations should act as the binding constraint on production. The capitalist system, driven by pursuit of private profit with systematic disregard of all considerations of broader social interest, is fundamentally unsuited to coping with these problems (one characteristic which was shared by the systems of the Soviet Union and Eastern Europe to an ever greater degree). Even if such slower growth were forced upon the system, no doubt long after it should have been deliberately decided upon, the fundamental question is how the slower growth should be distributed. Egalitarian solutions demand the expansion of non-resource intensive public services, the reduction of working time for all and the more even sharing out of income via erosion of wage differentials and progressive taxation. Yet the experience of the slowdown of the 1980s is that the logic of capitalism pushes in precisely the opposite directions – cuts in the public services, rises in unemployment, increased polarization of wage incomes and a less progressive tax system. 1990 may prove to represent a highspot of confidence in the universal superiority of market solutions which is as short-lived as it is undeserved.

Data Appendix

Sources and methods

This appendix first describes the basic series for profitability, capital accumulation and state spending which we constructed for the seven largest advanced capitalist countries since 1951. Many of the tables and figures in parts II and III are based on these data. The appendix tables present the series for profit shares, profit rates and the capital stock for each country, for both the manufacturing sector and the corporate business sector. Some discussion of sources and methods for these series follows this introduction. We also constructed aggregate series for the seven countries as a whole (labelled 'ACCs') and for the four European ones, France, Germany, Italy and the United Kingdom (labelled 'Europe'). The methods used are described below. The other data used in parts II and III come from standard international sources (notably OECD publications), as indicated in the tables and charts. The data for part I were put together from a range of national sources listed at the end of this appendix.

The stock of fixed capital at constant prices

Capital stock is calculated using the 'perpetual inventory' method. Each type of means of production is assumed to have a particular life, at the end of which it is scrapped. Each year the capital stock grows as the new investment is added to it, and shrinks as old means of production are retired. These figures are referred to as the *gross* capital stock. An alternative measure is the *net* capital stock. The essential difference is that when calculating the gross stock, means of production are assumed to retain their full initial value throughout their lives, whereas when calculating net stock the value is assumed to fall steadily, reaching zero at the point when they are retired (straight-line depreciation). Steadily falling values capture the fact that ownership of a means of production yields a steadily falling income as a result of competition from more modern equipment (see below). However, the productive capabilities of means of production change little with age. For this reason we have used changes in the gross stock to estimate accumulation.

The asset lives assumed in the different countries vary enormously. Since the statistical evidence on which the lives are based is very tenuous, there is little reason to believe that assumed differences accurately reflect real ones The assumption of unchanging asset lives is also dubious. For these reasons cross-country comparisons of the level of the capital stock should be treated with caution. Maddison (1982, appendix D) discusses the differences in estimation between the various countries and provides (table D6) estimates for various countries assuming the same life of assets for all countries (and assets). However, estimates of the growth of the stock should be more reliable (see Maddison, 1982, table D2). In any case, they are the best available.

The main source of the capital stock data are the OECD's *Flows and Stocks of Fixed Capital 1962–1987* and earlier issues, together with the EC's *Indicators of Manufacturing, Capital, Labour and Output* and *Indicators of Profitability, Capital, Labour and Output for the Non-agricultural Business Sector*. National sources have been used where the OECD does not provide data, and in order to extend the series back to 1951. The series for Italy (pre-1960) and for France (pre-1955) required extensive estimation and are less reliable. Estimates have also been made for 1988 and 1989, using investment data and our estimates of the amount of capital retired from use.

Additional sources for gross capital stock at constant prices

United States:	*Survey of Current Business*, October 1982 and earlier issues.
Canada:	*Fixed Capital Flows and Stocks*, 1926–78 and later issues.
United Kingdom:	*National Income and Expenditure*, various issues and un-published series supplied by the Central Statistical Office.
France:	Carré, Dubois and Malinvaud, *French Economic Growth*. Mairesse, *L'Evaluation du capital fixe productive*.
Germany:	*Volkswirtschaftliche Gesamtrechnungen*, Revidierte Ergebnisse 1960 bis 1981 and earlier years. Deutsches Institut für Wirtschaftsforschung, *Anlageinvestitionen und Anlagevermögen*.
Italy:	*Annuario di Contabilita Nationale*, tomo 1, 1982. *Bolletino Mensile di Statistica*, January 1978.
Japan:	*Estimates of the Stock of Non-Residential Business Capital*, March 1976 and other issues.

The measurement of profit shares and rates

The capitalist advances capital in order to appropriate a certain amount of surplus. Part of the gross surplus goes to replace worn-out or obsolescent equipment. The rest is net profit. Some net profit is used to extend the amount of capital, in the form either of such fixed capital as machinery or buildings or of stocks of commodities. So the value of capital is simultaneously both reduced, as means of production wear out or become obsolete, and increased, as a result of gross investment in new means of production.

It is difficult to estimate, either conceptually or practically, the depreciation of fixed capital. To construct national accounts, a simple general depreciation rule has to be assumed. This usually takes the form of straight-line depreciation. Both net profits and net capital stock can then be estimated, and hence the net profit share and rate. In order to avoid the difficulties involved in calculating depreciation, some authors have used the gross profit rate, which makes no allowance for depreciation in the estimation of either profits or the capital stock. Means of production are valued at their initial cost (after allowing for inflation) throughout their assumed lives. Hill (1979) has even suggested that the gross profit rate may be superior to the net as an estimate of the true rate.

The true, or economic, rate of profit is that which would be obtained from a discounted cash flow calculation of profitability. On this basis the rate of profit is the discount rate which equates the current value of gross profits to the cost of investment. Depreciation in any year can then be calculated: given gross profits, depreciation is set to ensure that net profit divided by the capital stock at the beginning of the period equals the net profit rate (previously calculated from the discounted cash flow). Figure A1 shows the depreciated value of the capital stock over the lifetime of an asset. The middle curve, 'depreciated stock', is that obtained when economic depreciation is subtracted each period. It is given the shape typically found when annual gross profits remain constant throughout the life of the asset. The distance AB represents the economic depreciation during the year n, and CD the assumed depreciation in national accounts terms, which is then used to calculate net stock and net profits. With the gross stock there is no depreciation until the end of the life of the asset, at which point the whole value is depreciated.

However, gross profits are seldom constant throughout the life of an asset. Most means of production are scrapped because they no longer earn profits. As the equipment ages, output may decline and running costs increase. Moreover, newer machines embody technical change and may enable the production of a superior product at a lower price. The consequence of lower gross profits as machines age is more rapid depreciation. The curve representing the depreciated capital stock, in figure A1, is flattened out, and more closely resembles the straight line of the net stock. So straight-line depreciation

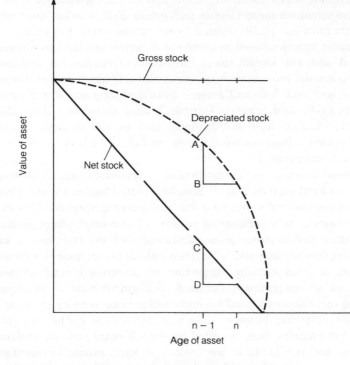

Figure A1 Economic and straight-line depreciation.

approximates closely to economic depreciation. The net capital stock is a good representation of the depreciated stock and net profits are a good estimate of true profits.

Our estimates overstate the level of the rate of profit in one important respect. Only the *fixed* capital advanced has been taken into account. But there is also a large amount of capital in the form of materials and fuels, work in progress, or finished goods waiting to be sold. (Capital is also advanced to pay wages, but this does not need to be considered separately. It very soon takes the form of commodities, which are sold or form part of the stocks.) Data on the value of the stocks held are rather sketchy. This is why they have not been included in the profit rate estimation. However, what data are available suggest that the ratio of stocks to net fixed capital varies little either over time or across countries, being about one-third of the value of fixed capital, for both manufacturing and total business. The United States is an important exception. It has a particularly high ratio of stocks to fixed capital in manufacturing, reflecting the very low ratio of fixed capital to output found there.

The basic OECD source for profit rates and profit shares is *National Accounts of Member Countries*, 1975–87 (Paris, 1989), and earlier issues, which gives net profits (value added less depreciation less employment incomes), net value added (gross value added less depreciation) and the net capital stock at current prices. It also calculates the net shares (net profits divided by net value added) and net profit rates (net profits divided by net capital stock). For earlier years, national sources have been used to construct the series needed (net profits, net value added and net capital stock). In some cases this has required a considerable amount of estimation on our part, especially the series for Japan (profit rates) and both Italy and France (manufacturing sector and business sector before 1960). In the cases of Canada, France, Germany and Italy, series for corporate business were not available and we had to construct series for non-agricultural business as a whole (including both corporations and unincorporated enterprises).

The national accounts series for profits in manufacturing, published by OECD and national sources, and for non-agricultural business which we have constructed from national sources are for 'net operating surplus'. This has an important weakness as a measure of profits: all self-employment income is included. Since self-employment is substantial in some countries, even in manufacturing (notably Italy and Japan), this inflates the estimates for the profit share. It can also substantially exaggerate the downward trend where the importance of self-employment declined. Self-employment is much more important in the non-agricultural business sector since services are included. So series for corporate business (which includes both public and private enterprises but excludes those operated by the self-employed) are preferable. Where these are not available we have calculated profits by subtracting an imputed 'wage' for the self-employed equal to the average wage in manufacturing or the business sector, whichever is relevant. For this reason our series for manufacturing profit shares and rates differ from those published by the OECD.

In addition to the national capital stock sources listed above, we have used the following national sources to construct the profits series needed to supplement those taken from OECD, *National Accounts*:

United States: *National Income and Product Accounts*, 1929–76 and later issues.
United Kingdom   *National Income and Expenditure*, various issues and unpublished series supplied by CSO.
France: *Les Comptes des entreprises par secteurs*, 1959–66
    Les Comptes de la nation, various issues.
    'Les bénéfices industriels et commerciaux', *Statistiques et études financières*, various issues.
Germany: *Volkswirtschaftliche Gesamtrechungen*, various issues.
Italy: *Annuario di Contabilita Nationale*, various issues.
Japan: *Annual Report on National Accounts*, various issues.

Other series

We also derived series for both manufacturing and non-agricultural business for productivity (output per hour), capital stock per person employed, and the product wage (productivity multiplied by the share of labour in net business output). The series for output were from OECD, *National Accounts*, and EC, *Indicators of Manufacturing, Capital, Labour and Output* and *Indicators of Profitability, Capital, Labour and Output for Non-agricultural Business Sector*, for employment (and self-employment) from OECD, *Labour Force Statistics*, and for hours worked from BLS, *International Comparisons*, and OECD, *Employment Outlook*. We also calculated the ratios to GDP (at current prices) of various categories of government spending (transfers, military, investment, current civil spending), the government deficit (government savings less government investment), consumption, privately financed consumption (private consumption less transfers) and various categories of investment (government, housebuilding, manufacturing and other business). The data came from OECD, *National Accounts*, supplemented by national sources.

Aggregation for ACCs

To derive series for the ACCs as a whole, series for the seven individual countries have to be combined in a suitable weighted average. The simplest approach is to add up the component countries, with the individual country's contribution (to output, for example) weighted by the current exchange rate (for example, converting everything into dollars). But the exchange rate is a poor indicator of purchasing power, as detailed studies first carried out by Kravis and his associates of the true 'purchasing power parities' (PPPs) of different currencies show. So absolute levels calculated using current exchange rates (for example, comparing output in Japan and the United States) would be unreliable, trends would also be masked (by progressive undervaluation or overvaluation) and totally spurious short-term fluctuations introduced (by rapid exchange rate gyrations such as were experienced in the 1980s). The detailed studies are not available for each year. So the approach used here was to combine the PPPs for one year (1980) with *constant price* data for the individual countries. Therefore, to combine Japanese and US outputs, the yen PPP in relation to dollars is used to convert Japan's series for output at 1980 prices on to a 1980 dollar equivalent. When this is done for all of the big countries (for the United States, of course, dollars are used; and for Canada, where no PPP is available, we have used the 1970 exchange rate, which must be very close to PPP) the 1980 dollar-equivalent outputs are added together to form the area figures, and the share of each component country in the total can be calculated.

We have also applied PPPs (1980 prices) directly to the capital stock (manufacturing and business) in order to calculate aggregates for the ACCs and Europe and to see how the different countries' shares have changed.

To calculate area profit shares and rates, we have simply weighted the figures for the individual countries using the shares of business output or manufacturing output. Current weights have been used in order to reflect the changing relative importance of the countries. The increasing weight of Japan (where the profit rate is high) means that the current weighted series declines slightly less than the fixed-weight one.

The main sources used for the PPP calculations were 'A note on the new OECD benchmark purchasing power parities for 1985', *OECD Economic Studies* (1987) by Derek Blades and David Roberts; 'International price levels and purchasing power parities', *OECD Economic Studies* (1986) by T.P. Hill; and 'International comparisons of labor costs in manufacturing', *Review of Income and Wealth* (1989) by Peter Hooper and Kathryn A. Larin.

Series for Part I

The major sources for the data on investment and capital stock (Tables 2.1, 4.1 and 6.1, and figure 6.2) are as follows:

United States	*Survey of Current Business*, March 1980, February 1981. *Long-term Economic Growth 1860–1970.*
United Kingdom	Feinstein, *National Income, Expenditure and Output of the United Kingdom 1855–1965.*
France:	Carré, Dubois and Malinvaud, *French Economic Growth.* Mairesse, *L'Evaluation du capital fixe productive.*
Germany:	Krengel, *Anlagevermögen, Produktion und Beschäftigung 1924–56.*
Italy:	Fua, *La Sviluppo Economico in Italia*, vol. III.
Japan:	Ohkawa and Rosovsky, *Japanese Economic Growth.*

These series are not always directly comparable to those used in part II and described earlier in this appendix.

We also used UNECE, *Economic Survey of Europe Since the War*, for changes in stock of machine tools (plus Cohen, *Japan's Economy in Wartime and Reconstruction*) and OEEC, *Statistics of National Product and Expenditure 1938 and 1947–55.*

The series for industrial production, employment, productivity and real wages and profits etc. (tables 4.2–4.5, 6.2–6.8 and figures 6.1, 6.3 and 6.4) are calculated from:

United States:	*Long-term Economic Growth 1860–1970.*

United Kingdom: Feinstein, *National Income, Expenditure and Output of the United Kingdom 1855–1965.*
        National Income and Expenditure, 1946–51.

France: Rioux, *La France de la Quatrième République.*
        Mouvement économique en France de 1938 à 1948.
        Annuaire statistique de la France, rétrospectif.
        UNECE, *Economic Survey of Europe*, various.

Germany: Bank Deutscher Länder, *Monthly Report, Annual Report,* various.
        UNECE, *Economic Survey of Europe*, various.

Italy: Fua, op. cit.
        UNECE, *Economic Survey of Europe*, various.
        Campanna, 'Economic Problems and Reconstruction in Italy'.

Japan: Ohkawa and Rosovsky, op. cit.
        Allen, *Japan's Economic Recovery.*

Europe: OEEC, *Statistics of National Product and Expenditure 1938 and 1947–55.*
        UNECE, *Economic Survey of Europe*, various.

Note to table 14.9, page 248

The purpose of the table is to 'decompose' the change in the profit rate (line 10) into changes in the profit share (line 6) and changes in the output capital ratio (line 9), and to further decompose changes in the profit share and output capital ratio into their respective determinants.

Influences on the profit share are approached via its complement the wage share (line 5). The focus here is on real wages (in terms of what workers can buy), not product wages, so productivity growth (line 1) has to be adjusted by the growth of consumer prices relative to value added prices (line 2) to derive the amount (line 3) by which real wages (line 4) can rise without increasing the wage share (sometimes termed the 'warranted' increase in real wages); if consumer prices are growing faster than value added prices (due to rising import costs or slow productivity growth in consumer services for example) then real wages have to grow correspondingly more slowly than productivity if the profit share is not to fall.

Lines (7) and (8) show how the change in the output capital ratio at current prices (line 9) depends on the real output capital ratio (line 7) and what has been termed 'relative capital costs', the main component of which is the change of the price of capital goods relative to the price of value added (see Glyn et al., 1990, p. 120 for more discussion).

The sources for the table are those described in this Appendix plus consumer price indices (from IMF *Financial Statistics*).

Table A1 Manufacturing net profit rate (percentages)

YEAR	ACC	ACC-USA	EUROPE	CANADA	FRANCE	GERMANY	ITALY	JAPAN	UK	USA
1952	30.2	24.3	24.3	29.6	22.1	36.8	23.1	17.1	17.2	33.9
1953	29.4	23.8	24.0	26.1	23.2	36.2	21.1	19.6	16.6	32.9
1954	26.6	24.1	23.9	23.5	23.6	34.6	20.3	26.0	17.3	28.4
1955	30.7	24.2	24.3	24.2	23.7	35.6	20.2	22.9	16.8	35.3
1956	26.6	22.7	21.8	25.0	21.6	32.0	17.2	27.9	14.7	29.5
1957	24.6	22.6	20.8	21.0	21.7	30.1	15.5	36.9	14.1	26.1
1958	21.1	21.7	20.8	18.4	23.2	29.4	15.5	30.6	13.6	20.6
1959	25.2	22.1	20.9	19.0	18.6	29.7	17.7	32.7	14.4	27.8
1960	24.7	24.6	21.5	17.4	20.2	28.6	19.2	47.3	15.6	24.8
1961	24.0	23.9	19.3	14.6	19.5	25.2	18.9	52.8	12.7	24.2
1962	24.3	20.7	16.7	17.7	18.7	21.0	15.9	42.6	11.0	27.9
1963	25.7	20.6	15.7	19.3	19.5	18.6	13.0	45.0	11.7	30.7
1964	27.5	22.8	16.8	21.0	21.6	20.0	12.4	50.6	12.9	32.3
1965	29.1	21.5	16.7	21.3	21.5	19.4	14.3	43.6	12.0	36.4
1966	28.2	21.0	15.9	18.6	22.4	16.7	16.4	43.3	10.2	35.2
1967	26.1	22.7	15.9	16.0	22.1	16.7	16.6	49.8	10.0	29.4
1968	26.8	24.9	17.4	17.2	22.5	20.6	17.8	52.8	9.5	28.8
1969	25.3	26.1	18.2	18.3	24.9	21.4	17.9	53.6	9.1	24.5
1970	21.9	25.0	16.8	11.9	23.2	18.5	16.0	52.7	9.7	18.0
1971	20.7	21.3	14.5	12.8	21.5	16.4	12.2	42.6	7.8	19.9
1972	21.3	21.0	14.7	14.1	22.4	14.8	13.0	39.3	9.1	21.6
1973	21.9	21.8	15.4	17.5	23.3	15.2	15.2	38.8	8.9	22.0
1974	16.4	17.3	13.8	17.6	22.1	13.7	15.9	26.1	4.3	15.1
1975	13.1	10.8	8.8	13.2	13.0	11.0	7.8	15.2	2.4	16.2
1976	15.3	13.1	11.2	11.9	15.1	13.3	12.2	18.0	3.0	18.2
1977	16.0	13.1	11.8	12.3	16.2	12.9	11.2	16.3	6.2	19.7
1978	16.2	14.3	12.4	13.4	17.5	13.0	12.3	18.9	6.5	18.5
1979	14.9	14.9	13.8	16.1	18.7	13.4	17.9	17.0	4.6	14.9
1980	12.3	13.5	12.1	14.1	14.0	9.5	21.2	16.2	2.5	10.6
1981	11.5	11.7	10.4	12.9	11.8	7.8	18.9	14.0	1.5	11.3
1982	10.2	11.4	10.5	6.5	12.0	8.8	16.6	13.9	3.3	8.5
1983	11.5	12.0	11.6	10.2	12.9	11.6	15.7	13.1	4.4	10.8
1984	14.2	13.8	12.7	14.7	14.5	12.2	17.5	15.3	5.0	14.8
1985	14.3	14.8	14.3	15.6	16.2	14.1	18.6	15.5	6.9	13.5
1986	15.1	15.7	16.7	15.3	19.1	16.2	21.6	14.3	8.5	14.2
1987	15.9	16.2	17.7	14.0	21.5	14.9	23.9	14.6	10.2	15.4

Table A2 Business net profit rate (percentages)

YEAR	ACC	ACC-USA	EUROPE	CANADA	FRANCE	GERMANY	ITALY	JAPAN	UK	USA
1952	17.5	17.8	18.5	18.1	19.6	24.8	20.6	12.8	13.2	17.3
1953	17.0	18.1	18.3	16.8	18.8	24.0	19.9	17.1	13.7	16.3
1954	16.4	18.7	18.8	14.7	19.6	23.3	21.6	18.0	14.3	14.9
1955	18.8	19.4	19.8	18.1	20.4	25.8	21.8	16.6	14.2	18.4
1956	17.1	18.9	19.3	18.5	20.7	24.9	21.8	16.6	12.8	15.9
1957	16.4	19.6	19.4	15.9	23.4	24.4	20.9	20.4	12.3	14.3
1958	14.8	18.6	18.6	14.4	22.7	22.5	21.6	18.4	11.5	12.1
1959	16.8	19.1	19.2	14.5	21.3	23.2	23.4	18.5	12.2	15.1
1960	16.9	21.0	20.5	14.0	24.2	22.9	25.3	23.3	13.5	13.8
1961	16.6	20.1	19.2	14.7	24.0	20.2	25.4	24.5	11.5	13.9
1962	17.2	18.8	18.0	15.7	24.1	18.0	23.8	22.2	10.3	15.9
1963	17.7	18.5	17.6	16.4	25.6	16.2	21.3	22.3	11.3	17.0
1964	18.5	19.0	18.0	17.5	27.5	17.0	19.5	22.8	11.8	18.2
1965	19.4	18.7	18.2	17.8	27.9	16.5	21.5	20.9	11.2	19.9
1966	19.5	19.3	17.9	16.5	28.5	15.1	23.0	24.1	9.8	19.6
1967	19.0	20.9	18.1	16.1	29.0	14.3	24.5	29.4	9.5	17.5
1968	19.3	21.9	18.8	16.3	27.1	15.9	26.6	30.8	9.6	17.1
1969	18.8	22.9	19.0	16.2	27.8	15.8	27.0	33.7	9.3	15.1
1970	17.1	22.4	17.3	14.7	27.1	14.5	23.5	34.8	7.5	11.9
1971	16.0	19.5	16.4	13.7	26.7	13.3	21.1	26.8	7.4	12.5
1972	16.1	19.2	16.7	14.1	26.6	12.8	22.3	24.6	7.7	13.1
1973	15.4	17.8	16.0	16.3	27.0	12.2	19.6	21.6	8.0	13.2
1974	12.6	14.8	13.7	16.8	24.5	10.4	17.3	17.3	4.5	10.4
1975	11.7	12.4	11.4	14.2	20.7	9.2	13.5	14.5	3.3	11.0
1976	12.3	13.0	11.9	13.6	18.9	10.9	14.5	15.4	4.1	11.7
1977	13.0	13.5	12.5	13.8	19.9	11.1	13.3	15.8	6.4	12.5
1978	13.2	14.3	12.9	14.0	19.9	11.6	14.3	17.4	6.6	12.1
1979	12.6	14.5	13.4	15.8	19.8	11.8	17.1	16.9	6.0	10.7
1980	12.1	14.9	13.5	15.7	21.7	10.0	18.6	17.4	5.0	9.2
1981	11.5	13.4	11.8	14.4	16.9	8.9	17.0	16.3	5.1	9.6
1982	10.6	13.2	11.7	12.3	16.3	9.0	15.6	15.9	6.7	7.9
1983	11.5	13.5	12.5	14.0	17.1	10.4	15.1	15.2	8.1	9.4
1984	13.1	14.4	13.6	16.0	18.4	10.9	17.0	15.9	8.9	11.7
1985	13.2	15.0	14.3	16.1	19.1	11.3	17.8	16.3	10.0	11.3
1986	13.5	15.9	15.7	14.1	21.6	12.2	21.2	16.2	9.0	11.2
1987	13.6	16.1	16.3	15.4	22.2	12.4	21.4	15.7	10.4	11.2

Table A3 Manufacturing net profit share (percentages)

YEAR	ACC	ACC-USA	EUROPE	CANADA	FRANCE	GERMANY	ITALY	JAPAN	UK	USA
1952	24.8	29.9	30.4	31.8	34.1	32.7	33.9	22.1	25.7	21.7
1953	23.7	28.9	29.3	29.4	33.6	32.3	30.4	24.2	24.9	20.5
1954	23.5	28.9	28.9	28.7	33.9	31.3	28.2	29.0	25.2	19.7
1955	25.2	28.5	28.6	29.5	32.8	31.5	28.3	26.1	24.5	22.9
1956	23.1	26.6	25.9	30.4	26.5	30.0	24.9	29.4	22.3	20.4
1957	22.8	27.1	25.8	27.8	27.4	29.8	24.1	36.0	22.0	19.5
1958	21.7	26.9	26.1	26.8	28.3	29.9	24.7	33.1	21.8	17.2
1959	23.5	26.9	26.0	27.2	22.9	30.2	27.2	33.2	22.5	20.6
1960	23.3	28.2	26.4	25.8	24.5	29.0	28.3	40.6	23.5	18.6
1961	23.1	27.5	25.0	23.1	23.7	27.1	27.8	43.3	21.5	18.6
1962	22.5	25.1	22.5	26.2	23.0	24.3	24.6	38.3	18.5	20.0
1963	23.3	25.0	21.9	27.6	23.9	23.4	20.0	39.4	20.1	21.5
1964	24.4	26.7	23.2	28.9	25.7	25.2	20.1	42.0	21.2	22.1
1965	25.2	26.1	23.1	29.4	25.9	24.5	22.8	38.3	19.7	24.3
1966	24.6	25.5	22.3	26.8	26.9	22.4	24.8	38.3	17.3	23.7
1967	24.2	26.5	22.7	24.4	27.3	23.6	23.6	41.1	17.6	21.8
1968	24.6	27.4	23.3	25.4	26.3	26.0	24.3	42.1	16.9	21.7
1969	23.8	27.8	23.4	26.3	27.9	25.8	24.0	42.3	16.1	19.3
1970	21.9	26.5	21.8	19.3	27.1	22.5	21.0	42.0	17.0	16.0
1971	21.6	24.2	19.7	21.0	25.4	21.0	17.4	37.5	14.9	18.3
1972	22.0	24.3	20.2	22.3	26.3	19.6	18.4	35.6	17.0	19.2
1973	22.1	24.9	20.7	25.9	26.9	19.3	21.0	34.9	17.0	18.7
1974	18.8	22.1	19.1	26.3	27.4	17.7	23.2	28.8	9.3	14.5
1975	16.2	15.4	12.9	22.4	17.1	15.4	12.9	19.8	5.3	17.4
1976	18.2	17.9	15.8	20.3	19.8	17.2	18.6	22.6	6.6	18.6
1977	18.6	18.0	16.6	20.8	20.0	16.3	17.0	20.6	13.1	19.4
1978	18.9	19.2	17.2	22.2	21.3	16.0	18.1	23.2	13.5	18.6
1979	17.9	19.6	18.1	25.2	22.3	16.2	23.7	21.9	10.0	15.7
1980	15.7	18.1	15.8	23.3	17.8	12.1	26.5	21.7	5.7	12.4
1981	15.1	16.2	14.1	21.7	15.6	10.4	24.9	19.2	3.8	13.6
1982	14.3	16.3	14.8	13.6	15.9	11.9	22.8	19.4	7.8	11.4
1983	15.9	17.2	16.2	20.1	17.0	15.3	21.3	18.3	10.2	14.1
1984	18.3	19.1	17.4	25.6	18.8	15.8	23.2	20.6	11.1	17.2
1985	18.4	20.3	19.1	26.0	21.2	17.3	23.5	21.1	14.5	15.8
1986	19.2	21.2	21.5	25.5	24.4	19.2	25.6	20.0	17.0	16.5
1987	20.0	21.9	22.4	25.5	27.2	17.8	26.8	20.6	19.5	17.5

Table A4 Business net profit share (percentages)

YEAR	ACC	ACC-USA	EUROPE	CANADA	FRANCE	GERMANY	ITALY	JAPAN	UK	USA
1952	24.7	29.6	30.0	23.4	37.4	29.7	35.1	26.2	24.7	21.8
1953	23.6	29.0	28.8	22.3	34.6	28.2	32.4	30.3	25.0	20.4
1954	23.5	29.0	28.8	19.3	34.1	27.8	32.9	30.5	25.1	20.1
1955	25.3	28.6	28.6	25.6	33.0	29.6	31.7	28.7	24.4	23.1
1956	23.6	27.9	27.7	26.3	31.6	29.2	31.3	29.0	22.7	20.8
1957	23.5	28.9	28.1	23.2	33.7	29.6	30.8	33.5	22.5	19.8
1958	22.2	27.8	27.3	22.3	31.9	28.5	30.9	30.8	21.7	18.3
1959	24.0	28.4	28.0	22.8	30.4	29.7	32.1	30.4	22.9	20.9
1960	23.8	30.1	29.2	22.3	32.8	29.4	33.3	34.6	24.5	19.1
1961	23.6	29.1	27.5	24.0	31.9	27.3	33.4	36.3	21.5	19.2
1962	23.7	27.7	26.5	25.7	31.8	25.7	31.8	33.1	20.6	20.6
1963	24.2	27.7	26.4	26.8	33.1	24.5	28.6	32.9	22.5	21.4
1964	24.8	28.0	27.0	28.4	34.4	25.7	27.2	32.1	23.2	22.1
1965	25.4	27.9	27.2	28.4	34.9	25.2	29.7	30.7	22.3	23.4
1966	25.2	28.1	26.5	26.2	35.5	23.8	30.5	33.9	20.2	22.8
1967	25.1	29.8	27.1	26.7	36.5	23.8	31.3	38.2	20.5	21.3
1968	24.9	29.9	27.3	27.4	33.6	25.0	32.8	37.3	20.8	20.8
1969	24.5	31.0	27.5	26.9	34.2	24.6	33.8	40.3	20.6	18.8
1970	22.8	29.8	25.5	23.3	34.2	22.6	30.6	40.3	17.5	16.1
1971	22.5	28.1	24.9	22.9	33.8	21.5	28.9	35.5	18.1	17.2
1972	22.8	28.3	25.4	24.0	34.0	21.0	30.1	34.8	19.0	17.5
1973	22.1	27.1	24.5	27.3	34.4	19.8	27.6	32.9	18.8	17.2
1974	19.5	24.1	22.0	27.9	33.5	17.6	26.6	28.8	12.4	14.9
1975	19.2	21.2	19.1	24.3	29.8	16.5	22.0	26.0	9.5	17.2
1976	20.0	22.3	20.3	23.2	28.3	18.6	23.3	26.6	11.8	17.7
1977	20.8	23.4	21.6	23.7	29.4	18.7	21.8	27.3	17.8	18.3
1978	21.0	24.5	22.3	24.9	29.5	19.5	22.9	29.2	18.3	17.7
1979	20.4	24.9	22.9	28.9	29.6	20.3	26.0	29.1	16.8	16.0
1980	20.3	25.9	23.2	29.2	33.8	18.0	27.8	31.1	14.8	14.5
1981	19.9	24.3	21.2	26.2	26.9	17.0	26.4	30.0	15.6	15.4
1982	19.3	24.6	21.8	23.2	26.4	17.5	24.9	29.8	19.4	13.5
1983	20.6	25.4	23.2	28.6	27.5	20.0	24.1	29.1	22.3	15.7
1984	22.3	26.7	24.7	32.4	29.0	20.9	26.2	30.3	23.8	17.8
1985	22.4	27.5	25.5	32.1	29.8	21.6	26.4	30.9	25.5	17.1
1986	22.6	28.4	26.7	27.7	32.3	22.9	29.5	31.3	23.3	16.8
1987	22.8	28.6	27.3	27.7	33.0	23.2	29.0	30.9	25.4	16.8

Table A5 Manufacturing gross fixed capital stock (1980 PPP dollars, beginning year)

YEAR	ACC	ACC-USA	EUROPE	CANADA	FRANCE	GERMANY	ITALY	JAPAN	UK	USA
1952	680.9	340.1	277.0	34.1	61.1	55.9	50.7	29.0	109.2	340.8
1953	710.2	354.6	287.5	36.2	63.8	60.0	52.9	31.0	110.9	355.6
1954	738.2	368.7	297.5	38.2	65.6	64.1	55.2	33.0	112.5	369.5
1955	765.8	383.7	308.7	40.2	67.2	69.3	57.8	34.8	114.4	382.1
1956	796.3	401.7	322.7	42.6	68.4	76.3	61.2	36.4	116.7	394.6
1957	837.7	424.0	339.0	45.5	70.1	84.0	65.2	39.4	119.7	413.8
1958	880.2	448.5	356.1	48.3	72.5	91.2	69.7	44.1	122.7	431.7
1959	911.3	471.1	372.6	50.5	74.8	98.3	73.8	47.9	125.8	440.3
1960	944.1	495.8	390.2	52.6	77.3	106.3	78.1	52.9	128.5	448.3
1961	990.2	530.3	413.6	54.8	80.4	116.1	83.7	62.0	133.4	459.9
1962	1043.1	572.7	441.3	56.7	84.2	126.9	90.5	74.7	139.6	470.5
1963	1098.0	616.1	470.4	58.5	88.7	137.4	99.0	87.2	145.3	481.9
1964	1152.4	658.1	497.9	60.9	93.1	147.2	107.7	99.3	150.0	494.3
1965	1213.7	702.1	523.6	64.4	97.6	157.7	112.9	114.1	155.4	511.6
1966	1278.5	740.1	548.5	66.4	102.0	169.2	115.4	125.2	162.0	538.4
1967	1355.8	782.7	575.3	71.1	106.9	180.4	119.5	136.3	168.6	573.1
1968	1438.0	832.8	599.9	77.6	111.8	188.8	124.5	155.3	174.8	605.2
1969	1521.6	887.3	625.4	81.1	116.9	197.1	129.8	180.7	181.6	634.3
1970	1617.1	952.3	656.9	85.4	123.5	208.9	135.6	210.1	188.8	664.7
1971	1722.9	1030.7	693.6	89.7	131.2	223.5	142.5	247.5	196.3	692.1
1972	1817.8	1103.5	729.2	93.6	139.3	237.5	149.4	280.8	203.0	714.3
1973	1903.7	1167.4	760.3	97.5	147.7	248.8	155.5	309.6	208.3	736.3
1974	1997.1	1234.0	790.8	102.1	155.8	258.2	163.1	341.0	213.8	763.1
1975	2096.7	1297.6	818.8	107.0	163.0	265.0	171.0	371.8	219.8	799.2
1976	2171.2	1344.1	838.8	111.6	168.3	269.9	175.6	393.7	224.9	827.1
1977	2241.0	1385.9	858.5	116.0	174.0	274.9	180.1	411.4	229.4	855.1
1978	2312.2	1426.7	877.7	119.6	179.1	279.9	184.7	429.4	234.0	885.5
1979	2385.8	1463.3	895.1	122.9	183.7	284.3	188.1	445.3	239.0	922.5
1980	2468.4	1508.0	913.9	127.3	188.1	289.7	191.7	466.9	244.4	960.4
1981	2557.8	1559.0	932.6	133.1	192.8	295.9	195.8	493.2	248.2	998.8
1982	2643.1	1607.5	944.1	138.6	196.2	300.5	197.7	524.8	249.6	1035.6
1983	2710.9	1647.9	951.6	142.4	198.8	303.0	199.4	553.9	250.5	1063.0
1984	2765.3	1688.2	959.0	145.2	200.9	305.1	201.8	584.0	251.1	1077.1
1985	2835.1	1736.4	966.2	148.6	203.2	306.0	204.4	621.6	252.5	1098.8
1986	2926.1	1800.4	976.9	152.8	206.2	309.4	206.7	670.7	254.5	1125.7
1987	3003.9	1860.3	988.8	157.4	209.4	314.6	208.8	714.1	256.1	1143.6
1988	3075.8	1916.2	1002.3	162.0	212.9	320.9	210.9	751.9	257.7	1159.5
1989	3171.9	1990.4	1019.4	168.7	217.8	327.3	213.8	802.3	260.5	1181.6
1990	3285.9	2079.6	1040.1	176.2	223.4	334.8	217.9	863.3	263.9	1206.4

Table A6 Business gross fixed capital stock (1980 PPP dollars, beginning year)

YEAR	ACC	ACC-USA	EUROPE	CANADA	FRANCE	GERMANY	ITALY	JAPAN	UK	USA
1952	2540	1008	804	116	183	173	120	89	327	1532
1953	2617	1044	830	122	190	181	125	91	334	1573
1954	2702	1081	858	129	193	190	131	94	343	1622
1955	2788	1122	889	136	197	201	138	98	352	1666
1956	2883	1166	921	144	200	215	147	101	360	1717
1957	2998	1221	962	154	205	232	156	106	369	1777
1958	3119	1283	1006	165	210	251	165	112	379	1835
1959	3220	1346	1052	175	216	271	175	120	389	1874
1960	3333	1413	1101	184	223	291	186	128	401	1921
1961	3463	1492	1159	193	231	313	200	140	416	1971
1962	3602	1582	1225	202	240	338	216	155	431	2019
1963	3754	1680	1295	211	250	363	235	174	446	2074
1964	3921	1782	1368	220	262	389	256	194	462	2139
1965	4091	1889	1443	231	274	416	273	215	480	2202
1966	4294	2000	1518	245	287	444	286	237	500	2294
1967	4517	2118	1597	260	302	472	301	262	521	2399
1968	4742	2244	1676	274	319	495	319	295	543	2498
1969	4989	2386	1762	288	337	519	340	336	566	2603
1970	5267	2547	1857	303	358	549	362	387	588	2720
1971	5560	2732	1961	319	380	584	386	451	611	2828
1972	5843	2915	2067	336	404	622	408	512	633	2928
1973	6137	3099	2171	354	430	658	428	574	654	3039
1974	6467	3291	2279	374	457	693	452	639	677	3176
1975	6786	3474	2381	395	484	721	477	699	699	3312
1976	7047	3635	2469	416	508	747	496	749	719	3412
1977	7303	3791	2561	438	534	773	515	791	739	3512
1978	7585	3951	2656	459	560	800	536	836	760	3634
1979	7893	4111	2751	481	586	830	555	879	781	3782
1980	8238	4295	2851	506	612	863	574	937	802	3943
1981	8589	4493	2955	535	638	897	597	1003	823	4096
1982	8942	4684	3046	563	663	928	617	1075	838	4258
1983	9250	4860	3129	586	686	955	635	1145	853	4390
1984	9548	5036	3210	608	706	983	653	1218	868	4511
1985	9897	5224	3293	630	724	1009	673	1301	887	4673
1986	10290	5432	3382	654	742	1039	694	1397	907	4858
1987	10667	5642	3468	677	760	1070	713	1497	925	5025
1988	11055	5866	3558	701	779	1102	733	1607	945	5189
1989	11512	6142	3668	733	803	1137	755	1740	972	5370
1990	12024	6465	3793	768	832	1180	781	1904	1001	5558

Table A7 Dollar values for GDP and imports, 1952–88

	Percentages of Gross domestic product			Percentages of Imports		
	USA	Japan	Large European country[a]	USA	Japan	Large European country[a]
In 1952 $1 billion represented	0.3	5.8	4.7	6.3	50.3	26.7
In 1970 $10 billion represented	1.0	3.2	5.4	18.4	51.5	38.9
In 1988 $10 billion represented	0.2	0.4	1.1	1.9	4.4	4.1

[a] Unweighted average of France, Germany, Italy and United Kingdom.
Sources: OECD *Historical Statistics 1960–88, National Accounts,* 1982 and earlier issues

Sources

For full details of publication, see the Bibliography.

Part I: Postwar Reconstruction, 1945–1950

Basic sources of statistical information used throughout part I:

J.-J. CARRÉ, P. DUBOIS AND E. MALINVAUD, *French Economic Growth*
K. OHKAWA AND H. ROSOVSKY, *Japanese Economic Growth*
C. FEINSTEIN, *National Income, Expenditure and Output of the United Kingdom 1855–1965*
US GOVERNMENT, *The National Income and Product Accounts of the United States 1929–76*
US GOVERNMENT, *Balance of Payments, Statistical Supplement*
US GOVERNMENT, *Long-term Economic Growth 1860–1970*
G. FUA, *La Sviluppo Economico in Italia*, vol. III
UNECE, *Economic Survey of Europe*
UN, *World Economic Review*
OEEC, *Statistics of National Product and Expenditure 1938 and 1947–55*
FRENCH GOVERNMENT, *Annuaire statistique de la France, rétrospectif*

See the appendix, pages 350–1, for further details on the more specific sources used for the tables and charts.

1. *Chaos and Despair*

The main sources for economic development after the First World War are:

A. LEWIS, *Economic Survey 1919–39*
D. ALDCROFT, *From Versailles to Wall Street 1919–29*

A general survey of conditions in Europe at the end of the Second World War is:

R. MAYNE, *Postwar*
See also the sources cited for chapter 2.

2. Behind the Chaos

The major sources used for the immediate economic consequences of the Second World War are:

UNECE, *Economic Survey of Europe Since the War*
J. COHEN, *Japan's Economy in Wartime and Reconstruction*
W. ABELSHAUSER, *Wirtschaft in Westdeutschland 1945–48*

The political and social consequences of the war are discussed in:

W. GRAF, *The German Left since 1945*
J. MOORE, *Japanese Workers and the Struggle for Power 1945–47*
J. HALLIDAY, *A Political History of Japanese Capitalism*
S. WOOLF (ed.), *The Rebirth of Modern Italy*
A. WERTH, *France 1940–55*
G. ROSS, *Workers and Communists in France*
A. PREIS, *Labor's Giant Step*
D. PRITT, *The Labour Government 1945–51*
J.-P. RIOUX, *La France de la Quatrième République*
P. GINSBURG, *A History of Contemporary Italy*

International relations, focused on the United States, are discussed in:

G. KOLKO, *The Politics of War*
G. KOLKO AND J. KOLKO, *The Limits of Power*
D. YERGIN, *Shattered Peace*

3. Great Power Policies

On the reconstruction of the world monetary system, see:

R. GARDNER, *Sterling Dollar Diplomacy*

On occupation policy in Japan:

J. HALLIDAY, *A Political History of Japanese Capitalism*
J. MOORE, *Japanese Workers and the Struggle for Power 1945–47*
J. COHEN, *Japan's Economy in Wartime and Reconstruction*

In Germany:·

J. GIMBEL, *The American Occupation of Germany*
H. ZINK, *The United States in Germany 1944–55*

On the policy of the Soviet Union:

I. DEUTSCHER, *Stalin*
F. CLAUDIN, *The Communist Movement*
M. DJILAS, *Conversations with Stalin*

4. *The First Two Years*

Sources are as for Chapter 2, plus the following.

On Japan:

G. ALLEN, *Japan's Economic Recovery*
S. LEVINE, *Industrial Relations in Post-war Japan*
JAPANESE GOVERNMENT, *Economic Survey of Japan*

On Germany:

I. TURNER (ed.), *Reconstruction in Post-war Germany*
H. WALLICH, *Mainsprings of the German Revival*

On Italy:

A. CAMPANNA, 'Economic problems and reconstruction in Italy'
E. SIMPSON, 'Inflation and deflation and employment in Italy'
M. POSNER AND S. WOOLF, *Italian Public Enterprise*

On France:

R. KUISEL, *Capitalism and the State in Modern France*
FRENCH GOVERNMENT, *Mouvement économique en France de 1938 à 1948*
UNIR, *Histoire du PCF*
G. LEFRANC, *Le Mouvement syndical*

On the United Kingdom:

J. DOW, *The Management of the British Economy 1945–60*
D. WORSWICK AND P. ADY, *The British Economy 1945–50*
A. ROGOW, *The Labour Government and British Industry*

5. *Marshall Aid: the United States Changes Tack*

See particularly:

M. HOGAN, *The Marshall Plan*
G. KOLKO AND J. KOLKO, *The Limits of Power*
D. YERGIN, *Shattered Peace*
A. MILWARD, *The Reconstruction of Western Europe 1945–51*

Also:

F. BLOCK, *The Origins of International Economic Disorder*

6. *The New Turn in Europe and Japan*

Sources are as for Chapters 2 and 4, plus:

T. BALOGH, 'Germany: an experiment in planning by the "free" price mechanism'
H. MENDERSHAUSEN, 'Prices, money and the distribution of goods in post-war Germany'

7. Towards the Boom

On the American recession of 1949, see:

H. VATTER, *The US Economy in the 1950s*

On the devaluations of 1949, see:

BANK FOR INTERNATIONAL SETTLEMENTS, *Annual Report*, 1949–50, chapter 6
A. CAIRNCROSS AND B. EICHENGREEN, *Sterling in Decline*

On the Korean boom, see:

UN, *World Economic Review*
OEEC, *The Problem of Rising Prices*

Part II: The Great Boom, 1950–1974

The main statistical series used throughout parts II and III, mainly derived from OECD national account, labour force and capital stock data, are described in some detail in the Appendix. Additional important sources of statistical material and analysis are:

OECD, *The Growth of Output 1960–80*
A. MADDISON, *Phases of Capitalist Development*
J. CORNWALL, *Modern Capitalism*
T. HILL, *Profits and Rates of Return*
C. KINDLEBERGER, *Europe's Post War Growth*

8. The Golden Years

Much detailed information on individual countries (in addition to the sources referred to for chapters 2 and 4) is contained in:

A. BOLTHO (ed.), *The European Economy*
M. FELDSTEIN (ed.), *The American Economy in Transition*

An orthodox Marxist interpretation of the boom is:

E. MANDEL, *Late Capitalism*

The literature on postwar economic growth in Japan is vast. The best general account of the Japanese postwar economy is:

A. BOLTHO, *Japan, an Economic Survey*
For this section on Japan we have also used:

S. BROADBRIDGE, *Industrial Dualism in Japan*
R. CAVES AND M. UEKUSA, *Industrial Organisation in Japan*
E. DENISON AND W. CHUNG, *How Japan's Economy Grew So Fast*
JAPANESE GOVERNMENT, *Estimates of the Stock of Non-Residential Business Capital*
JAPANESE GOVERNMENT, *Annual Report on National Accounts*

R. KOMIYA (ed.), *Postwar Economic Growth in Japan*
R. MINAMI, *The Turning Point in Economic Development*
K. OHKAWA, B. JOHNSTON AND H. KAMEDA, *Agriculture and Economic Growth*
K. OKOCHI, B. KARSH AND S. LEVINE (eds), *Workers and Employers in Japan*
H. PATRICK AND H. ROSOVSKY (eds), *Asia's New Giant*
K. TAIRA, *Economic Development and the Labor Market in Japan*
K. YAMAMURA, *Economic Policy in Postwar Japan*

9. *A New, Managed Capitalism?*

There is an enormous literature on the increased importance of the postwar state, including:

I. GOUGH, *The Political Economy of the Welfare State*
A. SHONFIELD, *Modern Capitalism*

On welfare, valuable sources are:

P. KOHLER AND H. ZACHER (eds.), *The Evolution of Social Insurance 1881–1981*
OECD, *Public Expenditure Trends*
G. RIMLINGER, *Welfare Policy and Industrialisation in Europe, America and Russia*

On German codetermination:

R. ADAMS AND C. RUMMEL, 'Workers' participation in management in West Germany'

On French planning:

S. COHEN, *Modern Capitalist Planning*
J. DELORS, 'The Decline of French Planning'
S. ESTRIN AND P. HOLMES, *French Planning in Theory and Practice*

On Japanese industrial policy:

I. MAGAZINER AND T. HOUT, *Japanese Industrial Policy*
E. KAPLAN, *Japan – the Government-Business Relationship*
R. KOMIYA, 'Planning in Japan'

10. *The Eclipse of US Domination*

Comparative productivity levels are calculated in:

I. KRAVIS, 'A survey of international comparisons of productivity'
A. ROY, 'Labour productivity in 1980 – an international comparison'

The development of trade patterns is analysed in:

A. MAIZELS, *Industrial Growth and World Trade*
R. BATCHELOR, R. MAJOR AND A. MORGAN, *Industrialisation and the Basis for Trade*

We based our factual analysis of multinational corporations on:

R. ROWTHORN AND S. HYMER, *International Big Business 1957–67*

J. DUNNING AND R. PEARCE, *The World's Largest Industrial Enterprises*

The major Marxist study of the US economy, emphasizing its monopolistic structure, is:

P. BARAN AND P. SWEEZY, *Monopoly Capital*

A more recent analysis is:

M. AGLIETTA, *A Theory of Capitalist Regulation*

The literature on the contradictions in the international monetary system is huge. The analyses which we found most helpful were:

M. GILBERT, *Quest for World Monetary Order*
H. ROBINSON, 'The Downfall of the Dollar'
B. TEW, *The Evolution of the International Monetary System 1945–77*
J. WILLIAMSON, *The Failure of International Monetary Reform*
R. PARBONI, *The Dollar and its Rivals*

11. Overaccumulation

An analysis which discusses falling profitability, while putting more emphasis on technology and less (than ours) on the labour supply, is:

E. MANDEL, *Late capitalism*

The next book reviews Mandel's in detail and also contains an excellent theoretical discussion of inflation:

R. ROWTHORN, *Capitalism, Conflict and Inflation*

A detailed analysis of the decline in US profitability is:

T. WEISSKOPF, 'Marxian crisis theory and the rate of profit in the postwar US economy'

An analysis rather similar to ours, though drawing very different conclusions, is:

J. SARGENT, 'Capitalist Accumulation and Productivity Growth'

See also the references under chapter 14.

12. Overheating

The classic description of the late 1960s and early 1970s is:

P. MCCRACKEN, *Towards Full Employment and Price Stability*

The main source on the European strike wave of the late sixties is the extremely comprehensive study:

R. FLANAGAN, D. SOSKICE AND L. ULMAN, *Unionism, Economic Stabilisation and Incomes Policies* together with:

C. CROUCH AND A. PIZZORNO (eds), *The Resurgence of Class Conflict in Western Europe since 1968*

Events in Italy and France are also discussed (respectively) in:

P. GINSBURG, *A History of Contemporary Italy*
C. SABEL, *Work and Politics*
G. ROSS, *Workers and Communists in France*
C. POSNER (ed.), *Reflections on the Revolution in France: 1968*
V. FISERA (ed.), *Writing on the Wall*

13. *Oil and the Crash of 1974*

Sources are as chapter 12, plus the most comprehensive review of contemporary developments in OECD countries:

OECD, *Economic Outlook*

For the oil crisis:

J. BLAIR, *The Control of Oil*
A. SAMPSON, *The Seven Sisters*
L. TURNER, *Oil Companies in the International System*

Part III: Coping with the Slowdown, 1974–

See sources for part II for a note on the statistical series used. In addition to sources mentioned there we have drawn extensively on:

GATT, *International Trade*
IMF, *International Financial Statistics*
OECD, *Economic Outlook*
OECD, *Economies in Transition*
OECD, *Historical Statistics*
OECD, *Employment Outlook*

14. *The Great Slowdown*

There is a vast literature on the stagnation since 1974. See the following for various interpretations:

M. BRUNO AND J. SACHS, *The Economics of Worldwide Stagflation*
J. CORNWALL, *The Conditions for Economic Recovery*
A. MADDISON, *Phases of Capitalist Development*
S. MARGLIN AND J. SCHOR (eds), *The Golden Age of Capitalism*
R. MATTHEWS (ed.), *Slower Growth in the Western World*
OECD, *Economies in Transition*

R. ROWTHORN AND J. WELLS, *Deindustrialization and Foreign Trade*
R. LAWRENCE AND C. SCHULTZE (eds), *Barriers to European Growth*

15. *Workers and the Organization of Production*

Major sources for European developments are:

R. FLANAGAN, D. SOSKICE AND L. ULMAN, *Unionism, Economic Stabilisation and Incomes Policy*
OECD, *Economies in Transition*
R. BOYER (ed.), *The Search for Labour Market Flexibility*

The Japanese industrial relations system is discussed in

M. AOKI, *Information, Incentives and Bargaining in the Japanese Economy*
M.A. CUSUMANO, *The Japanese Automobile Industry*
K. KOIKE, *Understanding Industrial Relations in Modern Japan*

A very clear statement of the death of Taylorism is:

R. WALTON, 'From control to commitment in the workplace'

16. *International Relations*

Developments in the Soviet Union, Eastern Europe and their economic relations with the West are analysed in:

UNECE, *Economic Bulletin for Europe*

The LDCs are analysed in:

UNCTAD, *Trade and Development Report*

The debt crisis is discussed in:

J. SACHS (ed.), *Developing Country Debt and the World Economy*

Developments in the international monetary system are regularly surveyed in:

BANK FOR INTERNATIONAL SETTLEMENTS, Annual Report
IMF, *World Economic Outlook*

The position of the dollar is analysed in:

S. MARRIS, *Deficits and the Dollar*

17. *Reversing the Consensus*

Sympathetic and critical accounts of Thatcher's economic policies are given in, respectively:

G. MAYNARD, *The Economy under Mrs Thatcher*
F. GREEN (ed.), *The Restructuring of the UK Economy*

Our main sources for Reagan's policies were:

F. ACKERMAN, *Reaganomics, Rhetoric and Reality*
S. BOWLES ET AL., *Beyond the Wasteland*

18. *Against the Tide*

Our discussion of the Labour government was based on:

A. GLYN AND J. HARRISON, *The British Economic Disaster*
D. COATES, *Labour in Power*
K. COATES (ed.) *What Went Wrong?*

The experience of the Mitterrand government is analysed in:

A. LIPIETZ, *L'Audace ou L'Enlisement*
J. SACHS AND C. WYPLOSZ, 'The economic consequences of President Mitterrand'
H. MACHIN AND V. WRIGHT (eds), *Economic Policy and Policy-Making under the Mitterrand Presidency*
OECD, *Economic Survey of France*

The performance of the Swedish economy is analysed in:

B. BOSWORTH AND A. RIVLIN (eds), *The Swedish Economy*
J. PEKKARINEN ET AL. (eds), *Social Corporatism: a Superior Economic System?*

Bibliography

Note: official publications are listed under the government concerned.

ABEGLENN, J. AND STALK, G. (1986). *Kaisha: the Japanese Corporation*. Basic Books, New York.

ABELSHAUSER, W. (1975). *Wirtschaft in Westdeutschland 1945–48*. Deutsche Verlag-Anstalt, Stuttgart.

ABELSHAUSER, W. (1982). 'West German economic recovery 1945–51: a reassessment'. *Three Banks Review*, September.

ACKERMAN, F. (1982). *Reaganomics: Rhetoric and Reality*. Pluto Press, London.

ADAMS, R. AND RUMMEL, C. (1977). 'Workers' participation in management in West Germany'. *Industrial Relations Journal*, March.

AGLIETTA, M. (1979). *A Theory of Capitalist Regulation*. New Left Books, London.

ALBER, J. (1981). 'Government responses to the challenge of unemployment', in P. Flora and A. Heidenheimer (eds), *The Development of the Welfare State in Europe and America*. Transaction Books, New Brunswick.

ALDCROFT, D. (1970). *From Versailles to Wall Street 1919–29*. Allen Lane, London.

ALLAM, P. AND SASSOON, D. (1977). 'Italy', in M. McCauley (ed.), *Communist Power in Europe*. Macmillan, London.

ALLEN, G. (1958). *Japan's Economic Recovery*. Oxford University Press.

ALLSOPP, C. (1982). 'Inflation', in A. Boltho (ed.), *The European Economy: Growth and Crisis*. Oxford University Press, Oxford.

AMPO, *Japan Asia Quarterly Review*, Tokyo.

ANASZ, W. UEDA, H. AND YAMAMOTO, H. (1986). 'Industrial structures in Japan: pyramidal organization in the automobile and electrical/electronic industries'. *Annals of the Institute of Social Science*, Tokyo.

AOKI, M. (1988). *Information, Incentives and Bargaining in the Japanese Economy*. Cambridge University Press, Cambridge.

APPLE, N. (n.d.). 'The historical foundations of class struggle in late capitalist liberal democracies'. Mimeo, Sydney.

BAGGULEY, J. (1967). 'The World War and the Cold War', in D. Horowitz (ed.), *Containment and Revolution*. Beacon Press, Boston.

BAILEY, R. (1982). 'Impact of the Euro-Soviet gas pipeline'. *National Westminster Bank Quarterly Review*, August.

BAILY, M. (1982). 'Productivity and the services of labor and capital'. *Brookings Papers on Economic Activity*, 1.

BAIN, G. AND PRICE, R. (1981). *Profiles of Union Growth*. Oxford University Press, Oxford.

BALFOUR, M. (1981). *The Adversaries*. Routledge and Kegan Paul, London.

BALOGH, T. (1950). 'Germany: an experiment in planning by the "free" price mechanism'. *Banca Nazionale del Lavoro Quarterly Review*, April–June.

BANK DEUTSCHER LÄNDER, *Annual Report, Monthly Report*, various issues.

BANK OF ENGLAND, *Quarterly Bulletin*. London, various issues.

BANK FOR INTERNATIONAL SETTLEMENTS, *Annual Report*. Basle, various issues.

BARAN P. AND SWEEZY, P. (1968). *Monopoly Capital*. Penguin, Harmondsworth.

BARJONET, A. (1968). *La CGT*. Seuil, Paris.

BATCHELOR, R., MAJOR R. AND MORGAN, A. (1980). *Industrialisation and the Basis for Trade*. Cambridge University Press, Cambridge.

BATT, W. AND WEINBERG, E. (1978). 'Labor-management co-operation today'. *Harvard Business Review*, January/February.

BAUER, M. (1989). 'The politics of state-directed privatization: the case of France 1986–88' in J. Vickers and V. Wright (eds), *The Politics of Privatization in Western Europe*. Frank Cass, London.

BAUM, W. (1958). *The French Economy and the State*. Princeton University Press, Princeton.

BERNANKE, B. AND CAMPBELL, J. (1988). 'Is there a corporate debt crisis'. *Brookings Papers on Economic Activity*, 1.

BISHOP, M. AND KAY, J. (1989). 'Privatization in the United Kingdom: lessons from experience'. *World Development*, May.

BLAIR, J. (1977). *The Control of Oil*. Macmillan, London.

BLOCK, F. (1977). *The Origins of International Economic Disorder*. University of California Press, Berkeley.

BLOOMFIELD, J. (1979). *Passive Revolution*. Allison and Busby, London.

BLUMENTHAL, T. (1968). 'Scarcity of labour and wage differentials in the Japanese economy 1958–64'. *Economic Development and Cultural Change*, October.

BOLTHO, A. (1975). *Japan, an Economic Survey*. Oxford University Press, Oxford.

BOLTHO, A. (ed.). (1982). *The European Economy: Growth and Crisis*. Oxford University Press, Oxford.

BOSWORTH, B. AND RIVLIN, A. (eds.) (1987). *The Swedish Economy*. Brookings Institution, Washington.

BOWLES, S., GORDON, D. AND WEISSKOPF, T. (1983). *Beyond the Wasteland*. Anchor Press, New York.

BOYER, R. (ed.) (1988). *The Search for Labour Market Flexibility*. Clarendon Press, Oxford.

BOYER, M. AND MISTRAL, J. (1982). *Accumulation, Inflation, Crises*. PUF, Paris.

BRANSON, W. (1980). 'Trends in United States international trade and payments since World War II', in M. Feldstein (ed.), *The American Economy in Transition*. University of Chicago Press, Chicago.

BRAVERMAN, H. (1972). *Labor and Monopoly Capital*. Monthly Review Press, New York.

BRECHER, J. (1972). *Strike*. South End Press, Boston.

BRITTAN, S. (1975). *The Role and Limits of Government*. Temple Smith, London.

BROADBRIDGE, S. (1966). *Industrial Dualism in Japan*. Frank Cass, London.

BRUMBURGH, D., CARRON, A. AND LITAN, E. (1989). 'Clearing up the depository institutions mess'. *Brookings Papers on Economic Activity*, 1.

BRUNO, M. AND SACHS, J. (1985). *The Economics of Worldwide Stagflation.* Blackwell, Oxford.

BRUS, W. (1974). *Post-war Reconstruction and Socio-economic Transformations in Eastern Europe.* St Antony's College Paper in East European Economies, **41**, Oxford.

BUITER, W. AND MILLER, M. (1982). 'The Thatcher experiment: the first two years', *Brookings Papers on Economic Activity*, **1**.

BUITER, W. AND MILLER, M. (1983). 'The Macro-economic consequences of a change in regime'. *Brookings Papers on Economic Activity*, **2**.

Business Week, various issues.

CAIRNCROSS, A. AND EICHENGREEN, B. (1983). *Sterling in Decline.* Basil Blackwell, Oxford.

CALMFORS, L. AND DRIFFIL, J. (1988). 'Bargaining structure, corporatism and macroeconomic policy'. *Economic Policy*, no. 6.

CAMBRIDGE ECONOMIC POLICY GROUP (1980). 'World trade and finance: prospects for the 1980s'. *Cambridge Economic Policy Review*, December.

CAMPANNA, A. (1951). 'Economic problems and reconstruction in Italy'. *International Labour Review*, June/July.

CANADIAN GOVERNMENT, *Fixed Capital Flows and Stocks*, Statistics Canada, Ottawa, various issues.

CANADIAN GOVERNMENT, *National Income and Expenditure Accounts*, Statistics Canada. Ottawa, various issues.

CAPDEVEILLE, P. et al. (1982). 'International trends in productivity and labour costs'. *Monthly Labour Review*, December.

CAREW, A. (1987). *Labour under the Marshall Plan.* Manchester University Press, Manchester.

CARLIN, W. AND JACOB, R. (1989). 'Austerity policy in West Germany: origins and consequences'. *Economie Appliquee*, tome XIII.

CARRÉ, J.-J., DUBOIS, P. AND MALINVAUD, E. (1976). *French Economic Growth.* Stanford University Press, Stanford.

CATALANO, F. (1972). 'The rebirth of the party system', in S. Woolf (ed.), *The Rebirth of Modern Italy.* Longman, London.

CAVES, R. (1980). 'The structure of industry', in M. Feldstein (ed.), *The American Economy in Transition.* University of Chicago Press, Chicago.

CAVES R. AND UEKUSA, M. (1976). *Industrial Organisation in Japan.* Brookings, Washington.

CHAN-LEE, J., COE, D. AND PRYWES, M. (1987). 'Microeconomic changes and macroeconomic wage disinflation in the 1980s'. *OECD Economic Studies*, no. 8.

CLAIRMONTE, F. AND CAVANAGH, J. (1982). 'Transnational corporations and global markets'. *Trade and Development*, Winter.

CLARKE, R. (1982). *Anglo-American Economic Co-operation in War and Peace 1942–49*, edited by A. Cairncross, Oxford University Press, Oxford.

CLAUDIN, F. (1975). *The Communist Movement.* Penguin, Harmondsworth.

CLOSON, F.-L., (1950). '1938–48 ou les similitudes trompeuses', in French government, *Mouvement économique en France de 1938 à 1948.* Paris.

COATES, D. (1975). *The Labour Party and the Struggle for Socialism.* Cambridge University Press, Cambridge.

COATES, D. (1980). *Labour in Power*, Longman, London.

COATES, K. (ed.) (1979). *What Went Wrong?* Spokesman, Nottingham.

COHEN, J. (1949). *Japan's Economy in Wartime and Reconstruction.* University of Minnesota Press, Minneapolis.

COHEN, S. (1969). *Modern Capitalist Planning: the French Model.* University of California Press, Berkeley.

COLE, A., TOTTEN G. AND UYEHARA, C. (1966). *Socialist Parties in Post-war Japan.* Yale University Press, New Haven.

CONFERENCE OF SOCIALIST ECONOMISTS (1980). *The Alternative Economic Strategy.* CSE Books, London.

COOPER, C. AND MUMFORD, E. (eds.) (1979). *The Quality of Working Life in Western and Eastern Europe.* Associated Business Press, London.

COOPER, R. (1982). 'The gold standard, historical facts and future prospects'. *Brookings Papers on Economic Activity*, 1.

CORIAT, B. (1980). 'The restructuring of the assembly line'. *Capital and Class.* Summer.

CORNWALL, J. (1977). *Modern Capitalism: its Growth and Transformation.* Martin Robertson, Oxford.

CORNWALL, J. (1983). *The Conditions for Economic Recovery.* Martin Robertson, Oxford.

COVENTRY TRADES COUNCIL et al. (1980). *State Intervention in Industry: a Workers' Inquiry.*

CREDIT SUISSE FIRST BOSTON (1990). *East Europe Databook.* London.

CROSLAND, A. (1956). *The Future of Socialism.* Jonathan Cape, London.

CROUCH, C. AND PIZZORNO, A. (eds) (1978). *The Resurgence of Class Conflict in Western Europe since 1968*, 2 vols. Macmillan, London.

CUSUMANO, M.A. (1985). *The Japanese Automobile Industry.* Council on East Asian Studies, Harvard University, Cambridge MA.

CUTLER, A., HASLAM, C., WILLIAMS, J. AND WILLIAMS, K. (1990). *1992 – the Struggle for Europe.* Berg, Oxford.

DALZELL, C. (1961). *Mussolini's Enemies.* Princeton University Press, Princeton.

DE CECCO, M. (1972). 'Economic Policy 1945–51', in S. Woolf (ed.), *The Rebirth of Modern Italy.* Longman, London.

DELION, A. AND DURUPTY, M. (1982). *Les Nationalisations 1982.* Economia, Paris.

DELORS, J. (1978). 'The decline of French planning', in S. Holland (ed.), *Beyond Capitalist Planning.* Basil Blackwell, Oxford.

DENISON, E. (1983). 'The interruption of productivity growth in the United States'. *Economic Journal*, March.

DENISON E. AND CHUNG, W. (1976). *How Japan's Economy Grew So Fast*, Brookings, Washington.

DERTOUZOS, M., LESTER, R. AND SOLOW, R. (1989). *Made in America: Regaining the Productive Edge.* MIT Press, Cambridge, MA.

DEUTSCHE BUNDESBANK. *Annual Report.* Frankfurt.

DEUTSCHER, I. (1967). *Stalin.* Oxford University Press, Oxford.

DEUTSCHES INSTITUT FÜR WIRTSCHAFTSFORSCHUNG (1976). *Anlageinvestitionen und Anlagevermögen.* Beiträge zur Structurforschung, Heft 41, Berlin.

DJILAS, M. (1962). *Conversations with Stalin.* Hart-Davis, London.

DJILAS, M. (1977). *Wartime.* Secker and Warburg, London.

DOW, J. (1964). *The Management of the British Economy 1945–60.* Cambridge University Press, Cambridge.

DROUCOPOULOS, V. (1981). 'The non-American challenge'. *Capital and Class.* Summer.

DUNNING, J. AND PEARCE, R. (1981). *The World's Largest Industrial Enterprises.* Gower Press, Hants.

Economist, London, various issues.

EDELMAN, M. AND FLEMING, R. (1965). *The Politics of Wage-Price Decisions.* University of Illinois Press, Chicago.

EDWARDS, R. (1979). *Contested Terrain.* Heinemann, London.

EINAUDI, M., BYE, M. AND ROSSI, E. (1955). *Nationalisation in France and Italy.* Cornell University Press.

EMERSON, M. (1988). *The Economics of 1992* (the 'Cecchini Report'). Oxford University Press, Oxford.

ESTRIN, S. AND HOLMES, P. (1983). *French Planning in Theory and Practice.* Allen and Unwin, London.

FEINSTEIN, C. (1972). *National Income, Expenditure and Output of the United Kingdom 1855–1965.* Cambridge University Press, Cambridge.

FELDSTEIN, M. (ed.) (1980). *The American Economy in Transition.* University of Chicago Press, Chicago.

FELS, G. AND FROELICH, H.-P. (1987). 'Germany and the world economy: a German view'. *Economic Policy*, no. 4.

FFORDE, J. (1983). 'Setting monetary objectives'. *Bank of England Quarterly Bulletin*, June.

FIELDHOUSE, D. (1978). *Unilever Overseas.* Croom Helm, London.

Financial Times, London, daily.

FISERA, V. (1978). *Writing on the Wall.* Allison and Busby, London.

FLANAGAN, R. (1987). 'Efficiency and equality in Swedish labour markets', in B. Bosworth and A. Rivlin (eds), The Swedish Economy. Brookings Institute, Washington.

FLANAGAN, R., SOSKICE, D. AND ULMAN, L. (1983). *Unionism, Economic Stabilisation and Incomes Policies.* Brookings, Washington.

FLEMMING, J. (1976). 'Trends in company profitability'. *Bank of England Quarterly Bulletin*, June.

FORESTER, T. (1979). 'Neutralizing the Industrial Strategy', in K. Coates (ed.), *What Went Wrong?* Spokesman, Nottingham.

FREEMAN, C., CLARK, J. AND SOETE, L. (1982). *Unemployment and Technical Innovation.* Frances Pinter, London.

FRENCH GOVERNMENT (1950). *Mouvement économique en France de 1938 à 1948.* Ministère des Finances et des Affaires Economiques, Paris.

FRENCH GOVERNMENT (1960). *Statistiques et études financières-annuaire 1930–1959.* Ministère des Finances, Paris.

FRENCH GOVERNMENT (1971). *Annuaire statistique de la France, rétrospectif.* Paris.

FRENCH GOVERNMENT *Les Comptes de la nation.* INSEE, Paris, annual.

FRENCH GOVERNMENT *Les Comptes des entreprises par secteurs.* INSEE, Paris, various issues.

FRENCH GOVERNMENT *Statistiques et études financières.* monthly.

FRIEDMAN, A. (1977). *Industry and Labour.* Macmillan, London.

FRÖBEL, F., HEINRICHS, J. AND KREYE, O. (1980). *The New International Division of Labour.* Cambridge University Press, Cambridge.

FUA, G. (1969). *La Sviluppo Economico in Italia*, vol. III. Franco Angeli Editori, Milan.

GARDNER, R. (1956). *Sterling Dollar Diplomacy.* Oxford University Press, Oxford.

GARTMAN, D. (1979). 'Origins of the assembly line and capitalist control of work at Fords', in A. Zimbalist (ed.), *Case Studies in the Labor Process*. Monthly Review Press, New York.

GENERAL AGREEMENT ON TARIFFS AND TRADE (GATT). *International Trade*. Geneva, annual.

GERMAN GOVERNMENT. *Volkswirtschafiliche Gesamtrechungen*, various issues, Statistisches Bundesamt, Wiesbaden.

GILBERT, M. (1980). *Quest for World Monetary Order*. John Wiley, New York.

GILMOUR, I. (1977). *Inside Right*. Quartet, London.

GIMBEL, J. (1968). *The American Occupation of Germany*. Stanford University Press, Stanford.

GIMBEL, J. (1976). *The Origins of the Marshall Plan*. Stanford University Press, Stanford.

GINSBURG, P. (1990). *A History of Contemporary Italy*. Penguin, Harmondsworth.

GLYN, A. (1990). 'Productivity and the crisis of Fordism'. *International Review of Applied Economics*, **4**, no. 1.

GLYN, A. (1991). 'Corporatism, patterns of employment and access to consumption', in J. Pekkarinen, M. Pohjola and R. Rowthorn (eds), *Social Corporatism: a Superior System?* Oxford University Press, Oxford.

GLYN, A. AND HARRISON, J. (1980). *The British Economic Disaster*. Pluto Press, London.

GLYN, A., HUGHES, A., LIPIETZ, A. AND SINGH, A. (1990). 'The rise and fall of the golden age', in S. Marglin and J. Schor (eds), *The Golden Age of Capitalism*. Oxford University Press, Oxford.

GLYN, A. AND SUTCLIFFE, R. (1972). *British Capitalism, Workers and the Profit Squeeze*. Penguin, Harmondsworth.

GOLDTHORPE, J. (ed.) (1984). *Order and Conflict in Contemporary Capitalism*. Clarendon Press, Oxford.

GORDON, A. (1985). *The Evolution of Labor Relations in Japan: Heavy Industry 1853–1955*. Harvard University Press, Cambridge, MA.

GOUGH, I. (1979). *The Political Economy of the Welfare State*. Macmillan, London.

GRAF, W. (1976). *The German Left since 1945*. Oleander, Cambridge.

GREEN, F. (ed.) (1989). *The Restructuring of the UK Economy*. Harvester, Brighton.

GREEN J. (1980). *The World of the Worker*. Hill and Wang, New York.

GRIMM, B. (1982). 'Domestic non-financial corporate profits'. *Survey of Current Business*, January.

GRUNDROD, M. (1955). *The Rebuilding of Italy*. Oxford University Press, Oxford.

GUERIN, D. (1979). *100 Years of American Labour*. Ink Links, London.

GUPTA, P. (1983). 'Imperialism and the Labour Government', in J. Winter (ed.), *The Working Class in Modern British History*. Cambridge University Press, Cambridge.

HADLEY, E. (1970). *Anti-Trust in Japan*. Princeton University Press, Princeton.

HALLIDAY, F. (1983). *The Second Cold War*. New Left Books, London.

HALLIDAY, J. (1975). *A Political History of Japanese Capitalism*. Pantheon, New York.

HARRIS, S. (ed.) (1943). *Post-war Economic Problems*. McGraw-Hill, New York.

HAYEK, F. (1972). *A Tiger by the Tail*. Institute for Economic Affairs, London.

HECLO, H. (1974). *Modern Social Politics in Britain and Sweden*. Yale University Press, New Haven.

HELLER, W. (1950). 'The role of fiscal–monetary policy in German economic recovery'. *American Economic Review*, Papers and Proceedings.

HENDERSON, P. (1983). 'Trade policies: trends, issues and influences'. *Midland Bank Review*, Winter.

HERDING, R. (1972). *Job Control and Union Structure*. Rotterdam University Press, Rotterdam.

HILDEBRAND, G. (1965). *Growth and Structure in the Economy of Modern Italy*. Harvard University Press, Cambridge, MA.

HILL, T. (1979). *Profits and Rates of Return*. OECD, Paris.

HOGAN, M. (1987). *The Marshall Plan*. Cambridge Univesity Press, Cambridge.

HOLLAND, S. (1975). *The Socialist Challenge*. Quartet Books, London.

HOLLAND, S. (ed.) (1972). *The State as Entrepreneur*. Weidenfeld and Nicolson, London.

HOOPER, P. AND LARRIN, K. (1989). 'International comparison of labor costs in manufacturing'. *Review of Income and Wealth*, December.

HOROWITZ, D. (1965). *The Free World Colossus*. MacGibbon and Kee, London.

IKEDA, M. (1979). 'The subcontracting system in the Japanese electronic industry'. *Engineering Industries of Japan*.

INCOMES DATA SERVICES. *International Report*. London, monthly.

INTERNATIONAL MONETARY FUND (IMF) (1982). *Developments in International Trade Policy*, Occasional Paper No. 16, Washington.

IMF. *Annual Report*. Washington, annual.

IMF. *International Financial Statistics*, monthly and annual yearbooks.

IMF. *World Economic Outlook*. Washington, April and October.

ITALIAN GOVERNMENT. *Annuario di Contabilita Nationale*. ISTAT, Rome, annual.

ITALIAN GOVERNMENT. *Bolletino Mensile di Statistica*. ISTAT, Rome, monthly.

ITOH, M. (1980). *Value and Crisis*. Pluto Press, London.

JAPANESE GOVERNMENT. *Annual Report on National Accounts*. Economic Planning Agency, Tokyo, annual.

JAPANESE GOVERNMENT. *Census of Manufactures*. Tokyo, various issues.

JAPANESE GOVERNMENT. *Economic Survey of Japan*. Economic Planning Agency/*Japan Times*, Tokyo, annual.

JAPANESE GOVERNMENT, *Estimates of the Stock of Non-Residential Business Capital*. Economic Planning Agency, Tokyo, periodically.

JAPANESE GOVERNMENT, *Japan Statistical Yearbook*. Office of the Prime Minister, Tokyo, annual.

JAPANESE GOVERNMENT, *Monthly Statistics of Japan*. Tokyo, monthly.

JAPANESE GOVERNMENT, *White Paper on Small and Medium Enterprises in Japan*. Ministry of International Trade and Industry, Tokyo, annual.

JOHNSON, P. AND STARK, G. (1989). *Taxation and Social Security 1979–89; the Impact on Household Incomes*. Institute for Fiscal Studies, London.

JONES, J. (1955). *The Fifteen Weeks*. Harcourt, Brace, New York.

KALECKI, M. (1971). *Essays on the Dynamics of the Capitalist Economies*. Cambridge University Press, Cambridge.

KAMATA, S. (1982). *Japan in the Passing Lane*. Pantheon Books, New York.

KAPLAN, E. (1975). *Japan – the Government–Business Relationship*. US Department of Commerce, Washington.

KASER, M. (ed.) (1986). *The Economic History of Eastern Europe 1919–75* (by W. Brus). Oxford University Press, Oxford.

KATZENSTEIN, R. (1967). *Die Investitionen und ihre Bewegung in Staatsmonopolistischen Kapitalismus*. Berlin.

KAY, J. AND VICKERS, J. (1988). 'Regulatory reform in Britain'. *Economic Policy*, no. 7.

KENDALL, W. (1975). *The Labour Movement in Europe.* Allen Lane, London.

KENNAN, G. (1967). *Memoirs 1925–50.* Hutchinson, London.

KINDLEBERGER, C. (1967). *Europe's Post War Growth.* Oxford University Press, Oxford.

KING, M. AND FULLERTON, D. (eds.) (1984). *The Taxation of Income from Capital.* University of Chicago Press: Chicago.

KOHLER, P. AND ZACHER, H. (eds) (1982). *The Evolution of Social Insurance 1881–1981*, Frances Pinter, London.

KOIKE, K. (1988). *Understanding Industrial Relations in Modern Japan.* Macmillan, London.

KOLKO, G. (1969). *The Politics of War.* Vintage Books, New York.

KOLKO, G. AND KOLKO, J. (1972). *The Limits of Power: the World and US Foreign Policy.* Harper and Row, New York.

KOMIYA, R. (1975). 'Planning in Japan', in M. Bornstein (ed.), *Economic Planning East and West.* Ballinger, Cambridge, MA.

KOMIYA, R. (ed.) (1966). *Postwar Economic Growth in Japan.* University of California Press, Berkeley.

KRAVIS, I. (1976). 'A survey of international comparisons of productivity'. *Economic Journal*, March.

KRAVIS, I., HESTON, A. AND SUMMERS, R. (1979). *International Comparisons of Real Product and Purchasing Power.* Johns Hopkins University Press, Baltimore.

KRENGEL, R. (1958). *Anlagevermögen, Produktion und Beschäftigung der Industrie im Gebiet der B.R.D. von 1924–56.* DIW, Berlin.

KUISEL, R. (1981). *Capitalism and the State in Modern France.* Cambridge University Press, Cambridge.

LAWRENCE, R. AND BOSWORTH, B. (1987). 'Adjusting to slower economic growth: the external sector', in B. Bosworth and A. Rivlin (eds), *The Swedish Economy.* Brookings Institution, Washington.

LAWRENCE, R. AND SCHULTZE, C. (eds) (1987). *Barriers to European Growth.* Brookings Institution, Washington.

LEFRANC, G. (1969). *Le Mouvement syndical.* Payot, Paris.

LEONHARD, W. (1979). *Child of the Revolution.* Ink Links, London.

LEVINE, S. (1958). *Industrial Relations in Post-war Japan.* University of Illinois Press, Chicago.

LEWIS, A. (1949). *Economic Survey 1919–39.* Allen and Unwin, London.

LICHTENSTEIN, N. (1982). *Labor's War at Home.* Cambridge University Press, Cambridge.

LINDBECK, A. (1983). 'The recent slowdown of productivity growth'. *Economic Journal*, March.

LIPIETZ, A. (1985). *L'Audace ou l'Enlisement.* Éditions la Decouverte, Paris.

LLEWELLYN, D. (1982). 'Avoiding an international banking crisis'. *National Westminster Bank Quarterly Review*, August.

LOCKSLEY, G. AND WARD, T. (1979). 'Concentration in manufacturing in the EEC'. *Cambridge Journal of Economics*, March.

MACAROV, D. (1982). *Worker Productivity.* Sage, Beverly Hills.

MACHIN, H. AND WRIGHT, V. (eds) (1985). *Economic Policy and Policy Making under the Mitterrand Presidency.* Frances Pinter, London.

MADDISON, A. (1964). *Economic Growth in the West.* Twentieth Century Fund, London.

MADDISON, A. (1982). *Phases of Capitalist Development.* Oxford University Press, Oxford.

MAGAZINER, I. AND HOUT, T. (1980). *Japanese Industrial Policy.* Policy Studies Institute, London.

MAGDOFF, H. AND SWEEZY, P. (1981). *The Deepening Crisis of US Capitalism.* Monthly Review Press, New York.

MAIER, C. (1987). *In Search of Stability.* Cambridge University Press, Cambridge.

MAIRESSE, J. (1972). *L'Evaluation du capital fixe productive.* INSEE, Paris.

MAIRESSE, J. AND DELESTRE, H. (1976). 'Rentabilités économique et comptable des sociétés en France de 1959 à 1975'. INSEE, Paris.

MAIZELS, A. (1963). *Industrial Growth and World Trade.* Cambridge University Press, Cambridge.

Management Today. London, monthly.

MANDEL, E. (1975). *Late Capitalism.* New Left Books, London.

MARGLIN, S. AND SCHOR, J. (eds) (1990). *The Golden Age of Capitalism.* Clarendon Press, Oxford.

MARRIS, S. (1987). *Deficits and the Dollar.* Institute for International Economics, Washington.

MASON, E. AND ASHER, R. (1973). *The World Bank since Bretton Woods.* Brookings, Washington.

MATTHEWS, R. (ed.) (1982). *Slower Growth in the Western World.* Heinemann, London.

MAYNARD, G. (1988). *The Economy under Mrs Thatcher.* Blackwell, Oxford.

MAYNE, R. (1983). *Postwar.* Weidenfeld and Nicolson, London.

McCAGG, W. (1978). *Stalin Embattled.* Wayne University Press, Detroit.

McCRACKEN, P. (1977). *Towards Full Employment and Price Stability.* OECD, Paris.

McKINNON, R. (1979). *Money in International Exchange.* Oxford University Press, Oxford.

MENDERSHAUSEN, H. (1949). 'Prices, money and the distribution of goods in post-war Germany'. *American Economic Review.*

Midland Bank Review. Sheffield, quarterly.

MIKESELL, R. (1952). *United States Economic Policy and International Relations.* McGraw-Hill, London.

Militant. London, weekly.

MILLER, D. (1982). 'Social partnership and the determinants of workplace independence in West Germany'. *British Journal of Industrial Relations*, March.

MILWARD, A. (1984). *The Reconstruction of Western Europe.* Methuen, London.

MINAMI, R. (1973). *The Turning Point in Economic Development.* Kinokuniya Bookstore, Tokyo.

MOORE, J. (1983). *Japanese Workers and the Struggle for Power 1945–47.* University of Wisconsin Press, Madison.

MORGAN, D. (1979). *Merchants of Grain.* Weidenfeld and Nicolson, London.

MORGAN GUARANTY BANK. *Survey.* New York, monthly.

MUET, P.-A. (1985). 'Economic management and the International environment, 1981–83', in H. Machin and V. Wright (eds), *Economic Policy and Policy Making under the Mitterrand Presidency.* Frances Pinter, London.

MÜLLER-JENTSCH, W. (1981). 'Strikes and strike trends in the Federal Republic of Germany 1950–78'. *Industrial Relations Journal*, July/August.

NATIONAL RAILWAY WORKERS UNION (Japan) (1980). *The Japanese Railwaymen's Struggle.* Tokyo.

NOSWORTHY, J. et al. (1979). The slowdown in productivity growth'. *Brookings Papers on Economic Activity*, 2.

OHKAWA, K. (1968). 'Changes in national income distribution', in J. Marchal and B. Ducros (eds), *The Distribution of National Income*. Macmillan, London.

OHKAWA, K. AND ROSOVSKY, H. (1973). *Japanese Economic Growth*. Stanford University Press, Stanford.

OHKAWA, K., JOHNSTON, B. AND KAMEDA, H. (1970). *Agriculture and Economic Growth: Japan's Experience*. Princeton University Press, Princeton.

OKOCHI, K. (1957). *Labour in Modern Japan*. Science Council of Japan, Tokyo.

OKOCHI, K., KARSH, B. AND LEVINE, S. (eds) *Workers and Employers in Japan*. Princeton University Press, Princeton.

ORGANIZATION FOR ECONOMIC AND COOPERATIVE DEVELOPMENT (OECD) (1970). *The Growth of Output 1960–80*. Paris.

OECD (1976). *Public Expenditure on Income Maintenance Programmes*.

OECD (1976). *Public Expenditure Trends*.

OECD *Employment Outlook*, annual.

OECD (1983). *Flows and Stocks of Fixed Capital 1955–1980*.

OECD *Economic Outlook*, July and December annually.

OECD *Economic Survey of France, of Germany, of Italy, of Japan, of United States, of United Kingdom*, annual.

OECD *Historical Statistics*, annual since 1982.

OECD *Labour Force Statistics*, annual.

OECD *Main Economic Indicators*, monthly.

OECD *National Accounts of Member Countries*, 2 vols, annual.

OECD *Trade by Commodities*, annual.

OECD (1985). *The Future of Social Protection*. Paris.

OECD (1988). *Economies in Transition*. Paris.

ORGANIZATION FOR EUROPEAN ECONOMIC COOPERATION (OEEC) (1957). *Statistics of National Product and Expenditure No. 2, 1938 and 1947–55*. Paris.

OEEC (1961). *The Problem of Rising Prices*. Paris.

Oriental Economist. Tokyo, monthly.

PARBONI, R. (1981). *The Dollar and its Rivals*. New Left Books, London.

PATRICK, H. (ed.) (1976). *Japanese Industrialisation*. University of California Press, Berkeley.

PATRICK, H. AND ROSOVSKY, H. (eds) (1976). *Asia's New Giant*. Brookings, Washington.

PEKKARINEN, J., POHJOLA, M. AND ROWTHORN, R. (eds) (1990). *Social Corporatism: a Superior Economic System?* Oxford University Press, Oxford.

PETIT, P. (1984). 'The origins of French planning – a reappraisal'. *Contributions to Political Economy*, March.

PIORE, M. (1982). 'American labour and the industrial crisis'. *Challenge*, March/April.

PLUTO PRESS (1983). *Thatcher's Britain. A Guide to the Ruins*. Pluto Press, London.

PONTUSSON, J. (1987). 'Radicalization and retreat in Swedish social democracy'. *New Left Review*, no. 167, September/October.

PONTUSSON, J. (1989). 'The triumph of pragmatism: nationalization and privatization in Sweden', in J. Vickers and V. Wright (eds), *The Politics of Privatization in Western Europe*. Frank Cass, London.

PORTES, R. (1981). 'East, West and South: the role of the centrally planned economies in the international economy', in S. Grassman and E. Lundberg (eds), *The World Economic Order: Past and Prospects*. Macmillan, London.

POSNER, C. (ed.) (1970). *Reflections on the Revolution in France: 1968*. Pelican, Harmondsworth.

POSNER, M. AND WOOLF, S. (1967). *Italian Public Enterprise*. Gerald Duckworth, London.

PRAIS, S. (1976). *The Evolution of Giant Firms in the UK*. Cambridge University Press, Cambridge.

PRAIS, S. (1981). *Productivity and Industrial Structure*. Cambridge University Press, Cambridge.

PREIS, A. (1964). *Labor's Giant Step*. Pathfinder Press, New York.

PRICE, R. AND MULLER, P. (1984). 'Structural budget indicators and the interpretation of fiscal policy stance in OECD economies'. *OECD Economic Studies*, Autumn.

PRITT, D. (1963). *The Labour Government 1945–51*. Lawrence and Wishart, London.

RAY, G. (1972). 'Labour costs and international competitiveness'. *National Institute Economic Review*, August.

RAY, G. (1976). 'Labour Costs in OECD countries 1964–75'. *National Institute Economic Review*, November.

REGGIO, G. (1968). 'Italy', in G. Spitaels (ed.), *La Crise des relations industrielles en Europe*. de Tempel, Bruges.

RIMLINGER, G. (1971). *Welfare Policy and Industrialisation in Europe, America and Russia*. Wiley, New York.

RIOUX, J.-P. (1980). *La France de la Quatrième République: l'ardeur et la nécessité*. Seuil, Paris.

ROBINSON, H. (1973). 'The downfall of the dollar'. *The Socialist Register*, London.

ROGOW, A. (1955). *The Labour Government and British Industry*. Blackwell, Oxford.

ROSS, G. (1982). *Workers and Communists in France*. University of California Press, Berkeley.

ROUSSEAS, S. (1982). *The Political Economy of Reaganomics*. Sharpe, New York.

ROWTHORN, R. (1980). *Capitalism, Conflict and Inflation*. Lawrence and Wishart, London.

ROWTHORN, R. AND GLYN, A. (1990). 'The diversity of OECD unemployment since 1973', in S. Marglin and J. Schor (eds), *The Golden Age of Capitalism*. Clarendon Press, Oxford.

ROWTHORN, R. AND HYMER, S. (1971). *International Big Business 1957–67*. Cambridge University Press, Cambridge.

ROWTHORN, R. AND WELLS, J. (1987). *Deindustrialization and Foreign Trade*. Cambridge University Press, Cambridge.

ROY, A. (1982). 'Labour productivity in 1980 – an international comparison'. *National Institute Economic Review*, August.

SABEL, C. (1982). *Work and Politics*. Cambridge University Press, Cambridge.

SACHS, J. (1983). 'Real wages and unemployment in the OECD countries'. *Brookings Papers on Economic Activity*, 1.

SACHS, J. (ed.) (1989). *Developing Country Debt and the World Economy*. University of Chicago Press, Chicago.

SACHS, J. AND WYPLOSZ, C. (1986). 'The economic consequences of President Mitterrand'. *Economic Policy*, no. 2, April.

SAGA, I. (n.d.). 'Labour relations in Japan: the case of the Nissan Motor Company'. Mimeo, Tokyo.

SAINT-JOURS, Y. (1982). 'France', in P. Kohler and H. Zacher (eds.), *The Evolution of Social Insurance 1881–1981*. Frances Pinter, London.

SALTER, W. (1966). *Productivity and Technical Change*. Cambridge University Press, Cambridge.

SALVATI, B. (1972). 'The rebirth of Italian trade unionism', in S. Woolf (ed.), *The Rebirth of Modern Italy*. Longman, London.

SALVATI, M. (1975). *Il Sistemo Economico Italiano: Analisi di Una Crisi*. Il Mulino, Bologna.

SAMPSON, A. (1975). *The Seven Sisters*. Penguin, Harmondsworth.

SAMPSON, A. (1982). *The Money Lenders*. Coronet, London.

SAMUELSON, P. (1943). 'Full employment after the war', in S. Harris (ed.), *Post-war Economic Problems*. McGraw-Hill, New York.

SARGENT, J. (1982). 'Capital accumulation and productivity growth', in R. Matthews (ed.), *Slower Growth in the Western World*. Heinemann, London.

SCHMIDT, E. (1970). *Die verhinderte Neuordnung 1945–52*. Europaische Verlaganstalt.

SCHMIDT, U. AND FICHTER, T. (1971). *Der Erzwungene Kapitalismus: Klassenkämpfe in den Westzonen 1945–48*. Wagenbach, Berlin.

SCHUMPETER, J. (1943). 'Capitalism in the post-war world', in S. Harris (ed.), *Post-war Economic Problems*. McGraw-Hill, New York.

SEABROOK, J. *Unemployment*. Quartet, London.

SENGENBERGER, W. AND LOVEMAN, G. (1988). 'Smaller units of employment: a synthesis report on industrial reorganization in industrialized countries'. Discussion paper no. 3, ILO.

SHINOHARA, M. (1970). *Structural Changes in Japan's Economic Development*. Tokyo.

SHONFIELD, A. (1965). *Modern Capitalism*. Oxford University Press, Oxford.

SIMPSON, E. (1949–50). 'Inflation and deflation and employment in Italy', *Review of Economic Studies*, **44**.

Socialist Economic Review. London, annual since 1981.

SOSKICE, D. (1978). 'Strike waves and wage explosions 1968–70: an economic interpretation', in C. Crouch and A. Pizzorno (eds.), *The Resurgence of Class Conflict in Western Europe*. Macmillan, London.

SOSKICE, D. (1984). 'The UK economy and industrial relations'. *Industrial Relations*, Fall.

SPIRO, H. (1958). *The Politics of German Co-determination*. Harvard University Press, Cambridge, MA.

STEINDL, J. (1952). *Maturity and Stagnation in American Capitalism*. Blackwell, Oxford.

STEINDL, J. (1982). 'The role of household saving in modern economy'. *Banca Nazionale del Lavoro Review*.

STEWART, M. (1983). *Controlling the Economic Future*. Wheatsheaf Books, Brighton.

STOFFAES, C. (1985). 'The nationalizations 1981–84: an initial assessment', in H. Machin and V. Wright (eds), *Economic Policy and Policy Making under the Mitterand Presidency*. Frances Pinter, London.

STRANGE, S. (1971). *Sterling and British Policy*. Oxford University Press, Oxford.

STREEK, W. (1985). 'Industrial relations in West Germany 1974–85: an overview'. Research Unit Labour Market and Employment, discussion paper 85–19, Wizzenscaftszentrum, Berlin.

SUTCLIFFE, B. (1983). *Hard Times.* Pluto Press, London.

SWEEZY, P. (1955). *The Present as History*, Monthly Review Press, New York.

TABATA, H. (1988). 'Changes in plant-level trade union organizations: a case study of the automobile industry'. *Annals of the Institute of Social Science*, no. 30.

TAIRA, K. (1970). *Economic Development and the Labor Market in Japan.* Columbia University Press, New York.

TEW, B. (1977). *The Evolution of the International Monetary System.* Hutchinson, London.

TEW, B. AND HENDERSON, R. (eds) (1959). *Studies of Company Finance,.* Cambridge University Press, Cambridge.

THERBORN, G. (1986). *Why Some Peoples Are More Unemployed than Others.* Verso, London.

TOTSUKA, H. (n.d.). 'Japanese trade union attitudes towards rationalisation'. Mimeo, Tokyo.

TROTSKY, L. (1973). 'The curve of capitalist development'. *Bulletin of the Conference of Socialist Economists*, Spring.

TSURU, S. (1958). *Essays on the Japanese Economy.* Kinokuniya Bookstore, Tokyo.

TURNER, I.D. (ed.) (1989). *Reconstruction in Post-War Germany.* Berg, Oxford.

TURNER, L. (1983). *Oil Companies in the International System.* Allen and Unwin, London.

UK GOVERNMENT (1971). *British Labour Statistics, Historical Abstract.* Department of Employment and Productivity, London.

UK GOVERNMENT. *Economic Survey.* HM Treasury, London, annual, 1947–62.

UK GOVERNMENT. *Employment Gazette.* Department of Employment, monthly.

UK GOVERNMENT (1989). *The Government's Expenditure Plans 1990–91 to 1992–3.* HMSO, London.

UK GOVERNMENT. *National Income and Expenditure.* Central Statistical Office, London, various issues.

UNIR (n.d.). *Histoire du PCF.* Paris.

UNITED NATIONS. *Statistical Yearbook.* New York, annual.

UNITED NATIONS. *World Economic Review.* New York, annual.

UNITED NATIONS. *Yearbook of National Accounts Statistics.* New York, annual.

UNITED NATIONS CONFERENCE FOR TRADE AND INDUSTRY (UNCTAD), (1983). *Commodity Issues.*

UNCTAD (1983). *International Trade and Monetary Issues.*

UNCTAD (1983). *Production and Trade in Services.*

UNCTAD (1983). *Protectionism, Trade Relations and Structural Adjustment.*

UNCTAD (1983). *Trade in Manufactures and Semi-Manufactures of Developing Countries.*

UNCTAD. *Trade and Development Report.* Geneva, annual, from 1981.

UNITED NATIONS ECONOMIC COMMISSION FOR EUROPE (UNECE) (1953). *Economic Survey of Europe Since the War: a Reappraisal of Problems and Prospects.* Geneva.

UNECE (1982). 'Reciprocal trading arrangements in east-west trade'. *Economic Bulletin for Europe*, June.

UNECE (1982). 'Recent developments in east-west trade'. *Economic Bulletin for Europe*, December.

UNECE. *Economic Survey of Europe.* Geneva, annual.

US GOVERNMENT (1962), *Balance of Payments, Statistical Supplement.* Department of Commerce, Washington.

US GOVERNMENT (1973). *Long-term Economic Growth 1860–1970.* Department of Commerce, Washington.

US GOVERNMENT (1981). *The National Income and Product Accounts of the United States 1929–76*, Department of Commerce, Washington.

US GOVERNMENT (1983). *Underlying Data for Indices of Output Per Hour etc.* Bureau of Labor Statistics, Washington.

US GOVERNMENT. *Economic Report of the President.* Annual.

US GOVERNMENT. *Survey of Current Business.* Department of Commerce, monthly.

VAN PARYS, P. (1980). 'The falling rate of profit theory of crisis'. *Review of Radical Political Economics*, Spring.

VATTER, H. (1965). *The US Economy in the 1950s.* Norton, New York.

VICKERS, J. AND YARROW, G. (1988). *Privatization – an Economic Analysis.* MIT Press, Cambridge, MA.

VICKERS, J. AND WRIGHT, V. (eds) (1989). *The Politics of Privatization in Western Europe.* Frank Cass, London.

WALLICH, H. (1955). *Mainsprings of the German Revival.* Yale University Press, New Haven.

WALTON, R. (1985). 'From control to commitment in the workplace'. *Harvard Business Review*, March/April.

WEISSKOPF, T. (1979). 'Marxian crisis theory and the rate of profit in the postwar US economy'. *Cambridge Journal of Economics*, December.

WEISSKOPF, T. (1987). 'The effect of unemployment on labor productivity: an international comparison'. *International Review of Applied Economics*, 1.

WERTH, A. (1956). *France 1940–55.* Robert Hale, London.

WILLIAMSON, J. (1977). *The Failure of International Monetary Reform.* Nelson, London.

WILSON, T. (ed.) (1974). *Pensions, Inflation and Growth.* Heinemann, London.

WINTERTON, J. AND WINTERTON, R. (1989). *Coal, Crisis and Conflict.* Manchester University Press, Manchester.

WOOLCOCK, S. (1982). 'Textiles and clothing', in L. Turner and N. McMullen (eds), *The Newly Industrialising Countries.* Allen and Unwin, London.

WOOLF, S. (ed.) (1972). *The Rebirth of Modern Italy.* Longman, London.

WORLD BANK, (1980). *World Tables.* Johns Hopkins Press, Baltimore.

WORLD BANK, (1983). *World Debt Tables 1982/83.* Washington.

WORSWICK, D. AND ADY, P. (1952). *The British Economy 1945–50.* Oxford University Press, Oxford.

YAMAMOTO, K. (1972). 'The production control struggle'. *Annals of the Institute of Social Science*, Tokyo University.

YAMAMOTO, K. (1980/81). 'Mass demonstration movements in Japan'. *Capital and Class*, Winter.

YAMAMOTO, K. (1980). 'Labour–management relations at Nissan Motor Co. Ltd'. *Annals of the Institute of Social Science*, Tokyo University.

YAMAMURA, K. (1967). *Economic Policy in Postwar Japan.* University of California Press, Berkeley.

YERGIN, D. (1980). *Shattered Peace: the Origins of the Cold War and the National Security State.* Penguin, Harmondsworth.

ZINK, H. (1957). *The United States in Germany 1944–55.* Van Nostrand, Princeton.

ZOLLNER, D. (1982). 'Germany', in P. Kohler and H. Zacher (eds), *The Evolution of Social Insurance 1881–1981.* Frances Pinter, London.

Index

For the main entries, *see also under individual countries*.